Tropic of Venice

Margaret Doody

Tropic of Venice

UNIVERSITY OF PENNSYLVANIA PRESS

Philadelphia

PERSONAL TAKES

An occasional series of books in which noted critics write about
the persistent hold particular writers, artists, or cultural phenomena
have had on their imaginations.

10 9 8 7 6 5 4 3 2 1

Published by
University of Pennsylvania Press
Philadelphia, Pennsylvania 19104-4112

Library of Congress Cataloging-in-Publication Data

Doody, Margaret Anne.
    Tropic of Venice / Margaret Doody.
        p.   cm. — (Personal takes)
    Includes bibliograhpical references and index.
    ISBN-13: 978-0-8122-3984-3
    ISBN-10: 0-8122-3984-9 (cloth : alk paper)
        1. Venice (Italy)—Description and travel.   2. Venice (Italy)—In literature.
    3. Painting, Italian—Italy—Venice.   4. Venice (Italy)—In art.   5. Venice
    (Italy)—Social life and customs.   I. Title.
    DG675.6.D66   2007
    945'.31—dc22

                                                            2006050918

Frontispiece: Giovanni Antonio Canaletto, *The Basin of San Marco on Ascension Day*
(Permission of National Gallery, London)

To my cousin John Williams,
who loves Venice as much as I do

Contents

Illustrations

1

Discovering Venice

Arrival

"The images of memory, once fixed into words, cancel themselves out,"
said Marco Polo. "Perhaps I fear to lose Venice entirely all at once, if I
speak of it. Or perhaps, in speaking of other cities, I have already lost it
little by little."
—Italo Calvino, *Le città invisiblili*

Venetia, Venetia, che non ti vede, non ti pretia.
Venice, O Venice, who does not see you does not appreciate you.
—Proverb

A great while ago, I first saw Venice. I was a student at the time, living
in Lady Margaret Hall, Oxford. I had come to Oxford from Canada
in 1960, to undertake two years' study toward a B.A. with Honours in English, after completing a B.A. in Canada. Thus I would have time for extra
reading and other enjoyments, including the pleasure of travel. Having explored the British Isles a little, I was ready by the spring to venture farther
afield and explore the Continent. My first visit to Paris in March 1961 stimulated a desire to see more. For the summer, I planned a more ambitious trip
to Italy.

Like most—though certainly not all—of my mates in Oxford I had more
enthusiasm than money. Travel needed to be planned with the utmost pru-
dence. Looking back on that period, I remember how anxious we all were to
find something cheap, and how greatly trains and boats figured in all our
arrangements. Only once in my life had I been on a plane, certainly not a jet,
and in this inexperience I was far from singular. I had crossed the Atlantic
(Montreal to Southampton) on the (relatively new) Cunarder SS *Saxonia*. By
this time people did travel by air to and from America or Kenya, but few
would have thought of crossing the Channel by plane. Even the sons and
daughters of the well-to-do were expected, for the most part, to travel eco-

nomically in their student days. That was certainly a different era. We had suitcases but no backpacks. We carried cash, or traveler's checks if we wanted to be posh, but there was no ATM, no ready access to one's own bank account. Banking arrangements, if any, had to be made between one's own bank and a foreign one. (A bank could wire one money in a dire emergency, but it took time.) Currency difference faced the European traveler at each boundary. Credit cards had just appeared in the 1950s (indeed the first of these, Diners Club, was spoken of with reprobation in the film I had seen on the *Saxonia* coming over, Billy Wilder's *The Apartment*). But Diners Club was meant for rich businessmen, not for the likes of us; to me they were no more than a rumor. And there were no portable phones; one has to imagine a Europe—even an Italy—without *telefonini* or *cellulare*.

The poorer traveler also lacked the backup system a good hotel can provide. Very few of us students had money to spend on hotels, or nice meals, en route. Fortunately, the National Union of Students encouraged travel with delightful offers of cheap tickets, and enticing advertisements for tours at rock-bottom fares. Booking one of these expeditions with rooms and meals and transport paid for in advance was the surest way to avoid currency distress, or the waste of time entailed in trying to find low-priced but decent accommodation in a strange city. I wanted to avoid bus excursions and group activities entirely once I'd arrived at a destination. Soon I discovered a tour that I thought would do—cheap, suitable, and respectable—with some choice of destination and no group activity. These particular tours were run by an agreeable Anglo-Russian couple, who lived in a rather ramshackle but delightful villa outside of Florence, which served as the hostel (and the best one) during the Florence part of one's trip. They seemed to take perpetual delight in assisting young people of next to no means to discover Italy, and I am sure they would have helped me had I been able to get in touch with them during the period of trouble that was to befall me on my journey. The fares were excellently low, the seats on the trains third class, and the *pensione* Spartan. Rates were at their lowest during the hot summer months, which is why I took my holiday then.

The tour attracting my attention included three destinations: Rome, Venice, Florence. Or, to use their more exciting real names: Roma, Venezia, Firenze. One could take them in any order. I decided (very much in accordance with my usual character) to proceed from what I liked least to what I liked best. Therefore, I placed Venice first—to get it over with, as it were. Of course, like many others, I had already acquired mental images, beginning

with some gathered from the elegant and oft-reproduced paintings of Canaletto (see frontispiece). There were some images from movies, advertisements, periodicals, and descriptions in books. Venice sounded to me a showy,
vulgar, superficial place, a gaudy but faded resort town, so familiar from repe-
titious photographs that there hardly seemed any reason to see it. I didn't
want to skip it, especially when it seemed so unlikely I would ever wish to
return. In my view, there was nothing in Venice to compare with the grandeur
that was Rome—the classical sites, the wonders wrought by Michelangelo.
But then Florence was the home of Italian art, the core of the business, as
well as the home of Dante. I expected to like it best, so would visit Florence
last and Venice first.

Having made up my mind and my itinerary on this sound principle, I filled
in forms, paid for transport and lodging in advance, and was ready to set off
on the bright August morning when a large bunch of us met in Victoria
Station. The whole of the journey (save for Channel ferry) was to be by
train. (It would have been possible—just—to go to Venice by air at that
point, Marco Polo Airport having been opened in 1960, but most plebeian
travel was still done by train. Now there is a new and modern Marco Polo
Airport, but too far from the landing stage to be comfortable, especially in
rain or wind, so I miss the old one.) After we all listened politely to a briefing
by our guide, we set off on the first leg of our journey.

A short train ride to the coast successfully delivered us to the Channel
ferry; we got off it again in France, took another train—and there we were
in the great French *gare*, where gigantic trains were panting to go south. We
were shepherded aboard by the leader who held the party ticket, each of us
holding a coupon. She advised us firmly to find the correct coach or *wagon* of
the train going to our particular destination, and to remain with it. The Venetian segment of our group were particularly warned that the train was
going to divide in the middle of the night and that their coach would not
remain with the larger train. I found the Venice coach without trouble and
stashed my suitcase there. But on the Channel crossing I had fallen in with
some congenial souls who were bound for Florence, so I looked them up to
enjoy their company while partaking of whatever frugal meal we had provided
for ourselves; we chatted while watching the Continental scenery slide past
the window during the long summer evening. I thought I should have plenty
of warning about the severance of parts of the train, which sounded like a
dramatic business.

But when, at last feeling sleepy, I headed for the Venice coach, I found that it—and my suitcase—had gone off elsewhere. This was alarming! The guide assured me that all was not lost. "That other train arrives in the station at Milan a little later than ours," I was told, "so all you have to do is wait for it and hop on again." Thus reassured, I was able to enjoy the rest of the journey, though I no longer had a reserved seat. Standing, I hung out the window to marvel at sunrise spilling on the Alpine peaks, although pleasure was tinged with a certain nagging anxiety. After all, my traveler's checks as well as my clothes were in the suitcase now proceeding sedately in another train without me.

In a postcard home, all I wrote on 28 August was, "Trip exciting, if long—Alpine scenery glorious, sunrise colouring snow-capped peaks rose and gold. Italy *hot*—full of vineyards, vines seem to hold hands and dance across landscape." All of this was true enough, as far as it went, but there would have been more to tell. I did not want to upset or disgust my family by explaining my ridiculous blunder in parting from the Venice-bound coach, a mistake which certainly rendered the trip both exciting and long.

I found myself in the station at Milan, now definitely declared to be Milano, where I had to jump off the train and leave the only people I knew in Italy. The matter became more alarming when I realized that the train station in Milano was huge—and had multiple layers. There was no way I could just stand beside the entry to whatever track was supposed to hold a train bound for Venice. There were many tracks and people streaming back and forth at each of them. When I tried to linger in one place, I began to be pursued and harassed by unwanted male admirers (a hazard of my life at that period). In taking myself off hastily and "losing" myself in the crowd I assuredly lost all possibility of spotting the original Venice-bound party's train—which had now come to seem a dubious possibility anyway. I had very little money in my purse, enough for a cup of coffee but not for a meal—or for a long-distance phone call. How, I wondered, could I have been stupid enough to pack my traveler's checks in my suitcase? (An error, indeed, that I have never made again.) I tried to go to a Travelers' Information post, but they would only inform of the price of a ticket to Venice: "Due mille lire!" (two thousand lire).[1] I tried at a wicket to ask the man selling tickets if I could pay at the other end—when reunited with my *valigia*—but all he would say was "Due mille lire!" Scowling at me suspiciously, he slapped the window down.

It seemed miserably possible that I might stay in Stazione di Milano Centrale forever—or for as long as I could survive without falling over—without finding any assistance. It was mid-morning. My own party had long ago proceeded on their way eastward to Venice. What would happen to my suitcase when the train got to Venice without me, I preferred not to think. It was time to do something. But what?

"An adventurous person," I thought to myself, "would just get on the first train to Venice and see what happened." I would have to act like that adventurous person. It had long been clear to me that the crowds surged on each train in such numbers that nobody could take or check a passenger's ticket at boarding. I found the next train naming Venice as a destination, got in the crowd, wedging myself carefully between a couple of nuns, and got swept aboard. Like most people, or so it seemed, once aboard the train I had to stand, every seat being more than taken. But the heaving crowd subsided, after stowing numerous odd-shaped parcels and cases, the train gave a huffle and chuffle, and we were off. Soon we were sliding past suburbs and industrial outskirts, and it was not long before we were in the country, passing between vineyards. Eventually I realized that I had no idea now even where Milano was. If thrown off the train I would have some ado even to walk back to that city.

Not too long after, a determined though not loud voice cut through the crowd, saying with practiced distinctness, "Biglietti, signori e signore! Biglietti—biglietti!" I knew little or no Italian at that time, but that word I did know. Tickets. The conductor was collecting and punching tickets. And I had no *biglietto*, nothing other than my grimy coupon, which stated clearly in four languages: "Not Valid unless held in conjunction with a Party Ticket." I had studied the grubby slip long enough to realize that the Italian word for "party" was *gruppo*. What to do when the conductor confronted me? He did confront me, and said, as I seemed unresponsive to his first demand, "Biglietto, signorina." I handed him the grimy brown coupon. He pushed it back to me, uttering in Italian a speech which I entirely comprehended: "I cannot accept this, signora, it really isn't a ticket."

What to do? I had already made up my mind—despite my Canadian horror of making scenes, and my proto-feminist dislike of appearing weak. I swept all that away. Summoning up all the Italian vocabulary I could muster, I uttered the following remarkable oration: "Non ho biglietto, ho perduto il gruppo, non ho dinero—che farò?" And I burst into tears. The *che farò*— "what shall I do?"—was a particularly effective touch, an operatic help summoned up from recollections of *Orfeo ed Euridice* (Orfeo's lament, the aria "che farò senza Euridice").[2]

This performance was more effective than I had hoped. The conductor immediately exclaimed, "Non—non piangare, signorina!—vorrei che non pi-angessi—aspetta qui!" and went off, while others gazed at me in mild as-tonishment. I knew indistinctly that he had adjured me not to weep; presuming he had gone to converse with someone in authority, I dried my eyes and waited patiently on Fate. Eventually he returned, and with a beckon-ing forefinger addressed me, saying, "Veni qui, veni qui!" I obeyed this com-mand to come here, and followed him, clambering over people's legs and other possessions, expecting to be taken to some official up ahead. But no! My conductor now conducted me to—oh miraculous!—an empty seat on this overcrowded train. (I have often wondered how he contrived to get this, and whom he had pushed off to make way for me.) The seat was enormously welcome, as I had been standing by choice through much of the night and by necessity all of the day. I sat and waited for more events, for the interview with some alarming official. But at least the train was heading east in the heat and the sunshine, and I was proceeding toward Venice.

In mid-afternoon, the train changed, as the conductor (now my guide, philosopher, and friend) had carefully warned me it would; fortunately, he was with me on the smaller train as it chuffed slowly toward Venice, with many stops. I had plenty of opportunity to admire the vine-clad hillsides and the merry effect of the vines. In this second part of our journey, the train was becoming ever less crowded, and, as the conductor was less busy, he was able to come back and sit down and converse with me. He had only Italian, and I did not know the language save for a few words, but drew haltingly upon my knowledge of French and Latin. Yet with the help of signs and intuition on both sides, we got along famously and he understood entirely what country I had come from and how many siblings I had, and where I was studying—all sorts of things except the answer to the question "Come hai perduto il tuo gruppo?" My lack of vocabulary meant I was not up to ex-plaining exactly how I had lost my group in the middle of Europe.

Signs of another kind, at train stations, gave intimation that the train was drawing into the Veneto—we passed Verona, Padova (Padua); few passengers were left on the train and even I had enough geography to know that Venice (or, rather, Venezia) came next. There would soon be more tedious and dif-ficult explanations with some unpleasant official, I thought, but at least I would be in Venice at the time. The train tooted and slowed, we drew into an ordinary-looking sort of station, and my kind guide and friend made sure I got off. He said again, "Veni qui," and I trotted meekly after, expecting to be shown the bureau of some bureaucrat where I would have far less pleasant conversations for the next few hours.

But—no! My conductor took me into the café of the station, bought me a cup of coffee, and showed me photos of his grandchildren. Then he beckoned again, and I followed, like a happier Eurydice her Orpheus, and we went out the front door of the station—and Venice itself burst upon me! There was the Grand Canal, the boats, the people, and sparkling water. He took me to the *vaporetto*. (I am ashamed to say I do not recollect who paid for the water-bus, but now fear it may have been he.) He also found a woman on this water-bus who was going in the same direction to make sure that I got off this conveyance at the right stop (San Tomà) for my hostel, and waved goodbye.

It was written, then, on my page of the Book of Fate that around six in the afternoon of 27 August in the year 1961 I should see Venice for the first time. I found myself free of official explanations—free and in Venice and traveling between marble palaces along the Grand Canal. I wish I had had the thoughtfulness and courtesy to write down the conductor's name, so that I could have written to him later to thank him. Some of my acquaintances on the tour observed that had such an accident befallen me in other parts of Europe it would not have ended so happily, and gleefully (if perhaps unjustly) imagined the reaction of, for instance, a German conductor: "*Dienst ist mir dich hinauszuwerfen!*" (It is my duty to throw you off!) My miraculous conductor and friend is one of the chance met persons who have done me great good in this life of mine. Because of him, my opinion of Italy and especially of Italians shot sky-high during that journey—and has stayed that way ever since. And now I was in Venice, able to look about confusedly in the evening light at its wonders, until I got to my stop and found the right college dormitory, which was expecting me, though a rumor had begun to circulate that a Canadian had gone missing—and there was even a suitcase. (Two of the young men had kindly taken it in turns to lug it off the train and to the hostel from the station.) So all was well.

Now I was safe, able to enjoy this most miraculous city, to which I had traveled through so many vicissitudes (brought on by myself) and into which I was thankfully released, like a Psyche who instead of being handed over to a monster finds herself in the palace of Eros. I was taken aback by Venice. Or, it would be truer to say, overcome. Originally, I had given but little place to human productions, aside from literature and music. My life in North America had not given me a high opinion of manmade constructions and communities; the beautiful and sublime were both to be found in the works of Nature alone. (This now strikes me as quite a Canadian stance.) True, I had known New York since childhood, and recently learned to know London. I had been impressed by Oxford at first sight. By now I had seen Cambridge too, and wonderful Paris. These were all enjoyable, they were all enhanced by accessible pleasures and multiple literary associations, but they had not quite touched me. I liked them because they could give me something—zoo, planetarium, theater, friends, libraries. I did not quite love them in themselves. None of these stirred that depth of delight immediately produced by Venice—an ineffable delight something between painful longing and recognition. To put it simply, I had not known that human beings were capable of anything this good.

The next few days were animated discovery. Exploring Venice in those young days entailed a good deal of walking. We didn't want to spend money unnecessarily on *vaporetti*, and the gondolas were above our touch and remained so—in my case, until 2002. That did not mean we disregarded the gondoliers, or that they entirely ignored us. The girls of our party were abuzz with a recent piece of news, a rather George Sand-y story that a highborn English lady had run off with and married (I think married) a gondolier. When we looked at these handsome graceful men we all agreed we could see why. Yes, we should certainly have enjoyed a gondola ride, but did not want to be like those parties of raucous tourists who set a gondola abulge, shrieking and exclaiming, and requesting the latest pop songs from the conductor of the deep.

Breakfast was supplied by the hostel in the morning, bread and a cup of milky coffee. We were each furnished with a chit to take to a cheap trattoria for dinner. The trattoria itself was not without interest; I wish I could find it again, for I later realized later that some of the language I was hearing around me there was genuine Venetian. The Venetian language is fascinating and perplexing; it is intimately related to Tuscan Italian, but with some elements from the neighboring Alpine regions and other elements showing the Greek influence. The use of "z" where standard Tuscan Italian would use "gi" and English "j" seems in keeping with Greek practice; modern Greeks spelling the girl's name "Gina" put it thus "Tzina." So too the Venetians. The part of Venice that standard map makers insist on calling "Chioggia" is to Venetians "Chiozza." The church of San Giuliano or Julian is "San Zulian." Venetians also abbreviate and run words together, and omit consonants that seem superfluous. Thus "Guidecca" becomes "Zuecca." You may ask a

Venetian the way to the church of Santi Giovanni e Paolo, and he or she will understand, but is likely to render it as "San Zanipolo." Giovanni is "Zani," and our word *zany* comes from the Zani, a clown character in Venetian comedy. "Venetiano" or "Venexian" remains a real local language, a spoken tongue; it's what all Venetians use informally when talking to each other. Some foreigners have learned to converse in it, but I was at that elementary point where everything is simply "Italian" and puzzling, as I strained to make something out. Later, I was to take a six-week night course in Italian (in the hope of reading Dante) but in 1961 I was—not clueless, for clues were what I had—but without a language.

If I wish to find that long-ago trattoria again it would not be for the food. The chit allowed us to indulge in one of two choices: *vitello arrosto* or scampi. The roast veal was rather stringy and the scampi numbered six; these were accompanied by some fibrous salad. Our Venetian pleasures certainly did not extend to meals. In those far-off days I was slim, and had no inordinate appetite, but I was young and in motion and had the distinct impression that I could have put away a good deal more food without any harm. My first memories of Venice have a slight not unpleasing undertone of hunger. In those days we could seldom afford to sit about at Quadri or Caffè Florian— though I most probably patronized the Caffè Florian at least once. On 31 August I wrote on the back of a postcard with a view of the Basilica: "From where I am sitting now (drinking oh shame! Coca-Cola in the heat) I can see this wonderful building. A fascinating dream-like structure, bathed in sunlight."[3] (The "shame" was not for the café but for drinking something as commercial, American, and mundane as Coke.) Coffee and soft drinks were, however, usually taken at humbler establishments, away from central squares. We were on our feet most of the time, in museums or palazzi or art galleries, or just walking in the sunshine, in the sparkle of Venice, happy, and in my case with the happiness of slowly falling in love at long distance with a man who was not there—perhaps the safest way to fall in love in Venice.

I had arrived in happy time for one major event, the Regata Storica, which takes place on the Grand Canal on the first Sunday in September; this regatta delights the spectator with the energy of boatmen dressed in fifteenth- or sixteenth-century costumes. I have no photographs of this or any other Venetian scene of 1961, for I deliberately had not brought a camera with me. I had the theory that it is a mistake when going to an important place for the first time to take a camera, that one tends to try to frame reality narrowly with one's little box instead of looking everywhere, and hearing and smelling too. It would be better to live each moment as it came. I was of an age to have theories, though I cannot despise this one. So—no photographs. But also, no day was encumbered with the duty to "take pictures," and I enjoyed just walking and looking. Even when there was no special event, there was always something interesting to see in walking distance—for the whole of central Venice is in walking distance. Most reliable of all, the churches cropped up in the frequent *campi*, or squares, each with its treasure to discover. The churches were more zealously guarded then than now. I was about to go into one when a flock of black-clad women came about me, tsk-tsking: "È nuda!" they exclaimed. My offense was wearing a sleeveless dress; they shoved a hot shawl over my embarrassed arms, and, laughing, pushed me into the dark recesses of the church. It's the only time I have been accused of trying to go to church naked.

Wandering in twos and threes, leaving the beaten track we would meander through what felt like alleyways and secret corridors of the city, under balconies full of washing and bedding hung out to air in the sunlight. Many modern British and American tourists see something slummy in a balcony decked with washing, but that is a designed use. I was impressed by the cleanliness of the Venetians in thus daily sunning their mattresses. And from among the wash and the bedding would come the frequent gay piping of canaries. At that time, every Venetian seemed to keep a canary or two, and I supposed they were all fed in those innocent days on seeds of substances now forbidden, for they certainly sang *fortissimo* and *con amore*.

Another feature of Venice at the time was cats—there seemed to be thousands (happily, quite separate from the canaries). It has been suggested that some of these cats (especially those with one eye of a different color from the other) came from Saracen lands in the Middle Ages. James Morris, living in Venice shortly before I got there, also noted the profusion of these animals.[4] Where did all those cats go in the intervening years? Nowadays one rarely sees one. I am sure they were—and perhaps some still are—invaluable for keeping the vermin down. Most of these felines lived independent lives, some in a rather tattered condition. I remember an elderly Englishwoman feeding bread and milk to the cats in her particular *campo*. But some of these rough kitties were fed by elderly Venetian ladies in their *campi*. Almost every little *campo* had a beautiful well-head in it, some of these marvels of carved art; many were truly old. There were wells in Venice in those days (mostly antique cisterns to store precious rainwater). After the great flood of 1966 they were closed down, and many well-heads have disappeared. The singing birds and the cats likewise seem to have largely vanished, though occasionally one comes across a surviving canary, or stray cat, or one of the well-heads. I suppose the last (though not the canaries or the cats) have now gone to adorn gardens in California.

And then—one would pop out of the bewildering maze of the side streets and the piping of the caged birds to find oneself wrapped in the blaze of sun on water—and then, a little way off, the transparent and wavering watery street of the Grand Canal, sending every color into a thousand shivers, and proving that even Canaletto had been forced to dull it down in order to get on his canvas. And along the Grand Canal and the smaller side canals would come working boats piled high with goods, with fruits and vegetables for the markets. In those days before the excessive packaging of modern times, the fruit were piled high without exterior protection or wrapping, so that a heap of golden melons or oranges would be reflected in the water, with enough splendid scintillation of color, and fragmentation and reassembling of reflected form, to drive an Impressionist crazy.

*T*he impact of Venice was immediate and intense. My enthusiastic postcards don't capture the strength of the experience, though I tried a little to express it, drawing unwittingly on the clichés of everyone who has first tried to give an impression of Venice. "Here I am in Venice—which I think must be *the* most beautiful place in the world. It is fairy-tale and dreamlike, with the most marvellous light radiating everywhere. Everything glows and shimmers—full of colour and grace." So my message on 28 August assured my family. On 2 September I was trying to express an opinion of the interior of the Basilica of San Marco: "A golden light pervades everything from [by which I meant "radiating from"] the gold mosaics in the ceiling." Venice seemed to me a city of light, and so it was—of summer light, and constant coruscation. "Venice continues magnificent," I continued. "Sun, art galleries, (glorious Tintorettos), fabulous buildings, streets of blue-green-silver water—& water water everywhere & *no* motor cars."

As a nondriver (then and later), I had reason to appreciate a place with "*no* motor cars." I was on the same footing, literally, with everyone else. Venice is an irresistibly walkable city. One can only walk or take water transport. The effect of the "blue-green-silver" water and the thousand reflections is constantly exciting and somewhat unnerving. The traveler to Venice is destabilized, forced to live without the accustomed boundaries between land and water. No visitor can ignore this effect, and in me it immediately aroused a primary and intimate delight. In those days I was trying to be a poet, and Venice provoked my only poetic experiment with the sestina hitherto, a juvenile work in which (with rather more thought than in the postcards) I tried to set down what was enchanting:

> Once we have gone on ships and come home singing
> Amber and jet ships over foaming water
> Into a city floating like a dolphin,
> Arion city, where each splendid palace
> Glinting with marble, glows like new-blown glassware,
> And shimmers through lapping waves in golden sunshine.
>
> The sunshine paints soft reflections on the water,
> And there are streets down which we glide, like dolphins
> While diving oars cut, shake, each watery palace.
> In the bright morning, markets glow like glassware,
> And calls, and cries and waves curled up in sunshine
> Mingle to make a music for the singing.
>
> Arion, who with singing sailed his dolphin,
> Might sleep and dream a water-imaged palace,
> Or golden lions, globes of domes like glassware
> That gleam like bubbles floating into sunshine,
> The incense of old churches, holy singing
> That sends its music out across the water.
> ("Venice Observed," MS of 1961, stanzas 1–3)

The meter and cadence, as well as certain images, undoubtedly owe something to a line in Belvidera's mad speech in Thomas Otway's play *Venice Preserv'd* (1682): "Lutes, Laurells, Seas of Milk, and ships of Amber."[5] I make no poetic claim for my verses, but they interest me now like a diary, an attempt to capture a complex moment of intense experience. It is interesting to me also that I noticed not only the glassware everywhere sold in Venice, a part of its history, like marble palaces and images of dolphins, but that I also associated Venice with holy music, in the part quoted above and later: "The honey of Torcello, where pious singing / Echoed long ago" (stanza 4).

Venice is not always associated with holiness—not at all. It seems to most a very sensuous city. And its Greco-Byzantine architecture and ecclesiastical

style make it uncannily not quite Roman Catholic as well as not Protestant—although Ruskin with determination could find intimations of a natural or native "Protestantism" in the carving of leaves and the energy of its
details. Perhaps by comparison with the perfect Romanesque or pure northern Gothic styles, Venice's churches don't look perfectly serious, as it were.
There's something rather surprising about nearly every one. Certainly, there
are enough churches in Venice; not only every parish and every *sestier* but every
campo had to sport a church that vied with the neighbors', and almost every
one has something worth looking at—though now of course many of the
churches often lack congregations of any size, not least because so much of
the working population has been forced out of the housing market and must
find a home in industrial Mestre, on the coast at the other end of the railway
bridge.

Enough remains of churches and churchgoers in Venice to hint to the
Northern viewer at different possibilities of holiness, and ways of being holy.
Saint Mark's has shocked some visitors with its resemblance to a mosque, as
if there were something unChristian about the globose domes. (And as if the
mosques in turn did not owe something to the fifth-century Greek church
of Hagia Sophia in Byzantium.) For many tourists, including myself, Venice
is the first encounter with Byzantine style and the Greek Orthodox influence
on church architecture. I found out after I fell in love with Venice that I have
a particular penchant for what I call "interface cities," where the Orient and
the Occident meet—I later discovered and loved Istanbul-Byzantium itself.
Elements of Venice also look farther east than Greek Byzantium, just as Byzantium itself does.

Perhaps everything in Venice looks slightly too happy for our Northern
and Gothic eyes. Certainly this seems true of some of the big baroque productions. The church of the Salute is a major example of delighted piety, its
curly volutes like giant snails being ridden by celebrated and happy persons.
And there are other examples of extreme baroque ornament—the façade of
San Moisè for instance. This exuberant church of Saint Moses, which
aroused Ruskin's extreme dislike, is a celebration of an Old Testament hero,
with Moses horned at the very top and jubilating figures clambering about
the front. Some Anglo visitors of the past have been rather put out by the
Venetian habit of naming Old Testament heroes as saints (Saint Samuel and
Saint Job also have churches), not because these visitors thought that strange
custom a trespass against the Jews but rather because it confuses proper
boundaries, renders holiness as one. There still is holy music, with pious

singing, in Venice. I recommend attending Mass at San Marco and listening to the beautiful if invisible choir. Attending a church service also gets one out of the round of tourism, and allows one to recognize the enduring function of these buildings, which are still living places and not dead museums. Some of the great works of art remain stubbornly in their original situation, as part of a church for which they were designed, and not in an official culture-consumption site of exhibition, as a curious shell of the past.

Looking at my imperfect sestina, I see that, like all travelers in Venice since the end of the eighteenth century, I in the 1960s associated Venice with an experience of the past. It is simultaneously my own experience as a tourist in the now that I was trying to represent, and a reconstruction of something that was once and is no longer:

> Now though each shop sells dolphins made of glassware—
> Fountains and glass fancies glitter in the sunshine—
> The days of all the pomp and golden singing
> Have melted back into the moving water,
> Have dipped away in time, like singing dolphins,
> And left us with a memory and a palace. (stanza 6)

There are, however, hopes for something beyond mere memory:

> Yet joy still echoes in our evening singing
> For we have found a home on shifting water,
> Delight rides floating days like splendid dolphins
> We know each water-hued and shifting palace,
> Colours and forms as strong and frail as glassware,
> Where life blew, drew a home from sea and sunshine. (stanza 7)

There is a hope that color and form will survive in the future, and glass is strong despite its fragility; besides, Venice is the perpetual glassblower, creating its multi-hued yet translucent self.

On the whole, however, I yield a trifle too much to the trope of "Venice-as-past." Western literature, especially in the nineteenth century, constantly employs Venice as background for what *was* but is no more. As we shall see, Mme. De Staël and Lord Byron lead the way in this, but others are not slow to follow.

*A*fter the 1960s there was a long period in which Venice did not much figure in my life. I reconnected with the city in the early 1990s. By this time, I traveled by air, with no tedious train journey, and could stay in comfortable hotels. I came to Venice often in the early 1990s, when I was working on my book *The True Story of the Novel* (1996), and trying to reconstruct the history of fictional narrative. Venice proved a center of narrative in every sense—not only because of the numerous works of fiction in which it has figured, but for its own collection of fictional material, in visible icons and in manuscripts. After the fall of Byzantium to the Turks in 1453, Cardinal Bessarion (1400–1472), in his desperate effort to save the heritage of Greek Byzantine culture, collected all the Greek manuscripts of value he could find. Bessarion must have had a special love for the novel, for he collected diverse copies of the novels of Greek antiquity in his assemblage of precious documents that were to form the true nucleus of the Marciana Library. That library is a very grand and ornate building, with delicate decorations, designed (after forty years of wrangling) by Jacopo Sansovino. So fine is the Marciana, in fact, that it is now considered too good for the likes of mere scholars. We, the lowly, are required to conduct our reading in a rather dreary set of rooms on the ground floor, below the Marciana Library proper. It seemed a nice irony that in my effort to do as Bessarion wished, neither I nor any one of his manuscripts was to sully the purity of a library so ideal that readers had been excluded. Still, I enjoyed my time in these rather dumpy rooms with their indifferent light. It is, after all, the only library I have ever worked in where the waters lap against the walls and the cries of gondoliers can be heard through the open windows.

Work on my novel book allowed me to connect Venice more strongly with its Greek heritage. One beautiful library is in the custody of the small museum by the Greek church, San Giorgio dei Greci, not far from the lively Riva degli Schiavoni or "Slavic Shore," once the headquarters for traders from Dalmatia and ever the site of ship moorings and water traffic. The Greeks were near the Slavs in a kind of foreigners' quarter. Construction of this church of San Giorgio was begun in 1539, but the edifice contains valuable icons that are considerably older. At one time the major Greek Orthodox church in western Europe, San Giorgio can always be located by its insistently leaning campanile. The Museum of Icons in the Scuola di San Nicolo dei Greci has examples of work by Greek (mainly Cretan) artists living and working in Venice, and provides a visible bridge to the work of the greatest of these, known as El Greco. The Istituto Ellenico (Hellenic Institute) here has some manuscripts as well, among them an impressively illustrated Byzantine manuscript (late thirteenth or early fourteenth century) of the *Alexander Romance*; this manuscript had gone from a Greek owner to an Ottoman one and back again to a Greek. I used images from this manuscript in my book, but had reluctantly to forego the vivid colors; I was especially sorry to lose the bright red dresses of the Amazon ladies.

Having a good academic excuse to work in Venice and not just gape at it gave me a deeper familiarity with the city and a more relaxed sense of pleasure in its daily doings and gallant devices. Going year after year in the early 1990s, I could notice changes, not only in the place and its ongoing repairs, but in the visitors. A sudden flash of light—and lo! there were parties of Russian tourists, for the first time since the Revolution. And recently, in the blink of an eye, at the start of our new century, the Chinese tourists appear and fill the gondolas. Every phenomenon in Venice seems significant, and as ever the world touches it and it brings the world to itself. I began to notice how much I looked forward to coming to Venice, and how I would regret the loss when I no longer could plead a need to go there. Almost insensibly, I began to think of making Venice itself my topic; by 1998 I had decided that I would (someday) write about it. Thus I renewed my excuse for visiting Venice. By now, I have seen it in every season, and each seems perfect, or almost. June and September are best—or February for Carnevale. But I am not sure whether the best of all time was not the mad visit in January. Then the snow-capped mountains were clearly visible, and three days of bright winter light washed by the Alpine snows fell upon the Basilica's foaming heights, glossed the canals, and drifted into the churches clarifying all the pictures. (The bright days were followed by rain and then by snow which had interesting effects whirling around the Basilica.) Ah, January—when there are no crowds or queues, when a beautiful church may still display its Nativity Scene (*Presipio*) even after Epiphany, and green garlands linger in the arcades of the Piazza.

But why—apart from devising an excuse for visiting—did I wish to write about Venice? I realized that I was still trying to puzzle out an answer to the question "Why do I love Venice so much—more than Paris or Rome?" I began to widen the question, to think less about myself individually and more about Venice in relation to our culture at large. What has Venice done for us (in the West, and in the world), and how have we responded to it?

At the level of language there is something both attractive and slightly sinister about Venice. It has not only a number of cities named after it (like

Venice, California) but is the only city to have given a name to a whole country—Venezuela. It has contributed to an international vocabulary, yet the words it has contributed have an ambiguous ring: "arsenal," "ghetto," "zany," "casino." (Also "pantaloon"—hence "pants"—and possibly, if indirectly, "candy," at a remove from Candia [Crete], where Venetian plantations grew sugar in the Middle Ages.) Attraction and repulsion characterize our own responses to these Venetian words—yet, after all, these are words that the rest of us agreed to import, and not the only words at the disposal of Venetians themselves. The adopted vocabulary reflects our foreign vision of the city—our imagination of Venice—at least as much as the city itself.

What is it that we—or many of us—still love about Venice? Love, even if we are ashamed or abashed at loving a place that is sometimes represented as tainted or morally inferior—cheap and dirty, if you will. Or, worse, glossy and meaningless—contemptibly comparable to Disneyland. As we shall see, there have been some distinguished visitors who have not loved Venice. My own first impression of Venice before I ever went there was largely negative, and certainly condescending. I am still trying to puzzle out why I love Venice so much, an inquiry that has expanded to larger questions: "What exactly is Venice? Why is Venice so important to us?" It seems a city irreplaceable in the Western imagination—but what role does it play? Even those who express dislike or condemnation are betraying that Venice matters.

This book is an attempt to transmit reflections and a few discoveries in relation to these mysteries. I have called it *Tropic of Venice*, trying to convey our sense of Venice as an Otherwhere, a circle or space of its own kind. It is, at least metaphorically, a separate geographical space from the rest of Europe, occupying its own region in the mind, a region of difference. It is treated by Northern Europeans and their descendants in the New World—who fancy they inhabit in every way a temperate zone—with some of the mixed longing and nervousness that we reserve for tropical climes. But Venice is also a place or an idea fecund in "tropes," in the normal sense of "figures of speech" or turns of fancy, and in the less normative sense of figures of thought or experience, what we might call "figures of mind." I intend to try to deal with various of these "figures of mind" both those produced by others in relation to Venice, and those produced by the Venetians themselves—not least by the artists.

This book is not a guidebook, nor is it a history of Venice, though it inevitably has a few elements of both. It is centrally a meditation, a speculation, about what Venice means to us in the West, and why it is or has become an irreplaceable idea. Why does it have these meanings, and why was it the productive site of these tropes? In pursuing possible answers to such questions I draw on various impressions of Venice, in visitors' diaries and letters, and in novels, poems, and films.

As I am not bound to the chronological order of the historical narrator, not telling a history of Venice in the customary sense, I want to begin not at the historian's beginning. Impressions of Venice produced in the nineteenth century, which have been hauntingly repeated through the twentieth century, affect the contemporary view so greatly that discussion of them cannot be postponed to the back of the book. Consciously or not, modern visitors still see Venice through nineteenth-century lenses and suppositions. Our impression of its edifices and art are apt to be strongly colored (or discolored) by these visions. Rather than proceeding first through foundation and Middle Ages and Renaissance, awaiting a decorous arrival at the later periods, we must, I think, first embark boldly upon the salty deeps. The more immediate past has much to do with shaping both recent and current visions of Venice. These visions will go a long way toward shaping ourselves in the coming era and likewise Venice itself—including whether or not it survives.

So then, I begin with the ideas and images of Venice produced in the nineteenth century—ideas and images for the most part decidedly negative. We see through a dark lens, though with a good deal of fascination. After discussing and illustrating the negative and critical view taken in the nineteenth century, and the historical reasons for that view, I wish to take a step back to the period immediately preceding, the eighteenth century, to consider the versions of Venice that were developed in that last period of Venice's independence as a Republic and an empire. That Venice too has left many traces on the modern psyche. Here are ideas of power and pleasure. We can note the development of a certain "Gothic" literary effects circling about Venice in works created by foreign visitors, as well as tracing, especially in the works of Goldoni, the development of a native Venetian democratic vision of life. In the chapter that follows, we look at the experiences of travelers to Venice from the Renaissance through the Enlightenment.

Only after dealing with some experiences and versions of Venice from the late sixteenth to the end of the twentieth century, including what both Italians and foreigners have made of it, do I turn to what Venice made of itself, from its beginnings to the height of its power, prestige, and creativity. Most saliently and triumphantly Venice expressed itself in its architecture and its art, creating tropes of indelible importance. The great Venetian painters who flourished from the fourteenth century to the eighteenth offer us in their images many visions of Venice, and tell us how they would have us read the city itself. The last full chapter, "Labyrinth and Carnival," turns to persistently recurring images, and deals with two master tropes of Venice. Both Labyrinth and Carnival entail loss, finding, movement, and metamorphosis. They disconcertingly express time and space. These tropes are not only experientially important to the traveler, but central to Venice as an idea. The conclusion will grapple with why in this city what we call terrifying, disgusting, disorderly, or unstable mingles with aspects of what we call the beautiful. And why, in short, we cannot really do without Venice.

2

Ever-Vanishing City

But chief her shrine where naked Venus keeps,
And Cupids ride the Lyon of the Deeps;
Where, eas'd of Fleets, the Adriatic main
Wafts the smooth Eunuch and enamour'd swain.
—Alexander Pope, *Dunciad*, Book IV

Its terraces, crowned with airy yet majestic fabrics, appeared as if they
had been called up from the ocean by the wand of an enchanter, rather
than reared by mortal hands.
—Ann Radcliffe, *The Mysteries of Udolpho*

*T*he entry into Venice, the story in which I have been engaging on a
personal level, is a trope of literature. Arriving is a significant process,
and entry into this strange tropic, like a ritual of initiation, demands remark.
In her novel *The Mysteries of Udolpho* (1794) Ann Radcliffe imagines her heroine Emily advancing upon Venice in Carnival time (in company with her aunt
and the villain Montoni) after a barge trip along the Brenta:

so smoothly did the barge glide along, that its motion was not perceivable, and the
fairy city appeared approaching to welcome the strangers.

She looked round, with anxious inquiry; the deep twilight, that had fallen over
the scene, admitted only imperfect images to the eye . . . a chorus of voices and
instruments now swelled on the air. . . . Now it died away, and fancy almost beheld
the holy choir reascending towards heaven; then again it swelled with the breeze,
trembled awhile, and again died into silence. . . . The deep stillness, that succeeded,
was as expressive as the strain that had just ceased. . . . Emily . . . long indulged the
pleasing sadness, that had stolen upon her spirits, but the gay and busy scene that
appeared, as the barge approached St. Mark's Place, at length roused her attention.
The rising moon, which threw a shadowy light upon the terraces, and illumined the

porticos and magnificent arcades that crowned them, discovered the various company, whose light steps, soft guitars and softer voices, echoed through the colonnades.[1]

Holy singing, indistinctness, fragments of architectural splendor, varying illumination characterize not only Radcliffe's "Gothic" manner, but also descriptions of Venice, especially of arrival; "pleasing sadness" or some other oxymoronic half-negative emotion often alternates with the "gay and busy."

A real traveler of the eighteenth century, Johann Wolfgang von Goethe, notes his own arrival with a mock solemnity: "It was written, then, on my page in the Book of Fate that at five in the afternoon of the twenty-eighth day of September in the year 1786, I should see Venice for the first time as I entered this beautiful island-city, this beaver-republic. So now, thank God, Venice is no longer a mere word to me, an empty name, a state of mind which has so often alarmed me who am the mortal enemy to mere words."[2] Goethe describes in further detail the slow approach by a journey down "the lovely Brenta" (77). Goethe's discovery of Venice is represented—by himself to himself—as the happy result of a pursuit of reality.

Ruskin, in a stroke of narrative genius, divides his story of entry and first sight into two parts in *The Stones of Venice* (1851–1853). The first description, telling of the journey down the Brenta to Mestre and then to Venice, is ominously full of the decayed, the spoiled, the modern. The once-beautiful Brenta is ugly and "dreary," "with one or two more villas . . . of the old Venetian type . . . sinking fast into utter ruin, black, and rent, and lonely, set close to the edge of the dull water, with what were once small gardens beside them, kneaded into mud . . . and here and there a few fragments of marble steps . . . now setting into the mud in broken joints, all aslope, and slippery with green weed."[3] This uninspiring river journey ends at Mestre and a journey across the lagoon by gondola:

Now we can see nothing but what seems a low and monotonous dockyard wall, with flat arches to let the tide through it;—this is the railroad bridge, conspicuous above all things. But at the end of those dismal arches there rises, out of the wide water, a straggling line of low and confused brick buildings, which, but for the many towers which are mingled among them, might be the suburbs of an English manufacturing town. Four or five domes, pale, and apparently at a greater distance, rise over the centre of the line; but the object which first catches the eye is a sullen cloud of black smoke brooding over the northern half of it, and which issues from the belfry of a church.

It is Venice. (I, 354)

So ends the first volume of *The Stones of Venice*, letting the reader absorb Ruskin's disillusionment. If you are searching for reality, here it is. Everything is crumbling, or stunted, misshapen, or uncompromisingly ugly in the modern manner. There is apparently no escape from the ethos and aesthetics of an English manufacturing town. We have come to a place which is alien through being too familiar, depressingly modern and industrial, a base and brickish outskirts.

After taking the Via Negativa at the end of the first volume, Ruskin takes a different path at the beginning of the second. Having dealt with the initial "disappointment," he turns to the effect of the sea, the sky, the distant mountains, and the sunset light upon the mountains and upon "the nearer burning of the campaniles of Murano, and on the great city, where it magnified itself along the waves, as the quick silent pacing of the gondola drew nearer and nearer" (*Stones*, II, 2–3). Then he engages in one of his great proto-Proustian sentences:

And at last, when it its walls were reached, and the outmost of its untrodden streets was entered, not through towered gate or guarded rampart, but as a deep inlet between two rocks of coral in the Indian Sea; when first upon the traveller's sight opened the long ranges of columned palaces,—each with its black boat moored at the portal,—each with its image cast down, beneath its feet, upon that green pavement which every breeze broke into new fantasies of rich tessellation; when first, at the extremity of the bright vista, the shadowy Rialto threw its colossal curve slowly forth from behind the palace of the Camerlenghi; that strange curve, so delicate, so adamantine, strong as a mountain cavern, graceful as a bow just bent; when first, before its moon-like circumference was all risen, the gondolier's cry, "Ah! Stalì," struck sharp upon the ear, and the prow turned aside under the mighty cornices that half met over the narrow canal, where the splash of the water followed close and loud, ringing along the marble by the boat's side; and when at last that boat darted forth upon the breadth of silver sea, across which the front of the Ducal palace, flushed with its sanguine veins, looks to the snowy dome of Our Lady of Salvation, it was no marvel that the mind should be so deeply entranced by the visionary charm of a scene so beautiful and so strange, as to forget the darker truths of its history and its being. (*Stones*, II, 3)

Venice as a manifestation is a phenomenon that enchants. But its nature is to express illusion, as Ruskin reminds us, though we may want to imagine Venice as a timeless construct of adamantine will, immune to mutability, instead of subject to necessity and change: "Well might it seem that such a city had owed her existence rather to the rod of the enchanter, than the fear of the fugitive; that the waters which encircled her had been chosen for the mirror of her state, rather than the shelter of her nakedness, and that all which in nature was wild or merciless,—Time and Decay, as well as the waves and tempests,—had been won to adorn her instead of to destroy, and might still spare, for ages to come, that beauty which seemed to have fixed for its throne the sands of the hour-glass as well as of the sea" (*Stones*, II, 3). Such impressions, Ruskin reminds us, are illusions, though it is no wonder that the "hurried traveller" may "shut his eyes to the depth of her desolation" (4). In view of the task at hand for Ruskin and the reader there is no permission for the "great charities of the imagination." Modern culture has created a delusory Venice: "The Venice of modern fiction and drama is a thing of yesterday, a mere efflorescence of decay, a stage dream which the first ray of daylight must dissipate into dust" (4). Ruskin becomes hard-boiled; he will not tolerate any sentimental Byronic twaddle, recollecting in annoyance the well-known opening lines of Canto IV of *Childe Harold's Pilgrimage* (1818), "I stood in Venice on the Bridge of Sighs; / A palace and a prison on each hand,"[4] lines which had become part of British tourists' mental apparatus. "No prisoner," Ruskin proclaims, "whose name is worth remembering, or whose sorrow deserved sympathy, ever crossed that 'Bridge of Sighs' which is the centre of the Byronic ideal of Venice" (4). Only common modern felons crossed that bridge. (Oh, that's all right, then.)

It was probably William Beckford in the 1780s who began the fashion of referring to the bridge which he tells us is named by Venetians "Ponte dei Sospiri."[5] He describes his horror upon looking at the Doge's Palace and thinking of the "close stifling cells, between the leads and beams of the palace" and "the dungeons, deep under the canals . . . its majesty is contaminated by the abodes of punishment." It is not clear whether Beckford objects to the prison or to the aesthetically distressing combination of prison and palace, but he wishes some giant could "level it with the sea," and regrets that Neptune, god of earthquakes and tidal waves, does not hold his ancient power (106).[6] With this whimsical wish for punishment of the punishers, youthful Beckford (born 1760) is perhaps the first of the modern Romantics to wish Venice overwhelmed—though his wish, comically expressed, attaches to the palace and not the whole. Certainly *le Pont des soupirs* is made much of in Madame de Staël's *Corinne ou l'Italie* (1807). De Staël claims that those who passed by the canal could hear the prisoners crying: *"Justice, help!"* She also dwells on the idea that state criminals were taken out of prison alive, by night, transported by boat, and drowned "in a spot on the lagoon where it was forbidden to fish; horrible idea that perpetuates secrecy even after death, and does not leave the wretch the hope that his remains at least will inform his friends that he has suffered, and that he is no more!"[7] (The author acknowledges, however, that at the time in which the novel is set, ostensibly the late eighteenth century, the canal had not been put to this hideous use for over a century.)[8] These horrors attract writers, especially of a liberal or libertarian cast of mind, but for Ruskin they are mere staples of cheap fiction.

Forget fiction and sentiment, Ruskin commands. All we have are the remains of the great Venice, secreted in moldering fragmentation, "hidden in many a grass-grown court, and silent pathway, and lightless canal, where the slow waves have sapped their foundations for five hundred years, and must soon prevail over them for ever" (5). Ruskin is really looking for the remains of "a lost city," remains which, in a kind of wizardry, he can capture and reanimate on paper even while the transitory witnesses to greatness are doomed to destruction.

Western literature from the beginning of the nineteenth century constantly employs Venice as a revelation and a metaphor for what has disappeared—for that which *was* but is no more. Browning's dramatic monologue "A Toccata of Galuppi's" offers a complex use of the nineteenth century's vision of Venice as a failed and dying—or indeed dead—place. The title is a puzzle, as, strictly speaking, the eighteenth-century composer Baldassare Galuppi (1706–1785) never wrote a "toccata," but John Julius Norwich has ingeniously worked out that the poem is probably based on an Italian popular song of that name, the melody of which was actually transcribed by Browning in a letter.[9] The speaker of the poem seems to be listening to some real music of Galuppi being played, but the central melody may be that adapted by the popular song, which presumably (like most popular songs) already has a certain valence of eroticism. In the poem Venice's disappearance is combined with a fictive memory of its eighteenth-century living self, a reminder that comes through music. Browning's speaker in "A Toccata" projects his own lost erotic chances upon the idea of Venice and upon the audible wall of the music provided by Galuppi, representative of the last faint sparks of genuine Venetian life. This Venetian artist can (half-irritatingly) still be heard, although his phantasmal music, like that of a "ghostly cricket, creaking where a house was burned," emanates from a city that is dead (line 34).[10] In "Venice. An Ode," Byron praises the earlier lasciviousness of Venetians as merely "the overbeating of the heart, / And flow of too much happiness" (lines 27–28),[11] most unlike Browning's self-righteous but melancholic speaker who holds—or tries to hold—that Venice got what was coming to her because of erotic overindulgence and decadent manners. At once censorious and wistful, he sternly passes judgment: "'dust and ashes, dead and done with, Venice spent what Venice earned'" (line 35). So Browning's Victorian speaker hears the music say:

> As for Venice, and her people, merely born to bloom and drop,
> Here on earth they bore their fruitage, mirth and folly were the crop;
> What of soul was left, I wonder, when the kissing had to stop? (lines
>   40–42)

Venice stands for what is incomplete, foolish, fleshly, and human, mere "mirth and folly." In 1855 when Browning (sympathetic to Italian aspirations for freedom from Austria) published this poem written in 1853, he knew well of the Venetians' heroic stand in 1848–1849; it is his obtuse narrator who clings to the conventional notions of Venetian "mirth and folly." This Victorian forerunner of Prufrock partly loves to think that others (unlike himself) have failed through imprudence, folly, and sensuality. Yet within the poem Galuppi himself as an artist proves not to be quite "dead and done with"; paradoxically, art reconstructs itself on countless occasions—music when it is played, paintings when they are looked at. Art survives its own time, and thus subjugates time even while falling prey to it. All art is "a ghostly cricket." Art has the last ghostly laugh in Browning's poem, for the priggish Victorian speaker listening to Galuppi and thinking of Venice becomes uneasily aware at one level of his being of unsatisfied erotic desire—"Was a lady such a lady, cheeks so round and lips so red—" (line 13). Browning's speaker presages Thomas Mann's Aschenbach, who discovers erotic desire late in life in his journey—not his first but definitely his last   to Venice.

The speaker of "A Toccata" was "never out of England" (line 9). This speaker certainly cannot be equated with Robert Browning, who lived in Italy part of his life, and who fell intensely for Venice—as did his son Pen, who acquired a Renaissance palazzo, the Ca' Rezzonico (presently a museum primarily exhibiting eighteenth-century art and artifacts). It was at Ca' Rezzonico that Robert Browning died, on the Grand Canal within the sound of the bells of St. Mark's. So Venice numbered Browning's hours and saw him off, and his present was part of its present, and he then became part of the past of Venice, which survived him as it has survived Byron and will survive me and all of its other admirers. Venice lends itself to meditations and homilies upon time and the temporal—partly through jealousy on our part, for Venice in its very structure admits time and tides as part of its nature.

Why is Venice so consistently associated with what is dead and dying— with what *was* but is no more? There is one powerful reason for this phenomenon—though most tourists are ignorant of it. Venice was conquered in May 1797 by Napoleon, whose generals subjugated the city. Before yielding, Doge Ludovico Manin declared the governmental organizations dissolved and the power of Venice entirely devolved upon the people. The French soon made their own declaration abolishing the ancient constitution. The Tree of Liberty erected in the Piazza San Marco. Playing his own military chess game, Napoleon passed the city-state on as a sop to the Austrians in October 1797, but when he had risen to power in France he grabbed Venice back. The French troops marched into Venice again in 1806, and then began what Alvise Zorzi calls "the saddest period of the whole history of Venice."[12] Once a Republic, it was jammed together with other regions of North Italy under the nominal rule of Empress Josephine's son Eugène de Beauharnais. Eternally inimical to one-man rule, Venice now had to bow to a prince. Already suffering from the crash of its bank after the first invasion, and the loss of its overseas territories, it now had to endure the total blockade that prevented sustaining trade with England, and other perpetual indignities. Indigenous organizations, including the ancient *scuole* which had nourished so many artists, were shut down under the enlightened Napoleon, as well as other devotional or charitable groups and guilds—anything the citizens or *popoli* organized for themselves. Many churches were shut altogether or put to other uses. The church of Sant'Aponal became a political prison, Santa Maria delle Vergini a penitentiary. The culture received blow after blow—not least because Napoleon had taken a lot of loot with him over the Alps, and paraded it about Paris as a sign of victory, like a Roman triumph. Prince Eugene could take any piece of art he wished, and give it to whomever he liked—a Carpaccio to a general, for instance.

Despite officially handing over rule to his stepson, Napoleon took an active interest in redesigning the city. It was he (now emperor) who had the old church of San Geminiano, facing the Basilica of San Marco on the other side of the Piazza, torn down in 1807 to make way for a palatial ballroom. Napoleon's well-known (and contemptuous) comment that the Piazza was "the finest drawing room in Europe" indicates that he wanted it for his drawing room, with a ballroom to match.

With Napoleon's defeat and first exile in 1814 his role in redesigning the city came to an end. Austria (or the Austro-Hungarian empire) came fully into control. The empire was determined to take and control the Italian peninsula, and succeeded in holding down much of North Italy. The French changed their mind about Venice a while later, but their attempts to retake the city were repelled. The Austrians remained, visible and aggressive military occupiers. Soldiers and officers were everywhere, and fortified the city to further their own control. The island of San Giorgio Maggiore with Palladio's church and convent was turned into a military post and battery, its guns trained toward the Piazza. Most of the nineteenth century was a period of subjugation and occupation; the Austrians did not depart until the late 1860s.

That the Austrian occupiers were deeply hated by the Venetians could be noted by anybody who cared to look. Anthony Trollope, who spent some time in Venice in the summer of 1855, notes the hatred in his story "The Last Austrian Who Left Venice" (1867):

In the spring and early summer of the year last past,—the year 1866,—the hatred felt by Venetians towards the Austrian soldiers who held their city in thraldom, had reached its culminating point. For years this hatred had been very strong; how strong can hardly be understood by those who never recognise the fact that there had been, so to say, no mingling of the conquered and the conquerors, no process of assimilation between the Italian vassals and their German masters.

Venice as a city was as purely Italian as though its barracks were filled with no Hungarian long-legged soldiers, and its cafés crowded with no white-coated Austrian officers. And the regiments which held the town lived as completely after their own fashion as though they were quartered in Pesht, or Prague, or Vienna,—with this exception, that in Venice they were enabled, and indeed from circumstances were compelled,—to exercise a palpable ascendancy which belonged to them nowhere else. They were masters, daily visible as such.[13]

The Venetians dealt with the invader-occupier by employing hauteur and self-control. They cut down on or put an end to their public pleasures, for they would not enjoy themselves under the condescending eyes of these "masters." The masking and partying diminished. Carnevale continued for a while, though not as it had been, and it ceased altogether after the failure of the insurrection of 1848–1849 and its cruel aftermath. Venetians would not attend concerts and shows patronized by the Austrians, and their private and religious celebrations withdrew into the inmost Venetian recesses. They would not listen to the Austrian military bands that pom-pommed in St. Mark's Square, nor join the conquerors in their coffeehouse. Even now I feel a pang of guilt if I enter the coffeehouse Quadri—though it makes the best cup of hot chocolate in the world—for Quadri is the Austrian establishment, patronized by no patriotic Venetians during the nineteenth century. Florian's Caffè was patriotic, and Venetians would deign to take their coffee there (if they could afford it). But most Venetians were suffering too much hardship from an imposed régime and a decaying economy to worry about coffeehouses in the Piazza San Marco.

The memory of the Austrian occupation lies heavily on much of North Italy, and for Venice it is a particular dark and long-endured trauma. From having been an indomitable Republic, the virgin and unvanquished ruler of the seas, Venice became a ravished and impure site, a place of the vanquished. Once she was "all glory," as Byron says in *Childe Harold's Pilgrimage*, "Though making many slaves, herself still free/ And Europe's bulwark 'gainst the Ottomite" (canto IV, stanza xiv, lines 118–123). But now look at her! Unlike the other Northern Italian cities enduring Austrian overlordship, Venice, former seat of empire, was jeered at and derided for her immense loss. The change wrought was not the effect of the hand of time and natural alteration—Venice the great was overthrown. Oddly enough, much writing about the condition of the city-state or ex-city-state in this period treats the change from Venetian power and prosperity to Venetian subjugation and impoverishment as if this were in part or in the whole the result of an inevitable—and even welcome—sequence of natural change and decay, if not ultimately the consequence of supernatural judgment on her sins.

Byron might be expected to take account of political causes, but he depicts Venice as not only passé but dying in that fourth canto of *Childe Harold's Pilgrimage*. At first glance Venice still looks wonderful:

> She looks a sea Cybele, fresh from ocean,
> Rising with her tiara of proud towers

At airy distance, with majestic motion,
A ruler of the waters and their powers. (stanza ii, lines 10–13)

She was—but is no more—a goddess and a queen. The traveler bitterly regrets the loss of her empire and power, and her lack of spirit in giving in to
her conqueror without a real fight. Having lost her greatness, the best that
shamed Venice can do is to sink back into the water:

> Venice, lost and won,
> Her thirteen hundred years of freedom done,
> Sinks, like a sea-weed, into whence she rose!
> Better be whelm'd beneath the waves, and shun,
> Even in destruction's depth, her foreign foes,
> From whom submission wrings an infamous repose. (stanza xiii, lines
> 112–117)

The poem seems to will Venice to commit suicide (by drowning) in order
not to prolong dishonor. In his "Ode" on Venice (1819), written about the
same time, Byron expresses exasperated contempt for the conquered Venetians of today, who are in such marked contrast to their imperial forefathers.

> And yet they only murmur in their sleep.
> In contrast with their fathers—as the slime,
> The dull green ooze of the receding deep,
> . . . .
>   . . . . and thus they creep,
> Crouching and crab-like, through their sapping streets. (lines 7–13)

Modern Venetians are but "slime," ugly mark of an ebb, in contrast to the
dashing waves of a former advancing tide. It is only a matter of time, Byron
indicates, until Venice itself is erased. The image of the tide confusingly
changes from that which is lively and successful (Venice of old) to that which
must destroy her. The poet seems almost anxious to see the Venetians and
their city expire, vanishing beneath the Lagoon, though in his prophecy he
has the grudging generosity to admit that this inevitable disappearance will
cause regret in some quarters.

> Oh Venice! Venice! When thy marble walls
> Are level with the waters, there shall be

A cry of nations o'er thy sunken halls,
A loud lament along the sweeping sea! ("Ode," lines 1–4)

We may take Byron as an initial point in the procession of doom-laden prophecies of Venice's being about to be overtaken by time and the sea, in just retribution for her own faults and follies. In the 1730s Alexander Pope thought Venice needed to be reminded that her pride rose from "dirt and sea-weed";[14] Byron and Percy Bysshe Shelley go further in wanting to return the pride to the mud and weed. These two poets seem in a race, as it were, to express this view, though Byron got there first; *Childe Harold's Pilgrimage* circulated rapidly in England and beyond. In the same period (1818–1819), Shelley expresses a similar sentiment in "Lines Written Among the Euganean Hills." From his hilltop vantage point, the poet sees at a distance the enchanting marine city bright in the first shining light of morning:

Underneath Day's azure eyes
Ocean's nurseling, Venice lies,
A peopled labyrinth of walls,
Amphitrite's destined halls,

. . . .

And before that chasm of light,
As within a furnace bright,
Column, tower, and dome, and spire
Shine like obelisks of fire. (lines 94–107)[15]

But this morning vision of the bright city is a mirage, for Venice has fallen upon dark days. She is contemptible: "with thy conquest-branded brow/ Stooping to the slave of slaves" (lines 122–123). The best that can be hoped for is that this enslaved state will be ended by her final reclamation by the sea. She will become "A less drear ruin then than now" in a drowned future "when the sea-mew/ Flies as once before it flew,/ O'er thine isles depopulate" (lines 125–127).

Apparently, Venice is really not worth saving. It is more appropriate that it should sink into the deep. There is a beauty in the idea of its marble palaces turning into something like a reef, "with green sea-flowers overgrown" (line 130). As for the degenerate inhabitants, they appear to be beneath consideration, let alone rescue:

Those who alone thy towers behold
Quivering though aëreal gold,
As I now behold them here,
Would imagine not they were
Sepulchres, where human forms,
Like pollution-nourished worms,
To the corpse of greatness cling,
Murdered, and now mouldering. (lines 142–149)

Surely Percy Bysshe Shelley never wrote a more vicious simile. If Venice's people are but "pollution-nourished worms," it does not matter what happens to this vanquished and degraded place. The contrast between both Byron's and Shelley's blame-the-victim attitudes toward the Venetians and their hopeful vision of the modern Greeks—conquered but about to rise again—could not be more striking.

The English Romantics present us with a Venice conquered and spent, its people humbled and degenerate. Both Byron and Shelley seem angry at Venice for not being an empire any more, not acting as a power making many into slaves, while keeping itself still splendidly free. Having lost, Venice is about to disappear—*should* disappear. It is a place that was but soon will not be. The Irish poet Thomas Moore deals with its fate even more briskly:

MOURN not for VENICE—let her rest
    In ruin, 'mong those States unblest,
Beneath whose gilded hoofs of pride,
    Where'er they trampled, Freedom died.
. . . .
Mourn not for VENICE—though her fall
    Be awful, as if Ocean's wave
Swept o'er her—she deserves it all,
    And Justice triumphs o'er her grave.[16]

To call this unsympathetic would be an understatement. Moore, however, has a different point to make from Byron and Shelley; his complaint against Venice is its harsh imperial rule (for "Venice" read "England"). Byron admires the old Venice that enslaved others but kept itself free, whereas it is that time of greatness itself to which Moore objects. He is glad that the Venetian empire is conquered: "I feel the moral vengeance sweet" (86). Amidst such disapproval it is refreshing to come upon a dissenting voice in young Benjamin Disraeli's early novel *Contarini Fleming* (1832). Contarini, descended from Venetian nobles, loves Venice at first sight, even under the occupation. Rejecting the *Leggenda nera*, he is full of rebellious fervor: "I could not forget that, of all places in the world, Venice was the one in which I should most desire to find myself a conspirator."[17] Alas!—in 1848 "Dizzy," the rising statesman, friend of Metternich, supported the rights of the Austrian (as of the British) empire.

The poets writing in the early nineteenth century seem to collude in imagining, gloatingly, Venice's imminent and deserved final destruction, its merited and inevitable drowning beneath the waves. Browning's "Toccata of Galuppi's" encapsulates and even parodies this triumphing over the grave of failed Venice.

We have already heard Ruskin, almost as if unconsciously, repeat this trope of divinely appointed and inevitable disappearance back into the water: "where the slow waves have sapped their foundations for five hundred years, *and must soon prevail over them for ever*" (italics mine). The effect of the nineteenth century's vision of a dark and doomed Venice has been profound. In twentieth- (and now twenty-first-) century literature Venice has likewise and perpetually been presented as subject to immediate erasure, to disappearance beneath the waters. Most unfortunately, campaigns to "save" Venice inadvertently repeat the same trope, and even seem, like the words of the poets, to lend themselves to a certain hidden desire that Venice *should* fulfill all these prophecies and disappear. It would somehow be so fitting if Venice were to become an eternal absence, drowning in one last dramatic act! This yearning—stemming from Romanticism's encounter with the effects of the Austrian occupation—-is an unwholesome hangover from the nineteenth century.

The city itself at times does seem to collude with its own oft-prophesied destruction (as in the case of the admission of giant cruise ships, or the pollution-laden industrialized breezes). But some of the first crude symptoms of modernity that swept into the Venetian Lagoon and made its position more precarious were imposed. The land bridge for the railway, built in 1846, represents the first great bar to the natural flow of the Lagoon. The station was the Austrians' idea, and they destroyed the Church of Santa Lucia and quite a lot of Cannaregio in building the new terminus. (The relics of Santa Lucia were removed to another church, San Geremia, which carries an imposing sign on its apse, the side nearest the Canal, informing us that the relics of Lucia Virgin Martyr of Syracuse can be venerated here.)

It is not true that the Venetians remained in the spiritless state that Byron indicted. In 1848, led by Daniele Manin, the Venetians arose and shook off Austrian oppression. On 22 March 1848, Manin, standing on one of the tables of Florian's Caffè, told the crowd "Siamo liberi!" ("We're free!").[18] The Venetians formed a government, wrote a constitution, and held a remarkably democratic election in January 1849.

The Austrians, first defeated and then held in a stand-off by heroic troops at Marghera, returned with better arms and more zeal, and laid siege to the city, as described by Jonathan Keates in *The Siege of Venice* (2005). The bombardment begun in May 1849 increased in intensity in July. Venice has the dubious honor of being the first European city menaced with aerial bombing. The Austrians rigged up a kind of flying bomb made of a heavy grenade attached to a balloon. (This may have been the invention of Effie Ruskin's admirer, the Austrian officer Paulitsky.)[19] Fortunately for the city, these balloons blew back upon the Austrians, so full aerial warfare was postponed. Ordinary bombardment increased in ferocity. The hospitals were said to be marked as targets. By the end of the conflict, Austrian heavy projectiles almost reached Piazza San Marco. Shells had hit the Madonna dell'Orto, San Zanipolo, the Frari, and other historic buildings. Cannaregio was badly damaged. Venetians of all classes contributed everything they had to the war effort in remarkable unity, but they were ultimately reduced to starvation; cholera raged (among the enemy too), and the shelling continued relentlessly.

The city had to yield, though it was slow in coming to that recognition. During a cease-fire and negotiation for capitulation, a crowd of Venetians along the canal of Giudecca cried "Viva Venezia!" According to Alvise Zorzi in *Venezia austriaca*, this cry came to the ears of the Austrian field marshal, who was so irritated that the gave orders to start shelling again. "But the ancient sprit was not yet lost, if it is true that a gondolier, at the recommencement of the bombardment, exclaimed 'How melancholy it was, those last few days, not to hear some firing.'"[20] This is an inspiring David-and-Goliath story in which Goliath wins. At last, in August 1849, Venice had to yield, after a little over a year of hard liberty.

After the revolt, when Venice, like much of Italy, was under the control of General Radetsky, the Austrians carried on an even stricter régime, subjecting the Venetians to heavy taxation and drafting young men for military service in Austria. They forced the toughly taxed and impoverished Venetians to pay for the damage they themselves had wrought. The period from 1849 until the liberation was an era of intense misery for Venice and her people.

Venice was not allowed to join the new state of Italy now unifying under the guidance of Cavour at the end of the 1850s; the Austrians let some other territories go, but not the jewel in the crown. European opinion, however, was now swaying toward the side of Italy, and Garibaldi's heroic marches with his volunteers created excellent publicity. Italian men of fighting age (including volunteers from Venice and other fortified towns who had managed to elude Austrian checkpoints) joined both Garibaldi's guerrillas and the newly formed army of Italy. They endeavored to defeat Austria militarily by force of Italian arms, but were defeated at the battle of Custoza (June 1866). Austria, however, was being severely pressed by France and Prussia. Only after the Austrians had been thoroughly defeated at Sadowa was most of the rest of Italy, including Venice, free of the yoke. After a strange, short interval in which Venice was technically in the hands of France, who then gave it to Victor Emmanuel (in October 1866), there was nothing for the Venetians to do but join newborn "Italy" under its new monarchy. The year 1867 was Venice's first full "free" year since 1796, but it was no longer its own state. Nor was the Austrian empire far away in 1867. The border lay only a few miles beyond Verona. Other areas of the Veneto, like historic Aquileia and Grado, remained in Austrian control. The boundaries of the modern Italian state were drawn only seven years before my own visit, when in 1954 Trieste and environs were ceded to Italy.

The nineteenth century was in most respects a period of practically unmitigated disaster for Venice. Everything important that happened to the city and the Veneto during the period 1797–1866 was wrought by the invaders, and the occupiers cared little or nothing for the physical or economic health of the inhabitants. You will look hard in Venice for images of the nineteenth century before 1867. The Museo Correr, the museum of the city's history, does not even have an exhibition dealing with the heroic days of free Venice 1848–1849. This omission perhaps results from an aversion to the topic of subjugation, or from a consciousness of the need for niceness in the European Union, or from a commercial unwillingness to offend German-speaking tourists—or all of these together. The wall of the Post Office behind St. Mark's is the only effectual historical memorial, and some of its bronzes are new; the one to Lajos Winkler and his band of Hungarians who fought with the Venetians was put up only in 2002.

If you want pictures of men in top hats and ladies in crinolines enjoying St. Mark's Square, you must turn to Austrian, French, or English artists. There is a kind of unconscious Venetian suppression of images of the nineteenth century (the Ottocento). This ban makes Luchino Visconti's film *Senso* (1954) surprising and, in a way, refreshing; it is set in May–June 1866, and here you do see Venetian men in top hats and ladies in crinolines who have been missing so long from Venice—though it is a sepia-colored and forlorn Venice of the Ghetto area that is shown in most exterior shots. (This film, made less than a decade after World War II, seems an attempt to come to terms with more recent conflict and liberation.) Undeniably, Venice was changed completely by the long ordeal of cramping oppression and expanding poverty; nearly the entire nineteenth century is a spiritual and cultural waste. In the eighteenth century, even though its economic and political power had waned, Venice was one of the most culturally productive centers in the Western world: it produced new composers such as Vivaldi, new writers such as Goldoni, and new artists like Giambattista and Giandomenico Tiepolo. In the time of its subjugation, its creativity was sadly in hiding.

Venice responded to oppression with massive dignity, but to foreigners, many of whom found the Austrian officers jolly folk, Venetian dignity seemed like sullen ill-humor. William Dean Howells, who was sent as American consul to Venice (a sinecure post, his reward for writing Abraham Lincoln's campaign biography), learned the language (not only Italian, but also Venetian), and observed the customs, but evidently found the Venetians sulky. He feels a twinge in his own republican principles, tacitly put in question by his falling in with the imperial power that had put an end to the Republic. As Venice was becoming liberated, he admits that something in the people's conduct is worthy of admiration, though as we see in his *Venetian Life* (first version published 1866), Howells can still be grudging: "They were then under Austrian rule; and in spite of much that was puerile and theatrical in it, there was something very affecting in their attitude of what may best be described as passive defiance. This alone made them heroic, but it also made them tedious."[21]

Despite many unkind or patronizing comments about the Venetians, Howells admits that the weight is on the heroic side:

And it is impossible to believe that a people which can maintain the stern and unyielding attitude now maintained by the Venetians towards an alien government disposed to make them any concession short of freedom, in order to win them into voluntary submission, can be wanting in the great qualities which distinguish living peoples from those passed hopelessly into history and sentiment. In truth, glancing back over the whole career of the nation, I can discern in it nothing so admirable, so dignified, so steadfastly brave, as its present sacrifice of all that makes life easy and joyous, to the attainment of a good which shall make life noble. (*Venetian Life*, 398)

When Venice emerged into freedom from Austria, it had perforce to be welded to a new state, Italy, unknown to its past. No longer an autonomous city-state, it emerged from its long Sleeping Beauty coma to find itself with no option but a forced marriage. In the Veneto, a long and somewhat painful reconstruction took place; the still impoverished region had to make expensive changes to renew itself. The city tried to find ways once again to enhance its appeal as an aesthetic center. In 1893 the art festival, the Biennale, was planned, and has become an agreeable continuing institution. (I recommend going to Venice in a Biennale year; the most entertaining artifacts and constructions are likely to be the sculptures placed in the Lagoon itself.) In order to attract businesses and tourists, buildings had to be repaired, and much effort was put into reconstruction, physical and mental. More damage was to be endured, just after affairs had seemed on the mend.

Although Italy came out of World War I with a little more territory in the Veneto (including Aquilea and Grado), Venice itself had a terrible time. The Austro-Hungarian army advanced to only a few kilometers away, and Venice once again suffered heavy bombing—now including successful aerial bombardment—from 1915 to 1918. As Ralph Curtis explained to Isabella Stewart Gardner in September 1915, Venice had to invent its own blackout, which included covering up shiny objects, even the angels on the Basilica:

The mosquitos from Pola come buzzing over nearly every fine night, and drop bombs for half an hour or so. . . . Venice is a like a lovely prima donna in deep mourning. All the gilded angels wear sack-cloth painted dirty grey. Anything that shines is covered. At night all is as black as in the dark ages. "Serrenos" call out "all is well" every half hour. But when danger is signalled the elec[tric] light is cut off, sirens blow, cannon firebombs explode and the whole city shakes on its piles. All the hotels but the Danieli's are hospitals.[22]

Furious Austrian bombings of the night of 27 February 1918, when parts of central Venice were hit, sent the population fleeing to Giudecca and the Lido; a large number left Venice altogether and became refugees. Alvise Zorzi attributes to World War I the final rupture of the continuity of Venetian customs and culture.[23]

The twentieth century has not been much kinder to Venice than the nineteenth, though by the end a certain degree of prosperity had been reestablished. Rising tourism in the 1920s was cut down by the Depression years, but that was nothing compared to the rise of Mussolini, who began to direct local affairs more than people had bargained for. In 1932 the Venice Film Festival was initiated; the city thought it had worked out an express understanding with the government that there would be no interference with the films or the visitors. But after about five years Mussolini began to intrude, and soon the festival was nothing but a series of propaganda movies. Meanwhile, Mussolini had banned the rebudding Carnevale. As Italy was one of the Axis powers at the outset of World War II, Venice might hope to be free this time from open attack. But the Germans in effect invaded in 1943, and implicit subjugation led to unprecedented atrocities; Venice is shamed by the fate of the inhabitants of the Ghetto. In the event, some Venetians fought once again; a few valiant partisans were hiding out in the marshes chasing off the last of the German soldiers while the British prepared to enter. After the war, Venice again faced reconstruction, along with the rest of Italy and most of Europe.

Like other places, Venice has had to submit to central government and big business. When I first visited Venice, the city had not undergone the terrible flood of 1966, when Venice was drowned for a day. Since New Orleans experienced the flood of September 2005 (when I was writing this book), the reality of a city's destruction by water has been made vivid. It is all too easy to imagine Venice undergoing a similar fate, or worse.

After the flood of 1966, which damaged buildings and menaced its tourism, Venice and the Veneto felt a fresh need to shore up the economic resources of the area. In 1968, Venice was party to the decision to enhance the petroleum refinery and create a giant port at Marghera, allowing supertankers to come right up to the docks; this enterprise necessitated deepening the channel. The original decision regarding the industrialization of Marghera was made after World War I by the industrial firm of Count Giuseppe Volpi; the Fascist national government directed subsequent phases. Count Volpi's son Giovanni protested to John Berendt that the original development was good, and that Volpi was not responsible for the later errors:

Marghera . . . The Big Polluter, the Destroyer of the Ecology in the lagoon! Right? And my father is supposedly a villain for building it. When my father designed Marghera in 1917, Venetians were starving. They were wearing rags, living five in a room. Ten thousand jobs were needed. So he built the port, filled in some marshes, developed the site for the government, and sold parcels of land to various industries—shipyards and manufacturing. It was only . . . after he was dead, that the people in charge, the idiots, filled in two more big sections of the lagoon. . . .

But worst of all, also after he was dead, they built oil refineries in Marghera and brought big tankers into the lagoon . . . so an extremely deep channel had to be dug for them. . . . Water used to flow gently in and out of the lagoon with the tides. Now it whooshes in and out, and the bottom gets all stirred up.[24]

It is easy to forget how very poor Venice, like much of Italy, was after World War I. It is decidedly unreasonable to expect modern countries to do without power. The desire of Venice not to be reduced to the status of a museum is also admirable. The refinery at Marghera, however, seems particularly unfortunately sited; it interferes perpetually with the Lagoon and is in danger of polluting both air and water to an alarming degree. Venice was for centuries so noted for the purity of its air that invalids were sent there on that account, even in the early twentieth century. Now its air is often dirty. Acidity and heavy particles in the air are eating away at irreplaceable buildings. The smog is also damaging delicate, irreplaceable lungs. New proposals to slow pollution include banning driving for three days a week, though it is hard to see how this will be workable in terms of the economic life of Marghera and Mestre.[25] Cars are only part of the problem, minor in comparison to the belching smokestacks which should consume more of their unwanted product.

Dredging the Lagoon to make room for great oil tankers has raised the water level unnecessarily, and poses incessant problems. There has been too much governmental insouciance about *acqua alta*, and too much attention given to wildly dramatic schemes of locking off the waters—the Mose or "Moses" Project—rather than returning to the original brilliant engineering and working with the waters of the Lagoon. Sometimes Venice, along with the modern Italian government, seems to share in the dream of Venetian collapse.

It would (theoretically) be possible to get rid of this decadent dream of collapse, if either Venice itself or the Italian government would take some prosaic measure that would be truly helpful—starting with forbidding the behemoths of cruise ships from entering the mouth of the Grand Canal. I should not speak against this pleasure industry—for making cruise ships is important to the economy of Marghera. But there is no need for gigantic cruise ships to come up to Venice itself; their passengers could arrive at the city in tenders, as formerly. Dredging to create depths that will accommodate monstrous vessels has made channels into which water will and must rush. Water has to go somewhere. It finds its own level, which nowadays (especially in November and December) means it is nibbling at the doorway of the Basilica of San Marco—or even rushing over the threshold, seeking the mosaics. Presumably it is not realistic to think of reducing the oil-tanker traffic—not until we come to the end of the Petroleum Age—but every one of these tankers menaces Venice.

In the present era of the computer it would seem eminently possible for Venice to introduce or expand its industry; the Internet offers not only effective advertising but also primary relations with customers. Internet commerce would favor clean industry and small businesses, as it does that of the Venetian fabric designer Mirella Spinella. Venice's traditional products— boats, glass, fabrics, flooring, lace—should find greatly expanded markets. Venice's traditional painted furniture (including bridal chests or *cassoni*, etc.) could find customers worldwide. Venetian repute for artistic expertise might make Venice a favored location of Web site designers and designs. After all, marketing, advertising, and fashion were activities in which the Venetians formerly excelled.

A truly heroic measure would be cutting off the land bridge, and making every comer arrive by ferry—not realistic now, when so many of the working population of the city have been forced to live on *terra firma* (Terraferma), in Mestre or elsewhere. But in an ideal world—which would include a living Venice, not a museum—there would be a serious practical effort not only to introduce clean industry but also to accommodate those Venetians who wished to live in Venice proper. The corollary of such a measure, however, would entail forbidding outright sale of property in Venice to outsiders— limiting right of use to, say, ninety-nine-year leases but eliminating absolute ownership by foreigners. Such measures, however, would certainly be unpopular with those who are making a quick euro. I digress into economic dreams. And besides—who am I to tell the Venetians what to do?

After all, Venice still staggers on, though pressed heavily by *acqua alta* in the winters, high water that turns the Piazza San Marco into a shallow lake. Of course, this too has its own fascination—it is really almost impossible for Venice to be dull, at any time. Donna Leon made a good detective novel out of *Acqua Alta* (1996). And how readily one can imagine a great love story or tragedy, in opera or film, set in the dangerous Venice of high water.

*T*he destruction of Venice as a social and political entity in 1797 stamped its image on all nineteenth-century representations of the city. One of the first on the scene was Germaine de Staël, who traveled to Italy in 1804–1805 to obtain the necessary background material for her novel *Corinne ou l'Italie* (1807). The novel about the fascinating female improviser and her Scottish lover is officially set in 1794–1795, the period just before the conquest, but the author's impressions were all gathered during the early period of the Napoleonic occupation. In *Corinne* we find many of the tropes that become associated with Venice during the nineteenth century and beyond. De Staël indeed seems an important fount or origin for some of these. We have already noted her evocation of the Bridge of Sighs and the secret drownings. The narrator's impressions of Venice are not very favorable; the architecture is too Moorish, and "the aspect is more astonishing than agreeable: you first think you are seeing a submerged city." The place reminds one of death: "These black gondolas which slide along the canals resemble coffins."[26] The drowning city in which one glides about in a coffin becomes hereafter a commonplace of description in the work of foreign writers dealing with Venice. To Byron in *Beppo*, the gondola is "Just like a coffin clapt in a canoe."[27] Some, like Mark Twain in *The Innocents Abroad* (1869), vary the metaphor slightly: "We reached Venice at eight in the evening, and entered a hearse belonging to the Grand Hotel d'Europe. . . . This the famed gondola. . . . an inky, rusty old canoe with a sable hearse-body clapped on to the middle of it."[28] We will pick the coffin motif up again, not least in *Death in Venice*: "Who could avoid experiencing a fleeting shudder, a secret timidity and anxiety upon boarding a Venetian gondola for the first time or after a long absence? The strange conveyance, handed down without any change from ages of yore, and so peculiarly black—the only other thing that black is a coffin (*nur Särge*)."[29]

In the Romantic era and then in the period we English-speakers call the Victorian Age, Venice becomes intimately associated with death, decline, processes of decay and erasure. It is a place of darkness, of impending end. This is reflected by George Sand in her account of her desperate visit of 1834 with her lover Alfred de Musset. The poet was severely, apparently terminally, ill with tuberculosis, and George Sand (Mme. Dudevant) feared that his end would likely come soon. In fact, he was to live until 1857; their

Venetian adventure ended in a rupture when Sand switched her attentions to another object. The poet's diary records that on the third of February he and George Sand had lunch at a place he calls "restaurant du Sauvage" and then walked in the gardens of San Biagio (to which he gives the French name, Saint Blaise). On the fourth of February, de Musset was ill, the physician Pagallo was called in—and that was the beginning of Sand's betrayal of her sickly lover with his doctor. De Musset fled from Venice in March (although the passion of Alfred and George was to have a stormy reprise later in the year). Not surprisingly, de Musset's impressions of Venice as reflected in his later poems are largely negative. Venice is

> The poor old woman of the Lido
> Swimming in a pool of water
> Full of tears. ("A Mon Frère, Revenant d'Italie," lines 124–126)

Repudiation, even horror, can be mingled with longing:

> Proud roofs! Cold monuments!
> Shroud of gold on heaps of bones!
> That was Venice.
> There my poor heart remains. (lines 127–130)[30]

George Sand gives a full account in prose of their first arrival in Venice. The hapless pair arrived in the chill of New Year's Eve, 1833–1834. Alfred was coughing and probably should not have been traveling in the middle of winter. George Sand herself was fevered and suffering from the dysentery of which she later complains, as well as migraines. Her "Fragment of a novel which was not written" reflects her own experience, the arrival at Mestre and the night journey from Mestre to Venice by gondola:

It was a January night, dark and cold. We reached the shore in obscurity. . . . We could not understand a word of Venetian. Fever threw me into a profound apathy; I saw nothing, not the shore, nor the water, nor the bark, nor the face of the boatman. I shuddered, and felt vaguely that there was about this embarkation something horribly sad. This black gondola, narrow, low, entirely enclosed, resembled a coffin. Finally I felt it glide along the waves. . . . Doubtless we crossed that dangerous part of the Venetian archipelago where, at the least wind, terrible currents rush furiously along.

It was so dark that we did not know if we were in open sea or on a narrow canal bordered with habitations. At that instant I experience a sense of isolation.[31]

The scene is dramatically set in darkness. A little later, she gives us a description of St. Mark's, and the vision of San Marco, the Doge's Palace, and the whole Piazza under the efficient radiance of a red moon, silhouetting against its broad disk "these monuments of a sublime beauty . . . or of bizarre fantastic quality." She deliberately seeks the chiaroscuro effect, and long before Proust she is already affected by an artistic vision mediated by the work of Turner: "This picture, thus illuminated, so recalled to us the capricious compositions of Turner that we seemed to see Venice once again in a painting, in our memory or in our imagination."[32]

And so George Sand and Alfred de Musset went to stay in the Danieli in the cold of winter, where the unusual female writer who dressed in man's apparel from time to time was spotted sitting on the balcony and smoking, looking out at the view of San Giorgio Maggiore and the opening of the Canal Grande. Sand received a solid reward from her visit to Venice in material for three novels: *Les Maîtres mosaïstes* (*The Master Mosaicists*; 1838), dealing with artists old-style and new in the time of Titian; *La dernière Aldini* (1838), centering upon a handsome gondolier's attraction for a wealthy and sensitive women; and *Consuelo* (1842), drawing upon eighteenth-century Venetian music and theater.

Ten years after Sand, Charles Dickens visited Venice for the first time. His description in *Pictures from Italy* (1846), in a chapter entitled "An Italian Dream," is by far the best in that book, a tour de force. (It is also one of the best descriptions of what it actually feels like to ride in a gondola.)

We had floated on, five miles or so, over the dark water, when I heard it rippling in my dream, against some obstruction near at hand. Looking out attentively, I saw, through the gloom, a something black and massive—like a shore, but lying close and flat upon the water, like a raft—which we were gliding past. The chief of the two rowers said it was a burial-place.

Full of the interest and wonder which a cemetery lying out there, in the lonely sea, inspired, I turned to gaze upon it as it should recede in our path, when it was quickly shut out from my view. Before I knew by what, or how, I found that we were gliding up a street—a phantom street; the houses rising on both sides, from the water, and the black boat gliding on beneath their windows. Lights were shining from some of these casements, plumbing the depth of the black stream with their reflected rays, but all was profoundly silent.

So we advanced into this ghostly city, continuing to hold our course through narrow streets and lanes, all filled and flowing with water. Some of the corners where our way branched off, were so acute and narrow, that it seemed impossible for the long slender boat to turn them; but the rowers, with a low melodious cry of warning, sent it skimming on without a pause. Sometimes, the rowers of another black boat like our own, echoed the cry, and slackening their speed (as I thought we did ours) would come flitting past us like a dark shadow. Other boats, of the same sombre hue, were lying moored, I thought, to painted pillars, near to dark mysterious doors that opened straight upon the water. Some of these were empty; in some, the rowers lay asleep; towards one, I saw some figures coming down a gloomy archway from the interior of a palace: gaily dressed and attended by torch-bearers. It was but a glimpse I had of them; for a bridge, so low and close upon the boat that it seemed to ready to fall down and crush us: one of the many bridges that perplexed the Dream: blotted them out, instantly. On we went, floating towards the heart of this strange place—with water all about us where never water was elsewhere—clusters of houses, churches, heaps of stately buildings growing out of it—and everywhere, the same extraordinary silence.[33]

This romantic journey is very like the approach of the modern visitor to the city from the airport side, barring the silence—today's visitor arriving by water is likely to be in a noisy motor launch. The ubiquitous presence of motorboats certainly militates against the quality of stillness for which Venice was formerly renowned, a silence that some visitors found restful and others dismal. But we too come past the dark and cypress-laden bulk of San Michele, the cemetery island, to the Fondamenta Nuova and one of the ducts leading from it, through labyrinthine lanes of water out to the side of the Canal Grande. Dickens's narrative formula renders the entire journey into Venice as a dream—even though he admits torchlight and daylight, the spell of the dream is never broken. Despite the intermittent gleams, the whole is a study in darkness, with Venice as the ultimate "Unreal City." Dickens is here in advance of himself, for only in later novels like *Little Dorrit* and *A Tale of Two Cities* does he as effectively unite the dream-work of the mind with the reality of external things. He creates a bizarre and treacherous chiaroscuro—more *oscuro* than *chiaro*—that will become a resource for other writers and for filmmakers.

Not long after Dickens, Théophile Gautier, poet and persistent traveler, came to Venice; his approach is another nocturne. Gautier arrived by rail on 10 August 1850; there was a giant thunderstorm that evening, so his entry was even more dramatically dark than that of Dickens. Even the crossing of the railway bridge by train was dramatic: "On both sides, the lagoon, with that wet blackness more sombre than obscurity itself, stretched into the unknown. From time to time glaring lightnings shook their torches on the water, which suddenly revealed itself, and the convoy seemed to be journeying across the void like the hippogriff of a nightmare, for one could not distinguish sky or water or bridge."[34] The terrors of this Dantesque journey were not over with once he left the train, for Gautier went by what he calls "gondola omnibus" to the Hotel Europa, which seems to the nervous visitor a long distance away, requiring "a voyage in blackness, as strange, as mysterious as those made during nightmare nights" (ibid.).

The storm, drawing to a close, still illuminated the sky with some pale flashes betraying . . . bizarre dentillations of unknown palaces; . . . doors, whose sills were licked by the flood, opened on emblematic figures that disappeared; staircases bathed their steps in the canal and seemed to rise up in the shadows towards mysterious Babels. . . . On the arches, forms vaguely human watched us pass like the sad figures of a dream. Sometimes, all light was extinguished and we advanced in a sinister fashion through four species of darkness: the oily, humid and profound darkness of the water; the tempestuous darkness of the nocturnal sky; and the opaque darkness of two walls, on one of which the bark's lantern threw a reddish reflection which revealed pedestals, shafts of columns, porticoes and grilled doors at once disappearing.

All objects touched in this obscurity by some fleeting ray of light assumed appearances mysterious, fantastic, frightening, out of proportion. The water, always so formidable at night, added to the effect by its heavy lapping, its teeming and restless life. Occasional reverberations prolonged themselves here in long-drawn-out sobs, and its thick waves, black like those of Cocytus, seemed to extend their complicitous mantle over many crimes. We were astonished not to hear some corpse falling from the height of a balcony or from a half-open door; never has reality less resembled itself than on that evening.[35]

Gautier claims that the traveler to Italy expects blue skies, but one suspects he was not disappointed at having such a dramatic entry to relate, such effects of chiaroscuro, such a summoning of fear. With a touch of deprecating ruefulness, he admits (using the editorial plural) the influence of mediated and conventional imaginings: "The old stories of the Three Inquisitors, of the Council of Ten, of the Bridge of Sighs, masked spies, dungeons and leads, executions in the Orfano Canal—all the melodrama and romantic *mise en scène* of old Venice, returned to our memory in spite of ourselves" (ibid.).

There was of course a cheerful tourist-advertisement Venice of the nineteenth as of the twentieth century, and an abundance of kitsch graphics and souvenirs. Travel writers take the hint, supporting reconstruction in emphasizing modern communications and touristic pleasures (railway station, tourists offered a gondola ride); they exhibit charming scenes in which the picturesque and the contemporary combine. The illustrated article from which Figure 1 is taken, "Boats of Venice," in London's *The Graphic* (16 January 1892), dwells on the variety of craft, and the "jolly oarsmen . . . full of fun."[36] The writer thinks that Venice has improved since liberation, though still showing signs of poverty and dilapidation. He defends the unromantic addition of the new *vaporetto*. Yet even a relatively upbeat article like this ends with a Byronic quotation lamenting the disappearance of queenly rich Venice.

In the twentieth century, as in the nineteenth, travel articles may strive for the jolly, but all serious art has rendered Venice as compelling, treacherous, dark-edged, and melancholy. Venice, cruel Venice, is vanishing into obscurity, into the past, into darkness. It may be glimpsed only in partial flashes or dreamlike images, emerging from or disappearing into water. The only possible exception, at least in its commencement, seems to be Gabriele D'Annunzio's *Il Fuoco* (*The Flame*, 1900), a novel celebrating Venice as well as the author's love affair (since 1894) with the Venetian actress Eleanora Duse (1859–1924). The stature of this overwritten and egotistical fiction is debatable, but it does ask at the outset of the new century if Venice can be reclaimed for the future. The genius-hero Stelio asks, "Do you know any place in the world like Venice that sometimes has the power to stir great forces in human life and arouse desires to fever pitch?"[37] The novel imagines a Dionysian rebirth, rekindling great art to rival Richard Wagner's northern imaginings. In the climax of *Il Fuoco* Richard Wagner dies in Venice, as he historically did (but back in 1883), leaving the coast clear for Stelio. In the end, however, D'Annunzio (through his hero) rejects Venice as too autumnal and decayed; like his beloved beauty, the actress Foscarina (his version of Duse), she is too old and experienced and worn out. Venice in the end becomes "the ancient city tired from having lived too long."[38]

Thomas Mann in *Der Tod in Venedig* (*Death in Venice*, 1912) ignores D'Annunzio's initially more positive hints of a new Renaissance for Venice itself,

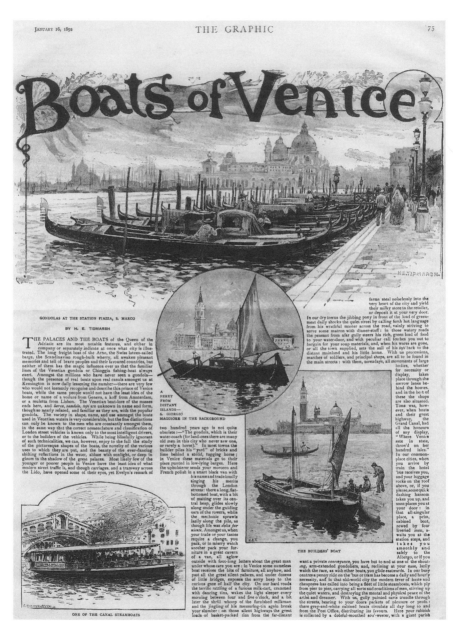

Figure 1. "Boats of Venice," *The Graphic*, 16 January 1892 (from copy in the author's possession)

although he connects with D'Annunzio in several ways, chiefly in associating the city with erotic and creative awakening. The death of Wagner had already provided D'Annunzio with a Teutonic death in Venice. The dark, treacherous, and melancholy Venice has never received a stronger representation than in Mann's novel. *Death in Venice* is set in the touristic Venice of the turn into the twentieth century, though one may still catch a flavor of the Austrian era and of a certain assurance that the Venetians could not manage their own affairs well. (Left to themselves they will be dirty and diseased.) Luchino Visconti's picturesque and Impressionist film version (1971) makes Aschenbach a composer, which is sadly beside the point, as it gives the hero a sensuous métier foreign to his nature.[39] Mann's Aschenbach is a writer, most essentially a word man; without his mental ruminations on history and Plato he is not himself. Mann's Germanic hero leaves his first destination because it is too Austrian, but in going to Italian-ruled Venice Aschenbach remains perfectly a tourist, to his end. He does not fall in love with an Italian, but with a young Pole. Venetians have only minor roles as waiters and boatmen and so on, or they are seen and sensed as sinister presences, like beggars or a threatening dwarf—a figure recycled in Du Maurier's story "Don't Look Now" (1970). The interface city lets uncleanness in, cholera from the Orient. The Venetians themselves in Mann's novel are the source and secretors of disease, like Shelley's "pollution-nourished worms."

This sort of public image was hardly what Venice required in 1912. The city had been working hard since liberation, repairing ancient monuments and returning to traditional crafts. At the turn into the twentieth century, Venice was still adjusting to its place in the new Italy while trying to maintain or reconstruct some degree of its ancient beauty. This endeavor received a shock in 1902 with the fall of the old Campanile, smashing into Jacopo Sansovino's sculpted figures on the beautiful Renaissance Loggetta at its base, but leaving the Basilica miraculously unharmed. (The collapse may have been hastened by efforts at repair.) In 1912 Venice had just completed its new campanile, a sign that the city intended not to yield its old glory; rather, it hoped to get positive publicity out of this achievement, and certainly did not need such a piece of negative propaganda as Mann's novel.

Mann's novel also associates Venice with homosexual fatal attraction. The period of reconstruction after 1866 is also the period of what one might call a kind of "gay Venice," as Mann must have known. In the late nineteenth century the half-forsaken city became a favorite haunt of aesthetes from England and America, men and some women with funds sufficient to allow them to rent entire palazzi, and hire a personal gondolier. The historian Horatio Brown and the poet John Addington Symonds (who fell in love with a gondolier and stayed in Venice) may be numbered among these new post-Austrian sexual visitors or refugees. Both writers contributed importantly to knowledge of Venice's history and its significance. Venice in the late nineteenth century and the early twentieth becomes an erotic ideal, a resting place for those who cannot wish for conventional marriage—persons as varied as Henry James and "Baron Corvo." It serves as the home and refuge of unorthodox couples, especially, but not only, gay males, who are able to create their own English society aside from that of the locals, and live in a world where they will not be much troubled by Puritanical inquiries.

Homosexuality has a long history in Venice. Most modern critics of Shakespeare believe that in *The Merchant of Venice* (1596 or 1597) the dramatist has drawn in Antonio a man of decidedly homosexual inclinations who generously helps the young male friend whom he adores to a lucrative heterosexual union. At one point in its earlier history the Venetian government was concerned at the idea that homosexuality was becoming too attractive to young males (thus endangering posterity), and the authorities therefore urged the famous Venetian prostitutes to redouble their efforts. It is, so legend goes, at this point that the Bridge of Tits (Ponte delle Tette) was so named, as the harlots were supposed to stand naked from the waist up— though this ploy seems ill calculated to appeal to the intended audience. Venice is paradoxical, always well policed and yet the home of sexual freedom, and countenanced pleasure.

Venice seems persistently to be associated with relationships that do not turn out well. We can hardly blame the Austrian occupation and its aftermath for the sufferings of Othello and Desdemona, or the disappointment of Lady Mary Wortley Montagu. But the percentage of unfortunate relationships associated with Venice seems to increase remarkably from the early nineteenth century onward. This seems to be true not only in fiction but also in "real life." For example, in the spring of 1963, the British MP John Profumo, soon-to-be-disgraced Secretary of State for War, took his wife, the actress Valerie Hobson, to Venice; the purpose of the jaunt was to break to her there the truth about his affair with the call-girl Christine Keeler. (This visit impresses itself as worthy of a play.) If Venice is traditionally a home of sexuality, sexual love is there consistently unsatisfied, tormented, secret, or exploded—or otherwise endangered and endangering. George Sand and de

Musset were separated by infidelity and jealousy, not by his tragic and beautiful demise.

The most curious, perhaps the most notorious, case of unhappy union
connected with Venice is probably the marriage of Euphemia (Effie) Gray
and John Ruskin. Youthful Effie had married John despite his bossy parents.
John was forging ahead with his ambitious plans for *The Stones of Venice,* and
Effie came to Venice with John in 1849. A strange time to choose! The grim
city was in pieces after the bombardment, and bitter at fresh subjugation.
Effie was a bride with a secret sorrow: she was still a virgin, her husband
would not unite sexually with her. Nor did Venice help them, as she might
have hoped it would; John fled her, spending most of his time drawing pillars
and mosaics in San Marco and gazing at paintings in the Madonna dell'Orto
and other cold buildings. At least Ruskin had an eye for a nice place to stay.
On their first trip the pair (like George Sand and Alfred de Musset) stayed
at the Danieli; on their second visit, in 1851, they hired a good suite of
rooms in the Casa Wetzlar, better known to us as the Palazzo Gritti, once
the palace of a Doge, Andrea Gritti. Yet, throughout, Effie remained a virgin
bride. There were pleasures and parties, organized by the wealthier Austrians
who were cold-shouldered by the Italians: as Effie blithely says, "Of course,
the Italians are not to boast of but they are not in society in Venice because
they don't choose."[40] That is, the Venetian Italians must be immoral, but
fortunately they keep out of the way. Some of my sympathy for Effie over
her cruel sham of a marriage is dissipated by disapproval of her insouciant
acceptance of Austrian rule and the charm of Austrian officers. Herself under
the yoke, Effie spends little time bewailing the yoke under which the Venetians labor. Effie eventually threw off her own yoke, getting free of her marriage in 1854 by claiming an annulment based on nonconsummation—to
the deep embarrassment of Ruskin and his family. She could assert later that
her time in Venice was never happy.

There are other disastrous loves. In May 1880, Marian Evans (born
1819), better known as the novelist George Eliot, following the death of her
long-time partner G. H. Lewes, married young Johnny Cross and made the
mistake of going to Venice for their honeymoon. John Cross leaped from
their hotel window into the canal below. (He survived; Marian Evans died
before the year was out.) Cynthia Ozick has written a shrewd—if not
kindly—semifictional account of the matter in her novel *The Puttermesser Papers* (1997); there the scene is reconstructed, under the supposition that
Cross's leap was the result of his horrified discovery that Marian expected a

full sexual relationship. Johnny Cross jumped into friendly water and was rescued, spared even by the bacteria of the Grand Canal.

Henry James's friend Constance Fenimore Woolson, less fortunate than Cross or more determined, committed suicide in January 1894 by jumping out of a window—but not into water. Constance Fenimore Woolson plunged upon the stones of Venice. It has been suspected that her suicidal depression was brought on by her unrequited affection for James. This incident is central to two recent novels about his life, David Lodge's *Author, Author* (2004), and Colm Tóibín's *The Master* (2004). Both of these novels deal, to varying degrees, with James's unfulfilled homosexuality, and both make a central scene out of James and the gondolier drowning the contents of Constance's wardrobe in the Lagoon. These two novels of the early twenty-first century thus revisit and replicate the nineteenth century's trope of Venice as an abode of loss, picking up too the Venetian motif of secret drownings which weighed so on Germaine de Staël. But we can relate the idea of Venice as an abode of loss (not a Venetian's idea) both to the trope of Venice as mud and weed, and the trope of Venice as magic. Whether boiling up out of the mud and slime, as dirt metamorphosed, or suddenly produced by "an enchanter" as an airy nothing, Venice is transient as a bubble. It has chimed (or been made to chime) with all our feelings about transience—the loss of health, faith, beauty, and love. And of course it can be made to express our ideas about the loss of life itself: Venice is not only a vanishing city, it is a place whence people vanish.

The consistent darkness in our view of Venice is evident in twentieth-century novels and films. Few stories about Venice—especially love stories—end happily. In James's *The Wings of the Dove* (1902), the schemers Kate Croy and Merton Densher consummate their physical union in his hired lodgings in Venice; that their first coupling takes place in Venice is in itself sufficient indication that their relationship will not endure. In this novel, death in Venice awaits Milly Theale, the American heiress with the magnificent reddish hair, victim of Kate's and Densher's intimate treachery and exploitation. Milly comes to a splendid palazzo in Venice to die. We see her as she appeared at her last party, encircled with a rope of pearls, symbols of tears, purity, and the wealth of the Orient. Milly is an emblem of the dying Venice herself, La Serenissima—at the point of beautiful decay, just before absolute death.

James had already drawn on Venice as a setting in *The Aspern Papers* (1888). The eager American researcher pursues love letters written by a famous dead

poet to his mistress—an object worth any amount of treachery and betrayal.
The dead author, worth infinitely more than his surviving lover, can be made
to speak—artificially, detached from incarnation—if the mortal but immortal letters enshrining his secret love can be brought into public life. The narrator's journey to Miss Bordereau's palace is a journey to a feminine and
worn site which must be broken into, but which is also apparently willing to
give way:

> The gondola stopped, the old palace was there; it was a house of the class which in
> Venice carries even in extreme dilapidation the dignified name. . . . It was not particu-
> larly old, only two or three centuries; and it had an air not so much of decay as of
> quiet discouragement. . . . But . . . the stucco with which in the intervals it had long
> ago been endued was rosy in the April afternoon. . . . I was given up to two other
> reflections. The first of these was that if the old lady lived in such a big and imposing
> house she couldn't be in any sort of misery. . . . The other idea that had come into
> my head was connected with a high blank wall which appeared to confine an expanse
> of ground on one side of the house. Blank I call it, but it was figured over with the
> patches that please a painter, repaired breaches, crumblings of plaster, extrusions of
> brick that had turned pink with time; while a few thin trees, with the poles of certain
> rickety trellises, were visible over the top. The place was a garden and apparently
> attached to the house.[41]

The house is dilapidated, decaying, quietly dying like Venice itself. A monument to a dead love, it is inhabited by the elderly and grotesque Juliana
Bordereau, formerly a great and imperious beauty (like Venice) now crumbling fast. This lady, whose name indicates being at the border of the water,
in the narrator's eyes resides here only as memory or caricature of the beautiful beloved—rather like de Musset's "poor old woman of the Lido." The
scholarly predator makes his way to the secret garden, but is not truly willing
to take on the secret sexual garden of Miss Bordereau's niece, whom he pretends to court only in order to get closer to the precious manuscripts.
  "Hypocrisy, duplicity are my only chance," says the narrator.[42] The pretense of loving seems to him a small price to play for such a prize as the
letters, which will offer an artificial resurrection to the dead poet. For that
he pays in counterfeit affection, bringing about an innocent erotic awakening
in the niece, a desire which he will never trouble even partially to satisfy. For
the women, the price of the researcher's duplicity is loss, physical and spiri-

tual death. Venice itself, figured in Miss Bordereau's sexually rosy and dilapidated palace, is here a dead love, a battered body with breaches and crumblings—on its way to absolute dissolution.

Death in Venice by contrast takes the side of the erotically awakened elder, but in Mann's novel Venice is not only crumbling but diseased. The sense of Venice as cracked and peeling, dirty and frightening, is caught in the film version of Mann's novel, as it is in the later Nicholas Roeg film *Don't Look Now* (1973), where a wintry Venice is falling to pieces, infested secretly with rats. The insistence on vermin seems to reflect the angry Romantic sense of the Venetians themselves as verminous, "crouching and crab-like," scuttling through their dishonored streets. *Don't Look Now* is Du Maurier's fable of grief. The bereft parents, who have lost their little daughter (through drowning, in Roeg's film version), struggle in and with an incomprehensible Venice which is closing down. In the novella, the couple are merely tourists, but in the film, the hapless bereaved father is appropriately turned into a restorer, working at resurrecting an old church that is crumbling away, as he remarks, in the acidic air. Venice itself is entering winter, a dying city with a dying faith. The movie's misty views offer us an abundance of the crumbling we glimpse in *The Aspern Papers*: chilly and faded buildings, forlorn in disappearing brick, patched plaster, and falling stucco. (The film gives one the chance to observe some of the effects of the flood of 1966.) The true object of the father's love is his dead daughter, who is mockingly everywhere and nowhere in Venice, a love denied. The beautiful blonde drowned child dressed in red in Roeg's film must be numbered among the latest images of the drowned female Venice. Her counterpart is the hideous female dwarf (elderly, like Musset's "poor old woman") who can repay kindness only by a stab—Venice also.

In a short novel of the following decade, Anita Brookner's *A Friend from England* (1987), watery Venice is the site of loss for the arid heroine. More cheerfulness is promised in Salley Vickers's *Miss Garnet's Angel* (2000), which at first seems to the hopeful reader to be a cozy fable about self-renewal and discovery. An elderly Englishwoman comes to her loved Venice to retire, and aids in the discovery of an old work of art. A principle of phoenixlike revival seems to be at play—but poor elderly Miss Garnet must die. Like Venice, she dies so that Venetian art may live a wider life. Once again, we experience Death in Venice. A dark Venice features in the work of the thriller-writer Massimo Carlotto, whose *The Colombian Mule* (*Il Corriere Colombiano*, 2001) gives us the ordinary and sordid Venice of airport, department store, hospital, strip clubs, and prison; the story of drugs and murder, often seen from a criminal's viewpoint, is lively, laconic, and contemporary. One cannot say the same of the pot-boiling mix of sex and cruelty in *Loredana: A Venetian Tale* (2004), a light entertainment by the historian Lauro Martines, claiming to unmask the myth of Venice by showing that in the sixteenth century the life of the poor was squalid, and legal penalties cruel. (True, and it would have been even truer if we had looked at crime, punishment, and the poor in Paris or London of the sixteenth century.) This novel is very much in line with the standard anti-Venetian propaganda.

After these works of loss and death, it is a relief to discover the light and pleasant film *Bread and Tulips* (*Pane e Tulipi*, 2002), an Italian story in which Venice features as happy background for renewal of life and love. In this film the Venetian milieu is cheerfully modest and working-class; scenes are set largely in the humbler residential area around the Piazzale Roma and the train station, and Venice is seen as a kind of escape from middle-class life and traditional hierarchies.

Witi Ihimaera, the Maori novelist, offers a rare positive representation of Venice by a foreigner in his novel *The Matriarch* (1996), but it is an odd positive. The Maori traveler values Venice for its glimpses of our Western totem animals, its departure from the glossy, the slime on the vaults of Rialto Bridge. In appreciating the slime and the animals, Ihimaera's book is an exception. Among recent English-language works figuring Venice, the city is seldom positively represented. The excellent detective stories of Donna Leon, however, make Venice fascinating and vital; while Leon does not spare us her vision of almost universal corruption in high places, Venice is a real locale with Venetian inhabitants, bakeries, and local bars and a daily life. Arguably, in Jeanette Winterson's *The Passion* (1987) Venice remains a positive site throughout. The time in which the story is set, however, is a fantasy version of the time of the Napoleonic conquest and Venetian loss; Henri, the hero, is Napoleon's inefficient cook. The heroine is a boatman—or boatwoman— with some connection to the female-male gondolier Zilda-Zildo in Frederick Rolfe's *The Desire and Pursuit of the Whole*. Winterson's fable of the waterman's daughter with the webbed feet seems to owe something also to Hans Christian Andersen's "The Little Mermaid," also a story of suffering; this amphibious heroine, Villanelle, must suffer something for both her art of rowing and her lesbian art of loving.

The strangest recent treatment of Venice in a work of fiction is to be found in a novel for children, *Die Fließende Köningen* (*The Flowing Queen*, 2001), by the prolific German writer Kai Meyer, translated as *The Water Mirror*.[43] This story (first of a series), rather along the lines of the Joan Aiken kind of children's tale, seems to owe something also to Winterson's *The Passion*. The late nineteenth-century Venice of steamboats and so on is also a Venice of strange and ill-used mermaids, crime, crumbling labyrinths, and magic mirrors. It is at war with—Egyptians! Revived, perhaps by the bumblings of Egyptologists, the Pharaoh has been able to rally his ancient forces and to invade, using armies of scarabs and unkillable mummies. The Egyptian enemy now besieges Venice, which resists, as it did during the Genoese siege in the fourteenth century—or the Austrian siege in the nineteenth. The city has its strength in its living stone lions, and above all in the "Flowing Queen," a goddess or spirit of the Lagoon and the canals. Yet Venice is decaying, impoverished, and famine-ridden. There is a certain comedy in imagining this misery foisted on the city by Orientals, when historically poverty, hunger, and fear were brought to real Venice by German-speaking people in the nineteenth and twentieth centuries. It is hard not to see in this attack of "Egyptians" a metaphor for the threat from immigrants from the East and from Africa as currently perceived and feared by northern Europeans. Venice, the interface city between West and East, is once again radically suspect, dirty, and dangerous, if also once again (rather as at Lepanto) a heroic bulwark against the alien threat.

In one of the most powerful not-quite-magical recent treatments of Venice, Ian McEwan's chilling novella *The Comfort of Strangers* (1981), Colin and Mary, lovers in the midst of a long and unsatisfactory affair, become lost in the labyrinth of a city that is obviously Venice, though it is one of the conceits of the novel (impossible to the film) that the city is never named. Lost in dark and winding ways, they are frightened by vermin. (The scene in the novel as well as in the film version of it owes a debt to Roeg's *Don't Look Now*.) The pair are, happily we may think, rescued by the loquacious native who gives his name in the English form, Robert. Robert and his Canadian wife, Caroline, offer hospitality; the English pair are taken in by the Venetian couple, reviving their sex lives but eventually becoming prey to their rapacious and perverse hosts. Looking at the beautiful naked bodies in the screen version directed by Paul Schraeder (1990), the viewer participates in the ambiguous and suspect pleasures of the designing Venetian hosts, save that viewers of any sex are likely to be as much impressed by the nakedness of Natasha Richardson's Mary as by that of Rupert Everett's Colin. Yet in the eyes of the sadistic and masochistic Venice dwellers, one of these bodies—

the luckier—is negligible. Only one, the lovely Colin, is truly desired by both his new lovers, who destroy him.

Not since Mann's *Death in Venice* were sex, treachery, Venice, and death more irresistibly and apparently naturally combined. The film version of *The Comfort of Strangers* is elegant—as how could it not be with costumes by Armani and a screenplay by Harold Pinter? It makes use of a rose-pink orange and blood-red Venice in a filmic symphony of reds (with early glimpses of Carpaccio). A glowing panoramic survey of Venice at dawn is strongly reminiscent of Shelley's dawn view: "As within a furnace bright,/ Column, tower, and dome and spire,/ Shine like obelisks of fire." As in Shelley's observation, the inner Venice, what Mary in the film naively calls "the real Venice," existing within the glow is a stinking sepulcher of the corrupt past. Once again, "pollution-nourished worms/ To the corpse of greatness cling."

Venetian passion—or passion experienced in Venice—is *more* than one wants, or other than one wants, or comes to grief in some fashion. For novelists, the temptation is to put the complications of love in Venice on the death trajectory. There seems nowhere else artistically safe to put it. Even in Vickers's little novel the heroine's passion for Venice is fey. In de Staël's *Corinne*, Venice is the site of the parting of the lovers. The trope of "death in Venice" is a trope of erotic pain, of what goes wrong with love, as well as a trope for our fearful relation to mortality—and not only the mortality of the body, but the mortal vulnerability of possessions, love, and hope.

Our sense of what is wrong or goes wrong with love has long been projected upon Venice, but that projection has greatly increased in agitation and intensity since the early nineteenth century. We notice in many of these stories (including tales from real life) that the characters who are strangers—*forestieri*—bring to Venice their inadequacies, sorrows, erotic pretenses, and denials. And Venice won't let them get away with it. It didn't let Othello off, though he was the perfect stranger; Othello is no longer in Venice after act I, but it is as if Venice pursues him for the next four acts. Othello resembles his successors in a burden of loneliness, and in being troubled with contradictory desires. In more modern fiction, interesting and melancholy persons come to Venice to remember, or to reconstruct or escape something, or to try to recover from illness. Or simply—but it's never simple—to die, like Milly Theale. Emotional torment, complexities of personality, restless desires of the soul, are brought to Venice to be revealed and intensified. Venice has become the center of a suffering. We use the city to explore intimately painful experiences, those which will not let themselves be recognized simply as soluble "problems." The city bears the terrific multiple charge of its golden-ness, its unconcealed material slime, its transience. The place that ever threat-ens to vanish tells us that we can vanish. No wonder that such use is readily combined with a desire to repudiate the place, the *topos* and *figura* of our suf-fering—to erase the Venice-place, have it sink into the sea. We have made it the tropic of pain, of coming to know Death.

3

A Dream of Pleasure, a Nightmare of Spies
Venice in the Eighteenth Century

Yes, you, like a ghostly cricket . . .
    —Robert Browning, "A Toccata of Galuppi's"

*T*he ghost that haunts nineteenth-century Venice is eighteenth-century
Venice.

The idea of Venice as it was—a self-governing city-state, prosperous (relatively) and free, the tourist center and mart of pleasure as of goods for East and West—this idea is last embodied in the city of the eighteenth century. It is thus not surprising that dominant and repeated images of Venice in the twentieth and twenty-first centuries play with recollections of the eighteenth-century world of Goldoni and Guardi. A nostalgia for the olden days of Venice touches much nineteenth-century reference to it, even though this nostalgia is stained by rebuke or some sort of *schadenfreude*. For Théophile Gautier the appeal of Venice resembles the appeal of slightly cheap music, a popular air recollected, "The air of the Carnival of Venice / On the canals once sung," in his "Carneval de Venise," first published in 1849—before he had seen Venice—and reprinted in *Émaux et Camées* (1852).[1] Possibly he is affected by the popular song "La Biondina in gondoleta" ("The Blonde Girl in the Gondola"). This song, with its image of a sleepy blonde beauty in a gondola, went all over Europe. Words and music were copied by Jane Austen in her own songbook, and the first verse is quoted in full by Sand in *La dernière Aldini*.[2] A description of the Grand Canal in Gautier's travel book recalls the amorous dreaminess of the earlier poem describing a Venice as yet imaginary. No other town could present a spectacle so beautiful, so bizarre, and so fairy like: "There, each palace has a mirror in which to admire her beauty, like a coquettish woman. . . . The water lovingly caresses the foot of these beautiful façades, kissed by a blond light, and cradles them in a double sky."[3]

In his "Carneval de Venise," Venice is charmingly feminine, a memory in light pastel to be conjured up at will rather than experienced directly. And no wonder. The Venetian Carnevale had just died out during the year of revolution, and from now on, like free Venice itself, would exist essentially as a memory. Gautier's speaker, not mourning the loss of a reality, is satisfied with the unperturbingly pleasing image.

> Upon a chromatic scale,
> Her bosom streaming with pearls,
> Rises the Venus of the Adriatic
> Her body rose and white, from the water.

> The domes, upon the azure flood
> Follow the phrase with pure contour,
> Swelling like the rounded breasts
> That raise a sigh of love, *amour.*
> . . . .
> With its palaces, its gondolas,
> Its masquerades upon the sea,
> Its sweet vexations, foolish gaieties—
> All Venice dwells within this melody.

> A frail chord which vibrates,
> Refashioned in a pizzicato,
> As in other times, joyous and free,
> The city of Canaletto![4]

Paganini had composed "Variations" on a Venetian popular song, and Gautier's poem is inspired by Paganini, rather than by the as-yet-unvisited Venice. The poem exemplifies an idea of Venice entertained from a distance, like that of Proust's young Marcel. Gautier seems satisfied, and does not attempt to introduce into any piece in *Émaux et Camées* a reference to the sublimely terrifying darkness that greeted him (or so he said) on his arrival.

The pleasure of Venice consists in imagining former days. Venice *once* was "joyeuse et libre." *That* Venus is really drowned, but can momentarily emerge from the water. The city of marble and masquerades and love sighs still sufficiently exists in imaginative evocations of the eighteenth century, memorialized in Canaletto's depictions. So Gautier proposes—in this poem that

seems a counterpart to Browning's "Toccata." Light music awakens a harm-
lessly delightful idea of Venice.

A charming image like that of Gautier is still proposed to visitors. Sweet
repetitive strains of Vivaldi, as well as costumes, masks, and sketches of Venice
and Venetians sold in souvenir shops everywhere—most of these memorialize
the eighteenth century, the Settecento, the beloved time before the destruction. The dark history of the nineteenth and the twentieth centuries, as well
as the abrupt and brutal ending of Venice not only as an empire but also as a
sovereign city-state, may explain this yearning for the eighteenth century, and
reiteration of images drawn from it. The silly film *Casanova* (2005) renews
Venice as a rococo abode of pleasures and dalliance. This vision comes as
rather a relief after what we have seen are a series of rather grim filmic fables
about Venice, although, as we shall see, the person Casanova is more complex
than debonair. The Settecento again asserts itself as the pleasure-time. As you
pass through the city itself, cheap—or expensive—artifacts, souvenirs, and
artworks incessantly hark back to the last Golden Age—not to mention the
indefatigable accompaniment of recorded music. (I once heard an Englishman
en route to heavenly Torcello declare that anyone who played the *Four Seasons*
one more time ought to be shot.) This reiteration of the eighteenth-century
idea is not to be explained merely by cynical calculations as to what will please
the tourists (though these play a part); rather, the operative cause would seem
to be some yearning or self-image deep in the psyche of Venice itself. I had
not thought my love of Venice had anything to do with my being an eighteenth-century scholar, but Venice is a perfect subject for an eighteenth-centu-
ryist. Venice never left the eighteenth century, where it was last seen as itself.
And eighteenth-century Venice is one of the ghosts that haunt Europe.

By the eighteenth century, as all the history books will tell you, Venice's
reign as a world power had essentially ceased. Both the discovery of North
America and the voyage of Vasco de Gama had slowly contributed to the
undoing of its empire. Venice was no longer the only door to the East, and
there were rich lands and new products in the Americas. New powerful nation-states had formed, acquiring their own colonies, competing in global
outreach and world markets. Yet its trade and commerce still boomed. Venice
was rich still in the eighteenth century,[5] if weakened by the unfortunate tendency of the "patricians" to try to keep an estate together under one heir;
they may have picked up this pattern from the feudal families of Terraferma,
the mainland. Marriage was endogamic, within the select families of Venice,
and brought no wealth in from outside; instead, wealth became concentrated

in a few families. Initiative and risk-taking were less rewarded than formerly. Unlike the English nobility and gentry, the Venetians had simply discouraged the noninheriting from marrying, and did not shove these extra sons downward into professions or trades. Gilbert Burnet in the late seventeenth century comments unfavorably but not untruthfully on a practice whereby "younger Brothers . . . are not stirr'd up by any Ambition . . . and are quite enervated."[6] From the sixteenth century on, there were too many unemployed men of blood and no money. These tended to congregate around the area of San Barnabà and were known as *barnabotti*.[7] One can see in Shakespeare's Bassanio of *The Merchant of Venice,* a sponge with a strong sense of privilege, an early example of a *barnabotto*. (I used to think that Shakespeare had never been to Italy, but work on the present book has persuaded me that he had indeed visited Venice; the insight into Venetian class relations—encompassing Antonio-Bassanio-Portia-Shylock—is acute, and these class relations differ from those obtaining in his England.)

Venice in the eighteenth century had successful businessmen and prudent councilors. By policy the city-state kept out of most of the eighteenth century's wars, artfully dodging alliances with one side or other during prolonged conflicts like the War of the Spanish Succession or the Seven Years' War that kept much of Europe inflamed. As a place of peace, prosperity, tolerance, and trade, Venice had strong attractions. Its traditional emphasis on and tolerance for pleasure made it a desirable stop for young gentlemen on the Grand Tour. There was always an elegant and multifarious company to join in the great Piazza, seeing and being seen, eating ices, drinking coffee. William Dean Howells in the nineteenth century comments that the Venetians have only one real meal a day, and that their supper is an ice and coffee at a café, and this seems to have been true of pre-occupation Venice. The Caffè Florian was established in the early eighteenth century; originally given the grandiose name "Alla Venezia Trionfante" ("To Venice Triumphant") by proprietor Floriano Francesconi, the celebrated coffeehouse became universally referred to as simply "Florian's."

The Venetians were notable coffee drinkers, which some observers set down to Eastern influence. Hester Lynch Salusbury Piozzi (formerly Mrs. Thrale), after traveling with her new Italian husband to Italy in the 1780s, comments in her *Observations and Reflections* that most ladies of Venice didn't seem to dine and everybody drank coffee all the time: "What, except being imbued with Turkish notions, can account for the people's rage here, young and old, rich and poor, to pour down such quantities of coffee? I have already had seven cups to-day, and feel frighted lest we should some of us be killed with so strange an abuse of it."[8] Perhaps in reaction to the superabundance of coffee, Venetians in the eighteenth century had the record now pertaining to the denizens of Barcelona, of sleeping the least of any Europeans. Apparently Venetians spent most of the hours of the twenty-four in pursuit of society and pleasure. (It may seem as if they were making up in advance for the long dark interval which was to follow.)

William Beckford suggests Venetians are really always sleepy: "The approaches of rest, forced back by an immoderate use of coffee, renders them too weak and listless to like any active amusement; and the facility of being wafted from place to place in a gondola adds not a little to their indolence. . . . I . . . am apt to imagine, that instead of slumbering less than any other people, they pass their lives in one perpetual dose [*sic*]" (*Dreams, Waking Thoughts, and Incidents*, 101–102). Perhaps Beckford at twenty felt annoyed that he couldn't keep up, and was jealous of this capacity for nonstop activity and "fidgeting about." Beckford discovers that the Erberia on the Grand Canal, the market for herbs and vegetables, fruits and flowers, was also a place of dawn resort for people who had been up all night. Casanova, who was walking in the Erberia just before his arrest, also notes, "Men and gallant ladies who have passed the night in the pleasures of the table or the fury of gaming are in the habit of coming here to take a little walk before retiring."[9] Casanova intends us to recognize that gallants and ladies had been spending the night in bed rather than just at dinner or at the gaming-table.

A good deal of entertainment was on offer even to the virtuous. By the eighteenth century, dramatic entertainments were produced more frequently than before, and not just packed into the two great seasons of high Carnevale and Ascensiontide. Lady Mary Wortley Montagu remarked in the autumn of 1739, "For those that love publick places, here are two playhouses and two operas constantly performed every night, at exceeding low prices."[10] Lady Mary also comments that ladies are able to walk in the streets and appear in public, simply by going masked; delighted by this freedom, she believes that there is less desire to censure female conduct here than at home. In the same letter she observes, "It is the fashion for the greatest ladies to walk the streets, which are admirably paved; and a mask, price sixpence, with a little cloak, and the head of a domino, the genteel dress to carry you everywhere. The greatest equipage is a gondola, that holds eight persons, and is the price of an English chair [i.e., hire of a sedan-chair, Georgian London's equivalent to our taxi]. And it is so much the established fashion for every body to live their own way, that nothing is more ridiculous than censuring the actions of another." Lady Mary may have enjoyed the freedom, but she hoped for even more pleasure; she had come away to Italy in the hope of linking up with her former lover, the Venice-born Francesco Algarotti (aesthetician, *philosophe*, and popularizer of Newton). She had misread the signals. Her bisexual friend was not interested in a permanent liaison, and avoided her, so the delightful freedom from censure was not as useful as she must first have hoped.

Females other than the "greatest ladies" walked the streets, or received selected guests at home. Long internationally renowned for the variety and expertise of its prostitutes, Venice remained notable for expensive and beautiful courtesans. A list of the best (and most costly) was circulated from the sixteenth century onward. (This sort of list was imitated in London by the eighteenth century.) Venice produced remarkably handsome women who specialized in blondeness, including the rippling gold-auburn tresses made famous by Titian. They are shown wearing remarkably sumptuous clothes; even when naked, in the guise of Venus, they lie on gorgeous satin displaying pearls or other jewels about their glowing flesh. Venice was undeniably the Renaissance leader in fashion. Although France's King Louis XIV in the late seventeenth century successfully determined that France should become the home of fashion (including style and materials), the Venetians did not entirely cede their eminent position. Eighteenth-century Venice still had access to the most luxurious fabrics of the East, the best imports of silk and damask, and could show how materials might be used to dramatic effect. When France went ornate, the Venetians could retort by becoming dramatically simple. Mrs. Piozzi reports that the ladies of Venice dress in black and go white-faced, "increasing the native paleness of their skins, by scarce lightly wiping the very white powder from their faces" (*Observations and Reflections*, 128–129). So we can see them in Pietro Longhi's picture of the fashionable audience looking at the rhinoceros (Figure 2). Fans, masks, shoes—the Venetians knew how to make such accessories effective and those who used them desirable.

As well as the pleasures and enticements of sex, Venice also provided gambling, in the luxurious Ridotto, which site the visitor today passes in going to Harry's Bar. The Ridotto was founded in 1638 when Marco Dandolo was allowed to open his palazzo in San Moisè il Ridotto as a public gaming house. There were ten rooms, in addition to two small refreshment rooms, and in each of the gaming chambers an identifiable and unmasked patrician male in perruque and "toga" kept the bank. The players were usually masked.

Figure 2. Pietro Longhi, *Exhibition of a Rhinoceros at Venice* (Permission of the National Gallery, London)

The company played and made bets silently, without chatter or cries, and won or lost "con un mirabile sangue freddo" (with a remarkable sang froid).[11] The Ridotto flourished until, in an attempt at reform, the Venetian state put an end to public gambling in 1774—but this did not greatly affect what could be done in private houses.

Thousands came to Venice for its famous Carnevale. Other cities had long held Carnival too, the celebration of the interval before the fasting period of Lent, a time when people say *carne vale*, or farewell to meat and other pleasures of the flesh, in a last fling. The period had become protracted, lasting from just after Christmas to the dawning of Ash Wednesday. In Venice the custom was the best kept up, its revelries the longest and the best, and it continued to be so despite constant objections from religious and civic worthies. (Carnevale is never universally beloved.) By—nay, even before—the eighteenth century such a touristic draw was a desirable prop to the Venetian economy. As a center of many attractions for the carnal-minded, eighteenth-century Venice drew upon itself increasing notice, and a different kind of power, which was at times more sinister in the eyes of others than its former supreme power in marine affairs and trade. We (often rightly) think of places depending on tourism as victimized, but the tourist center has an unusual power to refashion sensibility and desire. Tourism was long a source of anxiety to the visitors, as if Italy—and particularly Venice—could and would corrupt anyone who stayed in it very long. This is not a new fear, for we find Iago feeding the idea of Venetian corruption to Othello.

In Samuel Richardson's *Sir Charles Grandison* (1752–1753), an encounter with Venetian Carnevale offers a contrast between two young men, the virtuous hero Charles (later Sir Charles) Grandison and Lorimer, the spoiled son of a rich man. They are on the Grand Tour, Charles Grandison with a dissipated tutor whom he soon gets rid of and Lorimer under the tutorship of good Dr. Bartlett. Grandison does the Grand Tour aright, and Lorimer wrongly: "Mr. Grandison made almost the tour of Europe; and yet gave himself time to make such remarks upon persons, places and things, as could hardly be believed to be the observations of so young a man. Lorimer, mean time, was engaged in shews, spectacles, and in the diversions of the places *in which he lived*, as it might be said, rather than *thro' which he passed*."[12] We catch here the model of what might be called "imperial tourism," in which the good British visitor keeps up a brisk pace in full detachment, being self-consciously an observer and not a contaminated participant. Naughty Lorimer lowers himself to the level of the natives. Dr. Bartlett tries to keep him from the Venetian Carnevale, but in vain: "Lorimer, suspecting his intention, slipt thither unknown to his governor, at the very beginning of it; and the Doctor was forced to follow him . . . one of the most riotous persons there." Good Charles does not waste time in this vicious way, but continues traveling eastward to Constantinople. Lorimer and the courtesan to whom he has become attached try to get Dr. Bartlett in trouble, by suborning "a spy, who went to the Inquisitors of State, and accused the Doctor of having held a free discourse upon the nature of the Venetian Government, a crime, which in that watchful Republic is never overlooked. It is well known, that the city of Venice swarms with these spies."[13]

This somewhat sinister version of the Venetian authorities will recur. Since the establishment of the Council of Ten in the early fourteenth century, Venice had been noted for secrecy in matters of government, and for the use of spies. As John Julius Norwich points out, Venice as an open and global mart was full of spies in the Renaissance, and, with world powers like Spain and France plotting against her, the rich but slipping Republic had need of some counterespionage.[14] Some of its enemies disliked Venice partly because, as a Republic, it showed that a state without a monarchy was possible. In any case, there was a good deal of spying going on everywhere, as expanding (or contracting) states jockeyed for position and looked suspiciously upon rival powers, or nurturers of enemies. In the 1730s Lady Mary Wortley Montagu was nervous about going to *Rome*, where there were undoubtedly British spies who would be only too anxious to see or fabricate some rapprochement between herself and the obnoxious Stuart Pretender to the British throne. Lady Mary had few or no concerns about spying in Venice. Secrecy and spying, however, had become part of the city's mystique even before Jonson wrote *Volpone*, with its would-be spy, and in the eighteenth century the government took stronger measures to improve its policing and its ferreting out of enemies who might further weaken the state. There is thus some reality behind the fictional accounts of intrusion by the government. The very openness of the city posed in Venetian eyes a degree of peril, while in foreign eyes Venice is viewed as a dangerous if delightful place, capable of ruining young travelers, and as full of informers as of courtesans.

Venice was never more open than during Carnevale. It was the capital of Carnevale, almost synonymous with it, a city where visitors may lose their dignity, their virtue, and even their identity. People crowded to this center of delight and danger. A tutor traveling in the 1680s with the Earl of Arran as his ward on the Grand Tour, Maximilien Misson, a French Protestant, gives a disapproving account in much the style of Dr. Bartlett: "The Place of St. *Mark* is fill'd with a Thousand sorts of Jack-Puddings. Strangers and Courtesans come in Shoals from all parts of Europe: There is every where a general Motion and Confusion, as if the World were turn'd Fools all in an Instant."[15] Misson shrewdly conjectures the value to the revenue: "At the last Carnaval [*sic*], there were seven Sovereign Princes, and many thousand other Foreigners: How much Money all this Multitude must bring to *Venice?*"[16] Important people (as well as nobodies with some money to spend) did indeed flock to Venice; Lady Mary in December 1739 notes top people arriving: "The Carnaval [*sic*] is expected to be more brilliant than common from the great concourse of Noble strangers. The Princess of Holstein and the Prince of Wolfembutel [*sic*] (nephew to the Empress) are already arriv'd, and the Electoral Prince of Saxony expected next Week."[17]

Voltaire in *Candide* makes Venice during Carnevale time the unexpected rendezvous of six uncrowned or exiled monarchs—certainly Venice is about the only place where such a group might be imagined as meeting. In Voltaire's story, the ousted and idle kings are only the shells of power. Since these discarded or impotent men cannot quite continue their masquerade as kings or leave it off, it is implied, they might as well enjoy Carnevale.

Italy, and chiefly Venice, produced a style of entertainment which became the currency of Western European high life. From Molière to Frances Burney and beyond, we hear echoes of Venetian gaiety; masking and masquerades in Paris and London are an imitation of Venetian fashions and of the Carnevale. Sometimes very close ties linked a Western capital with the city-state of the Adriatic. The celebrated woman who called herself "Mrs. Cornelys" (née Teresa Imer) established brilliantly successful Venetian-style masquerade parties for London's élite in Soho Square in the 1760s and 1770s. (Frances Burney in her youth attended one of these.) In 1775 Teresa was the producer of the famous Venetian Regatta Ball at Ranelagh Gardens. The Venetian Teresa came from the same theatrical background as Goldoni and Casanova. Indeed, her father, impresario of San Samuele theater and producer of Goldoni, was enamored of Casanova's mother Zanetta. As teenagers Teresa and Casanova began an affair to be consummated in later life. (At least one of her children was his.)[18] Teresa knew in every respect what genuine Venetian style was.

A vocabulary of Venetian pleasure spreads through Europe: *ridotto, festino, casinò*. A "casino" means a "little house," and though to judge by Casanova such a room or set of rooms served principally for private sexual assignations, casinos in general were privately owned places of public resort, where coffee and other refreshments, as well as gambling opportunities, could be provided. Mrs. Piozzi describes a high-toned casino, very like a French salon: "We met at the Casino of the Senator Angelo Quirini, where a sort of literary coterie assembles every evening, and form a society so instructive and amusing, so sure to be filled with the first company in Venice . . . that nothing can now be . . . a higher intellectual gratification than my admittance among them; as in future no place will ever be recollected with more pleasure, no hours with more gratitude, than those passed most delightfully by me in that most agreeable apartment" (*Observations and Reflections*, 125).

William Beckford in the same period gives a more blasé description of a casino which induced ennui rather than gratitude:

She [Countess R.] very obligingly presented me to some of the most distinguished of the Venetian families, at their great casino which looks into the piazza, and consists of five or six rooms, fitted up in a gay, flimsy taste, neither rich nor elegant; where were a great many lights, and a great many ladies negligently dressed, their hair falling very freely about them, and innumerable adventures written in their eyes. The gentlemen were lolling upon the sophas, or lounging about the apartments. The whole assembly seemed on the verge of gaping, till coffee was carried round. This magic beverage diffused a temporary animation . . . but the flash soon dissipated, and nothing remained, save cards and stupidity. . . . It was one o'clock before all the company were assembled, and I left them at three, still dreaming over their coffee and card-tables. (*Dreams, Waking Thoughts, and Incidents*, 100–101)

What characterized Venetian life in the eyes of beholders was not so much that pleasure was available as that pleasure-seeking was openly the order of the day. Representations of Venice, embodied ideas of Venice, were in great demand. When Casanova first went to Paris in 1750, he was taken to a ballet-opera called *Les Fêtes vénetiennes* (*Venetian Festivals*). The Venetian-born adventurer writes (in *Histoire de Ma Vie*) that he was greatly amused at the spectacle:

After an overture which was very beautiful in its kind, performed by an excellent orchestra, the curtain goes up and I see a set representing the Piazzetta seen from the little island of San Giorgio Maggiore; but I am surprised to see the Doge's Palace on my left, and the Procuratie and the great campanile on my right. This too ridiculous mistake—a disgrace to my century—made me laugh. . . . I attribute it to the crass ignorance of the painter, who had made a botch of copying a print. . . .

The action took place on a day during the Carnival, when the Venetians walk about masked in the great Piazza San Marco, and the scene represented gallants, procuresses and women entering into and carrying on intrigues; everything in the way of costumes was false but amusing.[19]

We can compare the effect of the ultra-marbled and deliciously absurd Venetian Hotel in Las Vegas, which offers real gondolas and gondoliers going about a couple of shallow marble-lined ditches, as well as the Piazza San Marco—minus its Basilica—and large replicas of famous Venetian landmarks placed exactly wrong in relation to all the others. Rather than simply misreading an engraving, Las Vegas indulges in deliberate mistake; it is, as it were, "rewriting" Venice. The Venetian Hotel certainly exemplifies the desire to recycle eighteenth-century Venice as the abode of pleasure—of gambling and eroticism. Such a recycling was already going on in the eighteenth century, as Casanova's anecdote informs us. The Venice conjured up in Las Vegas with such pomp and expenditure seems also to reflect the Art Deco vision in the Fred Astaire–Ginger Rogers movie *Top Hat* (1935), which offers a stylized all-white Venice (apparently composed of pasteboard and icing sugar), where gondolas move along an implausible waterway beside a large dancing floor.

Masking, dancing, sex, and gambling were not the only pleasures on offer. Venice seems to have been a city full of musicians, and among the entertainments valued by visitors music was not the least. The city became prominent in the world of church music in the sixteenth century, after Adrian Willaerts came from the north as *maestro di cappella* at San Marco, and introduced the Venetians to the northern polyphony. San Marco's double choir loft encouraged antiphonal composition, and the church acquired not one but two organs. Subsequent *maestri* and organists like Gabrieli contributed notably to Venetian fame; many of these composers also produced less religious compositions. Claudio Monteverdi (born in Cremona, 1567) was made maestro in 1613, and directed the music in San Marco until his death in Venice in 1643. Monteverdi, known for secular works, had also produced important sacred music in his *Vespers,* and this and other religious works became well known, though perhaps not as famous as his operas.

To Monteverdi and to Venice must be given the credit not of originating modern opera but of establishing opera as a public form. The first public opera theater in Europe opened in Venice in 1637, bringing into the common arena what had been the preserve of the courts of princes, petty or great.

Monteverdi's *Orfeo* and *Arianna* set the scene for what followed.[20] His remarkable *L'Incoronazione di Poppea,* with a libretto by Giovanni Francesco Busenello, was first produced in the Teatro Santi Giovanni e Paolo in Venice in 1642. Monteverdi, an honorary citizen of Venice, remains there, buried in the Church of Santa Maria Gloriosa dei Frari.

Venice thus took the lead in this new—and, some would say, bastard—art of opera. After Monteverdi, successive composers produced operatic works. Tomaso Albinoni (1671–1751), son of a Venetian papermaker, produced as his first work an opera *Zenobia* in 1691. He later married an opera singer and produced operas indefatigably, as well as a number of instrumental works, including ninety-nine sonatas. His use of the oboe is accounted new; he wrested chamber music away from its former identity as the province solely of strings. Albinoni's most famous contemporary, Antonio Vivaldi, was an organist at the church of the Pietà and maestro for the Ospedale della Pietà. This latter is customarily spoken of as an orphanage for girls, and a certain pathos is not diminished by the fact that the plurality of the "orphans" would have been the female illegitimate children of well-born men and their mistresses. *Barnabotti* contributed to this pool, and the girls' likely blue-blooded origin partly explains the highly benevolent treatment of the officially parentless. The choruses of the Ospedale offered excellent performances, conducted by Vivaldi, of both vocal and instrumental works, the most celebrated of these last being *I Quattri Stagioni.*[21] He too wrote some operas.

A number of lesser known authors of Venetian music of Vivaldi's time are now being resurrected for recorded performance,[22] among them a female composer known as "Anna Bon di Venezia" (c. 1738–c. 1770); Anna, however, did most of her work for the court at Bayreuth. A better-known contemporary, Baldassare Galuppi (1706–1785), was, like Vivaldi, maestro at a charitable institute. Galuppi, outstanding and long-lived, by now has been honored with a centrally placed (modern) statue on his home island of Burano. In his own time he was spoken of as "il Buranello" (the little chap from Burano) and it is thus that Goldoni refers to him in his *Mémoires.*

Charles Burney in *The Present State of Music in France and Italy* (1771) gives a detailed account of the diverse excellence of Venetian music, including the chamber music, to which ladies of high birth contributed, such as Signora Bassa, "a noble Venetian lady . . . the best performer on the harpsichord of all the ladies of Venice."[23] Evidently fine ladies were not required to be above public performance. The composers are "good contrapuntists," but their "chief characteristics are delicacy of taste, and fertility of invention." All classes apparently enjoyed music: Burney tells us that "the Gondoliers have admission gratis" to all theaters, which he thinks "may account for the superior manner in which they sing compared with people of the same class elsewhere."[24] (We may prefer to think that the Venetians' general musical talent gave birth to those theaters.) Burney was especially assiduous in listening to the admirable Venetian church music, giving the palm to the productions of Galuppi. Though advanced in age by the time Burney met him, Galuppi, recently returned from Russia, was *maestro di capella* and composer for Saint Mark's, and also of the charitable institution the Incurabili. The composer was also privately employed as domestic organist to the Gritti family, whose palace must have at one time echoed to the strains of Galuppi's personal performance.

A devotee of composers and chamber and church music, Burney also notes the fine performance of unofficial musicians: "The first music I heard here was in the street, immediately on my arrival; performed by an itinerant band of two fiddles, a violincello, and a voice, who, though as unnoticed here as small-coal-men or oyster-women in England, performed so well, that in any other country of Europe they would not only have excited attention, but have acquired applause, which they justly merited."[25] The whole population seems musical, the whole city steeped in music:

The people here, at this season, seem to begin to live only at midnight. *Then* the canals are crowded with gondolas, and St. Mark's square with company; the banks too of the canals are all peopled, and harmony prevails in every part. If two of the common people walk together arm in arm, they seem to converse in song; if there is company on the water, in a gondola, it is the same; a mere melody, unaccompanied with a second part, is not to be heard in this city: all the ballads in the streets are sung in duo. Luckily for me, this night, a barge, in which there was an excellent band of music, consisting of violins, flutes, horns, bases and a kettle-drum, with a pretty good tenor voice, was on the great canal, and stopped very near the house where I lodged; it was a piece of gallantry, at the expence of an *inamorato* in order to serenade his mistress. . . . Whether the time, place, and manner of performing this music, gave it . . . collateral charms, I will not pretend to say; all I know is, the symphonies seemed to me to be admirable, full of fancy, full of fire; the passages well contrasted; sometimes the graceful, sometimes the pathetic prevailed; and sometimes, however strange it may be thought, even noise and fury had their effect.[26]

To *this* Venice, this city of constantly flowing extraordinary music, we cannot return.

A high percentage of the Venetians of the eighteenth century must have been musical to sustain all these performances in church and theaters and private chambers—and gondolas. In the late eighteenth century the Venetians decided to create for a new group of girls a special musical-theatrical space, a little gem of a music room in the Ospedaletto where Burney heard a concert. You can see this *sala della musica* now by dint of some effort; it lies behind and within the main hospital.[27] This delightful little space, with its elegant and amusing frescoes, was not long put to its designated use, for Napoleon put an end to all such projects. This small music box remains as a sad reminder of what might have been. On departing from the music salon one exits through a leisure room of the hospital populated by Alzheimer's patients, a somber memento of the passing away of all things.

Nowadays in Venice there are concerts in the church of the Pietà almost every evening—or so it seems—all performed by groups of competent and handsome young people of the city and the Veneto, playing and singing Venetian music with a spirit delightful to hear. (Be sure, however, to wear really warm clothes if you are attending one of these church concerts in the winter or spring. Churches tend to be pitilessly chilly.) Eighteenth-century Venice would have been full of music—new music, live music (there was none other). The constant performance of music in the streets and on the waters died away during the occupation.

The gondoliers were once musically famous, though these days, as by Marcel Proust's time, they can apparently rise no higher than the thoroughly non-Venetian "O Sole Mio." Of old the Venetian *gondolieri* sang passages of Torquato Tasso and other poets. Goldoni in his *Mémoires* describes how he and an actress were fooling about in a gondola in the laguna, when the gondolier sang passages of Tasso. Goethe, who found the music very moving, arranged in advance to have the boatmen sing Tasso to him, a symptom of his anxiety lest this music should have disappeared. Goethe knew what to expect, since Rousseau had written down a snatch of the song and published it in a book of music.[28] Rousseau interestingly classifies the vocal music with psalmody even if it exhibits quavers and long runs. Presumably this style left plenty of room for individual variation on any given day. Rousseau's tantalizing short recording transcribed in pen and ink is all that remains. Other late eighteenth-century visitors already feared that the custom had died out. Mrs. Piozzi expressed doubt upon the question, until she heard the singing: "But hark! While I am writing this peevish reflection in my room, I hear some voices under my window answering each other upon the Grand Canal. It is, it *is* the gondolieri sure enough; they are at this moment singing to an odd sort of tune, but in no unmusical manner, the flight of Erminia from Tasso's Jerusalem. Oh, how pretty, how pleasing! This wonderful city realizes the most romantic ideas ever formed of it, and defies imagination to escape her various powers of enslaving it" (*Observations and Reflections*, 123). Gautier in the mid-nineteenth century remarks that only a few elderly watermen could sing some passages of Tasso, and only for foreign visitors. Venetian watermen had other songs too, more their own, such as Goethe also describes in his account of the women of Malamocco and Pellestrina, wives of the fishermen on shore singing to their husbands out on the sea, and the husbands replying (7 October 1786; *Journey*, 92–93).

Horatio Brown at the beginning of the twentieth century describes spontaneous popular singing "in the more populous quarters of the city, little frequented by strangers" on Good Friday: "The people of the quarter, the shopkeepers, wine-sellers, fishermen, agree to sing the Twenty-four Hours, a long chaunt in twenty-four verses, following the life of our Lord through His Passion. The ceremony is a purely popular one; the Church has no part in it. . . . In harsh, but powerful voice, the leader of the band strikes up the first of the twenty-four hours, and the rest of his company join in as they catch the note. The tune is a grave and sombre chaunt, and the whole reminds one of psalm-singing in a Scotch kirk, with the precentor leading the way."[29] It seems a pity that such indigenous forms of popular music, which must have supported the musical flowering at the high cultural end of things, evaded the age of sound recording.

Venice is a leader in the arts of painting and of music. But it is not a literary nation, though the constant inspirer of literature by others. Astoundingly, Venice throughout the ages lacked true poets. That it has given the world no poetry is the more surprising as the poetic sense cannot have been lacking. Through the ages there must have been a good deal of anonymous poetry, folk poetry, as of popular song, in the Venetian language. Horatio Brown gives us an interesting example of the work song sung by the Venetian pile drivers.

E po lasèlo, e.e..e!	Yet let it go now,
Lasèlo andare, o.o . . . o!	Aye, let it go now
A baso a fondi, e.e..e!	Down to the deep depths,
A fondi del mare, o.o..o!	Depths of the ocean;
E va a ritrovare, e.e..e!	Down till it finds there

I suoi compagni, o.o..o!	All its companions;
Dele caverne, e.e . . . e	Down in the caverns
Orende scure, o.o..o!	Awful and gloomy
Dele caverne e.e . . . e!	Down in the caverns
Orende grote, o.o..o!	Grots full of horror
	(*In and Around Venice*, 132–133)[30]

This pile-drivers' chanty contains one of the few references to the "horrid" emanating from Venice itself—strangely rare, considering that the city is such an inspiration to writers of "horror" stories. It is the deep dark caverns of ocean which are horrendous, "orende." There must have been many other such productions, the creation of the working people. But no strong poet came along at the right time to drive such material into the high culture. Venice's poetry has been spread upon the waters in snatches of song.

With such an empire as it had acquired, Venice might surely have made its tongue the language of Italy—but it was comparatively mute, it lacked a voice such as Dante gave to Tuscan. When Venetians talk to each other they speak in Venetiano; when they write for themselves, as Marin Sanudo does in his *Diarii*, they write in their own language. But they didn't export that language, even though Aldus Manutius spread printed works and printing techniques throughout Europe. The rise of Tuscan meant that Venetian works remained for home consumption only. Venetiano or "Venexian" stayed a local language, later considered a dialect. There were some poets and writers, but none who became nationally and internationally renowned. Tasso's father came from Venice (which gave Venetians an added interest in him), but Tasso himself was born on the Amalfi coast. The most unusual of the local poets is the Cinquecento courtesan Veronica Franca (or Franco), whose reputation rose when she was chosen out of all the ladies of pleasure in Venice to give particular favors to the visiting King Henri III of France. Pietro Bembo (later Cardinal), born in Venice of good family and eventual historiographer of the Republic and librarian of Saint Mark's, was the nearest Venice came to an important poet, but he had been modernized by Urbino and Rome, and as a versifier was entirely of a humanistic and classicizing bent. Through the centuries, Venice has played host to important poets, including Alfred de Musset, Robert Browning, and Ezra Pound—and, most important, Francesco Petrarca (Petrarch).

Neither did the Venetians produce any strong practitioner of prose fiction, although Francesco Colonna is worthy of remembrance. He appears to have come from Treviso in the Veneto, but spent much of his life in the monastery of San Zannipolo; his strange, fantastic, and witty novel *Hypnerotomachia Poliphili* (1499), written in Venice and published by Aldus Manutius, was to be an influence on other writers of fiction, including Rabelais. (This work recently figures as inspiration and core text of the popular novel *The Rule of Four,* but the basic conceit of that novel depends on the idea that the author is *not* a Venetian—thus confiscating from Venice its only Renaissance novelist.)[31] On the whole, however, Venetian literary productions ran to histories, diaries, and autobiography—works combining the practical with the reflective, as in Marco Polo or Marin Sanudo.

In theater, however, as not in poetry and novels, Venice had been creatively busy over the years. The Venetians are inclined to the drama—opera, which Venice made its own, is a dramatic form, and composers such as Vivaldi and writers such as Goldoni contributed to it. Venice had long produced troops of comedians, and was a major contributor to commedia dell'arte.

The commedia is a production of many Italian regions, and some elements in it hark back to the theater of the Roman times. Essentially it draws on perfectly understood stock characters, such as Arlecchino (Harlequin), a ragged fellow of Bergamo dressed in patches; Brighella (a roguish servant type); and Columbina (the beautiful young soubrette). Pulcinella (our "Punch") is a figure from commedia dell'arte. A site in Venice gave one commedia character his name; Pantalone, or Pantalon, the miserly and grumpy old merchant, is taken from the name of the Church of St. Pantaleone (in Venetian, San Pantalon), because theatrical works used to be performed in the square outside this edifice. Hence we get our "pantaloon," as in Shakespeare's Jacques' description of an old man as the "lean and slippered pantaloon" (*As You Like It,* II.vii, line 158).[32] For Venetians, miserly old Pantalon is an ambiguous character, unamiable maybe, but also representative of the hard-pressed head of the Venetian household, the common man—"Poor Pantalon who pays for all."

Commedia dell'arte offers stock plots, with lots of room for fresh riffs. The stories customarily involve the unreasonable behavior of an old man blocking the love of two young persons; other characters foil the old man and advance the affair. There are stock actions, pieces of comic business, known as *lazzi* (a man concealing a sausage, an incompetent trying to put up a ladder, etc.). This tradition has spread itself through the dramatic art of Europe; any Marx Brothers film contains perfectly executed *lazzi.*

The effectiveness of a commedia dell'arte production depends on the quick wit of the actors, for much of the action is improvisatory. Goethe describes seeing "an improvised comedy, played in masks with great bravura." He comments on the delighted participation of the spectators, the common people of Venice, and their enjoyment at seeing "their actual life, presented with greater economy as make-believe . . . and removed from reality by masks" (4 October 1786; *Journey*, 86). Street life in Venice, as Goethe notes, is a kind of theater, and the genius of Venetians seems perfectly suited to such comedy. Venetians value quickness and have a strong vein of irony, the kind of comic sense visible in naming a street "Amore dei Amici" ("The Love of Friends")—a short street coming swiftly to a dead end.

That the old comic tradition did not die out with the coming of scripted drama, even after the occupation, is borne out by William Dean Howells's accounts of the native dramatic works that he saw in Venice. His description of the theater of the Marionettes tells us that in distress the Venetians were able to create a new commedia character, Facanapa (*Venetian Life*, 76–83).[33] Facanapa, unlike Pantalon the merchant, is low class, a boasting idler who gets nothing done; he perhaps represents the Venetians in the enforced state of worklessness and contrivance brought upon them by the Austrian occupation. "Low" theater, including the Marionettes, evidently remained a repository of the Venetian comic idea, even during the bad time.

Carlo Goldoni (1707–1753) is conventionally credited—as he credited himself—with escaping from the "dull" or "mechanical" commedia dell'arte—indeed, putting an end to it by his ingenious written comic dramas. He himself explains that he is trying to write modern comedies about characters. When one looks at Goldoni's work, however, it is quite evident that, despite his conscious efforts at modernization, the commedia has a significant effect upon him—and despite his critiques he really admires it. His plays frequently employ the plot structure familiar from commedia: an old man is a barrier to the happiness of young people, for instance; or a clever wife and servants get round the churlish master. Goldoni was quite happy to draw on the stock characters; sometimes the only difference is the substitution of a realistic name for a traditional one. The ever-popular *Servant with Two Masters* is a piece entirely in commedia style. The character of the coffeehouse keeper in *La Bottega del Caffè* (*The Coffee House*, 1750) was originally Brighella. The miserly Forlipopoli in *La Locandiera* (*The Landlady*) is a Pantalon type. Essentially Goldoni slightly remodeled old theatrical style to create a new written drama—a comedy aiming at further naturalism, with a wider variety of more subtly drawn characters, yet readily comprehensible to his audience because of their relation to the traditional personages.

Goldoni was a Venetian by birth. He was born in a very handsome house in the center of Venice (now the Museo Goldoni) and was brought up in Chioggia (Chiozza); after Carlo was born, his father became a largely itinerant physician of sorts (probably more like a charlatan). Carlo studied law, and practiced for a while. In the autobiographical prefaces to the multiple volumes of his collected dramas (1761–1768), Goldoni first wrote the story of his life. These handsome and well-illustrated volumes were published by Giovanni Baptista Pasquali, the printer, who, encouraged and partly funded by Consul Joseph Smith, had published translations of such writers as Locke, Voltaire, and Diderot.[34] Goldoni was linking himself to the progressive and enlightened of Europe. Yet, in his preface to the ninth volume of his collected *Commedie,* he presents us with something in his own life that we might think the reverse of enlightened; he chooses to discuss and even to order a graphic illustration of that phase of his life when he was a legal interrogator. "It took me aback at first to see a man strung up by Ropes and to have to examine him tranquilly, as you see in the Frontispiece to this volume; but habit is everything, and in spite of humanity, I heard nothing but what was demanded by justice and the duty of my position."[35] Goldoni explains that what gave him more pleasure was the "epilogue" to these trials or hearings (*Processi*), when he had to set down what had been elicited for the benefit of the judge, who would pronounce sentence; this was not an easy kind of writing, as he had to weigh his words exactly "so as not to aggravate the guilt in prejudice against the Wrongdoer, and not to diminish it to the detriment of Justice."[36]

Goldoni has the dubious distinction of being the only dramatist I know of to have participated in interrogation by torture. We see him in the frontispiece to which he refers, calmly taking notes while an unfortunate man, in no condition for writing to the moment, is being interrogated, apparently by the application of the *strappado* (Figure 3). The quasi-jocular use of the Virgilian motto Goldoni has supplied for this picture, *nunc animus opus . . . , nunc pectore firmo* (an exhortation to a hero about to descend to the Underworld), may hint at sympathy for the accused; "now is the time for a strong soul and a firm breast" encourages the unfortunate victim rather than his calm questioner. In his later *Mémoires* (written in French), Goldoni unabashedly defends this striking period of his career:

Criminal procedure is a most interesting lesson for knowledge of mankind. The guilty person tries to erase his crime or to diminish its horror; he is naturally adroit, or becomes so through fear. Though he knows that he has to do with well-educated

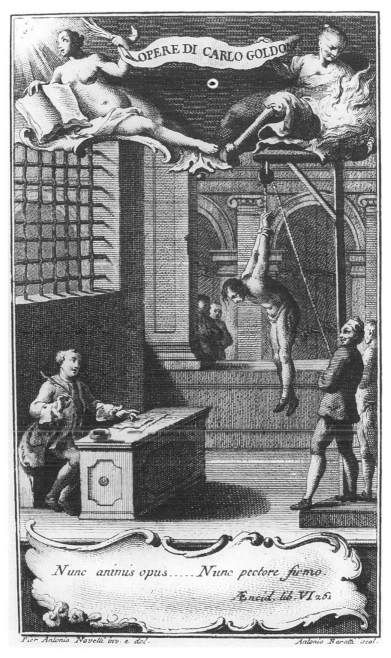

Figure 3. The young Carlo Goldoni as interrogator, in *Delle Commedie di Carlo Goldoni,* frontispiece to Vol. IX (Venice, 1761). (Permission of Biblioteca Marciana: 392D.156)

professionals, yet he does not despair of being able to deceive them. The Law prescribes to the Criminalists forms of interrogation, so that their questions are not captious, and so that mere feebleness or ignorance are not overwhelmed. One must, however, try to understand or unriddle the character and spirit of the man whom one has to examine, and taking the middle course between rigour and humanity one tries to disentangle the truth without constraint.[37]

Criminal interrogation, Goldoni indicates, is excellent practice for a dramatist in comprehending character, and seeing through behaviors. This seems a most disagreeable—if not shocking—milieu in which to discover a dramatist. One might expect Goldoni's works to be authoritarian, or full of harsh punishments. But they are nothing of the sort. The desire for fairness that he claims for himself indeed seems evident in his playful fictions, in which characters and author alike appear to search for some balance and harmony. In Goldoni's works we can see the contours of a Venetian democratic spirit (never entirely absent from Venice itself) beginning to take literary expression and work itself out, a development that might have been consequential if harsh history had not conjured the Venetian democratic spirit into silence—or near-silence—at the end of the eighteenth century.

Goldoni himself eventually and stubbornly chose the "lower" road of the theater over the "superior" upper-middle-class road of the law, in which his father and others were trying to set his feet. From childhood, he intimates, his love was for the theater. The young Carlo, aged twelve, took the part of a lady on stage in Perugia, and the frontispiece of the third volume illustrates that occasion when he appeared thus "in exercise of Comic Representations, for which he had a predilection."[38] He makes his first appearance as a lady. Goldoni himself is not at all abashed by this transvestism, just pleased with his own twelve-year-old cleverness. Looking at the picture uninstructed, however, we experience a shock, for we have been taken in—we first think we are looking at an actress. The game of the self is a game of gender, and Goldoni seems to play the game in a variety of ways.

A number of his plays involve gender issues. In *I Rusteghi* (*The Boors* or *The Rustics*, 1760) some lively Venetian women combine to frustrate their dull and unmannerly husbands in order that a young couple may at least be able to see and meet each other before being married off by their respective fathers. The time is Carnevale, and the young man is able to come in a mask and thus sneak a glimpse at Lucietta, the girl destined for him. But there is a slight shock, a kind of unease, in the fact that young Filipetto masquerades as a lady in a *bauta*, and is accompanied (like a lady) by a visiting gentleman, the foppish Count Riccardo. Should the young lover be so feminine? Is manifesting himself as "feminine" the right way for a man to signal that he is not coarsely masculine, not a surly despot like Lucietta's father Lunardo? *I Rusteghi*, written in Venetian, concerns Venice and its changing time, the mores of the middle class. We see how distant the distracting pleasures of Venice, of which we hear so much from the Renaissance on, may remain from average Venetians. Margarita, second wife to churlish Lunardo, complains to her stepdaughter about the dullness and privation of her married life, in contrast to her youth: "before I was married I did not lack for entertainment. I was well brought up. . . . But when the time came, we had our amusements. Only imagine, in the autumn we used to go two or three times to the theatre, and at Carnival five or six. If someone gave us a box, she took us to the opera; if not, to the play, and she bought good places and didn't grudge the cost. . . . Only imagine, we went sometimes to the Ridotto; to the Piazza for a while, and to the Piazzetta to see the fortune-tellers and the puppets; and once or twice to the fairground."[39] Now Margarita has these pleasures no more, and her stepdaughter has experienced none of them. Nor has Filipetto, who complains that he is not allowed to go to the Giudecca or Castello, or even Saint Mark's Square: "I don't think that in all my life I've passed through the Piazza three or four times."[40] Goldoni sympathizes with young people, and with women whose lives and legitimate desires are bound by the formalities and pretensions of Venetian male citizens. His urge, like that of any good dramatist, is always to let the suppressed persons out to play, to license their desires.

Many of Goldoni's plays involve the daily or seasonal pleasures of Venice—Carnevale masking, going to the villa for a holiday. Goldoni notices the little panics people get into, even on occasions of pleasure, as they try to arrange their lives; for instance, packing up for a holiday can cause confusion, even unhappiness. He delights in situations that bring a variety of persons together, creating a semi-public space in private life. A coffeehouse, a public square, an inn—these provide good settings. Goldoni likes exhibiting a variety of activities, as he does most notably in *The Fan*, where we have a female shopkeeper, a druggist, a barber, and a coffeehouse waiter nicknamed Limonado all performing their trades in the square of a small town, cheek by jowl with higher-ranking neighbors. *Le Baruffe di Chioggia* (*The Brawls of Chioggia*) opens on a scene of working-class girls of Chioggia making cushion-lace.

Goldoni seems permanently interested in working people, especially in those (including actors and actresses) who have to survive by serving and pleasing others. The owner of the coffeehouse in *Bottega di Caffè* is one such character, and so, outstandingly, is the landlady Mirandolina, heroine of *La Locandiera,* who acts as maid and cook in her boardinghouse. Goldoni's is a very material theater—we are always being asked to contemplate food, and utensils, and objects in action. His characters make things on the premises— they pound drugs or create lace or make coffee. Mirandolina is shown doing the ironing with a hot iron, with which she burns another of the characters. It could be said that his plays in this respect suit a Venice that is becoming more and more dependent on service industries for its livelihood. But there is more to the matter than that. What we are seeing in Goldoni's plays is a respect for working people and common life rare in drama, even in the age of Marivaux.

Goldoni represents an important democratic development—if we can take the word "democratic" at its broader and deeper meanings, indicating a vision of the worth of human beings and active respect for their significance and creative power. Goldoni's interest in working people makes it natural, perhaps, that the dramatist should pick up Richardson's *Pamela* (1740), a novel about a serving-maid, and dramatize it as *La Pamela* (1750–1751). As Goldoni explains, however, he had to change the ending of Richardson's novel, revealing Pamela the maidservant as really high-born, because, he claims, European audiences would not stand for seeing on stage such a misalliance as is shown in the English novel, in which a young woman who really *is* of the servant class marries her master, the wealthy and well-born landowner Mr. B. In Venice a man of the patrician oligarchy who married out of his caste doomed his children. Goldoni's anxious alteration therefore seems prudent, if disappointingly unrevolutionary.

Yet Goldoni is rarely on the side of the high-born. In his plays men of pretension to superior birth or noble caste tend to be non-Venetians, often poseurs or frauds; if genuinely well-born, such personages are frequently idiotic. Remarkably, too, in one who once acted as ancillary legal torturer, Goldoni has little taste for the harshness of law as a way of settling things. His stories customarily deal with compromise and accommodation. In *The Coffee House* the loose lips of the pretentious and chatty Neapolitan gentleman Don Marzio lead to the arrest of the rascally gaming-house owner. Don Marzio gossips away about the gaming-house and its doings to a man he has met in the coffeeshop, not realizing that this man is a member of the police, a spy for the government. The gaming-house owner Pandolfo is the villain of the piece, and Goldoni has to find a way of ending his career; at the same time, the dramatist dissociates himself from that end. The other characters, on hearing that Pandolfo has been arrested and will be whipped, turn fiercely on Don Marzio and expel him, accusing him of being a scandalmonger, an informer, and a spy. This seems a very believable reflection of the working-class view of the official law.

Goldoni's drama is patriotic. He is happy not only to use Venetian scenes but also to explain Venetian life to those who don't live there. Scene descriptions and stage directions often make it clear that we are to see his home city: "Night with a moon. Street with views of the Canal," as the initial directions for *Il Bugiardo* (*The Liar*) tell us. The play itself is an adaptation of a work by Corneille, but the new author has naturalized it in Venice. Not only so, but when he lists among the dramatis personae "Barcajuoli de Peota" (*peota* boatmen) he feels obliged to tell us what kind of boat a *peota* is, assuring us that this Venetian style of vessel is "commodious and can hold a number of persons, with good seats and a table in the middle." A *peota* is good for little voyages "and for diversion in the City"—there is a ring of enjoyment to the description.[41]

Goldoni's humor is gentle, and we are gently urged to desire reconciliation, recognizing the cloudy but stubborn nature of people's dreams and visions of themselves. As we are all vulnerable, social life requires tact—even with all the ambiguous dishonesty tact entails. Most human behavior is absurd. Despite his admiration for Molière, there is little of Molière about Goldoni's dramas, which lack the French dramatist's hard edge; the Italian dramatist's plays seem rather more like Menander crossed with Chekhov. The contemporary Venetian artist Pietro Longhi (1702–1785) is almost inevitably mentioned in connection with Goldoni. Longhi too gives us glimpses of the people of Venice in commonplace but vital life, though his favorite types are of a class slightly superior to Goldoni's. Longhi may mildly satirize, but, like Goldoni, he seems determined to enjoy. Yet Longhi's people give one the impression of more rapacity and bold determination than Goldoni's characters seem even to wish to possess.

Giacomo Casanova (1725–1798) is another literary Venetian of this period, and in Casanova too we can also see developments toward a democratic spirit, although very differently manifested. Unlike Goldoni, he is not in any sense gentle. Though a devotee of social life in all forms, he is not at all concerned with the well-being of others. He narrates lively scenes, but Casanova could never write dramas, for the only character who interests him is himself.

Casanova has, however, more in common with Goldoni than might appear at first glance: both are Italian pioneers in autobiography, and assist in the modern European development of this form. Casanova, rake and autobiographer par excellence, sprang from Goldoni's world. Casanova's father, Gaetano Giuseppe Giacomo, left his natal family at a young age, we are told, because he fell in with an actress. Gaetano learned to dance and to act; he left Parma for Venice with a troupe employed at the theater of San Samuele. (Traditionally, Venetian theaters were named after the nearest church.) He there fell in love with Zanetta, the daughter of a shoemaker who plied his trade opposite Gaetano's lodging, and Zanetta and Gaetano eloped. "Zanetta"—a very Venetian name, other Italians would say and write "Gianetta"—became an actress and continued her career with success even after the death of her husband. Their son Giacomo sometimes functioned as an instrumentalist in theater bands. The impoverished couple had patrons in the aristocratic Grimani family, owners of the Grimani theater; it was Alvise Grimani who supplied the delicate Giacomo first with the care of a physician and then with an education, intending that the poor but bright boy should pursue a career in the Church.

Despite his grand and noble last name, which may have been simply lifted from that of a really good Venetian family, the writer who calls himself "Casanova" is a "new house" of one. Son of a strolling player and a shoemaker's daughter, he is definitely *not* a nobleman of Venice—not even, by prevailing and important standards, a citizen, as his father is a foreigner. (Young Giacomo might, however, have secretly wondered if he were a by-blow of Grimani.) Giacomo Casanova is lower on the social scale than Goldoni, although he has enjoyed the education of a man of good rank, and can at times act like a man of the nobility. Part of the democratic point of Casanova's writing is the knowledgeable aping of the manners of the governing class, combined with a capacity to mock it. He makes us recognize the invention—the fiction—of class itself. Casanova is always an actor, eternally on stage, performing the artistic roles of his invented self and inviting us to enjoy and applaud his cleverness. Giacomo received a gentleman's education; he is fond of making allusions to classical literature and to the best Italian authors (Dante, Ariosto). But he is also fond of introducing "low" images or surprising facts with which he perpetually challenges the reader:

I have always liked highly seasoned dishes: macaroni made prepared by a good Neapolitan cook, *olla podrida*, good sticky salt cod from Newfoundland, high game on the very edge, and cheeses whose perfection is reached when the little creatures which inhabit them become visible. As for women, I have always found that the one I was in love with smelled good, and the more copious her sweat the sweeter I found it.

What a depraved taste! How disgraceful to admit it and not blush for it! This sort of criticism makes me laugh. It is precisely by virtue of my coarse tastes, I have the temerity to believe, that I am happier than other men, since I am convinced that my tastes make me capable of more pleasure. (*My Life*, I, 32–33)

So Casanova assaults the sensibilities of the reader of the preface to his *Histoire de Ma Vie* (*History of My Life*), which he seems fully to have intended to be published, but not until after his death—which is how it came to pass. In this writing, both private and public simultaneously, the author seems to play both sides of the street—as the gentleman and as the vulgarian. This is part of his charm. Casanova, so he assures us, will tell it "like it is." His reactions from moment to moment—whether he is being irrationally superstitious, cross, or greedy—will not be hidden.

Rousseau's *Confessions*, published after the author died in 1778, may well have served as an example and a spur to the writing of *The History of My Life*, yet the effect is very different. Casanova is truly unlike Jean-Jacques Rousseau in that he is interested only in a limited way in his interior consciousness. He is all for the exterior, almost entirely extrovert. Unlike the James Boswell of the *Journals*, he is not accompanied by guilt or a search for a super-ego. Casanova has a pronounced comic sense, which permits him to see himself as funny (not really true of Jean-Jacques); this is one of the attractions that pulls the reader in. *The History*—or *Story*—*of My Life* can become tedious and annoying in its piling up of sexual exploits. A modern reader is apt to become concerned as to whether Casanova understood what rape was. Certainly, as we can see also in Rousseau and in Boswell, the era still lacked any clear concept of child abuse. There is, however, more in Casanova's life than the amatory exploits. He fights a duel, he deals in the occult, he travels and encounters (and vies with) some of the major wits and *philosophes* of the time, such as Voltaire.

Above all, Giacomo Casanova the Venice-born had the unique experience of being a prisoner in the heart of Venice. And he made his escape from Venice's state prison, and lived to tell the tale. He evidently told the story scores of times to individual friends and mistresses and to admiring groups; after thirty-odd years he was moved to give it to the world in written form as *Histoire de Ma Fuite des Prisons de la République de Venise, qu'on Appelle les Plombs* (*History of My Escape from the Prisons of the Republic of Venice, Called the Leads*), published in Leipzig in 1787.[42] He tells us unromantically in his preface ("Avant-Propos") that he has to write the story down, now that he cannot tell it so effectively, as his teeth are going. Like Goldoni, Casanova decided to write his autobiographical account in French, an international language, which he uses too for the later unfinished *Histoire de Ma Vie.* Perhaps both authors felt more at home in the foreign French than in an Italian that might prove too Venetian for Tuscan critics.

The story of Casanova's imprisonment is nowadays recounted with gusto by the guides to the Doge's Palace. One can sign up for a special prison tour, inspecting both the Piombi ("Leads") above and the Pozzi ("Pits," "dungeons") below. (I recommend this tour, though not at the expense of viewing the Palazzo proper; ideally, it should be undertaken on a separate day and not in the heat.) The actual cells under the "Leads" disappeared in the nineteenth century, but a guide will show you where Casanova was incarcerated and how he tried to escape. Casanova's account is far better than that given in situ by Palazzo guides. The *Histoire de Ma Fuite,* a wonderful book in its way, should be much better known. It has the elements of a novel, and an adventure story. The hero is imprisoned. He plans an escape—the effort is frustrated. He makes another plan and at last succeeds, after much danger and difficulty, in finding his way to the fresh air. But the hero, the "I" of the narrative, is a comical "I" both self-conscious and spontaneous, both afflicted and funny. With panache, Casanova, describing himself about to enter an Inferno, makes a parallel with Dante, breaking into Italian quotation: "a happening which surprised me at the age of thirty *nel mezzo del camin de nostra vita* [in the middle of the journey of my life]" (*Ma Fuite,* "Avant-Propos," 5).

Casanova describes how he is abruptly arrested, his books and papers seized. In the *Histoire de Ma Vie,* he elaborates on the fact that he had been deliberately betrayed: "the jeweler Manuzzi had been the infamous spy who had accused me of having these books when he had gained entrance to my house, leading me to believe that he could arrange for me to buy diamonds" (*My Life,* IV, 200). Venice evidently does have real spies. The testimony written by Manuzzi for *Messer grande* ("Mr. Big," the chief of police) survives, and indicates that one of the reasons for Casanova's arrest may have been genuine concern over this con man fleecing his patron and friend, the wealthy and sickly Ser Giovanni (or Zuanne) Bragadin.[43] Quite possibly also the hero had engaged in too many affairs with married women of important families, or was suspected of corrupting the youth with whom he associated. He was also playing with magic and the Cabala, an accusation that the books and manuscripts in his lodgings had borne out. Casanova defends himself to the readers of *Ma Fuite,* saying these writings were like "drugs" which he kept on hand but never used personally. But as with any drugs, a possessor of quantities may be suspected of selling. There was reason to think that he was using magic and Cabalistic practices to extort money or favors from the gullible. He was not, however, tried formally for these offenses, presumably because the evidence would bring members of important families into disrepute.

Casanova is taken by boat to the prison, to *Messer grande*'s office, and left alone in a bare room. He is impressed by the fact that he needed to make water every quarter of an hour; even though he had not supped or drunk anything before his arrest "nevertheless I filled with my urine two large chamber pots" (*Ma Fuite,* 25). Such a detail, which another man would have suppressed, plays oddly against and with the *Inferno* reference, and substantiates his fear. Later he defends his inclusion of this detail: "I had a good laugh . . . when I learned that the fine ladies considered my account of the phenomenon a piece of swinishness which I might well have omitted. I would perhaps have omitted it in talking to a lady; but the public is not a lady, and I like to be instructive. Furthermore, it is not swinishness . . . despite the fact that we have it in common with swine, just as we have eating and drinking" (*My Life,* IV, 202). He insists he is never told why he is arrested and punished, nor what his sentence is. He is being slightly disingenuous; if he didn't know the term of his sentence he must have had a very good idea that he was meeting a severe check for his endeavors to fleece the patrician Ser Bragadin by bewitching him and others by means of (among other devices) occultism, "damnable impostures of the Rosicrucians and Angels of Light."[44]

Messer grande tells the inferior officer in Casanova's hearing to put him "*sous les plombs*" ("under the leads"), meaning a cell in the attic space just under the lead roof of the portion of the Palazzo Ducale allocated to the prison. Only thus does he find out what his fate will be. The cell would become frigid in winter and fiendishly hot in summer. The prisoner is tormented by fleas, which bite most persistently. The prisoner is not allowed books, save a mawkish religious treatise; after a time, his jailer relents and (ironically) allows him a copy of *The Consolations of Philosophy* by Boethius, the sixth-century Christian philosopher who wrote the book in prison, where he was at last put to death.

Casanova is eventually able to get some luxuries from home, or from friends, such as a fur cloak in winter. But these amenities do not make the situation much more endurable. The hero never reconciles himself to his fate.

He keeps hoping he will be set free on one auspicious day, then on another, but the lucky day never arrives.

The hero then decides to make his escape and, obtaining a tool, begins the laborious task over many months of making a hole in his floor. But it is a good Venetian floor, made of "what they call in Venice *terrazzo marmorin*. It is the ordinary flooring of rooms in all the houses in Venice that don't belong to poor people: the great folks (*les grands seigneurs*) themselves prefer *terrazzo* to parquet" (*Ma Fuite*, 104). This hardened marble mixture is tough to get through. Casanova has trained the jailers to sweep his cell floor to keep the fleas down; now he has to think of an excuse so that they won't do that any more. The hidden pit slowly gets bigger. And then—he is moved to another cell! The jailer expects he will be pleased, as this spot has two windows "where you will see half of Venice, a place where you can stand up" (121). This piece of bad luck was actually a piece of good luck, for had his attempt in that first cell succeeded, the hole would have landed him in the council chamber below.

Casanova acquires an ally, Père Balbi, a monk in the next cell (whose name indicates that he is of a very good Venetian family). The two now plan to escape through a hole to be created in the roof above Balbi's cell. In order to bring this about, Casanova must get his metal tool to his associate, but he has nothing large enough to hide it in. The only available portable and innocent object of size is a great Bible, and the tool is a couple of inches longer than the book. Casanova thinks of a ruse. With much precaution and parade, taking the jailer into his confidence only as far as cookery is concerned, he prepares for Père Balbi a special dish of macaroni, ostensibly as a gift in gratitude for the loan of books.[45] Three pounds of the pasta are to be cooked in a cauldron of boiling water, and then Casanova will carefully prepare a sauce of butter and Parmesan cheese, which the jailer is to bring him ready grated. The jailer understands he must deliver the hot dish straight away. Beneath the plate of pasta swimming in sauce there is the large Bible with Casanova's metal tool (his *esponton*) hidden within it. The jailer will be so anxious not to slop cheese sauce on the holy book that he is unlikely to investigate further (*Ma Fuite*, 150–151).

The pasta-and-Bible ruse is successful, and the pair eventually escape, not without many perils sliding around the roof of the Palazzo Ducale in the middle of the night. Having changed their clothes, they make their way to the Piazzetta and take a gondola to Mestre, where Casanova is surprised and annoyed to find Balbi stopping to take refreshment in a café, "and he said to me, 'sit down and take some chocolate too, since you have to pay for it'" (*Ma Fuite*, 230).

The book is full of obstinate details: the fleas, the macaroni, the untimely chocolate. The very writing of the story is connected with the unglamorous loss of teeth. In this narrative Balbi (without whose hard exertions they would not have got free) is unjustly treated as an annoying and inferior personage, but Casanova himself is never treated as heroic. Casanova tells us that this is by design "for an author who praises himself is not worthy of being read" (*Ma Fuite*, "Avant-Propos," 4). The hero of the narrative never becomes grand in our eyes, not even in his own. Giacomo as character has persistence, a certain grumpy humor, and an abiding self-love that is never mistaken by himself for greatness. He is proud of his ingenious trickery, thus knowingly reflecting one aspect of the traditional Venetian character. (Pious Giovanni Bellini, we shall see, is said to have tricked another artist into revealing the secret of painting in oil.) Throughout, and on many levels, Casanova defines himself as a Venetian. There is truth in what the Hungarian writer Sándor Márai imagines the escaped Casanova saying in the mountain town of Bolzano when Balbi attempts to join him in cursing Venice: "No one except me is allowed to curse Venice! . . . I bless my fate and I go down on my knees in gratitude to the destiny that decreed I should be born in Venice. . . . It is a source of pride and delight to me that Venice exists."[46] Casanova in real life never left off being a Venetian. In the 1770s, while he lived in Trieste, he actually made himself useful to the Republic by acting as a diplomatic liaison with Austria. He may have been something of a double agent as well. Casanova returned to Venice, and left again. In 1797 he thought of visiting conquered Venice, but died before getting there.

There is always a certain stubborn patriotism in Casanova, an identification with his city. Even in *Ma Fuite* there are a few flickering fleeting moments of Venetian beauty, like the reference to the Erberia; the hint of the scent of herbs, vegetables, and flowers stealing through a misty early dawn is the more effective as this outdoor scent of freedom is about to be shut out by the prison walls and leaden roof. Casanova offers many small comments on Venetian matters—as in the little disquisition on the *terrazzo*. He notes that the circumspect secretary of the Inquisitors "was apparently ashamed to speak Venetian in my presence, for he pronounced my arrest in good Tuscan" (26). Either (it is implied) the man is being uppity or he is ashamed of what he is doing.

The second illustration to *Ma Fuite*, depicting a moment that must have been chosen by the author, shows the Palazzo Ducale, massive and impressive and beautiful even in its back view, under the stars by whose light the hard-put escape artist attempts his escape. It is a beautiful and comic allusion to the Venice of the publicity mongers, the tourists' Venice in which the palace figures so centrally—here we see its backside and an untoward incident (Figure 4).

I have already remarked that Venetians were not novelists. Though a few writers (Casanova included) made some attempts at fiction, the great novels of Italy are not written by Venetians. All the same, we can see in life-narrative some of the traditional qualities of the novel put to use in the way that appeals to a Venetian sense of action and character. Novel and autobiography alike must take account of pesky details. and of an urgent and insistent material world that is hard to bend to the desires of the mind. Marco Polo's narrative—another prison book—was written out by a novelist who heard his fellow-prisoner Polo dictate the story, and Polo's surprising adventures and unexpected sequential experiences have something in common with Casanova's. Both characters are survivors par excellence. That Casanova in *Histoire de Ma Fuite* does at last make the Palazzo Ducale at least bend to his will makes him a Venetian, like the men who built the Palazzo and San Marco and the whole lovely edifice of Venice out of determined effort, hard planning, and bricolage.

Casanova's account of his escape has its political aspects, sharpening the propaganda weapons of the opponents of the Republic. It is democratic in that it is a critique of the exercise of arbitrary power. Moreover, it is a reaffirmation of the vital importance of the commonplace and of the flesh. But Casanova's account of his escape only underscored the associations of La Serenissima with spies, secret tribunals, and imprisonment. For foreigners who visited Venice—and for those who only dreamed of doing so—the idea of Venice's union of pleasure, secrecy, and danger was fascinating. Spies, secret tribunals, tortures, and desperate imprisonments were about to become staples of literature about Venice.

In Friedrich von Schiller's early Gothic novel *Der Geisterseher* (*The Ghost-seer*, 1787–1789), Venice is the central setting of the adventures of the hero, a young German prince, and his more stolid companion, the narrator. Schiller had never been in the city, but presents a recognizable Venice of named landmarks and habits: "The following evening we arrived earlier than usual in St. Mark's Square. A sudden shower forced us to shelter in a coffee-house where people were gambling."[47] At this gaming establishment the Prince is insulted

Figure 4. Casanova on the roof of the Doge's Palace, illustration of *Histoire de Ma Fuite* (Permission of the British Library: C.71.h.2, facing p. 213)

and an altercation takes place that renders him liable to Venetian revenge. Before the Prince can leave, he and his companion are frighteningly accosted and abducted:

Several servants of the Inquisition entered. They showed us orders from the Government requesting us both to follow them immediately. Strongly guarded, we were led to the canal. Here a gondola was awaiting us, in which we were required to embark. Before we stepped out of it, our eyes were blindfolded. We were taken up a long stone flight of steps and then through a long winding corridor, over vaults, as I deduced from the multiple echo that resounded beneath our feet. Finally we came to another flight of twenty-six steps that led us downwards. The staircase opened onto a hall, in which our blindfolds were removed. We found ourselves in a circle of venerable old men, all dressed in black; the whole room was hung with black drapes and dimly lit.

After this mystifying dark trek through a Piranesi-like edifice, characters and reader may expect astounding arbitrary punishments to follow. And so they do—but matters take an unexpected twist. The Venetian is brought in, and identified by the Prince as the man who insulted him. Asked by the "senior State Inquisitor" whether he intended to murder the prince that night, the prisoner says yes. "Immediately the circle drew back, and we were horrified to see the Venetian's head being separated from his body. 'Are you satisfied with this amends?' asked the Inquisitor.—The prince was lying in a faint in the arms of his escort. 'Now go,' continued the former with a dreadful voice, turning towards me, 'and in future be less hasty in your opinion of justice in Venice.'"[48] This is undeniably effective, though it has little or nothing to do with the administration of justice in real Venice. The public gaming house would signal a date prior to 1774, but Schiller isn't going to worry about such trifles when drawing upon the Venetian fantasy. One wonders, however, if his own Venetian idea has not been affected by Casanova's *Ma Fuite,* or perhaps an advance glimpse of it.[49] The story makes a knowing reference to the Piombi: "the most dreadful prison in Venice, situated under the roof of the St. Mark's Square's palace."[50] The touches of magical mystery in the characters of the Sicilian and the Armenian are interestingly reminiscent of the personae Casanova assumed to Bragadin and others, with his occult mysteries, and pseudo-Rosicrucian flummery about Angels of Light. Perhaps Schiller had also heard some various accounts of Casanova's life.

Schiller's narrative presses on, in a quest for both truth and pleasure. The characters go to the monastery of San Giorgio to look at Paolo Veronese's *Marriage Feast at Cana,* which the narrator thinks should be in some public place and not kept by a few monks in their refectory. (Napoleon agreed, and at his conquest of the city removed the great painting to Paris, where it remains in the Louvre.) The young Prince falls into an addiction to gambling, although for the first time in his life he also begins to feel the urgency of sexual attraction, becoming drawn to a mysterious Greek beauty in a black veil. Throughout, he is accosted by a mysterious "Armenian," who seems to have some of the characteristics of the Wandering Jew, to be a prophet and a seer.[51] The unresolved plot dances around a core enigma, something like "How does one find meaning in the universe?" Schiller's Gothic thriller seems to have become too much for him, and he left it tantalizingly unfinished, but vivid. Its montage is inspired by the idea of Venice, as dreamlike, shifting, arbitrary, seductive.

There were—and are—"real" Venetian ghost stories, tales of the macabre; Francesco Semi presenting local stories in *Leggende di Venezia* (2001) argues that they are folkloric. But the foreign improvisers of the Gothic mode did not bother with Venice's own tales; "Gothic" is a kind of international psycho-political language. In Schiller's unfinished novel, Venice emerges as a site ideally suited to certain Gothic effects, paving the way for the Venice of horror and disturbance to be found in literature and film of the twentieth and twenty-first centuries.

Many stages, however, separate Schiller and Nicholas Roeg. By the early nineteenth century, Venice had become a settled Gothic locale, in such works as Johann Heinrich Daniel Zschokke's *Abällino, der große Bandit* (1794), a novel influenced by Schiller, and the amplified "translation" of it by Matthew ("Monk") Lewis as *The Bravo of Venice* (1804), soon successfully rendered for the stage. It is worth noting, politically, that in these novels not all sympathy for the Venetian constitution is as yet lost. The Doge and some of the nobles are treated sympathetically, but a rebellion is plotted by discontented young nobles (read *barnabotti*?), and thugs (bravos) who live by more-or-less organized crime; only the Big Bandit can put a stop to them. James Fenimore Cooper follows suit after the conquest, with his sensation novel *The Bravo* (1834), a penny dreadful surprising from so good a writer. Cooper, who had visited Venice in the spring of 1830, claimed "the drift of the book is political" and that its objects were to "to demonstrate the manner in which men get entangled in the meshes of mystifications . . . and to expose the irresponsible nature of an aristocratic form of government."[52] By the mid-nineteenth century, such popular entertainments had canonized a now-familiar violent and Gothic Venice of the bad old days. Gautier in his first thundery night in Venice felt he was "circulating in a novel by Maturin, by Lewis or by Ann Radcliffe, illustrated by Goya, Piranesi and Rembrandt."[53] He also recalled *Aballino*. All of these works are influenced—and reinterpreted—by an effective barrage of criticism of the Republic of Venice. There is no parallel criticism of daft Hapsburg monarchs, or Austrian cruelty, spies, and tribunals in the bad new days.

Not all early Gothic treatment of Venice carries such a negative ideology. Gautier refers to Ann Radcliffe, but what catches Radcliffe's fancy in the Venetian section of *The Mysteries of Udolpho* is not the image of a cruel Venice but the image of the city of reflection and stillness: "The smoothness of the water, over which she glided, its reflected images—a new heaven and trembling stars below the waves, with shadowy outlines of towers and porticos, conspired with the stillness of the hour."[54] Radcliffe's Venice is not a set of standard gruesome Gothic preoccupations, but a meditation on the illusory nature of being. Her Venice is an image of Maya, the illusory veil of phenomena over which we sail. Mann's Aschenbach, who had written a novel entitled *Maya,* should have been better prepared for Venice and its disconcerting way with surfaces. Gautier, rather vulgarly we may feel, expects (perhaps wants) corpses falling from balconies.

During the French Revolution and in Napoleon's time it became increasingly desirable to say that the old Republic was all that was wicked. Hapsburg-ruled Austria had no reason to contradict. I sympathize with the patriotic Venetian historian Alvise Zorzi, who speaks of shadowy and denigratory sketches of Venetian history "diffused above all by the French propaganda after the killing off of the ancient Republic (a work of systematic defamation which served to construct an alibi . . . a justification in which Austria also associated itself)."[55] Zorzi thinks that the negative propaganda continues after the Risorgimento, a "systematic disinformation" that Italy didn't know how to contradict. Venice became an ideological screen on which some of the evils of Western history could be projected. There was little danger that Venice could answer back, but the projection itself stirred—and stirs—anxiety.

No one would argue for the faultlessness of the Venetian state. It required, like other European states in the eighteenth century, more justice, more openness, and a diminution of the power of old hierarchy. Both Goldoni the interrogator and Casanova the dishonest-honest prisoner point the way.

There was certainly need for a more open method of trial, not protecting members of the patrician class when their dirty linen was involved (as in Casanova's case). Goldoni exhibits the Venetian instinct for fair play, along with a desire for negotiation, which could have developed into a modified and evolving legal system. The eighteenth century Venetians in fact were not greatly given to executing people. They did not flog their own sailors to death like the English. Other nation-states (progressive Holland, for example) in the late eighteenth century used torture in interrogation—yet these states were not accused of fascinating wickedness. The Venetian government—unlike some superpowers of our day—was not in the habit of keeping gross numbers of the inhabitants in durance. There were very few prisoners of any description found to "liberate" when the French marched in.

The "melodrama and *mise en scène*" of Gautier's catalogue of horrors were in part the work of Venice's historic antagonists, from the rivalry of Louis XIV to the revolutionaries, Napoleon, and Austria. Perhaps there was a feeling among intellectuals that republicanism had to be invented anew, and that this reinvention necessitated the trashing of Europe's oldest and wealthiest republic. Whatever the cause, a body of fantasized propaganda becomes an aspect of the "normal" version of the ancient city-state, serving various purposes, especially that of Napoleon, who declared he would be "an Attila to Venice," and announced, "I will have no more Inquisition, no more Senate."[56]

Subjugated, Venice was forced to celebrate the end of the eighteenth century with a bonfire burning Venetian insignia and emblems, and a dutiful dance around a Tree of Liberty erected in the Piazza San Marco. Napoleon's generals uttered some impressive slogans about "Liberty" to a captive audience. Ten thousand French soldiers were quartered on the hapless citizens of Venice (they brought disease with them, to add to the city's woes). All the images of the Lion of Venice were to be removed or utterly defaced. The man charged with doing that was, happily, patriotically dishonest, and refrained as far as possible from destroying lions, though the lion and Doge on the Porta della Carta were too beautiful and conspicuous not to be demolished. (What we see now is a reproduction.) Venetian discontent was palpable, and perhaps feared. To shout *"Viva San Marco!"* became an offense punishable by death.

Having thus treated his captive audience to a fine exhibition of the rights of man, Napoleon passed Venice on to Austria, first helping himself to some superb loot, including many outstanding paintings, gold and silver vessels, and ornaments from the churches. The four bronze horses of San Marco were lowered and removed on 7 December 1797, and the Oriental Lion of San Marco on the pillar followed them. Before they left, in January 1798, the French army took everything else it could lay its hands on, including rope, canvas, and the very cauldrons (successors to the cauldrons Dante had seen) used to boil pitch for the Arsenale.

During the French and then the Austrian occupation, negative images of the excitingly unjust old Venice served to justify the then current (unjust) state of affairs. The *Leggenda nera* (Black Legend) becomes settled history. Austrian injustice and cruelty—their tribunals, reprisals, censorship, executions—never became the stuff of drama, in contrast to the fuss made about nasty Venice in the bad old days. As far as I know, no novel, drama, or film takes Napoleon's overthrow of Venice as its central story.[57] The account would, admittedly, be more dramatic had he personally been present at the conquest. Napoleon visited the city only once, for a cold and foggy week in November–December 1807, when he decided what to suppress and tear down. As John Julius Norwich points out, Napoleon didn't like Venice.[58]

Venice at the outset of the eighteenth century is still felt to be glorious, her beauty apparent, the pleasures she offers almost irresistible. But Venice was caught on the hop by the Enlightenment to which it had itself so handsomely contributed. Venice at the end of the eighteenth century becomes a fascinatingly negative figure of Enlightenment propaganda: it is the place of infamous luxury and sweet sin, and also the home of torture, prisons, arbitrary sentences, and sudden death. Ironically, most European states went in for some or all of these things too—not least, revolutionary France. But Venice had to pay—supposedly for its egregious inhumanity. Part of the revolt against Venice reflected in the repetitive images of the Bridge of Sighs, the secret tribunal, masked spies, and so on seems to arise from a revolt against pleasure itself. At very least, the negative images serve reassuringly as a bulwark against her seductiveness.

There is a particularly Venetian promise of human liberation, formerly adumbrated in the work of its great artists and in its use of commedia dell'arte, latterly finding articulate expression in works of literature. Goldoni makes us notice work and working people; Casanova speaks of the desire for liberty and the respect to be accorded the humble flesh. That Venetian "democratic" spirit honors the day-to-day, the contact of the soul with matter. It identifies social and psychological identity as constructed and labile. It is hospitable to diversity, materiality, joy, change, and transformation. It could have articulated much for the modern world, that spirit. And there was a brief tantalizing chance of realization. In 1848 the people took up the responsibility that old Ludovico had pointed out was theirs. They not only rose against Austria, but also created a new constitution. The first election by universal manhood suffrage of 1849 created an assembly "representative of every social class. There were members of the old nobility . . . merchants, lawyers, engineers, scientists, soldiers and sailors, teachers, priests, friars, Jews."[59] Venice was now probably now the most democratic state in Europe. Its people, high and low, pooled their resources, material and mental, in one great effort in 1848–1849. But the world went on repeating its Black Legend. It was in the interest of Austria as occupier, as it had been of Napoleon, to promulgate the myth of wicked old Venice, deservedly overthrown. Perhaps tourists who consented to enjoy themselves in an occupied city needed to believe it. But the sense of deathliness and melancholy that nineteenth-century travelers (and some twentieth century ones as well) reflect upon may have been picked up from an intuition of the great misery and resentment seeping through the very pores of the subjugated and impoverished city. Old Venice was treated as the abode of crime, but perhaps visitors harbored in some corner of their consciousness a stifled sense that they were accomplices in a new crime against Venice and mankind.

The fell nature of the sentence passed on Venice itself means that its own spiritual development in the political and even the artistic realm was abruptly ended. Something had been broken, and certain possibilities for the future were cut off. Yet, we may hope, not necessarily cut off forever—for some of us can believe that Venice has a future as well as a past.

4

Happy and Unhappy Travelers

I'm curious to know how this enchanted fortnight will strike me, in memory eleven years hence—for altho' I've got absurdly used to it all, yet there is a palpable subcurrent of deep delight. Gondolas spoil you for a return to common life.

—Henry James to William James, 26 September 1869

Although nineteenth-century visitors enjoyed themselves, there is nothing pleasing to Venetians in recollections of the nineteenth century. It is no wonder that Venetians are tempted to turn back toward a fancied good past, their eighteenth century, last era of magnificence. To remember the era of Goldoni and Canaletto is to recollect an independent existence, an identity. Now that we have arrived in the twenty-first century, however, it behoves Venice to forget from time to time the lures of the Settecento. Among the clutter of souvenirs, I yearn for sketches and images of us as we are now, and Venice and Venetians as they are now—so that we may all claim our share in the living history of Venice, the flow of time. Let us foreigners, the *forestieri*, be displayed and immortalized in the cheap shops and stalls, displayed wearing down jackets or silly hats, or the cheapest blue plastic galoshes sold in the streets during *acqua alta*, those temporary boots permitting the visitor to slosh through the squares and along the *passarelle*.

Why not exhibit these *passarelle* themselves?—the large trestle-supported planks, like huge picnic tables, laid about the Piazza San Marco, and along the streets. Depict the colorful procession trotting along this boardwalk above a miniature lake. Paint the Senegalese selling mysteriously high-quality knock-off bags outside the shops, and the gondolas full of Chinese tourists. Show us and posterity the gondolier of today, with his "traditional" straw boater on to be sure—and his *cellulare* at his ear. Yet one cannot expect alluring images of eighteenth-century Venice to disappear. That Venice could be—and was—loved without condescension. The anachronistic sketches and artifacts are an endeavor to revive that older love.

I certainly tumbled into that love with little instruction or preparation, turning from a notional contempt to a wondering passion in less time than it took to ride on a vaporetto up the Grand Canal. My own recollections of my first visit to Venice glow with a sense as of intoxication—though at that time I rarely took a drink, and the thin wine at the trattoria of the inevitable scampi could not have intoxicated anyone. It was Venice itself on which I got drunk. Many visitors long before myself have felt the Venetian delirium. In the fourteenth century Francesco Petrarca (Petrarch; 1304–1374) was so taken with it he professed himself willing to stay when the Venetians made him an offer he couldn't refuse: a house of his own in exchange for his library when he died. Some of Petrarch's letters joyfully observe his Venice, including the pleasure of living in his house on the Riva degli Schiavoni (then, as later, center of much bustle and sea traffic), where the tall masts of the ships passed by his upstairs windows. Petrarch notes that the ship that is departing at night from just outside his house will travel far off:

Such a loud shout from some sailors suddenly struck my ears that I rose. . . . I looked out; good God, what a sight, what a scare! Heartwarming, tremendous, delightful! Here at my door a number of ships were anchored to the glittering shore for the winter; equaling in size even this huge mansion, which this free and munificent city has provided for my use, their mastheads rose strikingly above its two corner towers. As the clouds veil the stars, as the wind shakes the walls and rooftops, and the sea bellows with an infernal roar, the largest of them is setting sail this very hour, and I do wish it Godspeed. . . . You would call it not a ship, but an image of a mountain floating on the sea, so weighed down with cargo that the waves hide a good part of its hold. It is going to call at the river Tanais. . . . Some passengers will disembark at that point, but it will not halt until, crossing the Ganges and the Caucasus, they arrive in India, farthest China, and the Eastern Ocean.[1]

Petrarch is struck with the wonder of the fourteenth century's global trade. On one hand the ship is an image of desire, of avarice; he muses, "how costly and, at the same time, how cheap life is to mortals." But it is also a sight that lifts the heart, and he wishes the great caravel Godspeed. Later, he is rapturous at the show the Venetians put on at their victory over their rebellious settlers in Candia (Crete). Venice seemed to him (for a while) "the one abode of liberty, peace, and justice."[2] Sadly, the love affair with Venice and the idyll by the Riva came to an end; Petrarch left Venice in something like a huff. He went to Arquà in the Euganean hills and built for himself and his cat a lovely house of his own design, with a prospect of fields and hills where no masts could pass by his window. Perhaps he forgot the salty view of the Riva.

In 1527 Pietro Aretino—*littérateur*, pornographer, satirist, and intellectual—came to Venice to escape papal displeasure and made himself thoroughly at home. From 1529 to 1551 he lived in a house just north of the Rialto Bridge. In a enthusiastic letter to his landlord in October 1537 he emphasizes his delight with the place:

Certainly the builder gave it the honor of the most worthy side of the Grand Canal. And as that is the Patriarch of all other canals, and Venice the Popess [*Papessa*] of all other cities, I can truthfully say that I am enjoying the most beautiful street and most delightful view in the world. I never go to the window but I see a thousand people, and as many gondolas, during the market time. The *piazze* under my eye on the right are the Beccaria and the fishmarket, and on the left, the bridge [old Rialto Bridge] and the Fondaco dei Tedeschi. In the centre of these two I have the Rialto, meeting place of men of business.

I see grapes in the sailboats, game and game birds in the shops, and vegetables in the open space. I have no wish to see rivers watering meads, when at dawn I can marvel at the water covered with every variety of things that can be found according to the seasons. And I have a great viewing point while those who bring the great copiousness of fruit and vegetables dispense them to those who carry them to their appointed places. But all is hurly-burly except the spectacle of the twenty or twenty-five sailboats, full of melons, which tied up together make a sort of Island to which the multitude pours in order to calculate, both by sniffing and weighing, the perfection of the melons. Of the lovely wives lucent in silk in gold and jewels, proudly seated in the central seat of honor in their gondolas, I shall not speak, in order not to diminish the reputation of such pomp. But I will say that I burst with laughter at the cries, whistles and shouts of the boatmen fulminating at those who had themselves rowed by a family servant without scarlet stockings. And who would not have pissed himself laughing upon seeing, in the height of winter, a bark full of Germans who had just left a tavern overturn into the water?[3]

Such a eulogy of Venice is in notable contrast to the moody moonlit views and general somberness of the Romantics and their followers. Clearly, Aretino preferred the busy hum of men—or speaks up for those who do. He is impressed with the wealth of Venice at its basic level—there is plenty of *food* here. He delights also in crowds and activity, and his busy Venice seems to match that of Carpaccio a few years earlier.

Aretino (unlike Petrarch) proved his devotion by staying in Venice until he died there. That is something foreign lovers of the city often profess to desire, but seldom achieve. Browning and Wagner died here but probably didn't quite intend it. Petrarch and Erica Jong settled and thought they would stay, but went elsewhere. Peggy Guggenheim (1898–1979) remained a faithful if belated lover of Venice. She took over an unfinished eighteenth-century palazzo and created a fine museum of modern art. So great was her gift to Venice that she secured the rare—nay, unique—privilege of being allowed to be buried there, on her grounds in Dorsoduro, and not in San Michele. Like Frederick the Great of Prussia, she lies at home by her favorite house, surrounded by the graves of beloved dogs. One feels she was satisfied by Venice.

Aretino's admiration for the Venetian wealth of food is not universal. Over the centuries, visitors have handed in mixed reports. The Venetians in general have a reputation for being (to say the least) frugal. There was a communal emphasis on temperance; the wealthy republic's ruling-class males were supposed to value simple *mediocritas,* a middle way, neither starvation nor gluttony. This cultural imperative was reinforced not only by constant regulations passed by the Maggior Consiglio, designed to rein in the wealthy patricians, but also by the traditional rule that the head of the house does the food shopping (just as in ancient Athens). Visitors from other countries found this odd and displeasing, a waste of time. William Thomas, a British traveler in 1549, utters a snort of contempt: a patrician "will go to the market himself and spend so miserably that many a mean man shall fare better than he."[4] As in Athens, no upper-class male would wish to be seen by his peers engaging in childish or feminine extravagance in mere food. Women, children, and servants may not have fared too well when nobles and burghers vied in the marketplace in a display of virtuous indifference to the pleasures of the palate and stomach. Launcelot Gobbo, Shylock's servant, cries, "I am famished in his service. You may tell every finger I have with my ribs"—a complaint that may illustrate Shylock the Venetian rather than Shylock the Jew (*Merchant of Venice,* II.ii; *Works,* 432).[5] In fact, Shylock has a lot of traditional Pantalon qualities, and many of his habits and attitudes illustrate the frugal and shrewd Venetian burgher. Venetians have an edge to them—Shylock, whetting his knife on his shoe, just takes this further than most.

As in ancient Athens, the custom of male shopping served as a check to overconsumption and waste in a region that did not produce a super-abundance of food. Even in the late Middle Ages and the Renaissance, when there were many luxury goods available in Venice, including spices from the East, oranges and lemons, and sugar from Candia, simplicity customarily prevailed. Dining rooms, however, became larger and glossier. Venice was a European pioneer in the use of the fork, an import from Byzantium. It took other people a while to get used to it. In a party scene by the school of Veronese, *The Feast of Saint Gregory the Great* (Vicenza), a moustached little man in yellow is shown handling a fork with great dubiety. "Then must you learn the use / And handling of your silver fork at meals," warns Jonson's Sir Poli-tick Would-Be.[6] Venetians also introduced transparent wine goblets. In fact, they invented the place setting with napkin, bread, silverware, and wine glass. They composed the archetypal model of the elegant private dining table, as we can see in works like Veronese's *Marriage Feast at Cana*. Although the Vene-tians led in producing what we might call a sumptuous dining mise en scène, Patricia Fortini Brown observes that a banquet offered the opportunity to share enjoyment of splendid rooms, furnishings, silver, and glassware rather than to revel in food. "To the English [and, we might add, the French] hos-pitality meant food and fine wine; to the Venetians . . . it meant display."[7]

To preserve *mediocritas,* the man of the house would purchase eggs, vegeta-bles, a few small fish, some apples. Fish and game birds, especially marsh birds, were staples. The Venetians have always liked strong tastes, gamey food, and onions (their remedy against scurvy). Casanova is not alone in his preference for strong flavors, as we will note if we sample a Venetian dish like sardines marinated in onion sauce (*sarde'le in saòr*).[8] If you like it, you like it a lot; you can almost feel your immune system being bumped up sev-eral notches. Thus marinated, the sardines could even be taken on a sea voy-age. A meal would include bread of some sort—the rowers on galleys made do with a special perdurable biscuit. After the introduction of maize in the late Renaissance, polenta became a Venetian staple food (pasta really came in after World War I). Wine from the mainland was permitted to be sold wa-tered. John Evelyn made his own (perhaps a typical resource of students).

Visitors by no means always admired this heroic simplicity in housekeep-ing. Among the discontented was Erasmus, who in the very early years of the sixteenth century visited Aldus Manutius in order to get his *Adages* properly printed. He resided with Aldus's father-in-law, another printer. However high his opinion of the Aldine Press, Erasmus did not think well of the conditions of his host's house (which had bugs), nor of the fare. Later, he ridiculed the household in a satire in his Latin *Colloquies* entitled *"Opulentia Sordida"* ("Sordid Opulence"), drawing a contrast between the immense riches of Venice and the mean way in which Venetians could live. In Erasmus's comically disgusting account, the host watered the wine from a cistern which held rainwater (and worse), and set before his guests and family amazing inedibles: hard stinking cheese, rotten eggs, the stomach of an old dead cow, unchewable bread, scanty salads—"seven lettuce leaves swimming in vinegar but no oil." The interlocutor inquires, "In a city so wealthy, could you be in danger of great hunger?" to which the speaker replies with laconic emphasis, *"Maximè"*—"the greatest," "to the max."[9] Erasmus expresses the opinion that Mercury, god of trade and trickery, was the only deity worshipped in Venice. He also found the place physically cold; Boreas the North Wind blew for three months straight, but the miserly host supplied a pathetic fire not lacking in smoke but without flame. Evidently they order these things better in Rotterdam.

An equally discontented visitor was the Anglican Bishop Gilbert Burnet in the late seventeenth century. He disliked even the rooms and furniture, and thought the Venetians lived very meanly, with iron bedsteads instead of wood "because of the Vermin that their Moisture produces."[10] His and Erasmus's unfavorable impression of insect life contrasts with Effie Ruskin's compliment (at least to the Danieli): "I have never been bit or seen a flea and in Switzerland I was half eaten up."[11] Burnet, however, is not alone in finding Venetian furnishing bony and inhospitable, and the city on the edge of the Alps does indeed get cold, as Erasmus had cause to observe. Henry Wotton, the English ambassador of James I, comments in 1607 on the January weather in which people were "breaking their heads with falls in the streets," noting ice on lanes and bridges, while sportsmen "that went afowling" were "frozen to death."[12] Venetian residences offered few comforts against the chill. They didn't have roaring fires in English-style fireplaces, nor snug Germanic stoves. Northern Europeans and the Americans after them appear to miss their stoves and fat feather beds and pillows. They also miss their own substantial pieces of furniture. (Venice has to bring wood from outside to make furniture, and tends to prefer the graceful to the heavy.)

By the nineteenth century there is an acute contrast between Venetian traditional (or, rather, eighteenth-century) style and the prevailing taste. The Venetians had bare floors, with small Oriental carpets, and a few items of delicate wooden furniture elegantly painted. (Of course in the nineteenth

century the impoverished Venetians had little money to waste on new furnishings.) They enjoyed a floor of *terrazzo* or of shining parquet, not only
because of the Venetian preference for a glassy and reflective surface, but
because such a surface is easy to keep clean. English and American visitors
in the Victorian era are rendered slightly miserable by their hankering after
overstuffed furniture and abundance of fabric in curtains, cushions, and giant
carpets. When William Dean Howells and his wife take a flat in the Palazzo
Giustiniani, he comments that the palazzo "had not all that machinery which
we know in our houses here as modern improvements. . . . Life there was, as
in most houses in Italy, a kind of permanent camping out. When I remember
the small amount of carpeting, of furniture, and of upholstery we enjoyed, it
appears to me pathetic" (*Venetian Life*, 406). Compare Dickens's description
of the faded palazzo rented by the Dorrit family, where Mrs. General sits in
a chair in her huge room "on a little square of carpet, so extremely diminutive in reference to the size of her stone and marble floor that she looked as
if she might have had it spread for the trying-on of a ready-made pair of
shoes."[13] The concept of area rugs was not yet appreciated by the *forestieri*.

Bishop Burnet, like Erasmus, not only found the accommodation uncomfortable, but judged the food execrable: "for above half the Year, the Wine is
either dead or sour. They do not leaven their Bread, so that it is extreme
heavy; and the Oven is too much heated, so that the Crumb is as Dough,
when the Crust is as hard as a Stone."[14] He alleges that he couldn't have
stood being in Venice for two weeks if it hadn't been for the kindness of the
French ambassador and his wife. Burnet was a thoroughly disgruntled traveler. The Anglican bishop had come abroad, however, with the purpose not
only of describing European countries but of detecting the frauds and folly
of "Popery," and was ready to be displeased. Yet the French ambassador was
surely Catholic, so there must have been something else, more inimical, about
Venice. Certainly it is a very odd traveler who thinks of two weeks in Venice
as an ordeal. But Maximilien Misson found the local wines "disgustful" to
the French palate, and he is entirely in accord with Burnet on the bread: "you
must break it as they do Bisket, with a Hammer."[15]

Hester Lynch Piozzi (formerly Thrale), visiting in the 1780s, speaks
warmly in favor of the food: "Such fish wait one's knife and fork as I most
certainly did never see before, and as I suppose are not to be seen in any sea
but this, in such perfection. Fresh sturgeon, *ton* as they call it, and fresh
anchovies, large as herrings, and dressed like sprats in London, incomparable;

turbots, like those of Torbay exactly . . . are what one principally eats here" (*Observations and Reflections*, 142–143). But then, Mrs. Piozzi is an enthusiast for fish. Some British and American visitors (and some Germans and Dutch, too, like Erasmus) miss their comfortably filling meals. Mark Twain finds Continental food in general unsatisfactory. In the Venice chapter of *A Tramp Abroad* (1880) he goes into a mock-patriotic rhapsody about the wonderful American breakfast that sounds to us like a heart attack spread out on a table: "a mighty porter-house steak an inch and a half thick . . . enriched with little melting bits of butter. . . . A township or two of tender, yellowish fat gracing an outlying district of this ample county of beefsteak . . . a great cup of American home-made coffee, with the cream a-froth on top, some real butter . . . smoking hot biscuits, a plate of hot buckwheat cakes, with transparent syrup."[16]

I can laugh at these travelers' nostalgia for their starches, butter, and beef, but cannot be so haughty when I remember my Venetian hunger and the six scampi. Hunger is a Venetian experience. In *The Comfort of Strangers* the lovers can find nowhere to have a late dinner. Even in the approbatory Italian film *Bread and Tulips*, the heroine, timidly venturing out to find something to eat, finds only one poor eatery open, and there is told that the cook has come down with appendicitis and she can have only cold food. Howells praises the Venetians for extreme temperance in eating, even among the wealthy, but at the same time he is obviously discontented with such abstinence: "I am ashamed to confess that I have not always been able to repress a feeling of stupid scorn for the empty stomachs everywhere, which do not even ask to be filled" (*Venetian Life*, 85). He complains that their poultry are much too lean, even the turkeys, "and as for the geese and ducks, they can only interest anatomists" (342).

Venetians over the centuries do seem to eat lightly, taking care to have fruit and vegetables in season. They enjoy some heavier foods, such as fried liver (*fegato*), and for a filling dish there is *seppie con polenta*, cuttlefish in its own jet-dark sauce on a slice of maize-meal polenta. Some foreigners may not like to approach so black-hearted a dish, and may even shy away from eel risotto. Venice offers either light repasts or hearty old-fashioned dishes with flavors disconcerting to moderns. Compared with Rome, Emilia Romagna, or, say, Sicily, Venice is not a place for elaborate dining. Of recent years restaurateurs, notably the Cipriani, have contributed to Venice's international fame in the eating line, but high restaurant cuisine is less local than *nouvelle*, though the restaurant Do Forni currently sustains Venetian culinary tradition while catering to modern tastes. Pino Agostini and Alvise Zorzi in *Venice: Tradition and Food* endeavor to draw favorable attention to the more traditional Venetian dishes. James Morris, writing of Venice in the late 1950s, comments that you can fare best "in some water-front trattoria eating a fine but nameless fish from the lagoon, garnished with small crabs . . . and fortified by a glistening slab of *polenta* . . . food fit for Doges."[17] These little fish-and-polenta places have largely vanished from central Venice, gone with the local population to Mestre. In Chioggia you can still find tiny cheap restaurants like those so lovingly described by Morris serving fresh salads and delicious fish. In general, body and soul can be successfully kept together at a middling seafood eatery in the city, though such a meal in central Venice is fairly expensive. If I lived in Venice for a while, as I long dreamed of doing (but something always happened to prevent it), I should enjoy shopping at the markets, especially the Pescaria, the fish market, and I could, like Aretino, experiment with salad herbs, though unlike him I could not expect to have game birds sent me by Titian.

Sensuousness—if not the stomach—is in every other way catered for in Venice. Sensuous pleasures—other than eating—abound everywhere: in the softness of fabric, the reflections in many mirrors, the iridescence of colors. Or, we might add, in silks, the carnation of flesh, the gold gleam of hair. Looking at women was always one of the pleasures Venice afforded to men, and women could enjoy dressing up, wearing jewelry, and making themselves beautiful with lotions and Oriental scents.

If a lady were not born blond, she could achieve blondness. The blondification of both high-born ladies and professional courtesans was achieved through bleaching; John Evelyn in 1645 tells us more than we may want to know as to how this could be accomplished: "They wear very long crisped haire of severall strakes and Colours, which they artificially make so, by washing their heads in pisse, & dischevelling them on the brims of a broade hat that has no head, but an hole to put out their head by, drie them in the Sunn, as one may see them above, out of their windos."[18] The bodily product had been used as a lye from antiquity to recent times, and at least there was a use for everything. Venetian women of the Renaissance dressed very finely, with many ornaments, and discovering a lot of themselves: "In their tire they set silk flowers & sparkling stones . . . & shewing their naked arme, through false Sleeves of Tiffany girt with a bracelet or two: besides this they go very bare of their breasts & back. Which they usualy cover with a kind of yellow Vaile of Lawn very transparant" (ibid.).

Evelyn obviously enjoyed watching these women, though he mocks them for the altitude of their *ciopppini* or high platform shoes of wood or cork. These chopines must originally have served like pattens to keep the wearer's feet above the dirt, but they grew more ornate, often painted or covered with colored leather, and so tall that the stilt-like shoes made movement difficult: "'Tis very ridiculous to see how these Ladys crawle in & out of their *Gundolas*." Evelyn comments that a man being asked how he liked "the *Venetian Dames*" replied "they were *Mezzo Carne, Mezzo Legno* [half flesh, half wood], & he would have none of them" (June 1645; *Diary*, 227–228). Three decades earlier, Thomas Coryat had commented unsympathetically on the dangers of this same extravagant fashion: "For I saw a woman fall a very dangerous fall as she was going doune the staires of one of the little stony bridges with her high Chapineys alone by her selfe: but I did nothing pity her, because she wore such frivolous and (as I may truely terme them) ridiculous instruments, which were the occasion of her fall."[19] We should hardly expect the pleasures of Venice to include laughing at the locals falling down. But observing and being amused at the mishaps of other people, natives as well as fellow tourists ("a bark full of Germans" overset, for example), is one of the less noble pleasures available to the visitor.

Certainly, not every visitor feels the enthusiasm expressed and enacted by Petrarch, Aretino, or Peggy Guggenheim. Venice may strike some as sinister, others as comically unnatural, an impression caught by the American humorist Robert Benchley, who is supposed to have wired to the *New Yorker*: "Streets Full of Water Please Advise." Some visitors have frankly hated the city at first sight, as the eighteenth-century historian Edward Gibbon seems to have done: "a momentary surprize . . . soon gives way to satiety and disgust. Old an[d] in general ill-built houses, ruined pictures, and stinking ditches dignified with the pompous denomination of Canals; a fine bridge spoilt . . . and a large square decorated with the worst Architecture I ever yet saw."[20] Many persons (chiefly North Americans, and some British) nowadays express their belief that they would never enjoy Venice because they heard it smells. (They don't seem to notice how their own cities smell.)

During its reconstruction period in the late nineteenth and early twentieth centuries, Venice in search of economic viability was ambitious to shine afresh as a tourist resort. The inevitable result   there were "too many" tourists. Travelers do not like to make way for too many of their own kind. The English poet Rupert Brooke in the early twentieth century was disappointed and even disdainful, his negative impression largely the result of the presence of those annoying others, and of modernization: "It is disheartening to wake next morning to electric launches and cosmopolitan hotels and Americans and all the other evils that our civilized age gives." Venetian painting seemed to him depressingly fleshy and soulless: "the stolid but respectable damsels of Bellini developed into the ponderous carnalities of Titian and Paolo [Veronese]." The Venetian people, Brooke sweepingly proclaimed, "were never purely young and never beautifully decadent, but always in a tawdry and sensual middle age." But he had a few happier impressions. Trying to persuade Ka Cox to travel with him in 1912, he writes, "My God, if you'd stay with me, somewhere down on the coast by Venice, while the spring woke: on and on! What we'd be there! (Oh, there's cafés in Venice—Florian's in front of St. Mark's)."[21]

It is hard to place the initial point of Venice's success in tourism. In the twelfth century the Republic gained from the Pope the privilege of remission of sins for pious visitors to San Marco, thus becoming a place of pilgrimage in its own right. But the first big influx came when Christians had control of the Holy Land, and pilgrims poured from west to east. Travelers found Venice an excellent transit point. There was even a kind of tourist agency, with branches in Saint Mark's and on the Riva; these *Tholomarii* (roughly, "bureaus for sea voyagers") aided the Jerusalem-bound in finding lodging in Venice, a berth on a ship to Palestine, and the goods they would need to take with them. So at one point the Piazzetta and Piazza (even when but a campo still) would have been full of pilgrims, in outlandish if travel-stained woolly garb. Individuals and tour groups, speaking in a gabble of languages, would have been trailing about to pilgrim tour agencies. The Maggior Consiglio recognized the need for legislation and passed *Capitulum Peregrinorum* (an act regarding travelers) regulating this trade in 1255. Hospices for pilgrims were dotted about greater Venice, especially on the islands.[22]

Saint Mark's Square sometimes arouses great admiration, and, at other times, annoyance over the crowds. People frequently imagine that the Piazza has become "spoiled," driven from some imagined earlier perfection. But Saint Mark's has had a variety of uses and occupations. In the time of Titian, painters of decorative cupboards and *cassoni* (the large wooden boxes in which Venetians kept valuable clothing and other goods) worked outside their shop in the square.[23] The Piazza was for centuries the official and permitted haunt of mountebanks and charlatans (Figure 5), so it makes sense for the cheating hero of Jonson's *Volpone, or The Fox* to sell his wondrous medicine there. Sellers of all sorts of goods drift to the Piazza. Mrs. Piozzi notes the auctions of

Figure 5. Charlatans ("li Ciarlatani") in Piazza San Marco with people of various nations, from Giacomo Franco's *Habiti d'Huomeni et Donne Venetiane*, 1609 (Permission of the British Library: C48.h.11, f. 25)

chickens and ducks. Howells comments on the hawking of fruit and—more oddly—of puppies. In Venice's great days the grave patricians in their togas used to meet by Saint Mark's for serious business, but the area just around the corner from the Doge's Palace in the arcade nearest the sea was an open and public (in every sense) privy. When in *Volpone* the English visitor Sir Politick Would-be notes in his diary "at St. Mark's I urined," he is doubtless correct (IV.i, line 144; *Plays,* III, 75). Goethe is not the only traveler to comment with disgust on the insistent presence of human manure. If all we have to complain of is pigeon-shit and too many tourists (oneself never counted among the "too many"), we should rejoice.

D. H. Lawrence in the 1920s rails against Venice in general, in describing Constance Chatterley's visit: "Too many people in piazza, too many limbs and trunks of humanity on the Lido, too many gondolas, too many motor-launches, too many steamers, too many pigeons, too many ices, too many cocktails . . . too many languages rattling, too much, too much, too much sun, too much smell of Venice, too many cargoes of strawberries, too many silk shawls, too many huge, raw-beef slices of water-melon on stalls."[24] Lawrence's "take" on life could be described as the neatly diametric opposite of Aretino's, for whom the *copia* hold deep charm and reassurance. They agree in seeing Venice as a place of copiousness, a home for crowds and multiplicity.

Venice loves crowds—indeed the crowd variously costumed and polyglot is itself one of the tropes of Venice. It is a standard observation to comment on the various nationalities to be met with, as John Evelyn does in 1645: "Nor was I lesse surpriz'd with the strange variety of the severall Nations which we every Day met with in the Streetes & Piazzas of Jewes, Turks, Armenians, Persians, Moores, Greekes, Sclavonians. . . . and all in their native fashions, negotiating in this famous *Emporium,* which is allways crouded with strangers" (June 1645; *Diary,* 228). Evelyn evidently didn't mind these other visitors "rattling" in their different languages. In an early guidebook to Venice, *Venetia Città Nobilissima, et Singolare,* first published in 1581, Francesco Sansovino boasts of the concourse of peoples in the city: "It is singular also in this, that being convenient to all nations, whether neighbouring or far away, they gather here from the most remote parts of the earth, all people (whence come different persons, discordant in faces, costumes, and language, but however all in concord in praising this so admirable City) to traffick and do business."[25] Sansovino takes his cue from Gasparo Contarini (1483–1542), the political theorist whose *De Magistratibus & Republica Venetorum* was published in 1543. Contarini's first page succinctly sounds the notes to be re-played and expanded by multiple writers on market and marvels:

Many visitors, prudent men nor ignorant of the arts, who first come to Venice and contemplate the extent of this city are struck with admiration and even as it were with stupor, open-mouthed, as never having had to bear before anything so wonder-ful (*mirandum*) or illustrious. Not all admire the same things. For some, the greatest wonder, even incredible to be seen, is such a great market filled with everything from all lands and regions, brought perpetually and without ceasing into this one city, and thence drawn away from it again to the most diverse peoples over land and sea. But others are held by the crowds frequenting the city, and the gathering of peoples of nearly all kinds, as if the city of Venice were the common emporium of the whole world (*veluti commune orbis emporium*). Others marvel at the magnitude of her empire, her rule far and wide over land and sea. But many of the more polite and acute-witted wonder at the plan for the site of the city, so it seems indeed to all as if it were the work of the immortal gods rather than human work and invention, and for this cause above all Venice takes precedence of all other cities which now exist among any peoples, or ever were.[26]

Régis Debray, our contemporary *philosophe*, in his *Contre Venise* ("Against Venice," 1995), asserts that in her glory days, which he equates with the time of the Battle of Lepanto (1571), Venice felt no need of touristic self-advertisement. This is not the case. Contarini in the 1540s advertises the glory of the Venetian marketplace, and Francesco Sansovino echoes him in *Venetia Città Nobilissima* (1581). Sansovino wrote puffs both before and after Lepanto. An indefatigable booster of Venice, he had published his *Dialogue Between a Venetian and a Foreigner* in 1564. The Foreigner ("Forestiero") com-plains that it is impossible to understand all these marvels; he requires inter-pretation. He has taken in the most delightful things by his eyes, but he needs no less to take in something at his ears, such as explanations of the antiquity of the city, its customs, modes of government, and so forth. Need-less to say, the "Venetiano" is happy to oblige, and the Forestiero's enthusias-tic admiration and eager ignorance make him a delightful target for information and instruction.[27]

Son of the immigrant architect Jacopo (who created the Loggetta), Francesco Sansovino may indeed be something of a pioneer in guidebook writing, but he is not the first. Venetians had started to publish descriptions of their city almost as soon as the printing press was available. As Patricia Fortini Brown and others have noticed, the burst of Quattrocento painting by Carpaccio and others, setting Venice out in detail, coincides with the production of important maps and detailed descriptions. What distinguished the sixteenth century is the production of guides in the vernacular, most explicitly aimed at visitors.[28]

Writers like Sansovino draw upon the political confidence so glowingly expressed by Contarini in his *De Magistratibus*, a work so analytical and far-reaching that (as Professor Eileen Hunt Botting has persuaded me) it constitutes his claim to be considered the West's first modern political scientist. Contarini, who was a Venetian senator before he was made a cardinal, has—for good and ill—an idea of the state as Jefferson or Disraeli will do. He is really discussing a constitution, as he describes and praises the government of Venice as a rational structure, a unique example of "temperature" and balance. He also admits the need for change; a man who has had lunch may still want dinner. A state is in essence what people do; one should not "account a Citie to bee the walles and houses onely, but rather the assemblie and order of the citizens. . . . and this is the true reason, manner, & form of commonwealthes, through which men enjoy a happie and quiet life: This is that rare and excellent thing, wherein *Venice* seemeth to shine, and to surpass all antiquitie."[29] Contarini pays attention to customs concerning marriage, public health, and so on. Sansovino evidently takes the hint from him in handing out profuse information about habits and traditions, as well as precise descriptions of buildings.

One of the remarkable things about his works is the detail in which they explain local customs. When, for example, Sansovino in *Venetia Città Nobilissima* writes about "Matrimony" and explains the marriage customs of Venice, past and present, he is in a sense performing an ethnographic examination of his own society. He is as fascinated by Venetian behavior as Goldoni will be. In former days, he explains, the marriageable girls collected in San Pietro, each with a box containing her dowry; the young men came and there was a mass wedding. Now weddings are arranged by a broker, and there is a party. The newly espoused bride of good family makes a special public journey: "accompanied then by diverse gentlewomen . . . she mounts a gondola, and sits outside the *felze,* on a raised seat covered by carpet . . . followed by a great number of other gondolas, she goes to visit the convents where she has sisters or other relatives."[30] Both the party and the journey through the city, he observes, make public the fact of the wedding. Giacomo Franco's *Habiti d'Huomeni e Donne Venetiane* (1609) picks up such points of interest, graphically producing the scene Sansovino described (Figure 6).[31] We see the girl setting

Figure 6. "A questo Modo vano le Novizze in Gondola" ("In this manner the Brides go by Gondola") from *Habiti d'Huomeni et Donne Venetiane*, 1609 (Permission of the British Library: C48.h.11, f. 13)

primly off, with blond ponytail and good clothes. Any visitor will now understand what is going on, should he behold an unveiled young woman of good family pursued by a fleet of gondolas. Sansovino admires his world, and expects others to do so, and yet he knows that the Venetians' world is made of customs, costumes, and habits of mind. Beneath his maintenance of Venice's perfection there is a sense of relativism. But he is prepared for the observer——with that self-reflective Venetian eye.

The entertainment to be found in looking at people of different nationalities is agreeably urged upon travelers in such explanatory pictorial works as *Habiti d'Huomeni e Donne Venetiane*. It is not a book of views of Venice, mere *vedute*, but a book about people. We are offered the chance of looking at Venetians and at foreigners. We are shown Slavs, Jews, and others in the concourse in the Piazza; the picture of course not only illustrates but also explains what or whom the traveler is seeing, just as a bird book explains what birds you have been or will be looking at (see Figure 5). An understanding of the touristic seems thoroughly developed by the sixteenth century. Not relying entirely on the attractions of its magnificent buildings and fine works of art, Venice offered many special occasions to delight spectators with a picturesque arrangement of peoples. There were not only the processions on conventional religious occasions but also unique celebrations of special days of the Venetian festive calendar. There was the sea-procession of the Doge in his highly decorated and gilded barge, the *Bucintoro* as the Doge went to wed the Adriatic off the Lido on Ascension Day (May or June) (see frontispiece). There was the *Regata Storica* in September. This regatta is not—as I first assumed when I saw it—a recent invention for the benefit of twentieth-century tourists; it was begun in 1315, though the big costumed boat parade dates from the fifteenth century, and the honors done Caterina Cornaro. The regatta has complicated rules regarding the style of vessels and the rowing, which must be done standing. There was—and is—even a women's boat race, as we see in an early seventeenth-century illustration, the girls' ponytails shown as flying behind them in hyperbolic sign of their speed (Figure 7). Come to Venice, the picture seems to say, and see something completely different.

Travelers of all sorts did come from abroad, for various reasons. Sir Philip Sidney was in Venice in the winter of 1573; his concerns were of the highest diplomatic order. The Grand Tour, first applicable only to young aristocrats, was originally a business trip. The coming member of the ruling class was to visit various courts and learn about Europe, spying out the land meanwhile, estimating the strength of fortifications and the military capacity of various

le donne, l'abitanti i ludi circostanti a'Ven.ª concorrono parimente à così fatta festa uogando insieme, et contendondo i premij con uniuersal piacere de riguardanti.
Giacomo Franco fo: Con Priuilegio

Figure 7. Girls' boat race, from *Habiti d'Huomeni et Donne Venetiane*, 1609 (Permission of the British Library: C 48.h.11, f 21)

nation-states. A noble traveler should model himself, as Sidney tells his younger brother, on Ulysses, seeing many men and many cities and considering the mores, laws, and military strength of every nation.[32] Sir Politick Would-be, Jonson's foolish visitor to Venice, parodically rejects "That idle, antique, stale, gray-headed project / Of knowing men's minds and manners, with Ulysses" (*Volpone*, II.i, lines 9–10; *Plays*, III, 25). (There are grounds for believing that Sir Politick is satirically modeled on the intelligent but political, pragmatic—and espionage-minded—ambassador Wotton.) Sidney notably excepts Venice from his generally harsh judgment of Italy—while the country is good for silks and wine, Italian governments, save that of Venice, can offer no useful model as they all exemplify "tyrannous oppression."

Increasingly, travelers who were not noble and had no diplomatic or other business were already going in for the Grand Tour, which became for many, as for Richardson's disreputable young Lorimer in the eighteenth century, chiefly a pursuit of pleasure and fashion. Venice had already seen to it that it was cried up as a place to visit; it was fast becoming de rigeur for aristocratic young gentlemen to prove that, as Shakespeare's Rosalind puts it, "you have swam in a gondola"—though she does not favor such travel (*As You Like It*, IV.i; *Works*, 645).[33]

Cervantes, who was in Italy for a couple of years from 1569, at first under the service of Giulio Acquaviva and then in the Spanish army, had a military interest in observing North Italy. Presumably he recorded something of his nonmilitary impressions in the experiences of his character Tomás Rodaja in the story "The Glass Graduate" (or "The Vitreous Licentiate"), published in *Novelas Ejemplares* in 1612. The hero's admiration for Venice is mitigated only by his admiration for Mexico City, Venice's New World rival. Tomás is so taken by the pleasure of the place that he forgets his other travel plans: "The pleasures and distractions which our curious traveller discovered in Venice were almost as compelling as those of Calypso."[34] Sidney had omitted to remark on some of the delightful dangers that threaten Homer's traveling hero; Venice impressed Cervantes as a place worthy of enchanting and entrapping Ulysses.

Rich visitors and the not-so-rich rented lodgings if staying for any time, but Venice was early a city of inns and hotels. A poor Scottish traveler in the early seventeenth century, William Lithgow, on his arrival perceiving a throng and "a great smoake," was delighted on being told "there was a gray Frier burning quicke at S. *Marks* Pillar . . . for begetting fifteene young Noble Nunnes with child." The fate of this unhappily prolific friar, who had been confessor to the convent of Santa Lucia, offered the Protestant visitors an enjoyable spectacle. Then, "being inhungred and also overjoyed," he and his companion "tumbled in by chance, *Alla capello Ruosso,* the greatest Ordinary [i.e., restaurant] in all *Venice,* neere to which the Friars bones were yet aburning." They got a good chamber, also two fine meals apiece, and were "nobly and richly served," but Lithgow was horrified next day on finding that they owed a large sum, "twenty shillings English." The brutal Lithgow in his excitement had made the classic traveler's error of not inquiring as to the rates before settling in. Then as now, hostelries near St. Mark's were costly.[35]

Inns and restaurants figure in Venice long before Lithgow's time. "Even in the fourteenth century," Morris claims, "it was a city of hotels—the Hat, the Wild Savage, the Little Horse, the Lobster, the Cock, the Duck, the Melon and the Queen of Hungary."[36] One of the early paintings of the cityscape, Carpaccio's *Recovery of the Relic from the Canal of San Lorenzo,* also known as *Miracle of the Relic of the Cross at Rialto Bridge,* clearly shows the already old Sturgeon Inn (Locanda dello Storione), with its fishy sign. In the eighteenth century William Beckford stayed in the hostelry to royalty, Albergo del Leon Bianco, which supplied orange trees and festoons of vines on the balcony. This "White Lion" was the converted thirteenth-century palazzo Ca' da Mosto, a luxury hotel from the sixteenth to the eighteenth century; it is very near Aretino's former lodging and Beckford too was awakened by the market boats.

Nineteenth-century travelers of means could rely on top notch hotels, most of which were converted *palazzi*: the Gritti, the Danieli, the Europa. All of these are flourishing today. The Europa, a Renaissance palazzo, had been turned into a hotel in the Napoleonic era, and remained popular with French tourists of means—like Gautier. Venice over the centuries was always determined to lure those rich and varied visitors with the promise of a good place to stay.

One of the more ambiguous if fascinating comforts offered by Venice was the persistent presence of the gondolier. A gondola could be hired for constant personal attendance by those who could afford it, but everyone had to hail a gondola upon first arrival, and the gondoliers were notorious for trying to take male visitors straight away to a fine courtesan or to a brothel. When hired on a permanent or semipermanent basis, they rapidly learned everything about their employer's doings and tastes, just as the Venetians' private gondoliers knew of their masters' business dealings and of the hideaways of their secret mistresses. *Gondolieri,* with their intimate knowledge of the laguna and the labyrinth of canals and *rii*, were—and are—mysteriously savvy as well as ineffably graceful. They are always noticeable, whether young or middle-aged, physically deft and exuberant, yet nonchalant in their athleticism. I know a man whose daughter is married to a gondolier. They do well financially, and go for Alpine skiing holidays in the winter. These strong, athletic—and balletic—men are frequently seen as erotic in their own right. An attraction to them as erotic objects tinges the appeal of hearing them sing Tasso. They possessed a nearly fatal attraction for John Addington Symonds and Frederick Rolfe. In George Sand's novel *La dernière Aldini,* the young gondolier becomes his lovely mistress's lover—though the youth Zorzi is not a very experienced gondolier: "I was a very mediocre oarsman, in spite of my zeal and my energy; I knew little of the lagoon, I had always been so preoccupied while crossing."[37] Their love affair is inadvertently furthered by his ignorance when, partly blinded by his emotion, he grounds their craft in the mud off San Giorgio in Alga.

Sand's Zorzi may be a sentimental boatman, but *gondolieri* in general are usually noted for sophistication and dry humor. How one would enjoy—and be horrified at—a collection of their jokes, sayings, and stories. They are up to anything; Constance Fenimore Woolson's gondolier Angelo helped Henry James to drown her clothes in the lagoon. It must be hard to surprise a gondolier. Howells notes their quick wit and wry comic sense, characteristics that have surely endured—though one imagines their best jokes are shared only among themselves. Yet through the centuries they have adjusted with aplomb to their unreasonable polyglot customers.

It is wonderful to find in the Renaissance such a boast as Sansovino's— that you will see people unlike in faces, costumes, languages. What is wonderful that it *is* a boast. What we would call Venice's "multicultural" quality is early felt to add to its appeal, emphasizing the singularity of the most noble and singular city. One of the attractions of coming to Venice, evidently, is that you will see everybody else here, including people from remote countries. There will be more folk here, and more *difference,* than you are used to. William Beckford is struck and entertained by the variety:

I observed a great number of Orientals among the crowd, and heard Turkish and Arabic muttering in every corner. Here, the Sclavonian dialect predominated; there, some Grecian jargon, almost unintelligible. Had St. Mark's church been the wondrous tower, and its piazza the chief square of the city of Babylon, there could scarcely have been a greater confusion of languages. . . . This instant, I found myself in a circle of grave Armenian priests and jewellers; the next, amongst Greeks and

Dalmatians; who accosted me with the smoothest compliments, and gave proof, that their reputation for pliability and address, was not ill-founded. . . . I was entering into a grand harum-scarum discourse with some Russian Counts; or Princes; or whatever you please; just landed, with dwarfs, and footmen, and governors. (*Dreams, Waking Thoughts, and Incidents*, 100)

Beckford evidently approves the "Babylon," even though he mixes in some condescension about muttering and unintelligibility. This mixture of peoples and tongues is a trope of Venice itself. Observation of the *discordia concors* of its mixture of peoples is a constant staple of commentary on the city, as in Effie Ruskin's account of her first evening in the Piazza: "a dense crowd in the centre of men, women and children, soldiers, Turks, magnificent Greek costumes. . . . I was walking there with John last night till past eight without any bonnet."[38] John Ruskin's father was most displeased to hear about a lady in a bonnetless state. Perhaps it seemed too daring amid a promiscuous crowd of Turks and Greeks.

Not all visitors approved the mixture. The singular "Babylon" could arouse dislike, even fear. My own philosophy teacher during my years at Dalhousie University, George Grant, a man who made an enormous intellectual impact on me, had not quite liked Venice when he visited it in 1938, at the age of twenty: "Venice is an amazing place, and I have been fascinated. Above all, I have got the impression that Venice is very much a temporal city. Commerce as its all engrossing element has left it no mysticism. It is a secular place and in many ways completely Babylonic. It is sensual and pleasure-seeking and yet remains a relic of the past. The queer mixture of the old Byzantine Venice, mixed with the Renaissance that came late, gives a queer impression."[39]

Venice did not bore Grant—he was "fascinated"—but it jarred. It was "Babylonic," and perhaps a Babel. It lacked spiritual dimension, it was worldly. It seems odd (to me) that San Marco and Torcello and the religious paintings gave the young George Grant no intuition of the Venetian style of "mysticism." It may be that a natural Platonist would always find Venice distasteful. There is a hint of challenge in this "queer" and "Babylonic" place. Both Babylon and Babel had figured in earlier travelers' comments, too, as in Gautier's view of staircases rising up "towards mysterious Babels." References to Babylon and Babel reflect a floating unease with the indigestible quantity and quality of difference that Venice proposes to normalize.

I am more sympathetic to that dogged and comical Renaissance traveler,

Thomas Coryat (sometimes spelled Coryate), whose book of travels is one of the liveliest English productions of the early seventeenth century. Coryat was a jester, a professional funnyman who was treated by all who knew him as if he were unintentionally funny, the butt of everyone's (more or less) good-natured laughter. One sees that was Coryat's way of maneuvering through life; he had no money and no family, and his position as buffoon had a certain value. He published his travels, giving the book the deliberately funny title of *Coryat's Crudities*—"crudities" as in *crudités*, mere uncooked antipasto, trifles that don't make a meal, let alone a banquet. Such self-deprecation is necessary because Coryat is a man of humble station, and practically penniless—he is the opposite of the proper traveler, the young aristocrat on the Grand Tour, like a Philip Sidney. Tom Coryat is no dunce—he is able to read Latin inscriptions, he recollects Latin authors, and he even recalls that the torture by the wheel is mentioned by Aristotle in his *Ethics*. But he is man of low class, with no need to travel abroad like a young nobleman, or a merchant, or even hopeful scholar. Coryat has no business to attend to. He travels for the sake of traveling. Coryat got persons of importance to patronize the book and write prefatory matter, at the cost of having them puff him off as an amiably ridiculous fellow, Ben Jonson leading the way, in his "The Character of the famous *Odcombian*, or rather *Polyptopian Thomas* the *Coryate* . . . *Done by a charitable friend*" (*Crudities*, b1R). Jonson tells us that Coryat is "irrecoverably addicted" to the idea of travel; he reacts even to a letter arrived from abroad: "The meere *superscription* of a letter from *Zurich* sets him up like a top: *Basil* or *Heidelberg* makes him spinne. And at seeing the word *Frankford*, or *Venice*, though but on the title of a Booke, he is readie to breake doublet, cracke elbowes, and overflowe the roome with his murmure" (b2R).

Acute lust for travel especially afflicts the person hampered by lack of funds. Coryat at last decided to go on his European journey, working his passage and writing it up. His grand object was to get to Venice, which he contrived to do by walking there most of the way. Coryat yearns to see *"the mayden Citie of Venice: I call it mayden because it was never conquered"* (158); one of the attractive things about Coryat is that he does humbly buy into what is now commonly called "the myth of Venice," her presentation of her ideal self. Venice the beautiful idea was nowise diminished by Tom Coryat's real experience—even though he came to the city in hot midsummer. He informs us very exactly that he arrived "on the twenty fourth of Iune being Friday . . . about two of the clocke in the afternoone" (157). He remained in Venice for six weeks, through July and into August, no light matter considering the steaming heat of Venice at this season; as he himself notes: "The heat of Venice about the hottest time of sommer is oftentimes very extreme." It was a world without ice or air-conditioning (as it is today in the humbler hotels), and presumably the poverty-stricken traveler from Odscombe had to endure an attic room. "For mine owne part," he confides, "I can speake by experience, that for the whole time almost that I was in Venice the heate was so intollerable, that I was constrained to lie starke naked most commonly every night, and could not endure any clothes at all upon me" (275).

In the seventeenth century it is a rare soul who would vouchsafe such a humble and humbling detail as his sleeping in the raw through hot nights. But Coryat consistently paints himself as a humble and very physical traveler. The comically emblematic frontispiece to his *Crudities* displays, as the symptom of the end of his journey, his worn shoes and louse-dropping old doublet, set up scarecrow-fashion, as a sign of the journey completed. Upon his return to England, he dedicated his shoes to his church in Odcombe (where they hung till they dropped to pieces).

Coryat takes appropriate note of the multicultural crowd in the Piazza: "Here you may both see all manner of fashions of attire, and heare all the languages of Christendome, besides those that are spoken by the barbarous Ethnickes; the frequencie of people being so great twise a day . . . that . . . a man may very properly call it rather *Orbis* than *Urbis forum*, that is a market place of the world, not of the citie" (171). A city that is the markerplace of the world—this was what the Venetians were hoping one would see. Though a poor traveler such as Coryat could not much enrich Venice, his published view disseminates her own propaganda about herself.

As Coryat was in Venice in July 1608, he was present for the ceremonial thanksgiving at the Redentore (Church of Christ the Redeemer), built as a fulfillment of a pledge in thanks for deliverance from the plague of 1576. Coryate admired the "marvailous solemne Procession" in which "every Order and Fraternity of religious men in the whole city met together, and carried their Crosses and candlesticks of silver in Procession to the Redeemers Church, and so backe againe to their severall Convents" (227). But not everything was solemn ceremony; the Venetians knew how to enjoy a day of celebration (and Coryat, how to obtain free treats): "Besides there was much good fellowship in many places of Venice upon that day. For there were many places, whereof each yeelded allowance of variety of wine and cakes and some other prety iunkats to a hundred good fellowes to be merry that day, but to no more; this I know by experience. For a certaine Stationer of the city, with whom I had some acquaintance . . . brought me to a place where we had very good wine, cakes, and other delicates *gratis*, where a Priest served us all" (227).

Venice persistently exceeds expectations. The buildings, the people (the beautiful courtesans included) all manage to be more than satisfactory. The traveler from Odcombe explores the famous architectural monuments, goes through the Doge's Palace and San Marco with dutiful attention to detail, and views numerous paintings. Thomas Coryat did all the touristic things, including ascending the Campanile (the old Campanile that was to collapse suddenly in 1902). He was most appreciative of the opportunity to have such a grand prospect, including the Euganean Hills and the Alps; one can see how the rage for extensive urban views was fostered by such ascendable religious objects as bell towers. Coryat urges his reader not to miss the sight—entry costs less than an English penny. (I, slightly acrophobic, never thought of ascending the Campanile until urged to do so by Coryat, who proved irresistible; the cost in 2006 is six euros, perhaps not a bad equivalent of one English penny in 1608.) Coryat tried the wines of the region, though he found them very dear, and had to make do: "a moderate and competent drinker may buy as much of their meaner red Wine in one of their Maga-zines, that is, cellars, for his sol, which is a little lesse then our halfe penny, as will serve for a reasonable draught." This moderate and competent drinker, however, evidently loved Lachrymi Christi, "toothsome and delecta-ble to the taste" (288); probably he would have drunk it rather than the meaner local red if he could have afforded it.

The tourist Coryat enjoyed some treats not so easy to come by, as when he was able to observe exactly how a Venetian woman does her hair: "For it was my chaunce one day, when I was in Venice, to stand by an Englishman's wife, who was a Venetian woman borne, while she was thus trimming of her haire: a favour not afforded to every stranger" (401). He went to a show at the playhouse, which he thought inferior to English plays, though it had its novelty for him: "I saw women acte, a thing that I never saw before" (247). He took a trip by gondola to "pleasant Murano . . . where they make their delicate Venice glasses, so famous over al Christendome for the incomparable finenes therof." Not content with looking at the work of the glass factories, Coryat took the opportunity to try his hand: "and in one of their working houses made a glasse my selfe" (248).

Coryat is one of the first travelers to give a detailed account of Venetian music, to which he listened in admiration at the feast of Saint Roche (6 August) in the hall of San Rocco:

This feast consisted principally of Musicke, which was both vocall and instrumentall, so good, so delectable, so rare, so admirable, so superexcellent, that it did even ravish and stupifie all those strangers that never heard the like. But how others were affected with it I know not; for mine owne part I can say this, that I was for a time even rapt up with Saint *Paul* into the third heaven. Sometimes there sung sixteene or twenty men together, having their master or moderator to keepe them in order; and when they sung, the instrumentall musitians played also. Sometimes sixteene played together upon their instruments, ten *Sagbuts*, foure Cornets, and two Violde-gambaes of an extraordinary greatnesse. . . . Of the singers there were three or foure so excellent that I thinke few or none in Christendome do excell them, especially one, who had such a peerelesse and (as I may in a manner say) such a supernaturall voice for sweetnesse, that I think there was never a better singer in all the world, insomuch that he did not onely give the most pleasant contentment that could be imagined, to all the hearers, but also did as it were astonish and amaze them. I alwaies thought that he was an Eunuch, which if he had beene, it had taken away some part of my admiration, because they do most commonly sing passing wel; but he was not, therefore it was much the more admirable. (251–252)

The only standard touristic luxury of importance that Coryat could not quite afford was a night with a courtesan, though the Venetian courtesans fascinate him. Perhaps, he indicates, his duty to the reader induces him to engage with the topic: "The more willing I am to treat something of them, because I perceive it is so rare a matter to find a description of the Venetian Cortezans in an Authour, that all the writers that I could ever see, which have described the city, have altogether excluded them out of their writings" (263). (Actually, Sansovino had discussed "Meretrici" in *Delle Cose Notabili Che Sono in Venetia—Of Notable Things in Venice*, 1570.) Coryat does obtain an interview with one, in order—so he assures us and probably himself—to find the opportunity to try to convert her from this sinful course of living. Throughout his Venetian tour, Coryat is troubled, at least in his official account of himself, by good intentions. He knows he ought to rebuke and reform the Catholics, endeavor to convert the Jews, and exhort the courtesan to change her way of life. But, as he comically presents himself, his efforts toward these good works always come to grief. His attempt to convert the Jews ends in an altercation with some Jewish merchants, "somewhat earnestly bickering with them" (236), a situation from which he is rescued by the English ambassador, Sir Henry Wotton, who happens to pass by this scene of heated argument on the Ghetto bridge and offers Tom Coryat a ride in his gondola (the one rented from a Jewish broker). Wotton presumably wanted to prevent an international incident and judged that the somewhat boorish English troublemaker would be sufficiently flattered by the offer of such a distinguished ride to leave off his doctrinal quarrel. Coryat would not have known of Sir Henry Wotton's own interest in Judaism, which he had pursued in Venice; it was presumably Wotton (acting on behalf of King James I) who had asked the learned rabbi Leon Modena to compose a written account of Jewish practices, a task resulting in the book first published in 1637 as *Viti, riti & costumi de gl'hebrei*, or *Historia de gli riti hebraici*.[40]

When Coryat meets with the courtesan, he tries to argue with her, but is argued down by her, and overwhelmed by a beauty he cannot possess—an encounter rich in the embarrassment he furnishes. Coryat perpetually presents himself as a man governed by his aesthetic sense. The Catholics are wrong—but their ceremonies are superb and the music in their beautiful churches is celestial. He admits to his surprise that the Jews in Venice are surprisingly "elegant" and handsome, particularly the women. And as for the courtesans—well! Coryat presents us with a representation of the richly attired beauty (a generalized courtesan given a conventional name) and his dogged homely (if dressed-up) self comically inserted as an illustration to his book, for which the courtesan becomes a kind of advertisement (Figure 8). The lady, "Margarita Emiliana," wears the beautiful damask such as we may see in full color on ladies in Veronese's paintings. Her hair is carefully crisped and patently blonde, and her throat is visibly encircled with a necklace of the pearls or "margaritas" suggested by her name—despite the official ordinance that prostitutes are not to wear pearls. The courtesan is like a dream of beauty. In his narrative the author seems consistently—and consciously—to be setting himself up to be "converted" by beauty at the expense of his Protestant ideology.

Coryat's love of Venice seems greater toward the end of his visit than it was at the beginning: "this incomparable city, this most beautifull Queene, this untainted virgine, this Paradise, this Tempe, this rich Diademe and most flourishing garland of Christendome. . . . The sight wherof hath yeelded unto me such infinite and unspeakable contentment" (290–291). There is *nothing* he would take in exchange for the chance of seeing Venice, he declares emphatically:

Il Signior Tomaso Odcombiano

Margarita Emiliana bella
Cortesana di Venetia

Gu: Hole sculp:

Figure 8. Thomas Coryat and the Venetian Courtesan, from *Coryat's Crudities*, 1611 (Permission of the British Library: C.32.e.9, facing p. 262)

I say, that had there bin an offer made unto me before I tooke my journey to Venice, eyther that foure of the richest mannors of Somerset-shire (wherein I was borne) should be *gratis* bestowed upon me if I never saw Venice, or neither of them if I should see it; although certainly those mannors would do me much more good in respect of a state of livelyhood to live in the world then the sight of Venice: yet notwithstanding I will ever say while I live, that the sight of Venice and her resplendent beauty, antiquities, and monuments hath by many degrees more contented my minde, and satisfied my desires, then those foure Lordshippes could possibly have done. (290–291)

This is an extraordinarily superlative declaration, considering that the English dream has always been to acquire a manor house. The value of four manors would be wealth beyond the wildest fancies. In asserting the superiority of experience to solid possession, Coryat is a modern man. By this I mean that he is like a person of the late twentieth or the twenty-first century, in setting a value on an experience (even a purchased experience) for its own sake. He also values the yearning for and search after experience. He is thus very well suited to Venice. "Manor houses" are precisely what Venice does not offer. Though there are some along the Brenta canal or in Friuli, this is not what we mean quintessentially by "Venice." Venetian wealth was created by experience, adventure, and exchange. Its goods, like the glass and lace for which it is still famous—or the ride in a gondola itself, or the Carnevale— offer a heightening of imagination, a dream-fabric rather than solidity.

Venice offers a sense of superabundance, of being given something better than one hoped for, something that manages to be unexpected, even if—as for Coryat—expectation has been fed by images, accounts, and well-designed propaganda, nurturing the imagination and prefiguring the experience. Théophile Gautier reflects such an instructed desire when he tells us that there are three places he has always wanted to see: Granada, Venice, and Cairo. Each man, he reflects, poet or not "chooses one or two cities, ideal fatherlands which he inhabits in his dreams, of which he imagines the palaces, streets, houses and aspects, according to an interior architecture."[41]

Proust develops Gautier's idea, capturing most fully that strange phase of mental development when one begins to acquire internally an image or a feeling about a place, without yet having been there. In *A la Recherche du Temps Perdu* the narrating Marcel longs to go to Venice, of which he has a dynamic internal composite impression: "I reflected . . . that the spring sunshine was already tingeing the waters of the Grand Canal with so dusky an azure, with emeralds so splendid, that when they washed against the foot of a Titian painting they could vie with it in the richness of their colouring."[42] This passage occurs in a chapter entitled "Place Names: The Name." Names are of great importance: "since I thought of names not as an inaccessible ideal but as a real and enveloping atmosphere into which I was about to plunge, the life not yet lived, the life intact and pure, which I enclosed in them gave to the most material pleasures, to the simplest scenes, the same attraction that they have in the works of the Primitives."[43]

Unlike Goethe, who proclaims his dislike of mere words and to whom "Venice" as still but a name is empty, Proust values the name for its intense suggestiveness. Nobody is better than Proust at capturing this strange capacity to reflect upon a place unseen, mediated by images, and reproductions of objects. Proust and his Marcel would have been able to see engravings, paintings, and numerous photographs of Venice itself, as well as careful reproductions of a Titian. Goethe himself becomes Proustian when his first trip up the canal in Venice reminds him that his father had a model of a gondola, souvenir of his own trip to Venice, which he allowed the child Goethe to play with: "When the gondolas appeared their shining steel-sheeted prows and black cages greeted me like old friends" (*Journey*, 74). Venice in Marcel's dreaming becomes a place not subject to normal spatial law; waters wash against a Titian painting in a dream state of desire. Part of the point here— even, one might say, the joke—is that Venice itself is indeed not subject to normal spatial laws—not the ones that govern more terrestrial urban centers. That the waves do indeed dash against the houses, museum, and churches is a fact, and the compression is only a salute to the material compression and strangeness of Venice itself. Marcel Proust had actually visited Venice with his mother and fallen in love with it. But his narrator is allowed centrally to dream of Venice, to fashion images of it, and that feeling remains slightly more intense than the experience of Venice itself when Marcel actually goes. One of the submerged links of Proust's vast novel is the desire for Venice— which remains even after the city has become one of the sites of memory.

Desire for the essence of all that is Venetian, the mingling of land and water, of stable and unstable, is never fully satisfied. Thomas Coryat once he has been to Venice also expresses a kind of continuing desire. For those who love that strange city, the affection is a kind of thirst that is never truly slaked.

5

Venice-Venus
The Brilliant Muddy History

Mark by what wretched steps their glory grows,
From dirt and sea-weed as proud *Venice* rose;
                    —Alexander Pope, *Essay on Man*

*N*ot all visitors are enthusiasts like Thomas Coryat. In some eyes, Venice has appeared from the outset but a debased enterprise. We don't find writers criticizing Paris (Lutèce) for arising out of mud (Lutetia). Although the unhygienic (even at times downright disgusting) aspects of Paris and London have called for occasional criticism, the cities themselves have been favorably treated—despite anxieties about the deleterious attraction of the Great Wen. Rome, Athens, Paris, London, New York—each of these can stand for the *Urbs*, for the Great City, for the City as vessel, even exemplar, of the best that has been said and thought in the world—or as magnet for the idle and unruly. But these human settlements have a kind of family likeness that Venice doesn't share. Venice is too different. It may seem magic, but it cannot be an escape from or a transcendence of the natural. Venice, arising "from dirt and sea-weed," has never been rid of its mud—nor can it treat mud as an accidental, best forgotten or ignored. The government of Venice (whatever it is from age to age) has to spend a lot of time, thought, and money on controlling mud, on acknowledging tides and dirt, on dredging itself out. It sits visibly in the unstable element, on the water—a slippery sort of thing altogether. Even before the decline of this imperial city, some did not like the place, feeling in some obscure sense affronted by its difference from the normal.

In *Venice Preserv'd*, Thomas Otway's play of 1682, Venice entire—not just its ruling class—constitutes the object of the revolutionary Pierre's scorn and detestation:

How lovely the *Adriatique* Whore,
Drest in her Flames, will shine! devouring Flames!
Such as shall burn her to the watery bottom,
And hiss in her Foundation.[1]

Venice is a prostituted female, dirty and slippery at the very bottom, the foundation or fundament, a piece of material and sexual dirt that should be purified by water's opposite element, the dry and cleansing flame. The sexual meanings in this passage are elucidated elsewhere in Otway's play, in which one of the important characters is a Venetian whore, with whom the would-be revolutionary Pierre has had relations that are still not broken off. However cleanly Pierre wishes to detach himself from the dirty courtesan that is Venice, or from his own personal *"Adriatique* whore," he is never able to separate from or overthrow either. The expression of significant hatred seems important in itself, and is picked up by the Romantics just after Venice's overthrow, as we have seen. Byron, who, unlike Otway, can rest his claim to speak with authority on a genuine traveler's knowledge of the city, regards the "sea Cybele"[2] as a feminine and ambiguous force, if now a spent force. She is experienced as decay, she "sinks like a seaweed." It is curious how Venice's slime and seaweed seem to be held against it as objective correlatives of internal fault, worthy of detestation—or erotically sadistic love.

Much late nineteenth- and twentieth-century imagery of Venice is ultimately derived from Ruskin's powerful *The Stones of Venice*. Ruskin carried out his researches in a city under military occupation, a fact of which he was entirely aware; he comments that the Austrians played military band music in the Piazza San Marco at the time of vespers and any Italian would be glad to stick a stiletto in them. But this does not bother him. As far as Ruskin was concerned, not only was modern Venice a mere residual shell, partly falsified, but the city-state had been going downhill since 1400 or thereabouts—a period which to others might seem still its high heyday. For Ruskin, Venice is itself only when Gothic—the Renaissance is a baleful spell, and Palladio an abomination. (It is only right to admit that I have come to share some of Ruskin's views of the inappropriateness of Palladian architecture to Venice.) Current Italian and Venetian feeling bothered Ruskin very little. Modern Venetians—in his view and that of a great many other nineteenth-century travelers—are in any case inferior and servile. Decadent and stupefied, they are unfit heirs of the great artistic productions of their city. Ruskin's views are subtly congenial to the interests of Austria, as it is usually convenient to imperial and colonial powers to represent (to themselves as to others) the culture of the native population as exhausted and outmoded, inevitably bound to die out.

We now recognize in such an insistence on the decadent nature of the Other, the cheerful emphasis on the ineluctable decline and disappearance of a culture or people, a trope pertaining to colonialism. (In different terms, much the same sort of thing was said about North American Indians and the Maori in New Zealand.) It is easy for superior invading powers (among which may be included tourists) to look down on "the natives" as inferior, decadent, or childlike, ignorant of their own good and fated to disappear. The dangers of operating according to such views attach to such benevolent societies as Save Venice or Venice in Peril. John Berendt in *City of Falling Angels* (2005) has explored some of these attitudes and their effects in recent years.[3] Organized or official "love of Venice" can readily become patronizing, even erotically sadistic——a warning to all of us who write about it. In the nineteenth century, easy negative generalizations abound. Ruskin thinks the Venetians are oblivious to the beauty and importance of their churches. He does not pause to consider that the popularity of San Moisè with the native Venetians might be partially explained by its relative lack of appeal to tourists, who (bedeviled by "good taste") will not pester them there. William Dean Howells is certain that a Venetian baptism is performed "without a ray of religious feeling or solemnity of any kind" (*Venetian Life*, 321). Such unwarranted assumptions are classic symptoms of the imperial frame of mind. The uneasy comfort of viewing the natives as undergoing dissolution seems largely to explain the incessant emphasis on the decay and deathliness of Venice in the works of nineteenth-century writers, the turning of love to death. Eros in Venice so often turns into Thanatos, as it does in Robert Browning's "Two in a Gondola," in which the eloping lovers are interrupted at the end, and (as in *Don't Look Now*) the man is killed, reflecting the lethal reveries of both partners while drifting in their black gondola, emblem of death.

Yet at the same time we can hardly pretend that there is not some consistency in the presentation of Venice both before and after the Austrian era. Plots, treachery, disappointment, death, and failure—and most particularly erotic excitement and erotic loss—figure in Western European writers' use of Venice in plays, novels, and poetry. Plots and treachery are comically featured in Jonson's *Volpone* (1605). Erotic gain and erotic loss figure centrally in *The Tragedy of Othello, The Moor of Venice* (1604), the play of Shakespeare's which turns most unusually on treachery alone as the great engine of its action. Other Shakespearean villains—Macbeth, Bolingbroke, and Edmund—are treacherous, but they have large ambitions, they are warriors and nobles, potential kings. Iago, a commoner masquerading as a common man, has no grand design; only a supersubtle Venetian (or is Iago part Spaniard?) could have such depths of malevolence. He finds the perfect prey in the alien Othello, who is unsure of himself and believes what people tell him. As Venetian women in general have the reputation for lust and deceit, it is easy for Iago to lie about Desdemona. Othello's wife is that rare literary creature, a spiritually beautiful and virtuous Venetian lady (if a little too outspoken), but of course her fate must be death.

Venice continues as the full rich tropic of itself, attractive and repulsive, at once extraordinary life-giving and thanatropic. All these examples (Shakespeare's *The Moor of Venice* included) are examples of what other Western Europeans have made of Venice, the attraction and repulsion they experience. Venice has obviously been an indispensable means of thought, provocative of much emotion. Here, then, is a mystery: why do European writers from other regions persistently see these same qualities in Venice? Or, rather, why is it *Venice* that is figured thus negatively? Perhaps, however, we should pose the question another way. Are the experiences of erotic frustration, death, weakness, and loss always truly negative? Or do we just pretend that they are?

Rather than dwelling too long on the fantasies of foreigners, it seems time to look attentively at the real history and achievement of Venice. Certainly, it was not founded an abode of wanton luxury, or of death, or of false or tragic passion—it is not inevitably what we have projected upon it. We should look fairly soberly upon the history of Venice itself, even though the history of what has been said about it may be for my purposes of nearly equal importance. After all, we are trying to track what Venice means to us, and not only that, but also why—so I insist—we cannot do without it. But we do need to give some central place to what the Venetians themselves say about Venice—"say" most of all through creating it in the first place.

*V*enice was founded as a place of refuge. People built it because they had to, because there was no where else for them. All the histories will tell you it was created by refugees from the Italian mainland, from a region called Altinum and from Aquileia. A major Roman city founded in the second century B.C.E., Aquileia was besieged first by Alaric's Visigoths, and then wrecked (after a three years' siege) by Attila the Hun in 452. The remains of the fourth-century basilica, especially the great variegated mosaic floor, prove that this was a flourishing and prosperous center of Christian culture, as was its seaport Grado. The little basilica (fourth or fifth century) of Santa Maria delle Grazie in Grado bears some resemblance to the more imposing cathedral on Torcello, first built in the seventh century. The inhabitants who fled the Aquileia region must have taken many memories with them. In the sixth century the Lombards (*i Longobardi*) invaded Northern Italy, chasing the native population before them. The mainland area near Venice called "the Veneto" was originally inhabited by tribes called the Veneti who had been overtaken by the Romans and conquered in the third century B.C.E. Verona provided a mighty Roman center, but the barbarian invasions from the fourth century onward soon weakened the Roman hold on the northeastern part of the Italian peninsula. Refugees fleeing eastward first picked the solid island of Torcello on which to settle. These early "Venetian" citizens have left two remarkable churches on Torcello, and some fragmentary remains—little enough to show for an island which at one time, it is thought, supported as many as ten thousand people. In seeking refuge from the Lombards, the early Venetians seem to have been eminently successful. It has been pointed out to me that the inhabitants of the surrounding Veneto on Terraferma are more often tall, stout, and blond, while the Venetians remain slender, relatively short, dark, and dark-eyed. Strange that the ladies would cultivate later what we might call "the Lombard look" in blondification.

In the seventh century Torcello seemed sufficiently permanent to be declared a bishopric. The Basilica of Torcello was founded in 639, under the control of the Exarch of Ravenna; like Ravenna, Torcello was then part of the Byzantine empire. Bishop Paolo, when he arrived, brought with him the bones of the first bishop of Altinum, the third-century Saint Heliodorus, placing the relicts below the high altar. But, going in as they did for saintly help and prestige, the Venetians were never going to be content with the bones of a mere bishop. On the contrary, they were to be very demanding in their quest for the remains of important saints.

The settlement of what we know as Venice (as distinct from Torcello) seems to have taken place over a period of time. It was recognized as an entity by Theodoric the Ostrogoth king, who in the year 523 had his prefect Cassiodorus write to these settlers asking for vessels to take Istrian oil and wine to his capital at Ravenna. Cassiodorus attempts to characterize the people to whom he writes in complimentary terms, though he succeeds in making them seem lonely and poor, if oddly exotic:

For you live like sea birds, with your homes dispersed, like the Cyclades, across the surface of the water. The solidity of the earth on which they rest is secured only by osier and wattle; yet you do not hesitate to oppose so frail a bulwark to the wildness of the sea. Your people have one great wealth—the fish that suffices for them all. Among you there is no difference between rich and poor; your food is the same, your houses are all alike. Envy, which rules the rest of the world, is unknown to you. All your energies are spent on your salt-fields; in them indeed lies your prosperity, and your power to purchase those things which you have not.[4]

This is the first historical glimpse given to posterity of how the Venetians lived and how they appeared to others. A recognizable community, these "sea birds" live in primitive fragile homes of clay and wattle scattered about on various little islands, and go upon the ocean in frail barks. They live by fishing, but they have one exportable product—salt—which brings in money. Indeed, the Venetians were to rely to some extent on salt for revenue even in later periods while building up their complex trade with the Orient. Today, walking along the Fondamenta della Zattere on Dorsoduro you can see the long cluster of salt warehouses, *Magazzini del Sale*, put up in the fifteenth century (but given a neoclassical facade in the nineteenth century). These efficient buildings reminds us that salt, the lagoon's own offering of natural wealth, was Venice's most important source of income in early life. Before the era of Orient pearls, the salty Venetians lived on a simpler product of the sea. A monopoly from the eleventh to the fifteenth century gave Venice an assured revenue. In a kind of sea-pastoral Cassiodorus represents the Venetians to themselves as blissfully contented and unenvious—comical enough when we think of the displays of wealth and the great marble palaces that are slowly to follow as time goes on.

Little muddy islets in the shallow lagoon offered small places of habitation. But the Venetians were not going to be content with their archipelago of wattle-and-daub settlements. They already knew—or some tribes among them did—the art of building with the use of piles, in use in spongy areas like that around Lake Garda for over a thousand years, as Alvise Zorzi points out.[5] They went vigorously to work in one of the most astounding feats of engineering in human history—making Venice. A settlement grew on the Rialto (*rivoaltus*) in the ninth century. The doge in that period, however, lived in Malamocco on the Lido (ancient Metamocco); here the Venetians-to-be heroically fought off the Frankish King Pepin's attempt to invade in 810. The deluded Franks, so the story goes, were lured onto the mud flats and then the Venetians picked them off, turning the waters red with blood, and making so many French orphans that the dread canal became called "Orfano."[6] (Perhaps later French travelers register so much horror at the grim punitive repute of the Orfano because they can both distract attention from the name's original source in their defeat, and punish Venice for it.) In 1107 Malamocco was to be buried under a tidal wave, which put an end to any interest in large settlement on that site.

What we call "the city of Venice" itself is a kind of composite large island (only connected to Terraferma at last by the railway bridge). Like a jigsaw map, it is composed of pieces, an island or archipelago of small islands—at least one hundred and seventeen of them. These groupings are subdivided into the six divisions or *sestieri* that make up central Venice: Castello, San Marco, San Polo, Santa Croce, Dorsoduro, Cannaregio. Just south of these there is the long skinny island of Giudecca. The six prongs of the *ferro* or iron comb that adorns the prow of every genuine gondola are said to refer to the six *sestieri*. (More on these later.) Chioggia is an important part of Venice, but it is on the periphery, a frying-pan shape with a manmade handle connecting it to the mainland. Chioggia, so close to the shore, was once a place of Roman habitation; resettled by the Venetians, it was an important center for salt-gathering and (even now) for fishing. One has the impression that everyone in Chioggia owns a boat—or has a brother who does. And the inhabitants still turn to their marshes for wealth, catching a particular kind of sea-sandworm much prized around the world for bait.

Water traffic is the essence of Venetian life. Public regulations seem to have required that some sites on the Grand Canal (and elsewhere) should have a gondola specifically and only for crossing the Grand Canal (which separates Dorsoduro from the other five *sestieri*), and also for crossing the canal between Dorsoduro and Giudecca. This requirement is still fulfilled by the traditional *tragehetto* or crossing. For twenty-first-century visitors a gondola ride is an expensive treat, but at some point you might avail yourself of a *traghetto*—a passage on that large, cheap gondola that takes passengers from a particular station along the canal to a station on the embankment directly opposite. To cross the Grand Canal properly at a *traghetto* you should travel standing up in the bark, as people availing themselves of this amenity have

been doing for many ages. Presumably in past centuries there were large gondolas or sailing vessels of moderate size provided to ship passengers from
the mainland to the islands at regular intervals. In *The Merchant of Venice* Portia
urges Balthasar to hasten from Padua bringing documents to the city: "Bring
them, I pray thee, with imagined speed / Unto the traject, to the common
ferry / Which trades to Venice" (*Merchant of Venice*, III.iv, lines 52–54; *Works*,
442).[7] The "traject" between the mainland and central Venice indicates that
there was something like a system of publicly regulated ferries in operation
in the Renaissance. Nowadays, you can of course take regular ferries from
and to Mestre, Chioggia, the islands of Murano and Burano, and the Lido.
Sailing boats (aside from private pleasure craft) have given way entirely to
motorboats. Gondolas, once the essential means of getting around—Venice's
coaches, luxury limousines, household cars, and plain cabs—now ply merely
for short pleasure trips for tourists. Yet—forget to fear vulgarity, and, if you
can afford it, take a gondola ride. Or even two—you see the architecture very
differently from that level, and appreciate much about the city that is not
seen even from a water-taxi, still less from a crowded vaporetto.

Wandering about Venice really means crossing salt water. Wherever you
go, you are making a transit over a piece of the sea, by boat or bridge. If you
wish to go from Salute to examine the Redentore you will have to cross the
Canale della Giudecca; as there is no bridge, you must figure out a vaporetto
route (or lavishly hire a *motoscafo* or gondola). If you are in central Venice and
want to get from the railway station to the Frari, or from the Frari to San
Zanipolo, or to go from the vegetable market (Erberia) at the foot of Rialto
Bridge to Castello, you have to cross the Grand Canal. In modern times, you
can take the bridge by Piazzale Roma, or one of the two main bridges at the
Rialto, or the Accademia. (There is talk of building another bridge.)

Then you will wind your mazy way through the streets, going up and
down the bridges traversing the small canals that thread the city. Francesco
Sansovino rather nicely compares them to veins in "lo corpo humano," thus
making Venice itself into a living body.[8] John Evelyn describes "this Miraculous Cittie which lies in the boosome of the sea in the shape of a Lute, the
numberlesse Ilands tack'd together by no fewer than 450 bridges" (June
1645; *Diary*, 227). One wonders if he actually tried to count the bridges
himself, or simply took Sansovino's word. But "tacked together" is a most
happy term. Each time we cross one of the small humpy bridges, we are passing from one islet to another. In the Middle Ages and Renaissance the brid-

ges had no walls and few rails, so the Venetian walker had to be wary and preferably sober—a lot of people must have fallen in. Rival gangs, the Castellani and Nicoletti who divided Venice between them, used to have ritualized fights on unrailed bridges, seeing which side could push the other into the canal.

Before the age of steam Venice was a wondrously quiet city. Gondolas and sailboats glided silently, there were no horse-drawn wagons on the streets and bridges—no familiar clip-clopping of equine hooves, no sound of wheels grinding on stones—or curses as wheels got stuck in mud. Visitors exclaimed at the absence of horses and carriages. True, in the Middle Ages there were some horses, donkeys, and other large livestock, but never a great many, and by the Renaissance they were disappearing. During his entire sojourn, Thomas Coryat saw only one horse, a little nag in the *campo* of San Zanipolo. Wheeled traffic beyond a handcart was—and remains—rather useless. The unusual quiet ceased in the late nineteenth century, with the advent of the coal-burning steamer puffing from island to island, a noisy "tea kettle" to whose advent Henry James bitterly objected, "the awful vaporetto."[9] Many years after he wrote *The Stones of Venice*, John Ruskin objected to the maltreatment of Venice by modernity, and rightly defined the nature of the pollution entailed: "The development of civilization now only brings black steam-tugs, to bear the people of Venice to the bathing-machines of Lido, covering the Ducal Palace with soot, and consuming the sculptures with sulphurous acid."[10] The water-bus is still termed a vaporetto, or "steamer," though now the "vapor" associated with it is gasoline fumes. The water transport the twenty-first-century tourist uses most often is likely to be this water-bus plying up or down the Canal, with stops on both sides. And if you, dear reader, like myself, are a tourist taking the vaporetto, then you act your part as one of the inconveniences that the working Venetians have to bear with while they struggle to get to work or back to their families on increasingly crowded vaporetti; there have been recent complaints that the "Linea 1" is practically unusable because of the mass of tourists (and heavy cases, vicious backpacks, etc.). Ferries, vaporetti, and water-taxis naturally all contribute to the air pollution. These vehicles, unlike their antecedents, also create noise. Venice has lost some of the quiet that used to be part of her charm—though some travelers in the past found the city *too* quiet. To nineteenth-century visitors, as we know, the hushed place could seem deathly, harmonizing only too well with the coffinlike black gondola.

Venice was a most ingenious and intelligent human creation, a delicate and conscious invocation of ecological balance. Flushed out by the tides twice a day, the city is designed to experience the gentle but determined flux and reflux of the seawater, moderated by the sheltering long islets of the Lido and of Pellestrina, which break the force of the Adriatic. Modern engineering has drastically interfered with the original plan. The industrial port of Marghera, once a fort, was, as we have seen, really the invention of the Venetian Count Volpi, Mussolini's finance minister, early in the twentieth century— but Volpi neither designed nor foresaw the horrors of the petrochemical works or the petroleum tankers. The stupidest thing done so far has been the dredging of a deep channel from Malamocco to Marghera for the tankers. Another modern piece of folly, with less excuse, was the deepening of the mouth of the Canal Grande to accommodate the monstrous behemoths of cruise ships. An old ordinance of Venice proclaims it to be high treason against the fatherland to meddle with or harm the waterways—the stone bearing this law is visible today in the Museo Correr, the museum of Venetian history founded by Teodoro Correr during the occupation in 1830.[11] Had Venetians only been able to live by this law in perpetuity! Another piece of folly, with less excuse, is the deepening of the mouth of St. Mark's Basin and of the Giudecca Canal to accommodate the monstrous behemoths of cruise ships, which flick their flukes like impudent whales above Salute.

The Venetians at present are yearly distressed by *acqua alta*, high water. That phenomenon was not unknown throughout its history—there was acqua alta when Napoleon visited in 1807. It is comical to find Burnet in the seventeenth century worrying about the opposite problem; he thinks that the laguna is getting shallower and will go dry, so that "if it continue to abate at the same rate, within an Age or two more, *Venice* may become a part of the *Terra firma.*"[12] Nowadays our fears run altogether the other way. In the past, the *acqua alta* was not as high, not so persistently damaging. By the end of the twentieth century, the phenomenon could occur in almost any month; winters are particularly hazardous to the fabric. The high water has not been as bad as in the great flood of 1966, when the surge brought in waters that rose over six feet deep in the Piazza San Marco, but the flooding of the great Piazza is a regular occurrence, with waters entering the Basilica and trying to sneak across the ancient mosaics. Global warming of course will not help. The planned construction of moveable mechanical barriers—the "Mose Project"—does not inspire confidence. The series of seventy-nine hydraulic gates placed at the inlets to the lagoon could wreak havoc on the whole physical and ecological system. Newspapers report that fishermen are particularly worried; there is constant discussion of the danger to the lagoon bed and to the portals, the natural gateways between the sheltering islands and islets that let the water in and out of Venice.[13] The barrier system will cause many more problems with changing patterns of silting and insults to the tidal flow than it could possibly cure—if it ever goes into action, that is. It was supposed to be opened in March 2003.[14] In delay there may be hope. During 2005–2006 organized opposition has grown, judging by posters plastered up in Venice, announcing anti-Mose rallies (see NoMOSE.org). A post-Berlusconi government is more likely to scrap the grandiose plan. Unfortunately, funds needed for regular upkeep and the essential humble dredging (so it is said) have been diverted into the Mose Project.

Venice still "hangs in there"—and it is as fair as ever. It may be that in the future stronger local control will make it possible for the city and the region to decide not to take ruinous steps to long-term detriment. It might be a good thing if a real "Save Venice" committee were founded, composed of local people, current Venetian *cittadini*; such a committee ought to include some of the watermen, who know the lagoon best. In the Middle Ages and Renaissance it was ordained that any committee dealing with the lagoon and waterways had to include two fishermen. It is worth pointing out that Venice did very well when this combination of islands was in charge of itself—for well over a thousand years.

The watery city did not exist during the Roman empire, so it never had to feel allegiance to Roman virtue and values. Venice gave itself a founding date, an official birthday: 25 April 421. The month and day are the anniversary of the Creation of the World, and also of the Annunciation. Venice is thus a holy creation. It has been its unique self—its own place. Other cities and states were founded by people just settling on land—sometimes felt to be "Promised Land," as for the Israelites, and for the English who settled in America. The Venetians had no Promised Land—God gave them no hectares to work. They had to make the land they were going to live in. Thus, they were privileged to share in the divine work of making the world. The creative Venetians took a very unpromising situation and saw its advantages. The muddy series of islets at the top of the Adriatic were very near the mouths of important and navigable rivers, the Adige and the Brenta. (Venice even changed the course of the Brenta, modifying it to make it more suitable for navigation.) It was relatively easy for Venice as it grew to create profitable commercial relations with the cities of the Veneto such as Treviso, Padua, and Verona, and at length to make use of the vineyards and farmlands of the

Plate 1. Jacopo Tintoretto, *The Removal of the Body of Saint Mark*
(Cameraphoto Arte, Venice/ Art Resource, NY)

Plate 2. Vittore Carpaccio, *Miracle of the Relic of the Cross at the Rialto Bridge* (Scala/ Art Resource, NY)

Plate 3. Vittore Carpaccio, *Two Venetian Women* (Scala/ Art Resource, NY) and *Hunting on the Lagoon* (The J. Paul Getty Museum, Los Angeles)

Plate 4. James Wilson Morrice, *Venice at the Golden Hour*, Montreal Museum of Fine Arts (949.1005), Bequest, Mrs. Gwendolen R. Caverhill, 1949 (Permission of the Montreal Museum of Fine Arts)

Plate 5. Titian, *Bacchus and Ariadne* (Permission of the National Gallery, London)

Plate 6. Paolo Veronese, *Saint Sebastian with Saints Mark and Marcellinus,*
San Sebastiano, Venice (Cameraphoto Arte Venice/ Art Resource, NY)

Plate 7. Giovanni Antonio Canaletto, *Rio dei Mendicanti* (Scala/ Art Resource, NY)

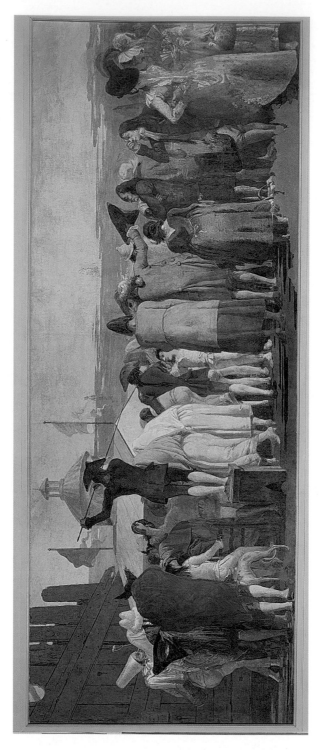

Plate 8. Giandomenico Tiepolo, *Il Novo Mondo* (*The New World*) (Scala/ Art Resource, NY)

Plate 9. Giovanni Bellini, *Madonna of the Meadow* (*Madonna del Prato*)
(Permission of the National Gallery, London)

Plate 10. Titian, *The Assumption of the Virgin Mary* (Scala/ Art Resource, NY)

Plate 11. Giorgione, *La Tempesta* (*The Tempest*) (Scala/ Art Resource, NY)

Plate 12. Titian, *Presentation of the Virgin at the Temple* (Scala/ Art Resource, NY)

inland area. From earliest times, Venice had to import essential building supplies from the wooded slopes of the Dolomites; the forests around Cadore (Titian's birthplace) supplied those strong tree trunks that served as the essential foundational piles, as well as material for houses and furniture. The great safety of Venice, however, lay in the shallow waters of the laguna, which placed a sly but strong barrier against any invader: any ship large enough to transport soldiers in significant numbers would run aground on the shoals and mud flats. It was this protection—a strength arising from a deficiency—that made Venice unconquered and unconquerable, "a mayden citie," as Coryat says. It could be La Serenissima, "most serene," because perfectly defended. The shallow waters were Venice's safety, but its advance in fortune lay in the mastery of the deep waters, the eastern Mediterranean.

From their first experiments with what must have been little better than reed coracles the Venetians became expert in boat-building, navigation, and commerce. Venice was to build up an empire on the basis of world trade. At first under the protection of the Byzantine empire, Venice had ready access to Byzantium (Constantinople), its original patron and trading partner, as well as to other ports and regions in the eastern Mediterranean. One of its first works in beginning its own age of empire was to gain control of the coast of Dalmatia (modern Croatia), including the peninsula of Istria with its valuable white limestone, so useful as an ornamental building material. By keeping pirates off the Dalmatian coast, Venice could gain entry to the Levant.

The patronage of the Byzantine empire was of importance when Rome had broken down under the barbarian invasions. But from the ninth century onward, Venice was a power on its own, able (when it wished) to bring ships and soldiers to the help of Byzantium. Venice became increasingly a force to be reckoned with, a formidable sea-power; it recognized that both its unusual security and its growing wealth were the gift of the sea. By the year 1177, the Doge of Venice was espousing the sea off the Lido in token of Venice's own lordship of the sea, as a husband to a wife. This ceremony, held annually at the feast of the Ascension, was still in use in the eighteenth century, as Canaletto records (see frontispiece); Mrs. Piozzi viewed one of the last occasions of the sea spousal.

The Byzantine emperor had given Venice a patron saint, San Teodoro. He is associated with slaying a dragon of some kind or other. The effigy of San Teodoro stands atop a tall column in the Piazzetta, one of the two columns brought in from the east and erected here in the twelfth century. The patron saint is planned to be one of the first images that the arriving traveler sees. (Actually, a modern copy now stands on the column in the Piazzetta, while the original has been removed to a museum.) The statue of San Teodoro is somewhat unimpressive, a fragment of a Roman bust with a substitute head; the saint stands over a small reptilian monster. Poor Theodore is not at all sublime, but looks like someone taking his pet alligator for a walk— simply no match for the terrific winged lion of San Marco that stands on the companion pillar.

Observers over the centuries have noticed that there is something a touch oriental about the winged lion on its proud shaft. The lion that we now see on the pillar in the Piazzetta has been restored and replaced (in 1991). But it apparently once had a singular splendor not copied in the twentieth century: this three-ton bronze lion was long ago covered with gold. Some think that this particular figure is Chinese, with added wings; others contend that it is part of a classical statue of a fabulous Chimera, others again argue that it is a work of Persian art from the fourth or fifth century. The lion of Saint Mark in its many representations, especially as *leone andante* (or walking), is wonderfully reminiscent of Babylonian lions. In late antiquity the lion was one of the important symbols of the sun, and something of this symbolism seems to carry over into the aggressive optimism and power displayed by the assertive and compelling multiple lions of Venetia—lions so strong that even Napoleon couldn't actually destroy them. The two shafts with the saint and the lion mark a kind of gateway to the sea at the end of the Piazzetta. Almost everyone has his or her picture taken nowadays between the two shafts; most tourists who do so don't realize that they are standing on what was traditionally the chosen site for Venice's public executions—although they may know this once they see the film *Casanova* (2005). Between San Teodoro and Saint Mark's lion, people were variously hanged, beheaded, and burned alive. The space between the columns also became a popular spot for gambling; some say the state at first allowed gambling only on that condemned spot in order to bring it into disrepute. More likely, gambling was allowed there because it was an open space directly under the eye of the authorities. It is a site of power and of luck (good and ill).

In its newfound position of strength, the growing city was not going to be content with a mere Theodore as a patron saint. They wanted a patron of the top rank. In 828–829 the Venetians got hold of the body of Saint Mark, originally buried in Alexandria. That the body of the Gospel-maker had originally been reverently buried after his martyrdom was—according to the accepted legend about the saint in the *Legenda Aurea* (*Golden Legend*)[15]—owing to the courage and intelligence of Christians of Alexandria, who bravely rescued the freshly killed corpse which the Alexandrians were going to burn. The traditional story tells us that God sent such a tempest of rain, wind, and hail that the Alexandrians scattered, giving up their attempt at forceful cremation, and so the saint's corpse was preserved by pious Christians who withstood the storm.

According to Venice's own new story, in the early ninth century two Venetians, merchants trading with what was by now Islamic North Africa, ingeniously stole the corpse of the apostle from Alexandria, hoodwinking the Muslim authorities. They brought Saint Mark "*back* to Venice." According to a legend known only to Venetians (and one which seems handmade expressly for the occasion), Mark was always reserved for Venice. When Mark was bishop of Aquileia on the mainland, the saint's ship had once anchored off the *rivoaltus* (Rialto). There he had a vision of an angel who spoke to him, saying, "*Pax tibi Marce, evangelista meo.*" According to the *Golden Legend*, this exact sentence was spoken by God to Mark in prison, just before he suffered martyrdom. But in this new story the event takes place in the Venetian Lagoon, and an extra sentence is added, so that the whole salutation is "*Pax tibi Marce, evangelista meo. Hic recquiescet corpus tuum.*" This does not seem a very reassuring message: "Peace to thee O Mark, my evangelist! Here your corpse will rest." Who would want to be buried on some empty salty mudbanks in the middle of nowhere? The prophetic utterance seems unhelpful to the saint in his missionary work. But it was a useful prophecy in that the Venetians could show that it had been fulfilled. Through their own agency and cunning, with of course divine help, they had recovered the sacred remains.

The story goes that the resourceful merchants concealed the stolen body of the saint under a cargo of pork. The Muslim inspectors at the port of Alexandria were not going to get near the unclean substance, so Mark was brought back under a pile of meat. (The story does not relate whether the merchants ate or sold the pig-meat afterward.) The seventeenth-century mosaic over the portal of San Marco on the right lunette (Figure 9) shows the Christian merchants in their boat, with the pork, and the Muslim officials holding their noses and glancing disdainfully away.

What the merchants brought back after centuries of entombment in Alexandria must surely have been a few ashes and bones, poor fragmentary relicts. Saint Mark's *body*, however, is always associated with the *flesh* (as in the story of the pork), and it is customarily represented in Venetian art and story as a

Figure 9. "Body of Saint Mark Leaving Alexandria," seventeenth-century mosaic lunette, façade of Basilica (south end) (Cameraphoto Arte, Venice/Art Resource, NY)

unitary corpse. Venetians obviously wanted to think of what had been brought back as an entire dead body in good condition. In Tintoretto's great painting of the first rescue of the body of San Marco by Christians in Alexandria, the gigantic corpse, dead flesh that is also somehow manly, healthy, and imposing, dominates the center of the picture (see Plate 1). Flesh is important, even when it is dead. The Venetians had secured the relics of a major saint—not just any old saint, but one of the four Evangelists. This put Venice practically on a par with the Rome of Saint Peter, spiritually speaking. The Venetians have always been proud of this theft of the corpse or remains of Saint Mark. The winged lion, an emblem of Saint Mark in traditional representations of the authors of the Four Gospels, becomes the triumphant winged lion of Venice. Saint Mark is a saint for people who believe in writing—Venice's lion commonly carries a book, if not a sword—sometimes both. (The Venetians claimed to have acquired a manuscript of the second Gospel handwritten by none other than Mark himself.) In the leonine representations, the book in the lion's paws always carries the words of God to Saint Mark: "*Pax tibi, Marce, Evangelista meo.*" This entirely unscriptural text emphasizes the good terms the saint is on with God, as well as the fact that the patron saint is a chosen Evangelist. One might have expected an empire adopting such an emblem and patron to have been vigorously evangelical. But in fact the Venetians were not much given to proselytizing, and a self-confident tolerance separates the Republic from most other European states.

The seizure of the remains of Saint Mark was not the only sacred body-snatch attempted by Venice. It went after Saint Nicholas of Myra, determined to seize the relics of the saint who was to be our Santa Claus, probably because he was the patron of sailors. But the Venetians were beaten on this rare occasion by the citizens of Bari, who got the corpse they wanted. Venice was to acquire relics of several other saints, including Saint Lucy, and Saint Stephen, the first martyr, as well as the body of a more modern saint who cared for plague victims, the fourteenth-century Saint Roche (San Rocco).

The acquisition of a major saint like Mark necessitated the building of a preeminent church. The first Church of San Marco was built in 832. During the whole era of Venice's empire Saint Mark's church was *not* the cathedral church of the city. It was declared such only during the Napoleonic occupation in 1807. Venice's traditional cathedral was the less well-known San Pietro in Castello, at a distance from the seat of power and commerce; in the sixteenth century St. Peter's became a Palladian building, with no sign of its (to us more interesting) medieval construction. Saint Mark's church was the personal chapel of the Doge, and thus connected with Venice's own government, rather than with the authority of Rome—a good way of ensuring that the bones of the Evangelist would be kept in his Adriatic home and not trundled Romeward. The shining edifice that we know as "Saint Mark's, Venice" is the later version, the ninth-century church having been damaged by fire in the tenth century. Rebuilding began in 1063, though the new building was not consecrated until 1094, when the "corpse" of the evangelist, which had mysteriously been "lost," was wonderfully "found" by the Doge and reburied in the new church.

The building of Saint Mark's in the ninth century shows how far the Venetians had advanced, and how much wealth they had obtained. They had already demonstrated what they could do in the way of building churches decorated with mosaics. When one looks at the mosaics in the great churches,

Figure 10. "Saint Mark's Body Carried into the Basilica," thirteenth-century mosaic lunette, façade of Basilica (north end) (Scala/Art Resource, NY)

especially on Torcello and Murano, the Byzantine origin of Venetian art is obvious. In the one remaining original mosaic over the portal of Saint Mark's, representing the founding of the Basilica, it is clear that the doge and the Venetian bigwigs are dressed like Byzantine people of importance (Figure 10).

*I*n a story of so much achievement, it is hard to admit the frequent presence of rupture and conflicts. The Venetians saw their founding as that of a holy city, unique among nations. Living close together as they had to do, united in their management of the sea, they resembled, as has often been remarked, people on a ship, who must work in united efforts in order to survive. The Venetians over and over again proved themselves well able to do this, pooling their entire national resources of personal treasure and courage in order to stand up against threats. But Venetian history, like the history of all other states, is a story of dissonance as well as union, of conflict as well as of cooperation.

The Venetians were heroic in driving off foreign invaders—as they did in fighting against the invasion of Pepin, King of the Franks; against their rivals in sea-power, the Genoese; against the French; and ultimately against the Turks. When they turned their attention to gaining control of some of the mainland land mass, they became unhappily involved in the many wars among the struggling Italian states and other growing powers like France and Spain. Venetians were not as well able to fight land wars as sea battles. Their attention had all gone to sea-power. Like other Italian states in the late Middle Ages, they fell into the bad habit of relying on mercenaries, *condottieri*, to fight their land wars. Venice itself was not to be molested, but remained unconquered, "a mayden citie" behind its watery wall. Venice and Genoa, however, were aggressive rivals. Both of these sea-trading powers share the blame for introducing the plague-carrying rat into Western Europe, and starting the Black Death; Venice was one of the first places in Europe to feel the effects. Terribly weakened by the plague, the city-state had to hold off the Genoese, who almost managed an invasion by sea. The Genoese fleet and fighting men got as far as Chioggia, which they held for a winter (1379–1380). Yet over and over, for more than a millennium, the Venetians kept themselves from being truly invaded.

But Venetians also fought among themselves, often over what we would term class issues. Venice started out with something like rough equality; the doge was elected by popular voice. This did not necessarily make for peace. A ninth-century doge was murdered. So was Doge Vitale Michiel II, unpopular for abject failure in prosecuting hostilities against Byzantium. He was assassinated in May 1172, while walking—or running—down the Calle de Rasse; this is now a street of harmless touristic eateries, but no doge would ever set foot on this street again. (The murderer's house was ordered razed to the ground and orders were given that no permanent building should be erected in that place, a ban broken only in 1948 when the site of the stabbing was covered by the extension to the Danieli Hotel.)[16] According to some accounts, the murdered doge staggered into the nearby church of San Zaccaria (not our lovely fourteenth-century building but the old brick convent church) and made his last confession before expiring.

As Venice became more prosperous, there was more visible difference between classes. In the late thirteenth century, in one bold move, those at the top of the Venetian hierarchy defined this difference. In February 1297 (1296 according to the old way of dating years), a new law required in effect that all who had a seat in the Grand Council be approved by stating their credentials of birth. No man whose ancestors had not been members of the

Council would be allowed to sit on it. Those with great wealth and good family connections had already been the members of the Great Council, and, as John Julius Norwich points out, "From the start the Council had been self-selecting."[17] Now the principles of selection were clarified. Essentially, a member sat on the Council from now on because he had already done so before 1297, or because an ancestor had been there before him. This measure of exclusion is known as the *Serrata del Maggior Consiglio,* the Locking—or Shutting—of the Great Council.

From this point on, it is customary to speak of the "patrician" caste in Venice, or the "nobles." The concept is oddly applied in Venice's case, as neither the standards and customs of a Roman landowning and warrior caste nor those of a medieval feudal aristocracy apply. The Venetians, unlike other Western Europeans, did not form in clans or groups around a military leader, an earl or duke, to whom they pledged fealty, and for whom they performed feats of prowess as armed fighters on horseback. There was no knightly class as that was understood in the rest of Europe—no horse-riding aristocracy. The Venetians first won their wealth and influence through trade and commerce. Their top class was a plutocracy rather than an aristocracy. Men of all classes were able fighters, to be sure, but their fighting was connected with the sea. They fought sea-battles against pirates, and, as time went on, they were to fight battles of invasion, conquering bits of Mediterranean territory. Although the leaders might be "patrician" in sea-fights, everyone on the ship would of necessity be engaged in defense and offense. As Venice's wealth and power increased, however, there was a firming up of the sense of "patrician" birth, privilege, and obligation. By 1315 there was a list of those eligible for election to the Great Council that excluded all bastards or offspring of a mother not of the noble caste. Naturally, this was followed by an exact register recording noble marriages and their offspring, the *Libro d'Oro* or Golden Book. One of the unforeseen consequences was the spawning of the *barnabotti,* men in the *Libro d'Oro* but without gold.

The number of males eligible to sit on the Great Council was extremely small by our standards: one thousand and seventeen in 1311, twelve hundred and twelve in 1340. This is in a city-state whose population was something like 150,000 souls—sometimes a bit more, quite often much less as after one of the devastating plagues. (The entire population of great Venice, we should remember, never quite rose to 200,000 persons, and the plague several times reduced this by a third.) A number of wealthy males were left outside this select group of "patricians"; in the second order were the *cittadini* or citizens of Venice. To be eligible to be a proper "citizen," one must not be a foreigner—though in special cases a foreigner might be admitted after twenty-five years of residence. To preserve one's children's citizen status it was absolutely necessary not to marry a non-Venetian, or one of the lower orders. It became a point of honor for the *cittadino* to be declared free of all taint of mechanical trades, base handcrafts, for three generations. The *cittadini* could look down on the remainder of the people, the plebeians or *popoli*.

A certain originary tendency toward democracy, whereby the people themselves had called for or approved the election of a Doge, was thus almost entirely suppressed at the beginning of the fourteenth century—at least as far as overt political practices were concerned. In setting up the republic in this way, the Venetians follow what might be termed Carthaginian practice, as Aristotle describes the Carthaginian constitution, sketching a structure of rule he defines as aristocracy deviating into oligarchy.[18] Certainly, there are similarities between the weakness of the king of Carthage and that of the Doge of Venice, as well as the lack of differentiation between courts of law and members of legislative bodies, and similarities also in the importance of certain consultative and legislative bodies, like the Carthaginian Board of Five and the supreme majesty of the Hundred. The *Serrata*—the great "Lockup" or "Lockout"—is likely to strike us as an unlovely achievement. In the eyes of many historians the ills of Venice have all followed from that act, which certainly counts as a turning point. But it is possible to defend the "Lockout" to some degree. Garry Wills argues that as well as a locking out it was more importantly a "locking in," a means of inducing those who would otherwise be rivals for power to work together.[19] The tendency was to encourage a uniform sense of duty, of responsibility to the state of Venice itself. Patrician males wore solemn black or red robes (something like the medieval robes of doctors of philosophy); these were called "togas." Their wives might wear silk and jewels, but the serious man looks serious.

In a patrician man's life there was one period of relaxation of this strictness, between school age and the age of twenty-five. In this adolescent period young men could wear the most brilliant colors, the most up-to-date and rich and sassy jackets and doublets. They sported the multicolored hose or tights, brilliant and stripey, fashionable at the time, which showed off the legs and the perky bum. Young men of noble life formed clubs, called Compagnie della Calza, or Companies of the Stocking, for their own jokes, games, get-togethers, theatricals, and other high jinks.[20] These colorful young men populate the canvases of Quattrocento artists, especially Carpaccio, and must have contributed a good deal of vivacity to the city. Yet once a "patrician" man reached the age of twenty-five, away it all went. No more club meetings, no more perky bum. The toga must be assumed and *gravitas* asserted.

In molding this ethos of a republican elite, Venice preserved itself from some of the rifts and feuds between rival families and contending warlords that afflicted other city-states. The distinction created or reinforced an ethos of obligation. Patricians were obliged to serve the Republic, to practice Republican virtue including the virtue of *mediocritas*—simplicity in dress, eating habits, and manners. They were expected to give freely of their personal wealth to the state in case of need. Garry Wills draws a comparison between this and the Athenian constitution, and there is a certain similarity in the way in which Venetian nobles drew on their wealth—for example, in paying for the creation and fitting of battleships, like the ancient Athenian grandees.[21] A Venetian nobleman might personally equip the ship he commanded. Rather than relying merely on taxation, the Venetians created a moral atmosphere which naturalized the giving of the best. Such a sense of things is probably truly available only to that state which is small and knows itself to be easily imperiled. Venetian patricians were supposed to be capable of strenuous sea-fighting, and of making arduous treks (which they would pay for out of their own purses) for the sake of diplomacy. The highest offices were reserved for men of advanced age. It is to the credit of the good health of Venetians and their longevity that so many men in their seventies and eighties—for the most part truly able—could be found to lead the Republic, even at times to lead in battle. Doge Enrico Dandolo, in his mid-eighties if not in his nineties, led the assault upon Constantinople in 1203, as the French historian Geoffrey de Villehardouin records: "For the Duke of Venice, who was an old man and totally blind, stood fully armed on the prow of his galley, with the banner of St. Mark before him, and cried out to the men to drive the ship ashore. . . . And so they did . . . and he and they leaped down and planted the banner before him on the ground."[22] Dandolo's modern biographer says that the old man did not do any leaping, but that it was undoubtedly he who gave the command that his galley "advance to the shoreline and run aground beneath the walls," thus making retreat impossible, and leading all the Venetians to the attack.[23] Venice in its rising was never in want of men of courage, even if in a dubious cause.

It is hard to understand Venice without understanding the emphasis it put on service. It was—to speak of the city-state itself as a sentient entity—always aware that the mode of enrichment through trade might lead to individual selfishness. The Venetian government—and even more important, Venetian ideology—endeavored to regulate and limit occasions of display. For example, at a certain point it was forbidden to go in for foolish private excess like the decoration of private gondolas—hence, all the gondolas are sober black. The traditional gondola did nevertheless allow of some interior decoration, such as cushions or pieces of lace, inside the sheltered cabin called the *felze* (no longer seen), and of course the shining brass dolphins at the rowlocks. Only the Doge was allowed a magnificently decorated and gilded ship, and that was the state barge, the *Bucintoro*, which was a reflection of the city and the possession of all. The gallant gilded *Bucintoro* was wrecked by the French, who not only stripped it of its gilding but meanly chopped up the ship itself. Happily, the Doge's *Bucintoro* appears in a number of Venetian paintings, and a model of it can be seen in the Museo Correr.[24]

Venice had no objection to private riches—as long as in a pinch these were to be available for the service of the state. Its great men were all rich men. But Venice seems to have feared above all things one-man rule. Strange! During the late Middle Ages and the Renaissance one-man rule was the norm in Europe, whether through the establishment of a settled linear monarchy or the more violent passages of regional control from one warlord to another. Venetians, without any feudalism in the background, perhaps lacked the motive and opportunity available to well-born feudal lords with a pack of armed vassals. Nor did Venetians regard vassalage with admiration. Their constitutional energies seem to have been bent—almost obsessively—toward preventing any one man from becoming too strong in Venice. To ensure the prevention of any faction from getting together and making a Doge of its own, an elaborate (and corruption-proof) election process was devised. This amazingly convoluted system described by Contarini is succinctly summarized by John Julius Norwich: "Briefly, the Great Council chose thirty of their number, then reduced them by lot to nine; these would vote for forty, who were reduced to twelve, who would vote for twenty-five, who were reduced by lot to nine again, who voted for forty-five, who were reduced to eleven, who finally voted for the forty-one" who would elect the Doge.[25]

The role of the Doge became progressively and deliberately weakened. It may have been in reaction to this leaching away of power that Marino Faliero (or, more in accord with Venetian usage, "Marin Falier") led a conspiracy of his own when he was Doge. He was seventy-six when elected in 1354, and lasted less than a year. During pre-Lent festivities at a party at the Palazzo Ducale there was an altercation with a drunken young noble, who was thrown out. This man retaliated by writing a two-line insult to the virtue of Falier's wife and leaving it on the Doge's throne. Deeply angered by this threat to his authority, and the lack of respect shown by the gilded youth, Falier was the more likely to be sympathetic when two sea captains complained that they had been insulted and physically maltreated by two other such young gentlemen. Falier conspired with the workers at the Arsenal. On a given time when the people, nobility and riff-raff alike, would be crowding into the Piazza, the conspirators were to strike down all the young nobles, and declare Marin Falier the Prince of Venice.

History, like life, has dealt hard with Marin Falier. To Byron he is a tragic example of a mistaken fighter for freedom, fated to act in madness of heart. But John Julius Norwich thinks it was fortunate for Venice that Falier was caught, his foolish conspiracy nipped in the bud. Margaret Oliphant in her *Makers of Venice* (1887) is more sympathetic:

His aspect is rather that of a man betrayed by passion, and wildly forgetful of all possibility in his fierce attempt to free himself and get the upper hand. One cannot but feel, in that passion of helpless age and unfriendedness, something of the terrible disappointment of one to whom the real situation of affairs had never been revealed before; who had come home triumphant to reign like the doges of old, and only after the ducal cap was on his head and the palace of the state had become his home, found out that the doge, like the unconsidered plebeian, had been reduced to bondage, his judgment and experience put aside in favour of the deliberations of a secret tribunal, and the very boys, when they were nobles, at liberty to jeer at his declining years.[26]

Oliphant later draws a parallel between the experience of Marin Falier and that of the poet Petrarch, who at the age of nearly sixty came to stay in Venice, he believed forever. He was charmed with the city for a long while, as we know, but received a rude check from four young men of high family, who had the impudence to find fault with his knowledge and tell him (like George Eliot's Ladislaw addressing the pedant Mr. Casaubon) that he is behind the times; the thing to read nowadays is Averroës.[27] Horrified and disgusted at their heresy, he comes off as a codger. Petrarch had a high opinion of himself and perhaps too little sense of humor; the great poet of the *Canzone* appears to have been susceptible to hurt feelings, and took such incidents—and insults—greatly to heart. He left Venice and never returned. "It was the insults of the *giovinastri*," comments Oliphant, "insolent and unmannerly youths, which drove Marino Faliero to his doom not very many years before . . . and

Petrarch, like the old doge, was now soulless, and had the less patience to support the insolence of other people's boys."[28]

Petrarch at least could depart from the source of his chagrin. Marin Falier could not, and his angry response was doomed to fail. The conspiracy came to light. The plebeian conspirators were hanged in a row outside the Palazzo Ducale. Marin Falier was taken from his apartment to the Council Chamber to hear his sentence, and then conducted to the landing at the top of the marble staircase that led to the courtyard. He was stripped of the ensigns of his ducal office, and then beheaded. It was later determined that his portrait should not only be removed from the row of portraits of Doges painted around the Council Chamber, but be replaced by a painted black veil with the legend *Hic est locus Marini Faledri decapitati pro criminibus:* "Here is the place of Marin Falier, decapitated for his crimes."[29] This black-veiled nonportrait was repainted, along with the portraits of the Doges, after the great fire of 1577 destroyed the Council Chamber, a fact displaying an unusual persistence in political hostility, an unyielding determination to warn doges how they would be punished if they aimed at too much leadership. (This memorable story of a black veil may have inspired the black veil in Radcliffe's *Mysteries of Udolpho*.)

The case of Marin Falier strongly marked a limit to ducal power. This boundary was again reinforced almost exactly a century later, in the treatment of Doge Francesco Foscari and his son Jacopo (another Venetian story that attracted Byron). Some suspicious feelings about dynastic power seem to have operated against the son (who appears no brighter than he should be) and his poor father, and both were zealously attacked by Loredan and others. The charge of murder against the son may have been trumped up. Jacopo was exiled to a Cretan prison, and died conveniently in four months, quite probably assassinated, though whether by his enemies or his own former supporters remains in question. Shortly thereafter (in October 1457) Doge Francesco Foscari was forced out of office, and died a week later. Giuseppe Gullino suggests that hostility had arisen against the family and its connections, the "clan," who were taking Venice further into the hinterland of Italy and away from its maritime traditions. For Byron, in *The Two Foscari*, the Doge and his son are suffering victims of a vicious patrician caste.[30] The troubles of the two Foscari were more likely political than personal, though the fact that Francesco had been made Doge young and ruled a long time was a factor. Never again would Venice elect a Doge who was not old, and thus free of ambitious handsome young sons.

Undeniably, the doge still had a good deal of power at the time of the *Serrata*, which was pressed into law by the pertinacious Doge Pietro Gradenigo. Perhaps it was resentment over this new order of things, perhaps anger over the fact that this Doge, by holding onto Ferrara, had brought a papal interdict upon Venice, that led to the revolt led by Bajamonte Tiepolo in June 1310. More probably, it was the fact that a Tiepolo had not been made Doge, though that had been called for by the people. Unfortunately for the conspirators, one of their number had given information to the authorities, and the Doge's soldiers were ready for the insurgents as they approached the Palazzo Ducale. Bajamonte was passing the entrance of the Piazza, where the great clock tower was to stand in later years. An old woman at an upper window threw (or dropped) a stone mortar at him. His standard-bearer was killed by this missile, and Bajamonte took to his heels, fleeing with his followers across the wooden Rialto Bridge, which the fugitives burned behind them. The traitor and his band were luckier than their fellows left in the Piazza, and were able to hold off their enemies long enough to come to terms which allowed Tiepolo to go into exile in Dalmatia, instead of being hanged or beheaded.

Bajamonte Tiepelo's house was taken over and dismantled, and a "column of infamy" raised on its site. Giustina Rossi, the aged woman who wielded her mortar in such a timely fashion, made two requests: her family were to be allowed to display the banner of Venice at that window, and her landlord was never to raise her rent. Both requests were honored. There is a modern marker on the wall as you turn into the Merceria, in commemoration of that heroine and her mortar.

Bajamonte's insurrection had involved members of other great families, the Querini and the Badoer, in addition to the Tiepolos. A new institution was established in 1310, the Council of Ten, given special powers to quell any unrest in the state. It needed to be strong enough to stand up to the patricians. The Council of Ten was first introduced as an emergency measure only, supposed to last a few months—but it lasted for nearly five centuries. Venetian secrecy was really initiated here; the objective was to prevent civil wars among the patricians and to keep them from tearing the place apart. There were controls on this body. The Ten were elected by the Great Council individually only for six-month terms, and had to act with the Doge and the Seignoria, a cabinet of six members. Thus, any decision really entailed the input of seventeen persons; the Ten did not act on their own. The swift rotation of the committee was designed to preclude the coagulation of power or leverage from favoritism or bribery. The conduct of the members of the Ten was strictly inquired into, and any sign of corruption meant death.

As John Julius Norwich points out, the existence of this subordinate Council or committee meant that swift action could be taken, such as was not readily allowed by the ponderous to-ing and fro-ing of the Great Council.[31] Monarchs had their cabinet or Privy Council, the Venetians had the Council of Ten. The Great Council was not a very good mechanism for decision, even though in practice the unwieldy large group was represented for day-to-day business by a special body called the Pregadi, or "the Invited" or "the Asked"—a body that we tend to call the Senate. That body itself had one hundred and twenty members, however, and was none too flexible. There had been no information-gathering apparatus in Venice before the establishment of the Ten. Other states as they grew in power and wealth also were beginning to keep such watch—by the time we get to Elizabeth I of England, for instance, we find an immensely important secret service. But the known existence of the secretive and discreet Ten helped to create Venice's reputation for espionage and secrecy.

A century before the establishment of the Ten, Venice itself had committed a most singular violent, criminal, and treacherous act. This deed was also the foundation of much of its greatness in trade and commerce, and of an empire at first wondrously profitable, if in the end expensive and impossible to defend. The Venetians turned against Constantinople, their former lord and friend, in the Fourth Crusade. Instead of going on to Jerusalem, the Venetian war party turned against a now weakening ally and unexpectedly attacked and conquered the Greek capital, effectually taking the Byzantine empire. It is a most unchristian "Crusade"—attacking other Christians. This is not the most savage act of European history, but it is one of the most strikingly treacherous—and yet the Venetians are very proud of it. Huge pictures celebrating this event decorate the interior of the Doge's Palace. The painting of the Conquest of Constantinople by Domenico Tintoretto (son of Jacopo) shows the event, like a D-Day landing, ships pushing up to the shore under the fire of enemy missiles, about to take on the Greek soldiery (Figure 11). This picture, painted after the fires of 1574 and 1577 had carried away earlier works, re-creates a scene that had taken place over three centuries before it was thus depicted. There is some respect for history: sixteenth-century ordnance is not introduced; the warlike action is convincing, and the towered walls of Byzantium dating from Theodosius (some of which still can be seen in Istanbul) are recognizable.

Figure 11. Domenico Tintoretto, *The Conquest of Constantinople* (Erich Lessing/ Art Resource)

The Venetians, despite their leadership, did not get the whole of the Byzantine empire; indeed, they would not have had the manpower to take it over. Run chiefly by the Franks, this "Latin" empire was lost again to the Greeks after sixty years. Venice, however, had been able to pick up choice bits of the Byzantine empire, and what she got she kept. The conquest of Constantinople meant that Venice acquired eastern Mediterranean bases from which to prosecute trading relations with areas further east, under Islamic rule. Their new footing in the Byzantine world brought the Venetians face-to-face with the Ottoman empire as that developed. It was always in Venice's interest to prevent—when it could—the Ottoman empire from moving further westward, while at the same time sustaining good relations and a trading system profitable to both sides. Venice long established a monopoly as the one Western trader who brought goods to Europe from the East. And through Venice all exports to the East from the West had to be shipped. All Western ships coming to Venice unloaded, and their cargo was transshipped in Venetian vessels. No goods going or coming from the East were to travel in other carriers, and the Venetians were strong enough to enforce this regulation.

So—whether you wanted to ship woolen fabric to Damascus or to buy silk fabric from the East, you had to go through Venice. If you wanted pepper, or pearls, or marble, you had to go through Venice. Their brilliantly unjust action of 1203–1204 obtained for the Venetians new power, control of sea routes, and a great deal of magnificent loot. New wider scope, new opportunities built up the wealthy "nobles" of Venice. This is probably why we come before the end of the century to the *Serrata*, the closing of the gate against new ruling families expecting a lion's share of the profits. From the early thirteenth century onward, Venice was a more complex and much wealthier state than before—and it showed everywhere. The Fourth Crusade changes the city's outlook forever; Venice now becomes an international empire.

This Eastern adventure also changed the look of the city of Venice. Not only Saint Mark's but many other churches and palazzi are adorned with Byzantine treasure. The four horses over the front door of San Marco were looted from Constantinople. The horses, stuck high at the front of the great church, are a salient instance of success in what might be called "Venetian appliqué": something from elsewhere is stuck upon another kind of fabric, creating a (sometimes disconcerting) three-dimensional multilayered effect. The north side of San Marco has a lot of this appliqué, bits of Greek art brought back from Constantinople after the Fourth Crusade and set upon the exterior wall of the great church. My favorite among these is the relief of Alexander being carried up to the heavens in a basket by two griffins—an illustration of an ancient piece of sci-fi.

It is striking how great a role theft (of a kind) plays in the story of Venice. Two of Venice's greatest legends concern the art of Mercury, theft employing both cunning and audacity. The stealing away of the body of Saint Mark displays the qualities of wit, audacity, and efficiency combined in a way that Venetians admire. Like Odysseus, Venetians are fertile in many wiles and devices. The attack upon the Byzantine empire was preceded by diplomatic feints and covered by a feeble pretense of putting the proper heir on the throne. Venetians also take what they can get by frank robbery when the time is ripe.

These talents were acknowledged by others, certainly not always with wholehearted admiration. From the Middle Ages, Venice is associated to some degree with chicanery. So it is in Boccaccio's *Decameron*: Venice is on the alleged itinerary of the super-fraudulent Fra Cipolla, and another scoundrel betakes himself to "Vinegia, d'ogni bruttura recevitrice" ("Venice, [feminine] receptacle of all iniquity").[32] No doubt Venice, with its absolute wealth and relative openness, was a magnet for confidence artists and ingenious thieves. Perhaps Venice's own national skill at extraction as well as its tempting wealth helped it to be viewed readily as a natural home of impostors, fraudsters, and mountebanks. Certainly, the Venetians themselves enjoyed what we call snake-oil salesmen, the artists of patter. A popular amusement was to enjoy the "Ciarlatini" or charlatans at their trade in Saint Mark's Square. Renaissance Venice is represented as spontaneously producing or fostering such con artists, as in *Volpone*. The untrustworthy characters of *The Merchant of Venice* can seem predatory cheats feeding off each other.[33] In the Venice of the 1950s Patricia Highsmith's Tom Ripley puts the finishing lucrative touches on his murderous masquerade. Robert in McEwan's *Comfort of Strangers* is only a recent addition to the gallery of deceptive Venetian rogues. It must be admitted that some elements in the negative view of Venice go back a long way.

The bronze horses of Saint Mark's are swag worth having. They are thought to be original Byzantine work of an early era, of the second or third century A.D., perhaps earlier. Magnificent, lively, whole, they are bronze work of the most extraordinary power. Once they were golden horses—gilded all over. In their original shining beauty they must have been breathtaking—and each horse had red eyes of real rubies. Most likely they were taken from the Hippodrome or racing track; they may have been part of a whole sculpture of a *quadriga* or four-horse racing chariot. They were not originally religious images in the strict sense—though chariot-racing was certainly a passion in Byzantium/Constantinople. But the image of the *quadriga* and the four horses is ultimately a religious image, the representation of the power of the sun god. So perhaps their coming to rest at the top of a temple is appropriate.

These stolen horses were again stolen by Napoleon, who took them to Paris. They were restored to Venice when Napoleon fell; the sculptor Canova was one of those who pleaded most successfully for their return. When they came back, the horses were blind, their ruby eyes gone. The beautiful bronze horses have now been taken down; they were restored in 1979 and not reinstalled because the polluted air of modern Venice is too hard on them. (Needless to say, there has been no suggestion of giving them back to Istanbul.) The horses we now see on top of San Marco are copies. Made by a very workmanlike foundry in Milan, they are serviceable but soulless. You can see the originals—above the nave of San Marco, there is a little museum where they are kept, looking both wistful and furiously impatient. Whether this museum stable does much to keep the baneful air particles from them, I take leave to doubt; they were nearly as well off outdoors. (I once wandered among them listening to strains of "Jesus Christ the Apple Tree" sung by a visiting American choir below—an odd experience.) I am glad that in 1961 I saw the Basilica with the original bronze horses—neighing and stamping (so it seems), rejoicing in their eminence, almost about to leap into Saint Mark's Square, "as if copied from life, and stampeding from above, of ancient workmanship and by a superb artist," as Petrarch says.[34] But it must be acknowledged that the four horses, not of an apocalypse but of secular jubilation, were beautiful loot placed on that basilica dedicated to Saint Mark as a most irreligious if exuberant sign of triumph.

6

The Engineering of Color

Once did She hold the gorgeous east in fee;
And was the safeguard of the west: the worth
Of Venice did not fall below her birth,
Venice, the eldest child of Liberty.
She was a maiden City, bright and free . . .
  —William Wordsworth, "On the Extinction of the Venetian Republic"

In domes of dim and ancient gold,
 In cloisters, where the lightning plays
Where gleam the gorgeous saints of old
 In aisles of jade and chrysoprase,

       —Herbert Asquith, "Venice"

Another point I wish the reader to observe is, the importance attached to *colour* in the mind of the designer.

       —John Ruskin, *Stones of Venice*

*T*he qualities of Odysseus—efficiency and intelligence, wiliness and persistence—characterize the Venetians. As we have seen, the Venetians developed enormous powers as sailors and navigators, and as sea-warriors, thus building up not only trade monopolies but an empire. Their engineering skills were unrivaled in the Middle Ages—and we have no modern project that has lasted as long or as well as Venice over time. In the first truly literary reference to the city-state, Dante refers to Venice and the Venetians first of all in terms of engineering and efficiency. The reference comes in the twenty-first canto of the *Inferno,* in a long simile in a description of a special pocket of hell. We are in a district of the "Bad Pockets" (Malebolge) of the Eighth Circle, the Circle of the Fraudulent:

We stopped to see the next fissure
 Of Malebolge and the next vain plaints;
And so I saw it wondrously obscure.

As in the Arsenal of the Venetians
        Boils in winter the tenacious pitch
Recaulking so what timbers be unsound—

For then they cannot sail—and in one place
        One shapes new timbers, while another stops
The sides of craft that has made many a voyage;

One hammers at the prow, one at the poop;
        Others make oars, and others still twist ropes;
And still another patches up the sail.

So, not by fire, but by divine art,
        Boiled down in that depth there a thick tar,
Which viscously stuck to banks on every side.

I saw it, but I did not see within
        Ought but ball-bubbles that the boiling raised,
And the whole swelled, and then fell back again.[1]

Dante in his simile is describing the Arsenale as a model of efficiency. In his riff about technology he uses the technical terms for sails familiar to boatmen (*terzeruolo, artimon*), and of course the great technical term *argana* or Arsenale. He directs our attention not to individuals casually mending their own vessels, but to the organized work being done in a Venetian division of labor. Rather strangely, as we may think, the Venetians are so proud of this description that some of these verses are displayed outside the (now ruinous and empty) Arsenale itself. All classes of Venetians were proud of the speed with which they could not only repair but build ships. In 1574 they showed the visiting King Henri III of France a ship's keel being laid in the early morning, and then took him back at the end of the day to show him the completed vessel. Their efficiency was partly the effect of a distinctive method of production that anticipates the discoveries of Henry Ford.

Dante associates Venice with this sort of assembly line, and above all with industry. His ostensibly admiring description of the wonders of Venetian industrial technology, however, is wrapped up in a description of a section of Hell devoted to cheating and stealing. In the boiling pitch are punished the "barrators," those who betrayed their virtue and the public trust in cheating the state which they were supposed to serve. It may be fitting that those who sinned against the state should take their penalty from the image of a most industrious state. But in this earliest of literary references to Venice, the city is associated, if indirectly, with treachery. Its rather alarming modern industrial energies are the energies of Hell.

The Arsenale, founded in 1104—and thus still relatively new, if not a novelty in Dante's time—made Venice "great." Its very name points to a certain foreignness—it comes from the Arabic word for "workshop," *d'arsina'a*. So happy were the Venetians with their *arzanà* that they were to make its entryway one of the first monuments of Renaissance art, setting up before it a gateway recycling Byzantine (or possibly ancient Greek) columns. The entryway did not allow all to enter—much of the Arsenale was or became top secret, off-limits to unauthorized persons. Venetians' power lay in their ships, including the fact that they could make new ones so rapidly that an enemy could not destroy a fleet, nor tempests ruin trade. The Venetian vessel which carried the national wealth was an oared galley. These galleys had enormous success for centuries, in the end sadly failing to develop sails and harness wind-power in the more sophisticated ways at last devised by the Venetians' initially slow northern competitors.

Venice is also interestingly associated by Dante with the viscous: with the tenacious pitch ("la tenace pece"), the everlastingly sticky: "bollìa là giuso una pegola spessa /che 'nviscava la ripa d'ogni parte"—which might be translated as "There boiled down there a thick tar/that *en-viscoused* the bank on every side." It is striking how often Venice is associated with the viscous, as if the thickly liquid and sticky substance from which it rose can never be shaken off. Her glory is in proportion to her obscure, even obscene, viscosity. Material triumph cannot be divorced from this uneasy adhesive materiality that shares the qualities of both solid and liquid while refusing to be strictly either. Certainly, in tracing the history of Venice, we should keep materiality strictly in view. Before she could become a political state, or an empire, Venice needed to become a *place,* needed to create the very physical terms on which she could function at all. She had no grounds of being until she made them. And wherever we look we catch her working.

The nature and work structure of the Arsenale resonate oddly in history. Where else have we heard of the construction of ships using the method of rational assemblage that Dante describes—an early assembly line? The answer is, in the world's oldest trading empire, Carthage. Founded by Phoenicians, a Semitic people who had been headquartered in Tyre and Sidon, refugees who may have spent their first years on the Tunisian coast living in boats, Carthage from the sixth century B.C.E. became a magnificent sea power. The Phoenicians on the coast of Africa set up trading routes with small colonies as far away as Spain and England. They ran up against the rising power of Rome, which would allow no rival; in 143 B.C.E. the Romans attacked Carthage. "Delenda est Carthago!" was the cry: "Carthage must be destroyed!" The overthrow of the city was very terrible. The Carthaginians fought back bravely. According to the historians Appian and Polybius, the Romans blockaded the harbor of Carthage and built a long mole. But the Carthaginians surprised them by re-creating a new navy out of scraps and damaged vessels, men, women, and children working together. When the new navy burst out of concealment, it gave the Romans a nasty surprise, and for a day or two Carthage again had a chance. The Carthaginians could perform this unheard-of feat because the island on which ships were built was specially set up for rapid assemblage. This island would seem to be the original Arsenale.[2]

The Carthaginians' capacity for rapid hard work is complimented even by the enemy propagandist Virgil, in relating the ill-fated love of Dido and Aeneas, presage of the ultimate destruction of the coastal city-state. Aeneas (who still has to build Rome) sympathetically watches the Phoenicians at the founding of their city, as they dig trenches and move stones and exert themselves to build walls harbors, towers, and a theater. They are working busily "As bees in early summer amidst rural flowers exert their labour in the sunshine."[3] Later, Virgil will prophesy unalterable antipathy between Carthage and Rome. The real Carthaginians built a splendid city on a narrow margin of hill and seashore, and went forth from it to dominate the known world's trade routes. Without any large land mass as a base, Carthage is really the first empire to depend primarily on trade and communication. As the city-state advanced, it seized some strategic bases (ports mostly) and went behind the coastal regions into the hinterland to take much of what is now Tunisia and Libya. But ships and seamanship were the origin of Carthage's power—along with comprehension of the value of trade, and a new technology of the alphabet that Carthage helped to spread, and to teach the world to use.

Venice as it rose was to follow almost exactly the pattern mapped out by Carthage a millennium earlier. With a very tiny center, made from scratch, Venice developed not only a home but also a method of keeping its sea power in constant repair, and dominating the Mediterranean. The Venetian empire was primarily based on trade and commerce; expansion of these commercial interests eventually brought it into conflict with its foster parent, Byzantium. Though a later period saw more territory claimed by the Venetians, with the semi-exception of Candia (Crete), Venice never really possessed "colonies" and "settlers" in the sense that the Roman, English, or Spanish empires did. Venice's enduring value was as a trading power, a communicator, an engine of commerce—and a medium, a mediator between East and West.

A certain resemblance between Carthage and Venice is perhaps only a curiosity of history, a coincidence. Yet, as every new treatise on such a well-worked subject as Venice should offer some strange new theory, I shall boldly offer mine. Suppose that the resemblance is not such a coincidence—because some of the founders of Venice really were Carthaginians? It's hard to say just what the Carthaginians were like, for Rome not only gave them a bad press but destroyed their culture. We have a few surviving images of the Carthaginians, for example from Plautus's Latin play *Poenulus (The Carthaginian)*, c. 195 B.C.E., based on a Greek original written a century earlier. The story makes the Carthaginian sympathetic, a dignified man looking for his lost children, stolen by pirates. From this and a few other works, we learn that Carthaginians were popularly supposed to be very serious, wear unbelted long robes, and eat grits. We can picture them as wiry, dark, and dignified, with decided noses. Of course, we don't know too much about the Semitic Carthaginians, as the Romans were so determined to erase them and their culture, including their library.

The destruction of the city of Carthage was a brutal and protracted affair. It took the Romans a week just to get up the central hill—they were opposed by men, women, and children, whom they killed in a sickening and desperate process of house-to-house fighting. In huge piles of debris, burnt beams, and house tiles, the living were swept away to the pit with the dead. The Romans made a thorough job, not only sacking the city but reducing it to ruins. Yet, it is hard to delete an entire people. In the nature of things, not all Carthaginians would have been in Carthage at the time the Romans came. A number must have been abroad—at sea in their ships, or in ports around the Mediterranean. These could have fled from the Roman might. One good place to go was the backside of the Italian peninsula, the muddy marshy oozy bit that nobody much wanted. After all, we know nothing about the inhabitants of the marshy islands and the coast except that they were called "Veneti." But a number of tribes and peoples may have amalgamated along that slightly dreary shore, where they could be left alone as long as they did not impinge upon the fertile river valleys beyond the dull coast. I suggest that the Carthaginian refugees, the Phoenicians, or Phoinikes or Fenici (Veneti?), combined with local peoples (including some earlier Phoenician settlers) to produce a distinct group that retained sufficient tribal or communal memory to know how to create a land base out of a space that had almost nothing to it. Moreover, they knew, these new Veneti, how to sail ships and conduct trading business. The Phoenician oligarchic constitution as described by Aristotle has a certain resonance with the Venetians' oligarchic arrangement of their state. And the Venetian face has a wonderfully emphatic Semitic nose, a quality emphasized in the local masks for characters like Pantalon, and not ignored in portraits. Important Venetian men had big noses, were serious and pious, wore long robes, and ate (eventually) a lot of grits in the form of polenta.

The foundation date the Venetians liked to give themselves—25 March 421—represents them as already Christian, self-conscious, self-sufficiently determined to build a city. As has been remarked, this is the anniversary of the Annunciation to Mary; Venice is in her own eyes a product of a special annunciation. Venice according to its own history is always a Christian state, and Venice invented a lively foundational story directly connecting it to a vision of God given directly to Saint Mark. The Venetians' valuable story about themselves is of a people quite distinct, owing nothing to Rome or to Romanness, as Garry Wills has emphasized.[4] The city is self authenticated without any Roman intervention—as a religious site on its own account; indeed Saint Mark's city is subtly self-presented as a rival, even a superior, to Saint Peter's. Although in one historical view its Christianity came from the Byzantine church, and the Greek Orthodox establishment, according to the preferred version and vision Venice is already on God's map, so to speak. An idea in God's mind before it was even built, Venice was always already Venice. It is thus a place of revelation, and has no need to humble itself to Constantinople or to Rome.

I used to think (rather like George Grant, for whom the city was a figure of "Babylon") that Venice represented a point absolutely opposite to the Holy City, figured as Jerusalem, Mecca, or Rome. I now see Venice as having a central concept of itself as a Holy City. But it is a Holy City on its own terms, in accordance with its own vision, and that vision requires exploration and meditation. Certainly, it is not Rome. It owed nothing to the Rome of antiquity (unlike some of the cities it took over in the Veneto, such as Verona, an important town in Roman times). Venice had never held an arena for wild beast shows and martyrdoms. It was never graced with Roman baths, administrative offices, or soldiery. And it never became Romanized. John Ruskin sensed this, and his fascination with Venice partly lay in a pursuit of something he wanted to feel was a kind of originary Protestantism. To Ruskin, with all his Anglo prejudices about him, that which is Roman Catholic represents that which is stereotyped, mechanically reproduced, while for him Protestantism stands for what is lively, truthful, and creative.[5] Rather engagingly, he recants some of these views in his later book on Venice, *Saint Mark's Rest:* "I have myself been forced to recognize the degree in which all my early work on Venetian history was paralyzed by this petulance of sectarian egotism. . . . There are few of the errors against which I have to warn my readers, into which I have not myself at some time fallen."[6]

Ruskin's importation of English sectarian terms may at times confuse issues, but he is not alone in considering Venice as representing a faith not entirely Roman. Catholic she is certainly, but not Roman. Throughout its long Catholic history the city insisted on its right to approve bishops. It would not allow the Inquisition free reign; the Inquisitors must work in concert with members of the Venetian government, and no accused Venetian could be taken to Rome for trial or punishment. (This did not help Giordano Bruno, arrested in Venice and taken to Rome where he was eventually burned at the stake, but Bruno was not a Venetian citizen.) As we have seen in Lithgow's anecdote, Venice in its heyday did take it upon itself to punish clerics without sending them on to the Vatican, and took a dim view of the sexual offenses of clerics in nunneries (not the less because most of the nuns were of good families). But Venice never burned a single individual for heresy. To the chagrin of Rome, laws were eventually made forbidding Venetians to will their property to the Church. Venice was fearful of losing control over its small land area, and thus losing authority and autonomy. In the sixteenth century, some of the Reformers thought Venice might become "Protestant"—which of course it never did. But Venice, to the occasional dismay of the pope, tolerated infidels and heretics within its borders, permitting not only Greek Orthodox services in the Greek church but also Jewish services in the several synagogues. Sir Henry Wotton, ambassador of King James I of England, was allowed to hold Protestant services in his residence, and, when the papal nuncio protested, the Doge said blandly that the law prevented Venetians from attending such services, so there was no danger. (But it was a great age for sermon-tasting, and some Venetians did go.)[7] Eventually there was a tolerated mosque in the Fondaco dei Turchi.

The Venetians, at the center of the book trade, had already resisted the *Index Expurgatorius*, or List of Forbidden Books, and in 1596 Venice refused to cooperate with the censorship regime demanded by Pope Clement VIII, which required printers to submit manuscripts to Rome for approval before publication.[8] In 1606, Venetian resistance to the imposition of an Interdict by Pope Paul V attracted world attention and was applauded by many. In the Middle Ages Venice (like other places) had been brought to heel by the power of the Interdict, which forbade the sacraments of the Church to all members of the erring state. But this time the mechanism didn't work. Resistance to the new Interdict took the form of outright disobedience. Despite the papal edict in May 1606 clergy in Venice simply continued to offer the sacraments to Venetians. In fact, more people went to Mass than usual. That was the last time the Vatican endeavored to put any nation under interdict. Paolo Sarpi, Servite monk and theologian to the Republic, acted as spokesman for Venice. Venice declared the Interdict invalid. Sarpi argued that it was against all law to punish groups for the misdeeds—or alleged misdeeds—of a few, and this appeal had a powerful attraction in terms of a developing national and international law. Having defeated the pope in October 1607, Paolo Sarpi was attacked by assassins and left for dead; badly stabbed as he was, Sarpi recovered, and wittily said he recognized the Roman style (or stiletto—*stilo*). Protestant visitors tended to be attracted to the story of the attempted assassination. Maximilien Misson looked up the bloody *stilo* (in a church), and William Dean Howells tried to figure out the exact site of the assault. That is easy to find nowadays, for in 1892 Venice put up a statue to Sarpi, near the site of his old monastery and just by the bridge where he was attacked. (There seems a touch of political feeling in the erection of Sarpi's statue in the early years of modern Italy, perhaps a little flick at Rome as the new Italian capital.) In the early seventeenth century Venice had shown that it could stand up to the power of the Vatican. It could do that because it reckoned it had truth—divine Truth—on its own side.

Everywhere as one goes about Venice, watching the flow of canal waters and the maneuvers of vaporetti and gondolas, standing on a bridge perhaps and contemplating, one hears as a kind of undersong: "Non so', non so', io non sono Roma!" This is a city determined not to be Roman. It is no more Roman than Dido. This means its history has a different twist from what we think of as "Italian history," and its accomplishments have to be seen in a somewhat different light. In this it has something in common with Sicily, but unfortunate Sicily has been the stamping-ground of every invader, riddled with piracy and turning to banditry as its only resource against imposed and occupying powers. Venice was anxious to keep banditry at bay, and to eradicate secret societies and criminal gangs. It was largely successful over the centuries in suppressing internal crime, and in putting a check on piracy, most vexing nearby along the Dalmatian coast. Despite the aspirations of new mega-states like Spain and then France, following very sharp conflict with the rival mercantile sea power of Genoa, Venice managed to hold off invasion. Even when Genoa brought war to its back door and took Chioggia in 1379, at a time when the city was weakened and depopulated by the plague, Venice did not give in.

The flourishing city-state managed at last to make peace with its inland neighbors. Padua joined peacefully and voluntarily with the Republic in 1406, as Vicenza and Verona already had done. The union was, on the whole, managed to the benefit of all. These cities maintained their own civic governments, with some restrictions. Venice worked with the city of Verona to create free primary schooling (for males), and to support education in law, medicine, and the humanities. Having no university of its own, it gave handsome support and protection (including protection from papal interference) to the University of Padua.[9] That institution grew enormously in stature during the ensuing centuries. It attracted students from other parts of Italy and from all of western Europe, including Pico della Mirandola, Erasmus, Sir Philip Sidney, Thomas Linacre, and William Harvey (discoverer of the circulation of the blood). Famous for medical studies, Padua created a beautiful anatomy theater in 1594, encouraged evidently by Venice, which had already opened an anatomy theater near San Giacomo dell'Orio in 1507, an area still marked by the name Corte dell'Anatomia. Padua's university was a center for what we would call "science"; a youthful Galileo Galilei became professor of mathematics there in 1592. It is famous for another unusual thing: a statue in the courtyard commemorates Elena Lucrezia Cornaro Piscopia, the first woman ever to be awarded a university degree (in 1678). Burnet, who admires her achievement, says she was the offspring of a Cornaro and a gondolier's daughter (thus she combined, one may think, the best genes Venice had to offer).[10]

All of this success is predicated on Venice's unusual wealth. Nibbling away at the formerly Greek territories, getting a station on this island and that, helped medieval Venice further to control trade and shipping in the east, in-

cluding not only the sea-lanes to Persia and beyond but also the routes to
the lands around the Black Sea and extending to the sea of Azov. Most of
Venice's empire building required little acquisition of land mass, although its
first takeover of Dalmatia (with its Istrian stone) was an important imperial
maneuver, as Larry Wolf has shown. (Croatians to this day are not best
pleased with Venetian rule.) What Venice needed was to hold enough seacoast
to safeguard trade routes, rather than to put down settlers. Venice in its apo-
gee chiefly occupied islands for bases. So it is that we find Venetian castles
and forts on various islands dotted about the Mediterranean. Venice took
Cyprus, Kos, Naxos, and Rhodes.[11] Venice was never shy of showing pride in
its battles and victories. Not far from the Palazzo Gritti is the church of
Santa Maria del Giglio, rebuilt by the Barbaro family in the seventeenth century; in their own honor they placed on the facade diagrams of the various
conquered places and fortifications (including Zara, Candia, and Corfu) with
which their family was associated—strangely warlike emblems for the exterior of a church dedicated to Saint Mary of the Lily.

The empire's value was not in its colonies, save as these provided support-
ive stations for patrolling shipping lanes and for refitting. Only in some instances, as in the cultivation of sugar in plantations on Candia, did Venice
gain a valuable product directly from its land holdings. The real value of the
Venetian "empire" lay in its dynamism as an engine of commerce. At one
point the Adriatic city-state controlled all the East-West trade. Giant cargoes
came back to Venice, which had first pick of spices (including pepper), marble, gems, fine tapestries, sweet perfumes, soft silks, rich damasks. Venice
was the first to have the most luxurious materials, the silk damascened with
intermixed threads of gold or silver. (This scintillating effect of woven silk
with metal threads inspired the Spanish designer and artist—and Venice-
dweller—Mariano Fortuny to revive it in twentieth-century form, using gold
and silver paints.)[12]

Among the highly valued imports none were as luscious and eye-catching
as the Orient pearls. Venice established these as a mark of rank and worth,
setting a fashion in pearls that only it could supply. The costumes of nobility
and royalty were studded or edged with these gems of the ocean. It became
customary for the betrothed of a Venetian patrician to be given a necklace of
such white and lucent pearls. They were a sign of the girl's high birth, as of
her chastity; their expense was a sure clue to both families' ability to sustain
conspicuous consumption. We see such a valued string of pearls in Tintoretto's picture of the Roman Lucretia. Lucretia's wearing of pearls spells out

Figure 12. Jacopo Tintoretto, *Tarquin and Lucretia* (Permission of Art Institute of Chicago: Art Institute Purchase Fund, 1949.203)

her constant chastity, but now—under the ruthless attack of Tarquin—her necklace is breaking, pearls spinning to the floor, in certain presage of the rape. The pair struggle in a hopeless moment, surrounded by dark and gleaming fabric, giving off angry metallic thrills of little lightnings (Figure 12). Courtesans were not supposed to wear pearls, these emblems of married purity, but they proved irresistible to most people (including loose ladies) who could afford them. Jonson appropriately has Volpone try to seduce Celia with a significantly valuable gift: "See, here, a rope of pearl; and each, more orient / Than that the brave Egyptian queen caroused" (III. vii, lines 190–191; *Plays*, III, 64). So too Shakespeare in his Venetian play *Othello* has the Moor speak in grief and self-reproach of himself as "Like the base Indian" who "threw a pearl away/Richer than all his tribe" (V.ii, lines 356–357; *Works*, 853). Othello is remembering the highest units of the chaste and the precious—the lustrous pearls, which the Venetians took, if at several removes, from unwitting "Indians."

Venice had a stranglehold on the dispersion and sale of luxury goods, and laid out this merchandise for the world to see. Medieval and Renaissance Venice was a paradise for shoppers, especially in the rich street of the Merceria, off Piazza San Marco in the Rialto direction. In the seventeenth century, John Evelyn is loud in his praise of this street:

I pass'd through the *Merceria*, which I take to be the most delicious streete in the World for the sweetnesse of it, being all the way on both sides, continualy tapissry'd, as it were, with Cloth of Gold, rich Damasks & other silks, which the shops expose & hang before their houses from the first floore, & with that variety, that for neere halfe the yeare. . . . I hardly remember to have seene the same piece twice exposd, to this add the perfumers & Apothecaries shops, and the innumerable cages of Nightingals, which they keepe, that entertaines you with their melody from shop to shop. (June 1645; *Diary*, 222)

The street was obviously designed to offer the stroller a sensuously rich and colorful experience, and to make a pause irresistible. It is no wonder that Venice for several centuries held the position of fashion leader in Europe. Ben Jonson can satirically imagine a Lady Would-be coming to Venice "for intelligence / Of tires, and fashions, and behaviour, / Among the courtesans" (*Volpone*, II.i, lines 27–30; *Plays*, III, 26). Actually, the top prostitutes and kept women would be much more elegantly attired than most European ladies, and for news (or "intelligence") about attire and modes Venice was the fount for all wanna-bes like the Would-bes.

The Venetians, though trading chiefly in imported goods, did have some products of their own. Much of their manufacture was for immediate practical use at home. They were, however, undisputed leaders for a long while in one luxury manufacture: glass. In 1292 that industry was taken out of Venice, because of the danger of fire, and sent to Murano. The craftsmen had gathered information from Syrians and others, and worked at perfecting the product. Glassmakers were treated as citizens (*cittadini*) and not common mechanics; theirs was not one of the base trades that disqualifies a man for citizenship, but a valuable contribution to the wealth of the state. Paul Hills describes the medieval search for transparency; the Venetians at last learned to make flawlessly transparent glass.[13] It was probably this purity that led to the story that a Venetian glass would shatter if poison were poured into it. Such a useful advertisement there was no need to contradict. Having learned and mastered the art of transparency, the Venetians introduced other substances, sandwiching gold between two clear layers. And then they cultivated the highly colorful craft of making *mille fiori,* the multicolored glass with a thousand cones of color. Venice also developed the mirror, eventually turning out perfect reflecting mirrors, which were much sought after. The Venetians were the first to use mirrors cunningly disposed in artistic interior decoration.[14] They also made imposing glass chandeliers, with delicate adornments of colored glass paste; if you go into the Museo Vetrario in Murano, you can see that the goblet or mirror or chandelier you buy now is the same design as one made in the Cinquecento. There was evidently some recognition of intellectual property in a discovery or design; when Hermonia Vivarini designed a glass pitcher in the form of a ship, a *navicella,* she was allowed to keep exclusive rights to its production for ten years.[15]

In the Renaissance, Venetian glass was admired and shipped all over Europe; every palace or great house had some memento of Venetian color, and something of the watery iridescent laguna in a piece of reflecting shimmer. The glassmaking art died out almost entirely under the Austrian occupation, except for bead-making (a women's craft), but the art was revived by the end of the 1800s. Since the nineteenth-century hiatus, Murano glassmakers have continued to develop the art—although a lot of the pieces are actually produced at their workshops in Marconi. Glassmakers produce new designs, although the pieces exposed for sale are customarily copies of Renaissance or eighteenth-century pieces. The glow and fragility can—like Venice—astonish.

The high art and *fantasia* of Murano glassmaking is reflected (pray endure the pun) in Francesco Colonna's dreamlike novel of a dream, *Hypnerotomachia Poliphili* (*The Strife of Love in the Sleep of Poliphilo;* 1499). In his dream-world, a precursor of Wonderland, Poliphilo is shown a uniquely beautiful garden:

instead of living plants, everything was made from clear glass, surpassing anything one could imagine or believe. There were topiary box trees moulded of the same material with golden stems. . . . The beds were filled with a marvellous imitation of various simples, elegantly trimmed as in nature, and with gaily varied forms of flow-

ers in distinct and delightful colours. . . . Sweet-voiced Logistica now made an eloquent speech with penetrating remarks in praise of the splendid craft, the nobility
of the material, the artistry and the invention (such as one would not find in
Murano).[16]

Not only the glassy description but also the praise of the substance itself
seem very Venetian. Despite the claims within the recent entertaining novel
The Rule of Four (2004), telling a story that depends on the author of *Hypnerotomachia* not being Venetian, tradition says the author was born in the Veneto
and was a resident of a monastery in Venice.[17] Reminiscences of Venice and
the Veneto can be found scattered throughout the narrative (an erotic and
mathematical predecessor of Carroll's *Through the Looking Glass and What Alice
Found There*). The living chess game is surely based on an actual living chess
game played in Maròstica, near Asolo in the Veneto, in 1454. (Revived, it is
now played there in September every two years.) Describing the glass garden,
the narrator claims that it is superior to the work of Murano, but the local
inspiration is everywhere apparent in this passage, not least in the gaily colored flowers of glass paste such as still adorn Murano chandeliers.

Another pleasing, if less glittering, art perfected by Venice is printing.
This art would probably not have arisen had Venice not been so well suited
to the making of paper. In those days paper was made from rags and not
from wood pulp; Venice was rich enough to have cast-off clothing, and lots
of raggedy old sails suitable for pulping. Gutenberg had gone bust, but Aldus
Manutius (1450–1515), who came originally from the Roman area, made a
great success of the printing business. He shrewdly married the daughter of
Andrea Torresano, a Venetian printer (and Erasmus's detested host). Aldus
used the Venetian resource of resident experts in Greek, and was the first to
print Greek works in the Greek alphabet. He also created italic type (said to
have been modeled on Petrarch's handwriting). The Aldine press produced
fine printings of the classics and of new writers at reasonable prices, and
spread literacy and humane letters about Europe as the Phoenicians had once
spread the alphabet. The Aldine logo, the anchor and dolphin, became familiar everywhere, though other printers also adorned Venice, which became a
center of learning. The Aldine Academy he founded in 1500 required members to speak Greek, and thus included the best Greek scholars in Italy. One
notes here again the Venetian movement toward inclusiveness and the polyglot. This background and outlook enabled Aldus to compile the first Latin-
Greek lexicon ever produced.

The growth of the paper industry permitted the introduction of a new and colorful refinement, the art of making multicolored paper. This art, which comes ultimately from Japan to the Near East, passed from the Arab world to the Venetians in the fifteenth century; elegant multicolored marbled paper (chiefly for holy books) was made by craftsmen in Venice until the invasion. Under the leadership of Alberto Valese, the art has been revived in Venice since the 1970s.[18] Nowadays the handcrafted paper is used for endpapers, book covers, wrapping paper, and various ornaments. Marbled colors are made by carefully putting one layer of dots of paints on another and then combing them out; the multi-hued swirls resemble (though they do not repeat) those to be found in multicolored glass.

*V*enice is an artful technological product, like the glass for which it was to become famous. The conditions of its own materiality were always present. The old names of parts or districts of Venice (*sestieri*) speak of the history of earth and water. The Rialto (not the name of an actual *sestier*, but the name of an area) gets its name from *rivoaltus* (high bank) because a bit of land there stayed above the tides; a settlement grew in the ninth century, when the Doge still lived in Malamocco. The Rialto became the trading center and most densely settled part of the city over the next two or three centuries as the great draining project developed. The Rialto Bridge connects the *sestieri* of San Polo and San Marco. The name of the district or *sestier* Cannaregio, though some think it means "royal canal," patently means "region of reeds." This reedy marshy part was not inhabited until the eleventh century, and required ambitious draining. The island called Dorsoduro (meaning "hard back" or "spine") has a spine of hard clay and is the firmest of Venice's regions. At the southeast end of the Grand Canal its tip it is marked by the Customs-house (Dogana) and the church of Santa Maria della Salute. Dorsoduro touches upon and seems unified with two other *sestieri*: Santa Croce and San Polo, each with its own history. The district of San Polo developed around the church of the same name, founded in the ninth century. Campo San Polo, the largest square in Venice aside from Piazza San Marco, was long used for exciting entertainments in certain seasons, including bullfighting and bull-running. Santa Croce was unhappy enough to lose its own church of the Holy Cross, near the present station bridge, in the Napoleonic era. Now Santa Croce has to make do with Piazzalle Roma and the view of the train station, though it does have San Simeone Piccolo, looking like a green bubble of copper bubblegum. At the other end of Venice, Castello, looking toward the Lido and Murano, was early given a fortress and is the site of the Arsenale, while the adjacent *sestier* San Marco contains the important buildings at the heart of Venice.

The island of the Giudecca (or in Venetian "Zuecca") was originally called "Spinalunga"—"long spine"; some think it would have acquired its other name from the Jews who settled there from the late twelfth century, though it is likely that this is merely folk etymology. (I myself think the name means "portion lying below," i.e., "the piece of land to the south.") Giudecca boasts a thoroughly Palladian church, the Redentore (the Church of the Redeemer) built in 1577–1592 in thanksgiving for deliverance from the terrible plague of 1575–1576. The Feast of Redentore takes place on the third Sunday in July, and traditionally a bridge of boats was set up between the Zattere and Giudecca so the people could cross over easily and with no expense. Nowadays the bridge is an ugly aluminum contraption, also put up—oddly—for the Venetian Marathon which is run in October from Mestre to San Marco (one would rather see the bridge of boats). As we have seen, Thomas Coryat felt himself lucky to be in Venice for this celebration. When the site for Redentore was chosen, Jews who had lived on Giudecca since the thirteenth century had to go and live with the rest of the Jewish population in the walled Ghetto on the island (or island group) of Cannaregio.

The Ghetto gets its name from the Venetian form of the word for "foundry," derived from *gettare* (to throw), that is, a place where things are "cast" or "thrown." The actual foundry had been removed from Cannaregio to the Arsenale in the fourteenth century, but the term "Ghetto" associated with a particular area of Cannaregio has lived on to become synonymous with enforced domicile for Jews. Nowadays the unpleasant but expressive word refers to any urban region assumed to be reserved for the habitation of those thought inferior or too different. In 1516 in an act of repression the Council had decreed that the Jews of Venice were all to live within the Ghetto, "as within a fortress (*castello*)"; they were to be enclosed, and the access bridges guarded and completely shut at night. The Jewish leaders put up objections, including the fact that this would be a breach of trust (which it was), but the law was passed.[19]

The context for this repellent act was an increase in the number of Jews flocking into Venice, refugees from the mainland. The pope and the Dominican and Franciscan friars were preaching strongly against them. Obviously, some thought it would be possible to expel the Jews from Europe altogether. (From the thirteenth to the late seventeenth century no Jews were allowed to

live in England under any conditions, so Anglos can hardly take a superior
tone in dealing with the original Ghetto.) The Venetian foundation of the
Ghetto represents a compromise, if a nasty and bitter compromise.

The law once passed was inexorable. The previous inhabitants moved out
of the island, and rents were raised in the blocks of housing on the island of
Ghetto Nuovo. Jews could now only rent, and only here; there was no chance
of their taking great houses or building *palazzi* on the Grand Canal, as they
had begun to do. The Venetian name of the area was used first for settlements on the island of Ghetto Nuovo, then for the Ghetto Vecchio (where
Levantine Jews came), and the Ghetto Novissimo (chiefly for recently arrived
Sephardic families). Land here was in extremely short supply, so the Jews,
constrained to stay in one small area, had to build upward; houses in the
Ghetto are much taller than in gentile Venice. The Jews were kept under
guard, but this policed enclosure at least prevented any outrages against
them. The inhabitants of the Ghetto had businesses there that brought gen-
tiles to them. As the pawnbrokers of the region (one of the few trades they
were allowed to engage in) they were a resource to poor and rich, even rent-
ing out very costly luxury goods to those who could afford them. Sir Henry
Wotton rented all the furnishings of his house, including the gondola, from
a Jewish broker,[20] a fact presumably picked up by Jonson when he has Sir
Politick boast: "I had read Contarene [Contarini], took me a house/ Dealt
with my Jews, to furnish it with movables" (*Volpone*, IV.i, lines 40–41; *Plays*,
III, 72). The Ghetto dwellers could also keep some people out; any Jew who
had converted to Christianity was forbidden, on pain of severe penalties, to
set foot in the Ghetto again.

Venice had to defend itself and its valuable Jewish inhabitants against sudden ebullitions of papal and other impatience at its harboring of "infidels."
Venice was much more tolerant of religious difference than most other areas
of Europe—in this imitating the Ottoman empire rather than Italy. The construction of synagogues was allowed in the early sixteenth century, and Jewish
worshipers could practice their religion openly. There are five historic synagogues in the Ghetto, the oldest, Scuola Grande Tedesca, dating from 1528.
In the sixteenth and seventeenth centuries the Jewish population grew to its
maximum of about five thousand. It is ironic that the period in which Shakespeare wrote of Shylock was the most tolerant era of Venice's history. Jewish-
Christian relations had never been so good. Venetian scholars would come to
hear sermons in the synagogues from teachers like Leon Modena. Tolerance
went backward in the mid-eighteenth century, with a desire to scapegoat

someone for Venice's ills. Napoleon grandly threw open the gates of the Ghetto—the only good thing that I know of that he did for Venice—but the Austrians closed—or half-closed—the gates again, though they did allow Jews to pursue more occupations. Cordial relations between Jewish and gentile Venetians may be gathered from the fact that among signatories to a petition in January 1848 requesting the release of Daniele Manin from prison are both eminent Jewish merchants and patricians bearing names that formerly graced the banned *Libro d'Oro*. (The Austrians thought them all nuisances alike.)

The rebellion against Austria in 1848, when Venice gallantly led the way in a revolutionary Europe, produced a new and essentially Jewish hero for Venice in Daniele Manin. His grandparents (named Medina) at their "conversion" in the mid-eighteenth century had been sponsored by Ludovico Manin's brother, and had taken his surname.[21] Daniele's Jewish ethnicity was well known but did not tell against him in Venetian eyes. In what must surely have been a conscious effort to reverse the pacific attitude of the passive Ludovico Manin, that last Doge with whom Daniele was so strangely connected, the new Manin led the valiant fight. Jews and Catholics, patricians and *popoli*, worked and fought and endured together when Venice briefly, if gloriously, threw off the Austrian yoke.

With the release from Austrian occupation and the union with Italy, the separation of the Jews ceased, but many people continued to live in their traditional homes, which meant that the Jewish population suffered when the Austrians shelled Cannaregio in World War I. The ugliest time of all was to come, during World War II, under Mussolini, when there were about fifteen hundred Jews living in Venice. In what is now a quiet and pretty *campo*, 289 Jews of Venice were rounded up prior to taking the train to the concentration camp—an event that many guidebooks fail to mention. Only a few families now live in the historic Ghetto. Luchino Visconti's film *Senso* (set in 1866) has many shots of his central characters in the Ghetto. Perhaps the area was easy for Visconti to use—probably the Ghetto in 1954 actually was as deserted and forlorn as he makes it in his film, where it stands for the whole of Venice under Austrian rule.

Surely the Ghetto's inhabitants in the seventeenth century must often have looked longingly on Giudecca (Zuecca), historic home from which they had been debarred. Zuecca was for a while a fashionable area, with wealthy homes and extensive gardens. Michelangelo had stayed here during his visit in 1529. It is the remembered setting of a perfect moment of love in a lyric by Alfred de Musset, celebrating his last happy day with George Sand in their Venetian love affair:

> At Saint-Blaise, on Zuecca
> You were, you were at your ease
> At Saint-Blaise.
> At Saint-Blaise, on Zuecca,
> All was well with us there. (*Nous étions bien là*)
> . . . .
> At Saint-Blaise, on Zuecca
> In the flowered fields to gather vervain,
> At Saint-Blaise, on Zuecca
>   To live and die there![22]

Théophile Gautier was enamored of this "Chanson" of Musset, but when he went to Zuecca expressly to pay homage to this site he found no happy mead for lovers' wanderings, and no vervain, but only strictly neat rows of dull vegetables in the convent plot. He comments sourly, "The morning was not favorable to illusions: at Saint-Blaise, on Zuecca, the pumpkin replaces vervain."[23]

At present even the Giudecca supplies little space in which to gather plants of any kind. There is a famous private garden called "Garden of Eden," but it remains closed to almost all. The Giudecca, however, even if most of us cannot enter its gardens, possesses practical current attractions as it is about the only area of central Venice where it is possible for a nonplutocrat to buy living accommodation. So, if you want to live with Venice forever in your eye, buy an apartment on Zuecca looking toward the Zattere at the back of Dorsoduro.

A friend of mine who teaches at the University of Venice but comes from Naples says what she misses in Venice is green space and growing things. It is certainly the case that gardens are rare and hard to find in Venice of the twentieth or twenty-first century, or even the late nineteenth, making plausible the expressed yearning for a garden on the part of the narrator of Henry James's *Aspern Papers*. Many private plots, however, evidently remain, small and hidden, providing the occasional teasing puff of honeysuckle or rose in season. The book *Secret Gardens in Venice*, by Cristiana Moldi Ravenna and Tudy Sammartini, offers handsome photographs and descriptions of remaining gardens. The Venetian garden, it seems, is a jealously guarded private area:

"Within the green world of the garden, space is broken up into ever smaller areas, in a search for personal expression. The habit of looking at things close at hand focuses our attention on passions, sentiments, and every nuance of our changing moods."[24] The small, intimate gardens, ornamented with old statues or ancient pieces of stonework, are occasionally framed against a vista of canal or lagoon, but for the most part Venetians evidently prefer in their gardens to shut out the water and play at being on Terraferma. There are some semiprivate gardens that visitors can enter, like that of Peggy Guggenheim's Museum or the Palazzo Querini Stampalia. Guests of the hotel Cipriani or diners in the restaurant can get into the Cipriani garden on the Giudecca. The authors of *Secret Gardens* believe this space is basically the same as the garden orchard described by Mario Sanudo where Andrea Dandolo gave a great party in 1520.[25]

In the search for gardens I discount entirely the Giardini Pubblici, which were Napoleon's idea. He cleared away a monastery and its grounds and several churches in order to achieve them; Alvise Zorzi says the public garden "cost the destruction of an entire area (*tutto un quartiere*)" of the city and scattered many works of art.[26] The resulting Giardini Pubblici have an imposed and official look; though they do offer space for the exhibitions of the Biennale, I cannot help regarding these enforcedly regular Public Gardens as remnants of the occupation.

In the earliest beginnings, Venetians would have wanted to create space in which to grow humble vegetables, pot-herbs to go with all that fish and salt. In its early centuries the muddy islands of Venice would have been streaked with green. A good deal of space would have been merely churned-up mud before the fashion came in of paving a *campo*; there was reason behind the Venetian invention of the raised shoes which evolved into those exaggeratedly high chopines. In later eras, farms and estates and villas were acquired by the well-to-do in the Veneto, along the Brenta, or northward in Friuli, and this perhaps alleviated the desire for greenery in Venice itself. Yet for a long while there were plenty of small fields and gardens on the main islands of Venice, in the Giudecca, and on the island of Murano. And the Venetians had important greenery to introduce for use or ornament. As the authors of *Secret Gardens* remind us, the city was on the main East-West botanical trade route. Venetians were often the first to get new and rare plants. Venetian artists, as they point out, "included botanical subjects" in their pictures; we have early glimpses in their paintings of the orange tree, the orchid, and the chrysanthemum.[27]

In every century the need for dwelling places and important buildings pressed upon the modest supply of handmade ground. The Piazza of San Marco itself was created by taking over the orchard belonging to the nuns of the convent of San Zaccaria. In the Renaissance, important houses on Castello had elegant gardens sloping down to the Lagoon, but these slowly got swallowed up. Maps of Venice from age to age faithfully follow the building of great edifices and houses, and record the amount of green space left, as one can see in the Museo Correr. The Plan of Venice engraved by Jacopo de' Barbari and published by Antonio Kolb in 1500 pays considerable attention to gardens, especially on the Giudecca. Even as late as Coryat's time there were many garden spaces to be seen from the vantage-point of the top of the Campanile: "Also many faire gardens replenished with diversity of delicate fruites, as Oranges, Citrons, Lemmons, Apricocks, muske melons, anguriaes [gourd plants]; and what not" (184–185). The list might be describing one of Venetian artist Carlo Crivelli's signature swags of fruit. John Evelyn praises the island of San Giorgio Maggiore, not only on account of its Palladian building but because "The Cloyster has a fine Garden to it, which is a rare thing at Venice . . . and has an Olive Orchard all invirond by the Sea" (July 1645; *Diary*, 233–234).

But as Venice became more and more prosperous it became more and more built upon. Houses were built cheek by jowl, in winding lanes following invisible contours of islets and banks. The dark windings made crime easy, and walking difficult. Fairly early, urban Venice went in for a form of street lighting; a shrine to the Virgin would be placed at dark corners and turns, with a candle ever burning before it. As space was hard to find, the fields, meads, and gardens had to go, leaving only the occasional hidden garden of a palazzo, such as the researcher of *The Aspern Papers* claimed to value. The city consoled itself with the pleasure of seeing what could be done with human construction. Natural materials could be honored by being worked with human fashioning, to create the city's own delicate diversity.

Nowhere is the riot of color and textures and the wonder of human ingenuity more fully realized than in the mosaics of Venetian floors. (These can be enjoyed at a distance in Tudy Sammartini's *The Floors of Venice*, 1999.) Their designs are partly derived from the Roman era, perhaps with memories of the astounding fourth-century pavement of the basilica in Aquileia destroyed by the Huns, but Venetian mosaics incorporate Byzantine techniques, and Syrian and North African motifs. Venetians like floors that glow and shine and wave and reflect—floors that do something and don't just sit there.

The medieval floors are an ordered wilderness of small pieces of color, cunning placed against one another. Rare materials shine: pure marble and travertine, porphyry and even lapis lazuli. Nothing outdoes the craftsmanship of tiny pieces; later Venetians continued to work in mosaic but with less minute tesserae. I do, however, have a soft spot for Longhena's roses on the pavement of Salute, a rich floral tribute to the Virgin of yellow and pink blooms. Venice could supply so many lovely colors in marbles, mosaics, and glass that one would not remember to miss even the flowers.

The Venetians themselves were aware of the paradoxes within Venice's appeal, and began to exploit these in advertising to the tourists at least as early as the sixteenth century. The Foreigner ("Forestiero") in Sansovino's *Dialogo* says it is almost impossible to know how to take in such a great thing as this city, "founded in the sea . . . in this respect outside the order of all other Cities."[28] The paradoxical nature of the place is a source of pride and elaboration. As a seventeenth-century writer of a book entitled *The Marvels of the City of Venice* says, "Venice is a City altogether wonderful, because it is entirely made of marvels" (*Venetia è una Città tutta mirabile, perch'è tutta fabricata di meraviglie*):

Consider her foundation so solid in the most unstable Element. . . . Her flux and reflux without laws; but so regulated. Her air so salubrious in the midst of Mud. Her strength, encircled and protected without walls. The security of her Port in the midst of the sea. . . . The copiousness of sweet water amidst saltness. The great abundance of all things amidst the greatest sterility. The perfect quality of the Elements among their confusion, so that one could say that the Earth is situated in the air, and Fire in the water—are not all these things the greatest marvels?

The author also lists specifically manmade "Marvels"—who could not wonder at "the magnificence of so many Palaces, the munificence of so many Convents and pious Places . . . the height of so many Towers . . . the prospect of so many Façades, the amenity of so many Gardens, the beauty of so many Strands, the deliciousness of so many Islands? All these things, planted simply on Piles seem to float immobile upon the waves, and as some ingenious wit has said, the impossible is founded on the impossible."[29]

Nearly a century before, Veronica Franca had waxed eloquent on the city of her birth, saying one could write poetry praising unique Venice with perfect honesty:

Without discoursing in poetic fashion,
>   Without the use of hyperbolic figure
Which lies too much and much too openly,

It would employ and repay your care
>   In praising Venice the singular,
Marvel and wonder of all nature:

This high dominatrix of the deep sea
>   Queenly Virgin pure, inviolate,
In the world without example, without peer.[30]

It may strike us as amusing that a courtesan should make Venice both a virgin and a dominatrix, but unvirginal Veronica is thoroughly grateful that she was born there. Venice, she says, is more beautiful than Verona as Paradise is more beautiful than the world; in fact, it is already something divine: "Fabricata è Vinegia sopra l'acque,/ Per sopranatural celeste aviso" ("Venice is fabricated on the waters / By supernatural celestial plan").[31] We can see she is picking up on an idea broached in Cantarini, whose Venice strikes visitors as work of "immortal gods." Dante in the *Inferno,* just after alluding to Venice, ironically refers to "divine art" (*divin arte*)—pertaining not to the beautiful city but to Hell. He may be satirizing Venice's already established mythical take on its divine nature.

Venetians lead the way in celebrating Venice as a divine paradox of beauty. It becomes a truism that Venice is a place of "marvels," of "wonders." Almost every traveler uses such words—and those who will not are suspect, like the superficial and supercilious Mrs. General in Dickens's *Little Dorrit,* who rebukes Little Dorrit for expressing wonder at Venice (since well-bred people never wonder). The seventeenth-century art historian Carlo Ridolfi builds "marvels" (*Meraviglie*) into the title of his book on Venetian painters—we are to marvel at the wondrousness of these artists.

The marvels of the city fabricated on the water were not achieved without great effort and labor. Almost entirely a human creation, Venice is a handmade work, with some stabilizing assistance from clay, marshland, and the slimy islets hovering at the surface above the clay and wet sand. If we could see Venice at its first appearance as an entity—apart from the settlement on Malamocco—we would likely be shocked and disappointed. What would we be looking at? A collection of wattle-and-daub buildings in the midst of muddy fields. This has already been imagined by Jacopo Tintoretto in his version of the immediate aftermath of Saint Mark's vision, *Saint Mark Blessing the Islands of the Lagoon*. Saint Mark, his lion just behind him, and under a flurry of angel wings and palm branches, blesses the huts with their inhabitants, the settlement in its first avatar that will arise on the islands in the future.

Could we look more closely, from our privileged time-traveler perspective, we would see muddy streams winding between unpaved banks, and some pigs rambling about. (Saint Anthony's scavenger pigs roamed the streets of Venice until the late Middle Ages.) Then, perhaps, we would see a real architectural edifice, a stone church, probably erected on the spot that the Venetians give as the sacred site of first foundation, near the marketplace at the Rialto. San Giacomo di Rialto, supposedly founded in the fifth century, is considered the oldest of Venetian churches; Ruskin in *St. Mark's Rest* pays homage to it as the founding site, where "the first stone of Venice was laid on the sea sand, in the name of St. James the fisher."[32] As Ruskin also describes, the church was repeatedly rebuilt, and in 1322 was even "moved out of the buyers' and sellers' way." An eleventh-century inscription remains, but San Giacomo's church was finally effectually rebuilt in 1601: "Lifted up . . . to keep the water from coming into it. and the thing finally patched together," as Ruskin contemptuously says, "the *Voice* of it—Sibylline,—left when its body had died."[33] Traditionally, the laws of the Republic were proclaimed nearby. From one doubtless small Greek church and very humble habitations, Venice bloomed into the city of churches and palaces, of the stones of Venice atop the mud of Venice. Petrarch was to hail Venice as "built on solid marble but held firm by the still more solid foundation of civic harmony."[34] But there was little solid about it, and the city was in no way built on or of "solid marble."

A book that ought to exist—but does not so far—would have as its title *The Engineers' Venice*. The settlement of what we know as Venice took place over a period of time. But the Venetians went vigorously to work in one of the most astounding—and long-term—feats of engineering in human history. In the Middle Ages they built Venice, made it by hand. They ordained its foundations by sinking piles into the underlying bottom and creating a manmade foundation. Every edifice required the expensive support of an artificial "land" created beneath it. Coryat offers a brief description, giving some glimpse of the great labor involved: "Most commonly they drive long stakes into the ground, without the which they doe *aggere molem*, that is, raise certaine heapes of sand, mudde, clay, or some other such matter to repell the water. Then they ramme in great piles of woodde, which they lay very deepe, upon which they place their bricke or stone, and so frame the other parts of the building. These foundations are made so exceeding deep, and contrived with so great labour, that I have heard they cost them very neare the third part of the charge of the whole edifice" (165).

When the old Campanile of San Marco collapsed suddenly on 14 July 1902, those who came to tidy up and rebuild had a first-rate chance of seeing the medieval understructure, which probably belonged to the eleventh century. There must have been an earlier bell tower, for a hospital founded by Doge Pietro Orseolo was attached to the tower's base in 997. The "new" Campanile (the one that figures in paintings by Bellini and fell down in 1902) was completed in 1148. The area in which the church and the Campanile were built is an area of firm clay, "a greenish compact clay mixed with fine shells" which when dry "offered the resisting power of half-baked brick." Horatio Brown cites Giacomo Boni's report on the excavations (as published in *Archivio Veneto*) in giving his own detailed summary of the findings:

The builders of the Campanile proceeded as follows. Into this bed of compact clay they first drove piles of about 9½ in. in diameter with a view to still further consolidating, by pressure, the area selected. That area only extends 1.25 metres, or about 4 ft. beyond the spring of the brickwork shaft of the tower. How deep these piles reach Boni's report does not state. The piles, at the point where he laid the foundations bare, were found to be of white poplar, in remarkably sound condition, retaining their colour, and presenting a closely twisted fibre. The clay in which they were embedded has preserved them almost intact. The piles extended for one row only beyond the superimposed structure. On the top of these piles the builders laid a platform consisting of two layers of oak beams, crosswise. The lower layer runs in the line of the Piazza, east to west, the upper in the line of the Piazzetta, north to south. Each beam is square and a little over 4 in. thick. This oak platform appears to be in bad condition; the timbers are blackened and friable. While the excavation was in progress, seawater burst through the interstices, which had to be plugged.

Upon this platform was laid the foundation proper. This consisted of seven courses of stone of various sizes and of various kinds—sandstone of two qualities, limestone from Istria and Verona, probably taken from older buildings on the mainland, certainly not fresh-hewn from the quarry. The seventh or lowest course was the deepest, and was the only one which escarped, and that but slightly; the remaining six courses were intended to be perpendicular. These courses varied widely from each other in thickness. . . . They were composed of different and ill-assorted stone, and were held together in places by shallow-biting clamps of iron, and by a mortar of white Istrian lime, which, not being hydraulic, and having little affinity for sand, had become disintegrated. Com[mentadore] Boni calls attention to the careless structure of this foundation proper, and maintains that it was designed to carry a tower of about two-thirds of the actual height imposed upon it, but not more. (*In and Around Venice*, 49–51)[35]

Despite the criticisms of the oak beams which had suffered from seawater and the inefficacy of the mortar, the foundation had been sufficiently well prepared to sustain a tower of three hundred and twenty-two feet (98.60 meters), weighing about eighteen thousand tons. And the foundation did not merely support the structure for a year or two, or several decades, or even a century—but for over seven hundred years. The campanile had experienced a lightning strike in 1383; more serious strokes in 1745 and 1761; several fires (1405, 1426, 1489, 1574); and several earthquakes, of which the most shaking occurred in 1511. Repairs and rebuilding undertaken after that quake may have weakened the tower over the long term, though blame was also cast on recent changes made by the custodian to the basement; he had created a chimney and a cupboard, weakening the pilasters. Ongoing restorations almost certainly precipitated the crisis in the summer of 1902. Yet one is more inclined to wonder at the formidable prowess of the twelfth-century engineers, who could not only build such a tall and weighty tower but also create the foundation for it. A tower that has stood for over seven hundred years (and has had people going up and down all the time) must be accounted a success.

The building of Venice, house by house, church by church, was a laborious process. Commonly a section of a muddy swampy area had to be pumped out—without benefit of electricity or any heavy earthmoving equipment. A wall would be built around the section, like a hollow cube. The Venice-builders sought the bottom of clay. Once drained, the section would be filled in, with piles and with heavy beams of oak and larch, on top of which would be placed the *zattaron*, a kind of raft made of two layers of hardwood planks cemented with stone and brick. The piles of oak, elm, or larch—all necessarily imported—were driven by hand into the clay bed streaked with peat that, as Horatio Brown says, "rests upon a bed of shifting, watery sand." It is important in driving the piles not to puncture the clay bed, but to get the pile deep into the clay, though the clay itself, as it were, floats. As Brown remarks, "the city is borne on a more or less elastic subsoil, and the resistance to the pressure of the buildings is a hydraulic resistance obtained from the watery quicksand below the clay. The heavier the weight the stronger the counter up-thrust" (125–126). The city is a play of forces—all ultimately depending on water in some shape—in some of its many shapes. All buildings are based on the *zattaron*. That term refers to something that floats. Water gives permission for the floating city to exist, though the city can deceive us with the wonders of brick and stone erected atop the hydraulic arrangement.

On top of the *zattaron*, stones could be placed and the stone foundations of houses, and the great churches, as well as paving stones for streets and squares. Not all of this was permanent, and archaeology occasionally is allowed to discover how multilayered Venice is. The Malibran theater is built over what is thought to be the ruin of Marco Polo's house, and Polo's house was put in above buildings going back perhaps to the sixth century. As we have seen in Ruskin's account, the church of San Giacomo was deliberately raised to a new level in the seventeenth century—and not all of us can share Ruskin's ire at the Venetians' trying to save their building, though we may regret their refashioning it in a later style. Other cities are built up on layers, but here everything ultimately rides upon a *zattaron*, a raft. The name "Zattere" was given to one long quay, the backside of the Dorsoduro, because it was there that workmen unloaded the timbers that had floated in rafts down the rivers, timbers expressly to be used in building Venice's edifices and ships. At one time the area would have been well furnished with boat-repairing or gondola-building yards, *squeri*; these still exist in Venice, but they are getting harder to find where once they were common in Castello and Dorsoduro. There is but one true *squero* left for the making of *gondole*, at San Trovaso, on Dorsoduro between the Accademia and the Zattere, but there are several yards for boat repair.

Venice, always repairing herself, might be thought of as a giant *squero*, and as a floater on her own pontoon raft. Venice makes—and *likes*—things that float. As you stand on the vaporetto landing-stage, waiting for the bus, you find that you are rocking up and down on a raft on the water—a sensation that can make some visitors feel vaguely seasick. Venice itself is all a bit like that, a delusive solid that is afloat. Venetians have long referred to the mainland as "Terraferma" (or in Latin *terra firma*). When you are in Venice you are not on Terraferma but on a manmade set of linked islands, like a series of rafts. Each edifice rises on its set of platforms. The islands are divided by canals and smaller canals or rios (*rii*), which allow the water to pass. The chief waterway, a sea road, is the Grand Canale, an elegant sinuous "S" (as prescribed in Hogarth's "Line of Beauty"). Orderliness of a straight kind, as is found in the grid pattern layout of Hellenistic cities in Asia Minor, or in the Roman four-square pattern of north-south road crossing east-west road, was never going to be possible in Venice, save in Chioggia. The city's designers had always to adapt to the sinuous patterns necessitated by the dottings of islands and the windings of water. Successful construction and adaptation resulted by the late Middle Ages in the well-known Venice of the maps, the always recognizable lute-shaped pattern of bodies in water.

The entity that we call "Venice," even when forming into recognizable shape, was always growing, adapting, changing—or, more prosaically, being pumped out, filled in, and built up. From the early Middle Ages to the Renaissance, Venice must have been full of the sound of saws, hammers, mallets. Rivers were crowded with logs to supply the precious necessary wood. At times, the laguna, almost choked with rafts of floating logs, would be more like our picture of the nineteenth-century Mississippi than gilded Venetia. The air must sometimes have been thick with sawdust. The whole enterprise would have made a good deal of noise. In March 1999 I was at first vexed when my room at the Gritti Palace was insulted well before dawn by a coughing and ungenteel motor-launch, but when I peered out I saw a working launch, freighted with materials to go into the building of the new Fenice, the theater first erected in 1792 (and burned down and rebuilt in 1836), which had burned down in 1996 in a mysteriously spectacular and thorough fire. It struck me then that this was as "Venetian" an experience as anything else; I was momentarily a spectator at Venice's constant energetic self-creation—and re-creation. The wrangling, brangling, and delay associated with reconstructing the opera house are also Venetian.

The pause in rebuilding La Fenice was not as protracted as, for instance, the delay formerly attendant upon the building of a new library in Venice. After receiving a major bequest of Byzantine materials from Cardinal Bessarion, the exiled Greek who trusted Venice to preserve Byzantine Hellenic culture after the disastrous fall of Byzantium in 1453, the Venetians started to talk about the great library they were going to build to house the collection and honor themselves. They wasted forty years discussing what kind of edifice they should build and who should be entrusted with the design, while the poor cardinal's precious Greek manuscripts lay about in one hundred boxes. Finally, the Florentine architect and sculptor Jacopo Sansovino (né Tatti) was commissioned to design the building often called the Libreria Sansoviniana, though it is—and should be—the Biblioteca Marciana. (As I have noted, that beautiful building has the disadvantage of being considered "too good" for the scholars who want to use it.) At the beginning of the twenty-first century, the Fenice, arisen from its ashes, has proven itself a true "Phoenix." (The Greek word refers to the legendary immortal bird, but also means "Phoenician.")

The Venetians are resigned to re-creation, because everything above ground needs to be shored up or readjusted in relation to water. That is not a one-time job. The laguna has to be dredged constantly, good old mud and weed thoughtfully and systematically scraped up and moved around to make the channels sufficiently deep not only for traffic but for healthy flow. The Lagoon is marked for purposes of seamanship and dredging—there is a novel called *No Signposts in the Sea,* but here the sea or at least the laguna is signposted everywhere, with buoys, and bollards called *bricole,* each consisting of three stout tree trunks fastened together. (Usually a *bricola* is seen with a thoughtful seagull on the top.) When you take your elegant motor launch from the airport and zoom to the city of marvels, you are likely to pass by dredgers at their serious work. The adventure of living with and in the sea in the Venetian manner calls for constant energy and labor—and intelligence, for energy wrongly directed could be disastrous. No wonder the Mose Project for blocking the waters inspires constant doubt and anxiety. The Venetians still live as seabirds.

This city, ingenious and intelligent human creation, is a monument to mankind's engineering skills and persistence—and ultimately, a monument to hope in the future. Manmade, constructed of imported materials, it does not sit in its own landscape as other cities do. It is a "cyber" place in way that Rome, Paris, London, New York, and so on, simply are not. Not only are its buildings and monuments human fabrications, but the very "solid ground" on which you stand is a human creation, an artifact, an ingenious bricolage cobbled together by dint of intellect from water, mud, clay, wood, and stones. Its ingenuity is part of its permanent appeal, but the Venetians made their strange city more than a refuge and a shelter—they made it a place of beauty.

*I*t is amazing that the Venetians, who had to build their city's space yard by yard and year by year, not all at once but over centuries, could create such a beautiful and elegant overall form. They never, as it were, "lost the plot." Never opposing the sea unreasonably, they continuously wrought pieces of land that would always fit in with the whole. That lute-shape is almost a miracle in itself, a result of that valuable and rare thing, human

vision and cooperation extended over time. Even without its splendid buildings, Venice is a triumph of design.

But of course there are the buildings. From being a place to survive in, a
new-found or new-made land, Venice became a place to glory in. The Venetians learned how to make land solid enough to support large edifices. Yet
these structures are often lighter than they appear, for they are not, like
Northern European castles and churches, heavy entities of solid stone. The
Venetians, who had no such thing to work with, wrought with basic brick
(local, usually cooked from the earth of Mestre) with a face of marble. They
are duplex and "duplicitous" in a special sense, as Ruskin points out: "The
substance is of two kinds, one internal, the other external, and the system of
decoration is founded on this duplicity, as pre-eminently in St. Mark's"
(*Stones*, II, 76). Ruskin hastens to add, "I have used the word duplicity in no
depreciatory sense." What he calls "the incrusted school" is one of the leading types of architecture, and, he insists, it is not insincere:

A northern builder . . . as soon as he gets acquainted with the incrusted style . . .
will find that the Southern builders had no intention to deceive him. He will see
that every slab of facial marble is fastened to the next by a confessed *rivet*, and that
the joints of the armour are so visibly and openly accommodated to the contours of
the substance within that he has no more right to complain of treachery than a
savage would have, who, for the first time in his life seeing a man in armour, had
supposed him to be made of solid steel. (II, 76-77)

What is "a nation of builders" to do, when any stone that they use must be
imported "from great distances"? If the expense is the same whether the
freight be common stone or marble, the builders will wish "to make each
shipload as valuable as possible." Either the pieces of marble must be lodged
"among his masses of brick" or it will be decided "to cut the coloured stones
into thin pieces . . . to face the whole surface of the walls" (77). Ruskin sees
the achievement of the Venetians as the perfect achievement—and perfect
understanding—of surfaces. Surfaces become depths, in more than one
sense, for the superficial, that is the superficies, can be—or can become—
divine.

The mosaic pictorial art is an art of making surfaces into depths. In the
cathedrals on Torcello and Murano the Venetians seem to have been able to
employ some of the best Byzantine mosaicists; their earliest efforts predate
the art of San Marco. Santa Maria dell'Assunta on Torcello, the cathedral
founded in 639, rebuilt in 1008, has an outstanding wall mosaic of the Last

Judgment (eleventh-twelfth century, restored). On Murano, the Basilica of Santa Maria e San Donato, founded in the seventh century, rebuilt in the eleventh century, very much in the Byzantine style, has a floor of twelfth-century mosaics. These beautiful figures have been aggressively "restored" in recent times, with the unfortunate result that they look tight and hard as if under a heavy varnish. (They looked more natural and beautiful in their slightly more damaged state in 1961.) There is still an appeal in its emblematic peacocks and griffins. Ruskin commented that the mosaics in the floor of Saint Mark's were more skillfully executed but less variegated, while "at Murano every fragment is itself variegated . . . showing thus early . . . the beginning of that mighty spirit of Venetian colour, which was to be consummated in Titian" (II, 52). The Murano mosaics of 1140 are certainly a sign that the Venetians were thinking about color well before they created palazzi like Ca' d'Oro.

Ruskin approves of the Venetians' decision to cut their marble into facing for their buildings, (and thus, as it were, to create a large mosaic surface). He shares their delight in the effect of the marble surfaces' multiple hues and soft reflecting lights. Ruskin quotes an opponent, one Mr. Wood (cited in *Seven Lamps of Architecture*), who had derided Saint Mark's, proclaiming "that the chief thing remarkable in this church 'is its extreme ugliness.'" The fact that Mr. Wood preferred the works of the post-Renaissance Caracci gives the game away, Ruskin retorts. This critic

had not any perception of colour, or delight in it. The perception of colour is a gift . . . and a deaf man might as well pretend to pronounce judgment on the merits of a full orchestra, as an architect trained in the composition of form only, to discern the beauty of St. Mark's. It possesses the charm of colour in common with the greater part of the architecture, as well as of the manufactures, of the East; but the Venetians deserve especial note as the only European people who appear to have sympathized to the full with the great instinct of the Eastern races. (II, 79)

Visitors long before Ruskin had not exactly failed to comment upon the "Oriental" nature of Saint Mark's, even its resemblance to a mosque. This similarity was observed with disfavor. Mme. de Staël's Corinne, no enthusiast for Venice, thought that Saint Mark's Square "gives one an idea of the indolent life of the Orientals," while the exterior of Saint Mark's "rather resembles a mosque than a Christian temple."[36] Some visitors actively disliked the edifice. Twain in *A Tramp Abroad* (1880) memorably descants on its "strong fascination" chiefly "because it is so ugly": "its details are masterfully ugly, no misplaced and impertinent beauties are intruded anywhere; and the consequent result is a grand harmonious whole, of soothing, entrancing, tranquilizing, soul-satisfying ugliness. . . . St. Mark is perfect. To me it soon grew to be so nobly, so augustly ugly, that it was difficult to stay away from it. . . . Propped on its long row of low thick-leggèd columns, its back knobbed with domes, it seemed like a vast warty bug taking a meditative walk."[37] Twain would seem to agree with Ruskin's opponent Mr. Wood—but at least Twain's complex negative description presents the building as oddly animated, having the appeal of a natural creature. Another American sightseer, James Fenimore Cooper, had already described "the quaint and venerable cathedral of San Marco" as a flatly hideous archaic affair: "Its Saracenic architecture, the rows of precious but useless little columns that load its front, the low Asiatic domes which rest upon its walls in the repose of a thousand years, the rude and gaudy mosaics, and above all, the captured horses of Corinth, which start from out the sombre mass in the glory of Grecian art."[38] For Cooper, writing in the 1830s, the only redeeming touch in the rude edifice lies in the captured Greek horses; the rest is "Asiatic," sinister and meaningless, its only value a sour and rude antiquity. Cooper is not fascinated (as Twain partly is) but righteously repulsed by this offense against the canons of architecture. We sometimes forget how much there was for Ruskin to put right, how difficult it was to persuade people to like "thick leggèd columns" or "gaudy mosaics," let alone "Saracenic architecture."

Ruskin is the first serious writer to acknowledge at length and with admiration the full power of the Eastern (Muslim) world in its influence on the architecture of Venice. The city's basic principles are those of "the Eastern races," which he prefers, almost defiantly, or so it seems, to Western principles, declaring his own personal allegiance to color and to the radiant duplicity of the Venetian "incrustation." Ruskin also recognizes that practical consideration of the weight of the building influenced the Venetians' decision only to face their edifices with valuable stones, lightening the load the ground is asked to carry. They knew that the foundation of all was not and could never be "solid ground."

Venetian architects had every encouragement from circumstance to pierce their surfaces, to allow as many windows and openings as they could get away with, further to lighten the load. But the formal examples they drew upon in creating the distinctive "Venetian" arch are the pointed windows and archways of Damascus and other Eastern cities. Use of colored marble columns dates from Greek and Roman antiquity, and many leftovers of ruined antique buildings were recycled in mosques and churches in the Near East and Eastern Mediterranean. The mosque at Kerouan in Tunisia has a courtyard, a forest of beautiful marble shafts, and, like San Marco, incorporates the most delicately polished marble columns. As Ruskin says, the shaft of jasper or porphyry is "a form of treasure," and he quotes Francesco Sansovino on a green column in San Giacomo dell'Orio, of which the Renaissance guidebook writer said it is rather jewel than stone (*Stones,* II, 82). D'Annunzio picks up the admiration for the same green column: "It is like the fossilized condensation of a great green forest."[39]

One of the earliest influences on Venice's architecture must have been the Fatimid architecture of Cairo. Abbasid grandeur and motifs also played a part. Deborah Howard in her learned and detailed study *Venice and the East* discusses the versatile designs of medieval Venetian *palazzi* in relation to the merchants' recollections of the Orient. "The intention behind the introduction of the ogee arch and its adoption as a trademark by the Venetian merchant class was to allude to a mental image of the Orient. . . . From soon after the *translatio* of Saint Mark's body in AD 829, Venetian merchants would have associated pointed arches with their experiences in Eastern emporia, long before the Gothic appeared in northern Europe in any form."[40] Howard suggests that portable objects such as Fatimid wood carvings or elaborately bound books were brought home by merchants and shown to local workmen, inspiring the pleasing production of related designs in a very different medium. "The urban merchants' houses from the great emporia of the East are more likely to have inspired Venetian palaces than rural houses a thousand years old on the Italian Terrafirma."

But memory, as Howard points out, is selective. What the Venetian merchants were creating on their manmade islands of mud was a construction of memory and a desire, in an amalgam of elements: "I shall try to suggest that the imagery of Venetian medieval palace architecture gave substance not only to historical memory, but also to a shared *geographical* imagination. Each reminiscence of a returning traveler may have dictated individual choices, but the ensuing process of recognition and emulation among the mercantile elite fed these alien elements into Venetian visual culture and into the city's social memory."[41] The wondrous medieval architecture of Venice is thus excitingly *impure.* It is a mixture of Eastern and Western elements fused in a matrix of memory and geographical imagination. Venetian architecture is not (until the advent of Palladio with his anxious classicism) a copy of anything else already in the world. These palazzi were *always* fantastic creations—with their facades and luxurious trimming, fantastic swirls and chains of dentellation. Their lacy arches and striped voussoirs were neither purely Oriental nor purely Western, but new productions, as befitted a city whose design was in the mind of God.

Venetian architecture is luxurious, and in a sense lawless. If one of the tropes of Venice is "the East," an even more compelling trope is the imaginary—the fantastic. The visual impact of Venice shockingly registers the importance of imagination. These structures are productions not of the earth itself, nor of the rules of reason, nor of the classical tradition, but of the associating mind. They reflect and embody the visions of a thousand minds. The watery marbled city excites the senses and the intelligence with a vivid impression of the mind's reflective and creative power. Venice can repel others with its illicit quality, its refusal of the steadfast rules of order, and even of repose.

One of the strongest tropes of Venice is *artifice*. It is impossible to look at Venice without seeing what is man-made, invented and recombinant. It is totally impossible to speak of Venice without speaking of artifice—and impossible for most of us not to speak highly of it. John Ruskin above all values the kind of artifice that Venice is. Ruskin's great description of Saint Mark's is irresistible:

a multitude of pillars and white domes, clustered into a long low pyramid of coloured light; a treasure-heap, it seems, partly of gold, and partly of opal and mother-of-pearl, hollowed beneath into five great vaulted porches, ceiled with fair mosaic, and beset with sculpture of alabaster, clear as amber and delicate as ivory—sculpture fantastic and involved, of palm leaves and lilies, and grapes and pomegranates, and birds clinging and fluttering among the branches, all twined together into an endless network of buds and plumes; and in the midst of it, the solemn forms of angels . . . their figures indistinct among the gleaming of the golden ground through the leaves beside them, interrupted and dim, like the morning light as it faded back among the branches of Eden, when first its gates were angel-guarded long ago. And round the walls of the porches there are set pillars of variegated stones, jasper and porphyry, and deep green serpentine spotted with flakes of snow . . . and above them, in the broad archivolts, a continuous chain of language and of life—angels, and the signs of heaven, and the labours of men . . . and above these, another range of glittering pinnacles, mixed with white arches edged with scarlet flowers,—a confusion of delight, amidst which the breasts of the Greek horses are seen blazing in their breadth of golden strength, and the St. Mark's lion, lifted on a blue field covered with stars, until at last, as if in ecstasy, the crests of the arches break into a marble foam, and toss themselves far into the blue sky in flashes and wreaths of sculptured spray, as if the breakers on the Lido shore had been frost-bound before they fell, and the sea-nymphs had inlaid them with coral and amethyst. (*Stones*, II, 67–68)

Ruskin loves the artificial things, the inorganic beauties; he sees no lasting opposition between the stony motionless and the motion-ful, or between the inorganic and organic. His one long sentence here is a paean to the unity-in-diversity of the exciting structure which refuses to form itself on classical canons. Just so, Ruskin's sentence defies alike both normal English sentence-shape and Ciceronian structure. (Proust learned English so as to be able to read Ruskin in the original, and one can see why, and believe it was worth the trouble.)

Ruskin's praise is a rhythmic chant of the glorious intermixing of natural life rhythms (snow, sea tides and spray, morning light) with the hard "trea-sure-heap." References to tides and sea spray are more than mere ornaments in the Venetian context, for everything Venetian is related to the sea, and reflects upon it. Ruskin can compare one hard inorganic object, alabaster, to others, both softer and both organic: amber, ivory mother-of-pearl—not present in the church, but serving dramatically to mix textures and effects in a description representing a building in which the elements are greatly mixed. Translucence and iridescence come to the fore. The entire iridescent sentence is built on changefulness, metamorphosis. Firm, hard, lasting objects find their affinity in what is mobile and transitory, as in the wondrous image of the frozen spray. The Venice to which Ruskin responds has produced a work of strangest art, of the transitory made permanent—or more truly perhaps, its effect lies in the permanent being rendered as if always beautifully transitory. Color never leaves for an instant this "confusion of delight." Nor does attention to the beautiful ever need to separate itself from interest in the surface.

Saint Mark's inside and out is glorified with colorful things, and with surfaces that turn into depths and depths that turn into surfaces. The edifice is meant to dumbfound the viewer with delight in color, including the flash of gilding. Within, the gold tesserae create an effect as of liquid honey that offers an idea of deep glory but leaves the eye unsatisfied. The eye wanders to the many-colored mosaics, pictured representations in intricate detail. The stir and glitter of the mosaics make the pictures changeable and demanding. Some of the tessarae are glass, introducing a lucent sparkle, and each stone or glass square borrows color from its neighbor. Paul Hills, in *Venetian Colours* (the best book on Venice since *The Stones of Venice*), examines the art of the mosaicists in relation to the changing theories of color from the thirteenth to the sixteenth century.[42] All mosaicists knew that the hue and effect of a little square of stone can be greatly affected by juxtaposed colors. Making shapes out of color—and color out of juxtaposed shapes—is a particularly Venetian occupation.

One of my own special favorites of the illustration in the great church, though less for aesthetic reasons than others, is the figure of Santa Tecla or Thekla in the right transept in the spandrels of the Dome of St. Leonard, along with Santa Dorotea. Thekla is splendid feminist saint. The story is that she was a native of Konya (in what is now central Turkey) who was converted by Saint Paul, ditched her fiancé, and went off with Paul as a missionary. When a local ruler made advances to her she snubbed him and was condemned to death—but was miraculously delivered. Spared by the land beasts, and then thrown into a tank of carnivorous sea creatures, Thekla baptized herself (with God's help) in the waters of the tank. She needed no priestly intermediary. She kept on going on her own. Thekla the tough is an Eastern saint, still recognized in Asia Minor. Although Thekla's story has not made a lasting impact in the West, she seems to have had an appeal in the Veneto, and Titian painted her picture in Este. It is nice to see her in San Marco.

The Venetians did not reserve their sense of beauty nor their rich "incrustation" for their construction of churches alone. The Palazzo Ducale or Doge's Palace is a sublime example of encrustation, with its façade of red and white marble in lozenge design. The red marble of Verona, faded over the centuries, is now a kind of bittersweet orange in some lights, rose-pink in others; the effect would have been bolder in earlier centuries. Almost everyone concurs with Ruskin—though not everyone dislikes the Renaissance so much—in being glad that after the fire of 1577, which destroyed much of the Doge's Palace, the Republic did not take up the offer of Palladio to design a completely new Ducal Palace in the modern neoclassical style. The Paduan Andrea di Pietro della Gondola (1508–1580) assumed the name of Palladio (after Pallas Athena) given him by an important patron of Vicenza who introduced him to Vitruvius and the principles of classical architecture. The self-styled "Palladio," who became a one-man academy for the revival of Roman architecture, never quite got his own way with Venice, though he did build San Giorgio Maggiore, the façade of San Francesco della Vigna, Redentore, and Santa Lucia. His commissions within the city were all from religious bodies—none were secular or civil. When it came to the Doge's Palace, the Venetians stubbornly rebuilt in the old style, so one of the most lively and amazing productions of the Gothic age was preserved in stripey red and white.

Venice everywhere sought the effect of mixed and multiple colors, and mixed and multiple substances. In the Quattrocento the Venetians had invented their own particular type of flooring, or *terrazzo,* made of chips of colored marble mixed in with an amalgamation of lime and ground brick or ground stone. Paul Hills calls this "marmoreal Russian salad,"[43] but *terrazzo* always reminds me of the English galantine we call "brawn." It is also strangely reminiscent of a Carthaginian style; as the excavated houses of Carthage reveal, the inhabitants covered their kitchen floors with pink marble chips. Terrazzo had the advantage of being capable of hardening and polishing; the floors that resulted met all practical needs, including the Venetian need for cleanliness. Making terrazzo became a special Venetian craft with its own guild. It is this style of multi-colored flooring with a variegated texture that gave Casanova such a deal of trouble when he was trying to make a hole in the floor of his cell in the Palazzo Ducale.

A private house, Ca' d'Oro or the House of Gold, constructed in the fifteenth century, followed the style of the Palazzo Ducale in using checkerdesigns in red Verona marble. Marino Contarini, wealthy member of a patrician family, had this peculiarly delightful palace built to his own design. He instructed that the red be as red as possible; he also wanted the carved tracery to be picked out in white against a black background, so as to show up. Contarini was evidently fond of emphasizing not only color but also color contrasts. The original palace would have been even more picturesque and striking than the beautiful edifice we see; the balls on the top of the ornamental crenellation were gilded, so a genuine "House of Gold" was set by the Grand Canal. The front of Ca' d'Oro, unlike the Palazzo Ducale, is completely reflected in the waters, forever breaking up and reforming, creating new patterns in the changeful ripples. The façade of encrustation gains an extra reality and unreality in the insubstantial water, which seems, after all, only to reflect the dreamlike insubstantiality of the glamorous structure. But this is generally the effect of the Grand Canal on the grand palazzi at its edge, though no other palatial mansion may be quite as beautiful as Ca' d'Oro. And the buildings flaunt their encrustation, and what I have called "Venetian appliqué," which is the application of an external ornament to a surface that is itself an ornament applied externally to another surface.

The play of surfaces is a strong trope of Venice, strong and disconcerting, for it seems to put to the question everything that we mean by "stability" and "sincerity." The stone is just cladding, the crenellations are mock-fortifications for buildings that were never fortified. Ornament resurfaces the surfaces, creating a dream of the East and West mingled. Surfaces advance and recede. Far from wishing to appear solid, far even from trying to deceive the viewer with the intimation of solidity, the buildings most characteristic of Venice yearn to appear light. They seem to endeavor—but that is too strenuous a word—to achieve a harmonious volatility, and a kind of transparency. Their gleaming delicacy resembles that of an iridescent bubble, always about to burst but never letting go. This nacreous metamorphosis, this threat of dissolving, offers a challenge to the viewer's sensibility. No wonder it has become mingled with the uneasy sense of Venice as an ever-vanishing city.

7

Venetian Painting
Design and Color

In this city the eye acquires an autonomy like that of a teardrop. The only difference is that it does not detach from the body, but subordinates it wholly. After a while—the third or fourth day after arrival—the body begins to consider itself simply as a vehicle for the eye, almost like a submarine in regard to its periscope, which now dilates and now contracts.

—Joseph Brodsky, *Fondamenta degli Incurabili*

The nobility of colour . . .

—John Ruskin, *The Stones of Venice*

*I*t is always the business of Venice to catch and please the eye. The art which above all appeals to the reason through the eye is one of the city's (and the region's) great achievements. No description of Venice, of whatever kind, can ignore the brilliance of its art, and its distinctive paintings, which inspire a certain fascination—even something like loyalty. Venetian art is now dispersed over the world, yet in Venice itself great riches remain, though you must travel to various churches and *scuole* and of course to the Palazzo Ducale to see them. But there is one great center of instruction and wonderment, the Galleria dell'Accademia on the Dorsoduro. The Accademia contains—or coagulates—the major collection of Venetian art in the world, and no visit to Venice is complete without a journey thither.

The Accademia Gallery is not purpose built. It has been made by knocking together the church of Santa Maria della Carità and the Scuola della Carità. Visitors are likely to imagine this a recent and ultramodern arrangement. It is not. The takeover was one of the early fruits of the occupation, and belongs to the Napoleonic ideas of civilization. The Scuola della Carità—with the other *scuole*—was shut down in 1806, and it was at once firmly put to another use—perhaps because it was considered a potential power base. In 1807, at Napoleon's command, the buildings, along with the church, were taken over to make a picture gallery. The resulting complex is likely to strike the modern gallery-goer as less than perfect. There is a shortage of the kind of amenities this spoiled contemporary museum visitor has by now been led to expect as his or her due: few postcards, no café, only one set of toilets mysteriously hidden away (which you can find if you are lucky *nell' mezzo del camin*). Individual rooms are narrow and can easily become crowded. The coatroom arrangements are primitive beyond belief; when I was there on a rainy day in October 2005 you were required (rightly) to park a backpack or large umbrella, but equally firmly required to take your small umbrella about with you, even if this object were (and mine was) well-used and dripping. So you trail damply about the gallery taking this wet rat along, and everyone else does the same, not only adding to the unpleasantness of proximity but also contributing excess humidity to the whole building. One trembles to think how many droplets of dirty water are added to the atmosphere surrounding some of the greatest paintings in the world. Yet you are likely to forgive all this, even to feel that few places are as significant or satisfactory as the Accademia, because of its contents.

The first room has a handsome fifteenth-century wooden ceiling (it was the former chapter house) and some examples of fourteenth-century art, which the viewer is likely to get through as rapidly as possible, in search of the great works, which are shortly going to burst upon him or her in the second room and beyond. Ah! the Bellinis, the Carpaccios . . .

Byzantine style was of major importance to Venetian art. The Byzantine influence can be seen in, for instance, the works of Carlo Crivelli (c. 1430–1493), with their solitary erect holy figures against a rich background of gold. Crivelli did not, however, live an entirely holy life; in 1457 he was imprisoned for adultery (which would mean stealing someone else's wife); he has something in common with Casanova. After that, he left the city for good, but signed his pictures "Carlo Crivelli of Venice." Florentine art as well as Byzantine has something to do with the development of painting in Venice. Jacopo Bellini (1400–1471) studied with Gentile da Fabriano, an important artist of the Florentine school. Jacopo was an innovator soon to be outshone by his sons Gentile (1429–1507) and Giovanni (1435–1516). Gentile da Fabriano came to Venice in 1409, commissioned to decorate with frescoes the Sala del Maggior Consiglio, the Great Council Hall of the Palazzo Ducale. (None of this work has survived, as the great fire of 1574 destroyed the Sala del Maggior Consiglio and all its magnificent paintings.) Gentile da Fabriano apparently gave the Venetians an idea of how to go about history paintings in important places. Jacopo Bellini, his pupil, may have visited Florence; his elder painter-son Gentile Bellini was evidently named after da Fabriano, and specialized in history painting. One of Florence's leading artists, Andrea Mantegna, working in the Veneto in the 1460s, became brother-in-law of Giovanni; their connection represents a nodal point in the history of Italian art.

Gentile Bellini is an important painter in his own right. But Giovanni—or (in Venetian) Zuan—Bellini (or "Zambellini" or "Zambellin'"), it is generally agreed, represents the start of the great tradition of Venetian art. This is slightly unfair; there are good painters earlier, and many conventional accounts of Venetian art have ignored the nobility and beauty of the remaining Byzantine works to be found in Venezia. The twelfth-century mosaic of the Madonna in the central apse of the Cathedral of Santa Maria dell'Assunta on Torcello is one of the loveliest things you will see in Venice.

The brothers Bellini come fairly late, well after painting had developed more fully in some other areas of Italy. The end of what we call the fourteenth century (and Italians the Trecento) and the beginning of the fifteenth century (the Quattrocento) brought new stimuli to Venetian artistic production of the painterly kind. For one thing, the power of Venice led to the creation of important new public spaces requiring decoration. At first, the Council members turned to outsiders, but were glad to be able to employ their own. In adorning the restored Palazzo Ducale at the end of the sixteenth century they could call upon incomparable native talents—Veronese and Tintoretto among them.

The Church had long been a chief patron of the arts; now the government followed. A new element was added in Venice with the development of the *scuole* or confraternities. The word *scuola* means "school," not in the sense of an educational building but in the sense of a group, a collection of people got together for a common purpose. The foundational purposes were religious; people gathered to do penance, to honor a particular patron saint, and to carry out charitable acts, such as visiting the sick and burying the dead. As the *scuole* grew older they grew richer through endowments, and offered the advantage to their poorer members of medical care and dowries for daughters. The *Scuole Grandi* grew from flagellant penitential communities to important and recognized institutions. The *Serrata* of 1297 had separated the

Venetians into sharply defined sociopolitical groups. The development of the *scuole* enabled these groups to unite. Patricia Fortini Brown in *Venetian Narrative Painting in the Age of Carpaccio* emphasizes the political importance of these institutions. "It was here in the lay confraternities that *cittadini, popolari* and even *stranieri* were given the opportunity to hold office and to engage in politics of a sort. The privilege was especially significant in the case of the Scuole Grandi. During the course of the fifteenth century, the *cittadini originari* were established exclusively as their ruling elites by government edict. This move was later presented by Contarini as a wise concession on the part of the nobility, calculated to reduce the temptation of sedition by the disenfranchised."[1] The *scuole* provided a forum for the coming together of people of different groups, from the humble to the extremely wealthy: "Although membership was confined to males, each Scuola Grande drew from the whole city and, in addition to patricians, encompassed every occupation and trade."[2]

The *scuole* represented an opportunity for encouragement and channeling of the collective creativity and energy of the nonpatrician Venetians. As important institutions, guarding the holiness and welfare of the whole city, the honored *scuole* built themselves large buildings, which needed appropriate ornament—leading to the patronage of individual artists of genius. The state itself had led the way, with its expanding need to employ artists of importance to adorn its important edifices. And for the *scuole*, Venice desired artists of its own breeding. And they developed their urgent, immediate public style, what Patricia Fortini Brown refers to as an "eyewitness style."[3]

If you look carefully at the work of Giovanni Bellini, you can see that he is strongly affected by the Byzantine tradition, just as much as by Florence. His paintings of Madonna and Child bear a certain relation to icons. But they are not icons, nor are they mosaics. The painters of Venice before Bellini's time worked most often in tempera, and Bellini is generally considered the first Venetian artist to have used oil fairly constantly, though tempera was still employed. Carlo Ridolfi, the seventeenth-century art historian, relates an amusing anecdote: attracted by the new form of painting practiced by one Antonello, producing "a certain concord and shading of colors not practicable in tempera," Bellini visited Antonello in disguise: "under the title of a gentleman, with the fiction that he wanted his portrait painted, and as he was dressed in the Venetian toga he easily succeeded, so that the deceived man without any other thought put his hand to work, and Giovanni, observing that from time to time he dipped his brush in linseed oil, learned the technique from his observation."[4] What a story to tell of the saintly Zambellin,

painter of Madonnas! Ridolfi wants to tell us this Venetian story; it seems
that Venetians must not be given things but should obtain them by their
wits.

Oil, introduced actually through the Flemish artists, offered a refreshingly
different medium in which to work, allowing the painter more time, more
changes, more layering of colors. The medium was significantly suited to
Venice, and the art works had a greater chance of survival. A sea power will
have plenty of canvas, and Venice had access to oil. Frescoes were tried, but
Venice's salt air has always been murder on frescoes.

Giovanni Bellini's Madonna and Child paintings are, like the icons, devotional works; it is thought many were purchased for private homes and private devotions. The Christ Child is shown most often with the genitals
revealed, a sign of Christ's full humanity. The Virgin's pose is somewhat sad,
haunted by the future, though she always appears strong also. Sometimes
there is complete joy, as in the *Madonna dei cherubini rossi*, in which the rosy red
heads of cherubim surround the holy pair in a jubilant semicircle. Each bodi-
less head coasts on a little puff of cloud, and the pink *cherubini* seem to express the tender and ardent feelings of the mother, feelings inexpressible, as
she gazes at her (rather heavy in this instance) infant. But the strongest Bellini paintings have something sad in them, or at least a tension, an irony.
Bellini is attracted to the feminine subject; his women are beautiful (round-
ish faces, wide-spaced eyes), but there is more to them than sweetness. And
he may do the most surprising things without fanfare, as in his *Annunciation*
in the Accademia, where the light blue robe of the saluting angel breaks into
nonnaturalistic shiny cubist masses.

Consider Bellini's painting of *The Madonna and Child with Saint Catherine and
Mary Magdalen* (Accademia). The Virgin looks out at us thoughtfully, full
face; where we stand seems to be the picture's source of light. The Virgin
has thoughtful brown eyes (her hair is hidden by a cap under her robe) and
a strong nose. Her head tilted a little to one side, as if she were slightly
skeptical—not of her baby but of herself, it may be, or of us, or of the two
women beside her, each a kind of daughter-in-law (given their respective stories). These two other women gaze on the child. Mary Magdalen has reddish
hair in somewhat disheveled curls, and a brilliant ornament, heavy but delicate, of pearls and rubies at the edge of her dress at the neck. (Pearls for
chastity, red ruby for passion.) A voluminous black sleeve gives weight to the
arm and the body, a black set off by a mantle of red velvety texture. Her
fingers are tapering and elegant, her face (seen in three-quarters) is youthful,

and she appears fragile and intense. On the left side of the painting Saint Catherine looks more sensible and adult. She is dressed in a robe and mantle of a duller red than that of the Magdalena, with an edging of gray pearls. Her hair, also of a dull red or auburn, is coiffed with elaborate pearl ornaments. She is seen in profile, and shows the beginnings of a double chin. Otherwise, Saint Catherine bears a slight resemblance to Susan Sarandon in the grave poise of the mouth and the cut of the nose—a serious saint who wouldn't put up with any nonsense.

There is a drink named after this artist, the "Bellini," a creation (in 1948) of Giuseppe Cipriani, proprietor of Harry's Bar. (He also created a "Titian" and a "Giorgione," but they didn't catch on.) The Bellini is meant to be a delicately innocent if alcoholic beverage, founded on peach juice and Prosecco. I have had one—for purposes of research—in Harry's Bar, and was not too pleasantly impressed with its bland mawkishness. As a reading of the artist, I consider the drink distinctly unfair. It wants tension, the touch of the bitter. Bellini is a visual poet of attentiveness, contemplation, and endurance. There is a *Pietà* in the Palazzo Ducale showing the Virgin and Saint John with the dead Christ. The Holy Mother in a purple mantle is trying to sustain the only too visibly dead body of her son; the disciple and she are with labor holding the corpse upright, a vertical posture the gray-green body resists; blood from the wounded side drips on John's right hand. The Virgin's left arm supports the right arm of the dead son, her right hand touches his chest just above the armpit, and her face is turned toward his. The Son's eyes are closed but his mouth is open, slack and flaccid in death, yet hideously imitating the appearance of speech. The Virgin has her mouth open similarly, but we know hers is a living mouth and we can almost hear the outcry and lamentation that pours forth from it. This Virgin is no longer beautiful, she has gone beyond all that, her face is discolored, blotchy from tears and grief, distorted by the open mouth, like a wound.

Some of Bellini's best work shows the Mother and Child alone. He shares the Venetian interest in multiplicity, however, and can present the Virgin and Christ Child with various saints. He developed an idiom of the altarpiece or *pala* in which the Virgin with the child on her lap is enthroned, within an apse beneath a domed ceiling and somewhat above groups of saints. The *Pala San Giobbe* in the Accademia (Altarpiece of Saint Job lifted from Saint Job's church) is the best known of these works. The apse in which the figures stand, richly decorated with gold mosaics above, seems a reference to San Marco. Saint Job (almost naked) is present, so too are Saint Francis and

Saint John on our left, and on our right Saint Dominic, Saint Sebastian (with only a couple of arrows in him), and Saint Ludovico. Those who cannot name all these saints will have no trouble identifying as happy angels the merry beings who play musical instruments at the foot of the throne—two lutanists and one playing the rebec. Such musical angels become an idiom and sign of Bellini. In the *Pala* in San Zaccaria he has an angel playing the viola. The *Triptych* in the Frari has two very sassy little angels, like chubby children, one playing the lute, the other a simple flute or recorder. Angels are traditionally always supposed male (if androgynously male), but these look like little girls of about five years old. One is tempted to say that—without being vulgar—they have a Shirley Temple quality.

Giovanni Bellini executed at least one large crowd scene, the picture of Saint Mark preaching in Alexandria (now in the Brera, Milan). The area in which Saint Mark is preaching looks like a revision of Saint Mark's Square itself. A huge religious building with many cupolas dominates the background; whether it is meant to be an anachronistic mosque is an open question, but it is certainly a variant on the Basilica of San Marco. There are crowds of various personages of different races; men with turbans dominate. This kind of "exotic" painting is more the province of the artist's brother Gentile, who executed a portrait of the Ottoman Sultan Mehmet. Gentile Bellini was also a genius in the creation of crowd scenes and Venice-scapes. He has a gift for the formal arrangement of human persons in a space, as we can see if we look in the Accademia at his *Procession in the Piazza San Marco*, honoring the feast day of Saint Mark (25 April). We tend to believe that here we can actually see how Saint Mark's and the corner of the Doge's Palace looked in the late fifteenth century. Gentile's ability to deal with crowds, both performers and spectators, is fully evident; we can also note that the Piazza San Marco was designed to feature throngs of people. It has by now reached its paved state, the canal which formerly ran through it having been covered over, the orchard of the nuns of San Zaccaria cut down to make the great square.

Crowd scenes are very much the province of Vittore Carpaccio (1455–1526). Like Giovanni Bellini, this artist has received the attentions of Giuseppe Cipriani, who named a dish after him, in honor of Carpaccio's reds. This may make it difficult to look at the artist without receiving from some vagrant cells of the brain an image of thin raw beef, lightly drizzled with olive oil and nesting on a bed of arugula. Carpaccio deserves to be remembered as more than a term of cuisine, though he does have unusual reds. His color palette differs from that of the Bellini brothers, but he has thoroughly taken in the significance of what they do. Carpaccio's *The Presentation of Christ in the Temple* (Accademia), for example, shows how he has picked up the idiom of Giovanni, including the three musical angels below the main party.

An ambitious artist, Carpaccio made his mark on history painting. He undertook a very large project for the Scuola di San Orsola, producing for this confraternity a series of grand paintings narrating the legend of Saint Ursula (Orsola) as told in the *Legenda Aurea*. This sequence has a room to itself in the Accademia, as it well deserves. Here is history painting or story painting in the grand style, with hosts of characters and superb edifices. It has been pointed out that Carpaccio's narrative was conditioned by a history "specifica veneziana," inspired by Venice's ceremonies, its grand buildings (including the Doge's Palace), its embassies; there is even an element of reportage. In 1489 there had been a great public festival to welcome the returning Caterina Cornaro, queen of Cyprus, "exemplary model of patrician fidelity to the State."[5] Caterina Cornaro, or Corner (1459–1510), member of a highly patrician family, had married in order to become Queen of Cyprus; once widowed in 1489, the new ruling queen dutifully handed Venus's island to Venice (according to plan). She was rewarded by the Venetian state with honors, and an estate in lovely Asolo in the hills (well away from the center of power). Her long engagement and her political mission offered a (tenuous) parallel with Saint Ursula.

At the beginning of the series, envoys come from the king of England to request the Princess Ursula's hand in marriage. She is shown in front of her rather harassed-looking father, who is sitting down with his head on his hand, as if talking to his serious and well-dressed daughter hurts his head. Ursula, standing before him, is earnestly ticking off on the fingers of one hand her own stipulations. Certainly these must include the conversion of the pagan prince of England, but she is also asking for a delay of three years so she can make a pilgrimage to Rome. Above the royal father and daughter a Bellini-and-Byzantine-style painting of the Virgin and Child hangs on the wall. In the next big picture, the English ambassadors are formally given the reply, in a document handed them by the king. A stream of people populates the formal marble rooms. *The Return of the Ambassadors* (with the answer "Yes") is particularly joyful—we seem to be in the landing space of the Mole, by the Piazzetta, and the buildings seem partly like dream buildings and partly like the real Venice. Such an effect is even more striking in the representation of the meeting of the betrothed. The public is jubilant, the walls of the city are draped in rich Oriental rugs—a Venetian style of celebration—and people are hanging from every coign of vantage. The quietest painting of the series is perhaps the most famous, *The Dream of Ursula*; the saint sleeps neatly supine in a well-appointed bedroom with all the luxuries the fifteenth century could provide.

Ursula journeys on, she meets the pope, goes to Cologne, and at last she is murdered by the Huns. Her martyrdom takes place in a wooded outdoor space. The massacre scene is confused and multiplex; as in the other paintings in this series, a lot of actions are taking place at the same time among and amidst a multitude of persons. We see from the back the young man who is shooting Ursula to death, as he holds his arrow poised in the string. The viewer must be struck by his personal beauty, more suited to a member of the Company of the Stocking than to a Hun. We cannot see his face, but the energetic jut of his perfect red-clad bum is assertive, and his long curly blond hair looks like that of the princess's betrothed prince of England. Gabriele D'Annunzio comments, "The archers have brought their finest bows, they are wearing their most lavish garments, their movements are elegant, as though they were going to a festival (*festino*). The golden-haired archer who strikes the saint with such grace and skill seems truly the young Eros, still in his chrysalis stage (*larvato*) and wingless."[6] The last scene of the series is calm, as Ursula is taken home to a fine funeral, and an apotheosis.

The entire Ursula sequence, with its rapid modelings of different actions, and its variety of detailed architectural elements and of other important features (ships, armor, weapons) in what yet seems a free-flowing human narrative, cannot but strike the viewer with astonishment. Carpaccio tells his story cinematically, and moves from frame to frame of major action. His is an action film, not a story of character and introspection. They are hard to look at in detail, these pictures, save for Ursula's dream, for the insistent multiplicity is meant somewhat to daze the viewer, as well as to satisfy. The people are variegated, like the colored marbles that appear almost everywhere as a sign of civilization. There are wonderful touches of detail—Ursula's little clogs arranged at the side of her bed in the scene of her dream, for instance. Or consider the old woman beneath the chamber where the king and his daughter meet. While Ursula is dictating her terms to her father, and the royal pair, secluded, considers matters of state, we see on the marble stairs outside and below the room a plainly dressed old woman sitting doggedly on a marble step. She is evidently Ursula's patient nurse—a lame old woman, for she holds a cane against her lap. The nurse recurs in the last scene, of

Ursula's funeral. She has had nothing to do with the adventure, the glamour, the danger; she did not choose the terrible risk, but she pays the price. She is simply heartbroken.

Carpaccio is an artist of the public life, public space, and public presence. Probably under the direction of Gentile Bellini, he was one of the contributors to a series of paintings illustrating "The Miracle of the True Cross" for the Scuola Grande di San Giovanni Evangelista. This series celebrated the most important holy relic, a piece of the True Cross, which had been given to the Scuola as long ago as 1369. (Interest in its advent in Venice may have been sparked anew by the fresh surge of relics rescued from Constantinople, including some donated by Bessarion.) The theme evoked all of these painters' ability to deal with Venice and with crowds.

We can see what a big thing Gentile Bellini makes of his subject. He gets to depict a miraculous moment, *Recovery of the Relic from the Canal of San Lorenzo*. The precious relic in its gold monstrance has just been jostled off the bridge by the pushing of the crowds, and hovers, not in but just above the waters of the canal near the Rialto Bridge. Several persons—so the story goes—jumped in and tried to retrieve it, but they were not worthy of the task. At last Andrea Vendramin jumped in and was allowed to handle and rescue it. This is the central moment depicted. We see Vendramin's hand touching the cross-shaped monstrance that holds the ineffably holy relic. The rescue takes place before the eyes of a watching crowd including important personages, one of whom is Caterina Cornaro. Not all the people depicted are bigwigs. In the foreground at our left there is an African woman, simply and neatly dressed with a scarfed head. Presumably she is the attendant of the golden patrician girl in front of her, an insouciant teenager who seems not to care much about whatever transpires. But the black woman has her hands clasped in anxious prayer—she has her own reaction. The crowds become individualized as we look, and we cannot but note the densely jostling buildings of rosy brick, their windows neatly outlined in Istrian limestone. The skyline is packed with stout chimney pots. We notice the people in the water, the swimmers or would-be swimmers in various states of undress, including the young black man (slave, servant, or visitor?) just about to jump in on the right. A stout man swims ponderously on the left, a look of anxiety on his face. Behind this swimming figure is the everyday sight of an empty *sandalo*, parked at the embankment, its temporarily disused oar jutting athwart the craft. The painting even indicates the high-water mark and a slight slime line on the embankment. All the variety is drawn by Gentile Bellini into a unified and flowing narrative, with a strong center.

Presumably, it was the luck of the draw that denied Carpaccio a big action scene in this series. The title of his scene, commonly the general *Miracle of the Relic of the Cross at the Rialto Bridge*, is sometimes given as *Cure of a Lunatic by the Patriarch of Grado* (see Plate 2), but perhaps the artist was unwilling to go indoors for this scene, even to exhibit a miracle; all he shows of this main narrative is a group of the pious ascending the stairs to assist at an exorcism. But what a narrative he makes of Venice! He and Gentile Bellini are surely the first inventors of the cityscape, the tribute to buildings and bridges and the pulsing reality of daily life. Carpaccio's canvas is superbly crowded. We seek to comb out the details. On the lower left are groups of Venetian nobles in their red and black "togas," and also Greeks or Armenians with hats on. To the right is the Grand Canal, with quite heavy canal traffic; in the middle distance and central is Venice's one bridge of the period, the old Rialto Bridge, a construction of wood, mobile in the center to allow tall masted ships to go through. (This is the bridge replaced in 1524 by the stone arch still in business today.) As Claudia Cremonini says, "Carpaccio grasps the opportunity to represent in his painting one of the most important sites of civic life—the nerve center of commercial Venice."[7] Patricia Fortini Brown acutely observes the need for narrative ("narratives are what keep societies sane"); Venetian painters such as Carpaccio create narratives that are emotionally credible to contemporaries, owing to "the note of authentication conveyed to us by the intervening narrator as eyewitness or self-proclaimed authority."[8]

That authentication conveyed by the "eyewitness" mode of painting can extend to reportage. Carpaccio's picture does offer us a valuable record of what buildings were there and what they looked like—we can see the old Fondaco dei Tedeschi (or German warehouse complex), soon to be destroyed by a fire in 1505. It is hard to keep one's mind on such static phenomena in a scene of such activity, a scene in which the artist dares to decenter the action and make our eyes dart about. We cannot keep our own eyes from the river traffic, with the gondoliers so elegantly dressed in red or striped tights and well-made nipped-in jackets, especially the black gondolier in the left foreground. The gondolas zigzag along the canal, each gondolier in a different posture from the others, each craft with different sorts of passengers under the *felze*. And who can ignore the little curly white dog, on the front gondola?—a Maltese dog, descendant of the kind that the ancient Greeks loved as house pets. The eyewitness does not offer us a restful eye.

The city has a vertical lift from all the chimney pots, up-thrusting shafts with inverted-cone tops, many decorated, and crowded so thickly as to remind one of Victorian London. The roofs, the dangling laundry at the top of a house, the many chimney pots—all push themselves up against a delicate sky, azure above and peach at the horizon—"a formidable atmospheric rendering of the lagoon *sky-line*, with the unforgettable forest of chimneys projected against a luminous sky," as Cremonini remarks.[9]

In the contributions of Gentile Bellini and Carpaccio to this series we see a fresh discovery of urban representation, scenes of a city as a human intense habitation, in which the place and its pulsing and various activities take on the role of the central subject. The big polyglot crowd that is such a trope of Venice—and that so appalls D. H. Lawrence—gets a good look-in here. As Patricia Fortini Brown has pointed out, paintings like these coincide with the production of new maps and the first guidebooks by Marcantonio Sabellico (in 1490) and Marin Sanudo (1493).[10] We can clearly discern not only the Venetians' pride in their city's structures, including common and secular things, but also their investment in representing their city as offering interesting differences, the presence of strangers and visitors who are not Venetian—nor even Italian. Here is a confluence and a marketplace, a moving scene of perpetual wonders, a resort of variety. We see Albanians, Turks, even veiled women who are presumably Muslim. Painted histories of public self representation explain not only to native Venetians but also to foreigners what Venice itself thinks it is. The inclusion of the *stranieri* as real presences in Venice might serve to attract more foreigners there. Painted histories also solidify the city's sense of itself as a holy and miraculous place. Perhaps being a multilingual emporium made the Venetians less likely to concentrate on literature as a means of communication. The appeal of Venice must be largely to the eye—whoso does not *see* thee, O Venetia, does not value thee: *che non ti vede non ti pretia*. Carpaccio and Bellini help even those who dwell permanently in Venice to *see* it.

Carpaccio has a sense of humor that does not interfere with his love of the grand subject, but serves to amplify it. In 1451 the Slavs (*Schiavoni*) of Dalmatia got permission to found their own *scuola*: its proper title is Scuola Dalmata dei Santi Giorgio e Trifone—the Dalmatian School (or Guild) of Saint George and Saint Tryphonius. They did not get their new building until 1501, by which time they were also well enough off to commission

Carpaccio to paint a series of pictures of the lives of Dalmatia's patron saints—George, Tryphonius, and Jerome—as well as representations of the Calling of Matthew and the Prayer in the Garden. Carpaccio had a friendly and rather compact space in which to work—compared with the grandeur of San Rocco and others, the Slavs' *scuola* is positively homey. His immediately lovable set of paintings are easily visible, all at eye level or just above.

The Saint George paintings are probably the most appreciated, featuring the always-popular dragon, including grisly remnants of his previous human meals. Carpaccio persistently includes animals, and obviously likes them, whether real or fantastic. In the picture representing a later stage of the action, Carpaccio's Saint George shows off to the royals his captured dragon, which now looks like a very sick, bedraggled monster, with a lance painfully piercing its mouth. One tends to hope the king and queen might let it live. There are other animals in the picture, too—Saint George's chestnut horse nuzzles a white one, in a promising if dumb friendship.

In the Jerome series, we meet the saint's lion. Saint Jerome is by now an old man; his beard and hair have gone quite white, he is somewhat stooped and walks with a cane. But like an Androcles, the aged man has rescued a lion by taking a thorn from its paw. It is as if Jerome after years of faithful service is now being *rewarded* with the splendid lion. The saint gazes in displeased wonderment at the monks fleeing in all directions away from the fearsome animal. The panicky monks are triangles of white skirts and scapulas, comically stressed. Behind them is the gracious pink bulk of a new building, the Scuola di San Giorgio degli Schiavoni itself.

In the last scene of the Jerome series, showing Saint Augustine in his study, Carpaccio exhibits his love of detail, his sense of the comic, and his sense of pathos. Saint Augustine, still robust and dark-haired, in contrast to the bent and white-haired Jerome, is found in the most perfectly appointed study that any early sixteenth-century scholar could wish. A generous selection of bound vellum books can be seen neatly packed on a shelf; open books, untidily arrayed for ready reference, clutter the bottom of the desk platform, signaling a real writer at work. The room also contains interesting and friendly objects: a red leather chair, some Greek pottery, astronomical instruments. The saint, obviously working hard and deep in thought, is looking away from the friendly presence of a Maltese dog sitting in the middle of the floor. The dog takes the place that a lion customarily has in the depiction of Saint Jerome's study. We can feel the puppy is waiting, not too patiently, for the next moment that the saint can spare to speak to him. But that will not be soon, for a miraculous light is flooding in upon the saint, who suspends his pen. The painting captures the (dramatic but interior) moment when, while Augustine was writing a letter to Saint Jerome hoping to consult him, he saw a light and heard a voice as Jerome informed him that he had died, and gone to be with Christ.[11] According to legend, Jerome at the same time warned Augustine against intellectual pride, and there are a few signs of that too in the collection of objects, the high place given to the pagan statue and the astronomical model.

What is probably Carpaccio's best-known painting, at least in our own time (and one with plenty of animals) is not found in the Accademia or the Scuola but in the Museo Correr. Conventionally this Carpaccio painting has been called *Two Venetian Women* or—less kindly—*Two Courtesans* (see Plate 3). Two women sit on a balcony. One, her yellow hair piled atop her head, dressed in a yellow gown and a pearl necklace, stares dully ahead, unseeing, ignoring the tame birds on the ledge at her side, or the other entertaining birds (including a parrot) at her feet, as well as the young page in front of her. In her right hand she holds a pendant white handkerchief. Toward the foreground another woman sits, well-endowed as to the bust, wearing a close-fitting black embroidered bodice and a red skirt. Her left hand holds the right paw of her little short-haired white dog, which sits in a begging posture, while her right hand pulls at her dog whip, still in the determined teeth of a larger dog. This more leonine dog has its left paw on a crumpled letter.

Oddly enough, considering its strangely feminine and erotic subject matter, Ruskin in *St. Mark's Rest* pronounced this painting (which he referred to as "two Venetian ladies with their pets") to be in perfection of execution "the best picture in the world." He praised its mingling of "breadth with minuteness, brilliancy with quietness . . . colour with light and shade." "The subject," he states with authority, "is a simple study of animal life in all its phases." He supposes the painter was commissioned to paint the portraits of two ladies whom he did not altogether like, but Carpaccio "painted their pretty faces and pretty shoulders, their pretty dresses and pretty jewels, their pretty ways and their pretty playmates— . . . he himself secretly laughing at them the whole time."[12] Perhaps Ruskin considers women alone as just another phase of animal life—did no recollection of his deeply neglected Effie ever cross even his subconscious mind as he looked at this painting? But there is more truth in what Ruskin says than even he knows; I think him acute in seeing the humor in the picture, though that is more complex and uneasy than he makes out.

We now know more than we used to do about this painting; it is part of a larger work (perhaps all part of a board plus letter rack, or a large chest); the other surviving portion of it can be seen in the J. Paul Getty Museum near Los Angeles. The two scenes are connected by the inappropriate Madonna lily set near the yellow-gowned woman on the far balustrade. The flower is in the foreground of a lagunar scene, which spreads before our eyes, appealing to our sense of distance (see Plate 3). Over the watery area, a number of figures are distributed, whereas the balcony scene plays with a number of figures caught in an enclosed space. This other part of the piece is in a subtly different palette. It represents a masculine activity on the dull silver lagoon, a scene of hunting ducks or snipe. The young men are evidently members of the Company of the Stocking; their legs are colorfully arrayed, in hues connecting them with the women, but the grayish lagoon light and hint of mist soften the color effect. These sportsmen are in flat-bottomed boats (such a boat is a *s'ciopòn* in Venice); tooling around the marshes, they take aim (with bows and arrows) at the birds in the water. Here is another study of animal life, and another view of our relation to animals and birds. Carpaccio plays with the wild and the tame, that which is petted and that which is killed. The young men, armed like Cupid (as was Ursula's Hun), are outdoors, unbounded and uncaring of love, whereas the two women are indoors, in a space strictly confined and marked by the balustrade. The men seek to kill wild birds; the women consort with tame ones. The men are associated with the liquid element; the women with the dry and heavily chromatic.

I am aware that there is a contemporary school of thought holding that these women are proper Venetian ladies. Patricia Fortini Brown says, "Here a young bride, identified as such by her pearl necklace, sits with an older woman—perhaps her mother or elder sister—in decorous elegance on the terrace of the family palace. Surrounded by symbols of chastity, nobility, wealth, and marriage, they become allegories of female virtue."[13] I don't believe a word of it. These women are not happy. The animal and inorganic clutter around them is more vital than elegant. We can overinvest in the significance of pearls, which were *theoretically* supposed not to be worn by loose women. We may recall Coryat's illustration and description of the courtesan "Margarita Emiliana," whose first name itself means "pearl." In Carpaccio's picture, pearls as symbols become suggestively excessive, as do the emblematic myrtle and the lily. I do not take the myrtle and the lily any more straightforwardly than the pearls. The Madonna lily is an irony—there is no

Annunciation here. This sulky young woman whose ultra-blond hair suggests determined bleaching is surely not a happy bride as she plays with the handkerchief into which she perhaps has been sniffling. We can connect the two scenes and realize that the two women have been forsaken by their glamorous young men for a day's sport. The crumpled note under the dog's paw is not an Annunciation but an announcement; it presumably says, "Sorry—gone shooting." Their lovers are not coming. These two females are fed up, yet there is nothing that they can do about it.

These women express that very modern form of consciousness which we know as boredom. They are the most bored ladies in the universe. They seem to belong to a different world not only from Saint Ursula but also from other Venetians we meet in Carpaccio. These ladies would chime in with denizens of Montmartre in the 1880s; one could imagine them taking to absinthe.

It has been suggested that his treatment of color and light in *Two Venetian Women* shows the influence upon Carpaccio of Giorgione (1478–1510).[14] Giorgione, however, is a very different artist from the extroverted Carpaccio. For one thing, he has much closer ties to the Bellini. Giorgione and Titian were both students of Giovanni Bellini, though Titian came from the better background. Giorgione we know only by his nickname, the diminutive "little Giorgio," "Zorzone." Little George was a nobody from the village of Castelfranco. Giorgio Vasari, the Florentine art historian, would make Tiziano Vecellio (1485–1576) a pupil of Giorgione, a hierarchy that Ridolfi, the Venetian art historian, flatly contradicts, insisting that both men lodged in the house of Giovanni Bellini and studied with him. Yet Ridolfi admits that Titian learned from Giorgione's manner: "This beautiful method of coloring put in use by his fellow-student (*condiscepolo*) was pleasing to Titian, and he practiced it himself, becoming at the same time both imitator and emulator."[15] The two young painters were both set to work making frescoes for the Fondaco dei Tedeschi—a lost labor, for these exterior adornments were destroyed by salt sea-wind and weather. (Pieces of Giorgione's fresco have been rescued and are now in Ca' d'Oro or the Accademia, but it is difficult to make much of these faded fragments.)

It is relatively easy to discuss what long-lived and prosperous Titian (Tiziano) is and does, but it is very difficult to define Giorgione. The artist died young, of the plague, in 1510—accounts blame his early death at least in part on his riotous living and insistence on seeing his mistress. His reputation is that of a young man perpetually pursuing music and parties and love.

Giorgione has left relatively few paintings that are fully and undeniably his—some left unfinished at his death were, according to credible report, finished by Titian. So one of his masterpieces, the *Sleeping Venus*, is also from the hand of Titian. The *Fête Champêtre*—forerunner of Manet's *Déjeuner sur l'Herbe*—is sometimes accounted his and sometimes Titian's. Our contemporary opinion has gone decidedly in favor of Titian, and in an exhibition of 2006 it is featured as his work.[16] Yet while the elegant naked women at both left and right seem like Titian, the appearance of the middle group of men, along with some of the background, looks to me very much looks to me very much in Giorgione's style, and one of the characters looks like Giorgione (who seems fond of self-portraiture). Learned opinion will probably fluctuate in ages to come.

Giorgione is lauded by his contemporaries and immediate successors for mingling art with nature in such a way as to produce a new nature. His landscapes are soft and subtle, he discovers a soft brushstroke, he naturalized painting ("naturalizzata la pittura").[17] At the same time as he is interested in naturalizing nature, creating new lights and soft shades and capturing halftones and subtle textures, Giorgione shares the liking for allegory and even riddles, which is one of the aspects of later Renaissance culture. New movements of knowledge interest him, including hermeticism and the occult. It is suggested that he may have been Jewish.[18] He painted *The Trial of Moses* and *The Judgment of Solomon* and represented himself as David, with Goliath's head in his hand. His *Three Philosophers* may represent a means of relating Jew, Christian, and Saracen—or the painting *may* depict a new version of the Magi. Giorgione is such a puzzling figure, always seeming to leave us with enigmas; David Rosand says with some exasperation, "On every level, then, Giorgione's art seems calculated to frustrate."[19]

The frustration may be part of the charm. I detect more than a hint of aggression in Giorgione, a quality really absent from Titian, even though some of his characters in legendary scenes may perform aggressive acts. In most of Giorgione's paintings there is aggression somewhere, and there is fear. It is perhaps naive to be surprised to find that the artist was such a party animal when his works are so stressful. A certain nuanced melancholy mixed with anxiety seems to hang about them. Giorgione's male characters seem less to act than to survive in some sort of damaged state, or in a pensive condition that appears troubling in some indeterminate way. It interests me that this tendency or motif comes though in a number of paintings uncertainly attributed to this artist.

In the National Gallery in London there is a strange painting entitled *Il Tramonto,* or *The Sunset,* often attributed to Giorgione. A young man (looking rather like Giorgione) who wears a blue velvety jacket and white trousers, is suffering apparently from a wounded leg. He is being attended to by another figure, an older, bearded, brawny man who is holding the leg. Beside the two men is a brown mere in whose unwholesome depths wallow strange beasts, largely hidden. An animal that looks like a tapir emerges from a hole in the bank, and a ducklike creature with a disproportionately large head swims to the bank nearest the two men. Beyond, on the right, Saint Anthony lurks in a cave, and in the near middle distance Saint George is fighting with a repulsively rat-tailed dragon, while an impending mass of hill threatens to fall on him. In the background are bleached wood houses or shacks; beyond these, a pale-peach sunset light would be pleasant if the fading light did not threaten to leave us in darkness with the blighted mere and the brown things. The whole may—or may not—represent a miracle of Saint Roche.

The National Gallery also possesses another painting more seldom and more dubiously attributed to Giorgione (and not often on view); it shows a poet, surrounded by pleasant landscape and the riches of the earth, who seems to be in a state of arrested melancholy. Another work, labeled *Double Portrait* (Rome), often given to this artist, shows a young nobleman with tapering fingers and soulful eyes gazing love-struck at an orange, while behind him another male figure, less good-looking, moves in on him, with a kind of concentrated rapacity that the dreamy-eyed man does not see. I am willing to entertain the attribution of these uncertain works to that painter because I take Giorgione as an artist whose constant subject is the difficulty of love, the tension of lust, and the monsters that lurk in the depths.

The paintings assuredly Giorgione's both invite and repel the rapacity of the viewer. They tend to be records of frustration and loss. The greatest of these certain attributions, which will be discussed in the next chapter, is *La Tempesta* (*The Tempest,* Accademia; see Plate 11). It is no exception to the pattern of fear, introspection, and melancholy.

How very different Giorgione is from Titian! For Titian dwells customarily in untroubled but not unstrenuous pleasure. Ridolfi in the illustrations chosen for his book on Venetian painters has ensured that the difference between the two is emphasized. The image of Giorgione (which resembles the young man who recurs in his works) looks youthful, tousled, defiant, unadorned, faintly apprehensive, while the picture of the elderly Tiziano is of an intellectual seeker who has yet achieved maturity and material success in life (Figures 13, 14).

With Titian we come to a rhapsody of self-confidence in Venetian art, a new sense of display. He learned from Giorgione the shadowing, the softness and inwardness of a picture, but a Titian painting is always executed in colors rich, assertive, and manifold. Any discussion of Venetian art leads ineluctably to the quarrel between Design and Color. Color is a leading trope of Venice. Its architecture, its mosaics, betray this before we even come to its paintings. And its paintings effloresce in colorfulness. Venetian art has taught other painters to see and use color. The Canadian James Wilson Morrice learned from Venice to dare to be colorful; his *Venice at the Golden Hour* (1901–1902) represents a departure for an artist often rather timidly beige and gray (see Plate 4).

Color is a complex idea masquerading as a simple one. We take it as "simple" because its appeal is so intuitive and immediate, so difficult to describe or to subject to reason. The colorfulness of Venice has itself been a bone of contention over the centuries. Is color not vulgar? To some it has seemed so, and Titian of all artists makes Venetian coloring unignorable.

Titian is also a new man of the Renaissance; he turns to treating classical mythological subjects and scenes—and on a grand scale. He is no longer an "eyewitness" reporter; he wants to achieve the same vividness of impression, and a rush of action, but the viewer cannot miss the fact that his painting of story is knowingly creative and deliberately enchanting. A major example is his *Bacchus and Ariadne* (National Gallery, London; see Plate 5), one of a series on "The Loves of the Gods" and one of the paintings on pagan subjects he turned out for the *camerino* (small private room) of the Duke of Ferrara. To appreciate this subject, one has to know (as we say now) the "backstory." Ariadne had assisted brave Theseus in his quest to kill the Minotaur of Crete, which was devouring an annual tribute of youths of Athens. The monster was in the center of a labyrinth, and Ariadne supplied the "clue," or thread by which Theseus could find his way. Having killed Crete's prized monster, Theseus quickly sailed away, eloping with his accomplice Ariadne, whose partnership had been accepted at the price of a promise of marriage. But Theseus didn't mean it. When the pair got to Naxos he left Ariadne sleeping and sailed off to Athens, leaving the Cretan princess stranded on the empty island. Fortunately for Ariadne she was discovered there by a more appreciative lover. She unites with Dionysius (or Bacchus) and in the end turns into a constellation, a crown of stars.

GIORGIONE DA CASTEL FRANCO
PITTORE.

Figure 13. "Giorgione of Castelfranco, Painter," from Carlo Ridolfi, *Le Maraviglie dell'Arte, ovvero Le Vite degl'illustri Pittori Veneti,* 1648 (Permission of British Library: 562*.a.1, p. 76)

TITIANO VECELLIO PITTORE,
E CAVALIERE.

G. Georgi f.

Figure 14. "Tiziano Vecellio, Painter and Knight," from Ridolfi, *Le Maraviglie dell'Arte, ovvero Le Vite degl'illustri Pittori Veneti*, 1648 (Permission of British Library: 562*.a.1, p. 134)

Ariadne may already have carried for Titian some emblematic suggestion of Venice, something made more explicit in Tintoretto's painting for the Palazzo Ducale of *The Marriage of Ariadne and Bacchus* showing the couple in the presence of Venus. Ridolfi in discussing that painting glosses Ariadne as representing Venice, "born along the sea shore . . . crowned with the crown of liberty by the divine hand."[20] Certainly Ariadne, who had pursued liberty, turns from yearning after an Athenian Theseus and Greek culture to take up a more divine place in the universe, as Venice had forsaken its Greek pupilage and reached for the stars.

In Titian's painting we see Ariadne, on the far left. She is barefoot and disheveled, in keeping with Ovid's description of forsaken Ariadne in *Heroides*. (The painting is inspired by Carmen 44 of Catullus, but other descriptions of Ariadne and of Dionysos-Bacchus play through it.) She has only just shrugged herself into her clothing, for her left shoulder is bare, though she is draped in a magnificent blue garment, achieved through paint of the most expensive and enduring of blues, made with lapis lazuli. She has been looking out to sea, where Theseus' heartless white ship sails on. Her lover has deserted her. Ariadne has just realized that she is abandoned in Naxos. But she is also beginning to turn with a start of surprise, for behind her, to her right, comes Bacchus and his train. The leopard-drawn chariot of the god is in front, and behind, to our right, comes a group of Bacchic revelers, dancing and playing and treading through blue iris and columbine. A barelegged woman plays the cymbals, a drunken naked man strains within a wreath of snakes like a comic if troubling Laocoön. In the background, Silenus, his belly round and pink as a peach, and crowned with grapes and vines, rides a donkey. In the foreground, a boy with a goat's legs (a baby satyr or *satiretto*) trails a calf's head.[21] A small dog is barking intently at the infant satyr.

Dominating this ambivalent procession of beings is the figure of the god, in the act of flying upward out of his chariot in order to rescue and console Ariadne—and to keep the leopards (really more like cheetahs) from bothering her. The god is in movement. That he is flying is indicated by the wonderful drapery that streams around him and behind him is tossed upward, like wings. The drapery is of candy-pink silk, it is irresistible and playful, like the handsome somewhat epicene god himself. Ridolfi, who spends a long time describing and celebrating this painting, praises the artist's achievement in presenting the countenance of the Dionysiac god: "his handsome face, just as Titian painted it, was described . . . by Marino as he was recounting the loves of Bacchus in his *Adonis*."[22] The god is caught in mid-leap, almost a new thing in art—the representation not of an action only but of a figure in the midst of bold movement. The bodies of both hero and heroine are slightly twisted in their action and reaction, bodies reflecting the fact that they have just taken notice of each other. It is a painting about rediscovering joy after sorrow, with emphasis on the movement of joy, and the promise of jubilation still to come. Above them the sky holds the constellation of Ariadne's crown. Where this sky is not dotted with puffy white clouds it is of a deep and hopeful blue, though not the splendid blue of Ariadne's garment.

This painting lives and breathes in its color—the deep blue, the light blue, the bright candy-pink swirl in the center. And that is just the trouble with Titian and the Venetians in general, according to some theorists. These Venetians are foolishly intoxicated with color, careless and superficial. The dispute about the merits of color seems already to have been hot in Italy by 1550 when Vasari took up the cause of Florence and Florentine art, and of Michelangelo as the paragon of artists. (The first edition of Vasari's *Lives of the Artists* appeared in 1550, the second amplified version in 1568.)[23] For Vasari, art is the offspring of *disegno*, design or drawing. *Disegno* is the father of art, its soul and meaning, though its mother may be Invention. The object of good art is to recapture the qualities of Roman classicism—and to forsake the vulgarity and crudity of the past. Vasari has as much contempt for mosaic art as any eighteenth- or nineteenth-century traveler. The strength of a painting is in its *drawing*. Here the Venetians are woefully lacking, seduced by the feminine amiability of color, which is altogether a weaker and more decadent thing. Giorgione didn't even bother drawing on the canvas but splashed around directly with a brush. Vasari presumably voiced the opinions of a number of Florentine artists when he maintained that the Venetians didn't know how to draw. Venetian painters tend not to obey outlines, even if they sketch them. They rely on the relation of color to color; brushwork, not line, is the organizing power. Vasari is particularly hard on Giorgione, seeing in him the epitome of carelessness, of inattention. Admittedly, Vasari himself did admire the free brushwork of Titian's paintings at mid-career, saying they "seemed alive." The conflict over Venice's artistic preference for color over form remained well enough understood for Hester Piozzi to make a joke of it in relation to female cosmetics: "A custom which prevails here, of wearing little or no rouge, and increasing the native paleness of their skins, by scarce lightly wiping the very white powder from their faces, is a method no Frenchwoman of quality would like to adopt; yet surely the Venetians are not behindhand in the art of gaining admirers; and they do not, like their painters, depend upon *colouring* to ensure it" (*Observations and Reflections*, 128).

The suspicion of color has a long history, as Paul Hills points out. The fourteenth-century writer Coversino da Ravenna had asserted, "When a painting is exhibited . . . it is the ignorant man who is attracted simply by the colour." Form and proportion are what is sought by the knowledgeable man. Angelo Decembrio in Ferrara in the mid-fifteenth century argued, as Hills summarizes, "that it is proper for the painter to exercise his skill in rendering the nude, whereas to depict ornaments in period or contemporary costume is suspect because it disturbs the timeless values of representation." Seek the permanent, not the transitory. Color is negligible, the province of tapestry-makers and other frivolous artisans, makers of stuff that will not endure. The highest value is to be given to the male nude, "essentially color-less or monochrome, like the sculptures in which the ideal forms of the naked body were transmitted by the Greco-Roman tradition. . . . Colourless-ness in this scheme of representation is linked to timelessness and to univer-sality."[24] Such a concept—or systematic set of concepts—can be traced back to standards inherited from antiquity. For Pliny in his *Natural History*, sculp-ture was worth mentioning and celebrating, while painting was obviously minor and unimportant. We can go further back, to Plato. The sophist and the cheap rhetorician employ the (figurative) ornaments and coloration. Sus-pect colors and flowers of invention distract man from the righteous appeal of pure Form.

Thus, Vasari and the Florentine and Roman brigades had a lot of support behind them when they attacked the color-mad Venetians. Even oil painting on canvas itself was felt to be a minor and unserious art. It is "feminine"— not that women engaged in it, but because it belongs to the weaker and less worthy class of things. The Venetians, as we have seen, had taken to produc-ing oil paintings on canvas, using materials readily available and more likely to endure in their air. Venice has never got over its love affair with color— which began in its mosaic age, even before it took to oil paints. Certainly, Titian does experiment with darker hues and with clouds and obscurity, as in *Cain Killing Abel* (Salute). This belongs to the artist's later period, in which he painted a number of works on mythological themes for the king of Spain, his *poesie*. Perhaps almost all of Titian's works could be called "poesie," they have a poetic rather than realistic relation to narrative, and they stretch cre-dulity and delight almost to the breaking point. If less concerned (save semi-parodically) with the "eyewitness" kind of realism attributable to Carpaccio, these works are as richly cinematic, and can be more deeply disturbing. In a new variation on "the Loves of the Gods," *The Rape of Europa* (1559–1562), a late and turbulent piece of *poesie* for King Philip, Titian uses darkness for water and deepening brown for a distant land mass, while Europa, being carried away toward the dark unknown, is all pink and white, her genital area— almost directly before the viewer's eyes—just covered with a light chemise. In her hand she waves like a distress signal a cloth of bright orange-pink, which complements the orange clouds of a sky that is almost Turneresque, and certainly invokes Titian's younger contemporary Tintoretto.

There is always a dramatic strain in Titian, as in the other great Venetian painters. He came at a time when there were more and more commissions to fill large and imposing spaces with compelling events and generous movement. The Franciscans, who had begun the church of Santa Maria Gloriosa dei Frari in the thirteenth century, added to their plan in the fourteenth century and finally finished the gigantic building in the mid-fifteenth century. Among other things, the large Franciscan church held monuments of the famous and important. (It is an irony that a rather ugly monument to Titian was put up over his grave in the Frari church in the nineteenth century, whereas Canova's own tomb in the same church is based on his unused proposal for the monument to Titian.) In 1519 Titian was commissioned by Bishop Pesaro to create an altarpiece for a side chapel for the Pesaro family in the Frari. The resultant *pala* shows the Virgin and Child with saints, and also the donors, members of the Pesaro family, as worshipers. We can see what Titian learned from Giovanni Bellini, and what he changed. The Virgin no longer appears with absolute symmetry at the center of an arch or apse— she has now been moved way over to the column on the right, before which she sits, robed in glowing red, looking down and to the right at Saint Peter, in the central position but not as central subject, for the light emanates from the superior position of the Virgin. Part of the strength of such a painting lies in its use of architectural elements to set off the idea. The marble columns seem here to shoot up to infinity. Titian plays games with space. One may wonder, however, if the idea of the divine level is to be served sufficiently by the little bottomy cherubs flying about at the top; the viewer who raises his eyes will be looking directly into the crack of the cherub nearest us. The effect is disconcerting—almost flip, like a parody of Bellini, like a joke at the end of a sermon. The cherub's-bottom effect may be another manifestation of Titian's game.

In search of a Venetian who had no qualms at all about color, we can look confidently to Paolo Caliari, the artist known as "Veronese" (1528–1588). This artist from Verona—hence his appellation—loves large architectural spaces, crowd scenes, and multiplicity. To Ruskin at moments, Veronese represents the epitome of everything that went wrong with Venice, and his influence is seen everywhere in the further degradation of its art: "the rags and ruin of Venetian skill, honour, and worship, exploded all together sky-high. Miracles of frantic mistake, of flaunting and thunderous hypocrisy."[25] So Ruskin in *Stones* thunders against the church of San Pantalon, site of Veronese's last painting as well as of his successor Fumiani's large baroque ceiling.

Veronese's pictures are often dramatic scenes, strongly set with the help of balustrades, stairs, columns, and parapets. His works dealing so constantly with spectatorship demand internal spectators. Veronese seems to be most himself when there is a long horizontal space, a walkway on which various persons can travel and take in a view. In his *Triumph of Venice,* in the ceiling of the Maggior Consiglio (Grand Council, Doge's Palace), he has a loggia or walkway with important people moving about it, looking upward toward the heaven where Venice reigns triumphant. Everything laughs and is festive, and burns with gold, yellow, and blue. Venice could not be triumphant without a crowd.

Veronese's *Wedding Feast at Cana*, originally painted for the refectory of the monastery at San Giorgio Maggiore (now in the Louvre), shows this biblical wedding as a fashionable mob of people (Figure 15). William Beckford, impishly deadpan, comments, "I never beheld so gorgeous a group of wedding-garments before: there is every variety of fold and plait, that can possibly be imagined. The attitudes and countenances are more uniform, and the guests appear a very genteel, decent sort of people; well used to the mode of their times and accustomed to miracles" (*Dreams, Waking Thoughts, and Incidents*, 91). The viewer is—and is supposed to be—impressed with the elegance of the principal group at the beautifully appointed banquet table, and stunned by the multiplicity of things and persons. You have to search to make out Christ and the miracle in the background. You feel like a hapless guest at a wedding of folks not too well known to you—who *are* all these people? And how shall we find our way thought the crush? The bridal party gathered at table is obviously enjoying the best fare, to match their well-fed looks and sumptuous garments. Behind the bride shimmer marble pillars, catching the light and gleaming, softly and roundly, as attractive as flesh without losing their marble solidity and their mirror-like smoothness.

Figure 15. Paolo Veronese, *The Wedding Feast at Cana* (Réunion des Musées Nationaux/ Art Resource, NY)

A great dinner-party painting famously got Veronese into trouble. He intended the painting to be *The Last Supper*, a picture for the refectory of the convent of San Zanipolo to replace a Titian on the same subject destroyed by fire. But he was summoned before the Inquisition (the local Venetian-controlled one) to answer charges regarding having defiled the Last Supper: "Interrogatus se li par conveniente, che alla cena ultima del signore si convegna depingere buffoni, imbriachi Thodesci, nani, et simili scurrilità?" ("He was asked if it was suitable at the last supper of our Lord to depict buffoons, drunken Germans, dwarfs and similar scurrilities?").[26] Veronese protested mildly that he had thought them suitable and ornamental. Contrary to the Inquisitors' wishes, Veronese would not change his painting, but he would change the ostensible subject, giving it a different biblical reference. And here at the Accademia we can see the work of 1578, a huge wall of painting entitled *Feast at the House of Levi* (Figure 16). Facing us with confusing multiplicity and chromatic detail are the richly varied activities of the inhabitants of a great house, including the servants, the German halberdiers, a dwarf, a parrot, and dogs. All of these are coming and going in the foreground, busy in contrast to the more serene interior space, framed by marble arches, where the

Figure 16. Paolo Veronese, *Feast at the House of Levi* (Scala/ Art Resource, NY)

dinner itself is taking place. There are a number of black servants, and two little girls. But as Veronese remarked in explaining himself to the Inquisitors, wealthy people had a lot of servants. It probably didn't quite escape his interrogators that Veronese is painting rich Jews, who appear to be allowed to own palazzi—in biblical times, though not in contemporary Venice of the Ghetto.

On our left, the young man in yellow, presumably an upper servant, has just suffered a nosebleed, from accident or strife; he holds awkwardly in his hand a bloodstained white napkin or handkerchief. Perhaps this was originally a strange prefiguration of Christ's sacrifice. Here, the effect of the bloody white napkin is disturbing—almost shocking, like the appearance of menstrual blood in a sacred or "clean" space. Veronese is bringing in dirt, as he does too with the animals and bones under the table. It is as if Veronese were chiefly concerned with the things and beings that are apt to be left out. A little like Chris Ofili with the elephant-dung paintings, he will remind us of our common earth-embedded nature. When Veronese is at his best, his interest in the flesh is neither simply decorative or whimsical. In this mixture of objects and people, this regard for common things and unsentimental sympathy for the working persons—and even animals—we sense something of the same democratic spirit that comes over in a different way in the work of Goldoni. Veronese at his best expresses a kind of spiritual sense of the importance of the least.

I was going to say "pace Ruskin" in that last sentence—but did Ruskin really dislike Veronese? *The Stones of Venice* is not the critic's last word. In his autobiography *Praeterita* (1885–1889) Ruskin describes a remarkable change of heart. In Turin for the autumn of 1858, one Sunday after attending an evangelical service in which the preacher gave a sermon "on the wickedness of the wide world, more especially of the . . . city of Turin" and on the "exclusive favour with God" of his own small congregation, Ruskin "walked back into the condemned city, and up into the gallery where Paul Veronese's Solomon and the Queen of Sheba glowed in full afternoon light." At the same time, the sound of a military band (playing music of the Risorgimento, one hopes) seemed "more devotional . . . than anything I remembered of evangelical hymns." At this moment, as Ruskin tells it, he underwent a kind of conversion: "And as the perfect colour and sound gradually asserted their power on me, they seemed finally to fasten me in the old article of Jewish faith, that things done delightfully and rightly were always done by the help and in the Spirit of God." On that day, Ruskin claims, "my evangelical beliefs were put away, to be debated of no more."[27]

It was Veronese who brought about this change. Why? Not just because of Veronese's dazzling and subtle color, though that energy got to Ruskin, who was a devotee of color. But in Veronese he sees color put to fully human use, which is also thus a religious use. After all, it is a picture of Solomon that helps Ruskin to that Jewish revelation about delightful and right works. And John Ruskin copies from the picture an image of a black woman in the train of Sheba's queen "to my father's extreme amazement and disgust, when I brought the petticoat, parrots, and blackamoor, home."[28] Veronese induces an unusual respect for the diversity of "the wide world," for the multitudes who met in Venice's islets and crowded canvases. Fortified by Jews and blacks, Ruskin could handle the psychological reversal that he called "the queen of Sheba crash."[29] Veronese brings the world to us; he is not merely decorating with crowds of exotic people. Some critics maintain that Veronese lacks human interest: "the last thing that interested Veronese was psychology."[30] Yet to say so is to ignore the touches of grief or tension, the possibility of mistake and suffering, the confusion of human interaction and the tentativeness of human relations, that lie within Veronese's luminous and textured works.

A great picture by Veronese, *The Family of Darius Before Alexander* (National Gallery, London)—great in all senses, for it is extremely large—has an important cast of characters. The center is full of the women of the family of the defeated Persian King Darius, each a mass of billowing silk and damask, kneeling gracefully before Alexander the conqueror. The women have just mistaken Alexander's best friend and lover Hephaistion (in green and with armor) for him, and the two men are laughing at the joke, while Alexander, dressed sexily in brilliant red (transparently only pseudo-covering for his belly-button), assures the women that it doesn't matter, that he and Hephaistion are one. Dramatically, the scene is about to resolve its tensions in the utterance of Alexander's promise of good treatment. The scene illustrates the Macedonian king's celebrated continence in refraining from raping these helpless women (an act of virtue classically considered noteworthy). Above this central main action is a walkway, a marble loggia, and many spectators are leaning over it, craning to see what the important people are doing—some spectators are looking down so intently that we can see only the tops of their heads. Behind the women and Alexander there is a lot going on, too; soldiers and horses are moving to and fro. A chained monkey on the parapet grins and scolds excitedly at the men and horses, turning its back to Alexander, and facing the party of less important persons on the left.

One of these is a frightened dwarf, of the Persian party evidently; he nestles for comfort against two Persian attendants, recognizable as such with their exotic costumes and brown skin. These grave-faced Persians on the far left are holding a couple of delightful little dogs, and the dwarf, childlike, throws his left arm for consolation about one of these cute doggies. The sentiment of the scene is officially in the momentous meeting of high personages, and unofficially in the conflicting hints of sexuality between Alexander and his friend, and between Alexander and the elegant young woman. But the true emotion of the scene, the shock of overthrow and helpless people's fear of maltreatment—these are captured by the dwarf, the attendants, the monkey, and the big-eyed little dogs. These express the fear, anxiety, and tension not allowed to the calm of the main company. In his "low" characters and in his animals is Veronese's truth.

Among Veronese's big "party pieces" perhaps we ought strangely to include *Saint Sebastian with Saints Mark and Marcellinus*, one of the series of paintings of the life of Saint Sebastian that Veronese made for his own parish church of San Sebastiano near the Zattere (see Plate 6). The subject of this picture is Saint Sebastian encouraging the young men Mark and Marcellino to go forward to martyrdom. According to tradition Sebastian, an officer in the Roman army, encouraged the young martyrs when they were already languishing in prison, awaiting their end. But Veronese has chosen to make

it more dramatic, to show Sebastian arousing them to go off and be martyred. In the center of this big painting Saint Sebastian, in armor as a knight
of the Cross, holds in his left hand a banner which already intimates a cross,
while with his right he imperiously summons away the two handsome
bearded young men, already fettered and in charge. The party are in front of
a handsome marble building, with many columns. (The steps were put in by
a nineteenth-century restorer to make sense of Veronese's unorthodox use of
perspective.)[31] This building has been read as a hall of justice, but the presence of the women, including a little girl, and the pets makes it more legitimate to read it as a wealthy family's home, in which the young sons have
been arrested and from whence they are now being hauled off to the outer
world where curious spectators await them. The crowd looks almost as if a
dinner-party has been broken up and streamed outdoors. The agitated parents are trying to stop the ineluctable progress of the arresting officers, and
the imperious "Forward!" of Saint Sebastian's raised arm.

In the midst of the action, left of center but sharing with the saint domi-
nance of the scene, is an aging woman, the mother of the two young men.
She is still dark-haired but her face is haggard, deeply lined, and currently
red at the nose and eyes. Disheveled, she accidentally displays unbeautiful
bony neck and collarbones, but she cares nothing for the impression she
makes—all her energies are engaged in expostulating, imploring, stretching
out her arms, trying to hold back the dreadful event. She is dressed in Veronese's favorite golden yellow, with deep touches of saffron; the mantle flows
importantly about her. I choose to reproduce this painting which is in such
a contrast to the oft-reproduced picture of the *Triumph of Venice*. Unlike
golden Venice in similar drapery, this woman is distinguished by her agony,
her nightmarish incapacity to prevent the worst. She is deeply interesting.
Age and dishevelment do not diminish her; Veronese treats her with full respect for her suffering. One can feel how much the agonized mother hates
Sebastian at this moment.

Below these groups, beggars marvel confusedly at the chaos taking place
among these rich people. A blotchy dog with a furry neck, some kind of set-
ter, trots delicately, not knowing what the trouble is. Behind the futilely active mother is a plinth, perhaps a pagan altar, and on it a monkey innocently
lifts its paw, mimicking the important gesture of imperious Saint Sebastian.

In the *Golden Legend,* much time elapses between Sebastian's encouragement of the young martyrs and his own martyrdom. Converted, he is sentenced to
be shot to death by flights of arrows. This attempt actually fails; the youth

survives, nursed by Saint Irene. But after expostulating with Diocletian, Sebastian is again sentenced, this time to be pounded to death. Veronese collapses the time. He has contrived his two big companion pieces so that it feels as if Sebastian went straight from leading the young men on to their death to his own death—as if, when he is moving down the steps in glorious armor, he is already rushing ahead to his final scene.

The companion picture on the other side of the sanctuary shows Sebastian no longer armed and heroic. His armor has been removed, he has no shell, his recumbent and compacted body looks flabby, soft and fetal, as men handle his parts with hideous familiarity (they seem to be about to do something dreadful to his scrotum). This is not our usual picture of the upright, handsome, arrow-shot Sebastian. No other martyred saint has been presented in such an embarrassing and reductive physical form. Sebastian lifts his arm in the old gesture, but the arm, defamiliarized, is like a stick, as the arm of the pagan priest overlays it. We are sent back to the monkey's gesture on the opposite wall. The monkey helps us to count the cost of martyrdom.

This monkey in the Sebastian scene resembles the one found in other Veronese pictures, and it goes a long way to explain those. Veronese's favorite monkey in its innocent physicality echoes the human gestures, and represents the vulnerable human and animal body. Veronese's "monkey talk" is an appeal in the name of the needs of the natural, the pathos of the human at its simple animal level. Veronese's monkey is what must never be left out, the reality of physical life, of corporal vulnerability and of human suffering. When I first came to Venice, I agreed (without knowing it) with the earlier Ruskin, seeing in Veronese the most shallow and jolly of Venetian decorators. Respect grew over the years. At last—like Ruskin—I have changed my mind, but it was the church of San Sebastiano that truly pushed me over. Now Veronese seems to me a theological painter, a spiritual painter, searching for the immanent truth in the experience of the flesh. The virtue he pursues in the incarnate and the mundane is compassion—a compassion that will not omit the lowly and the physical.

Jacopo Robusti, best known as Tintoretto (1518–1594), son of a citizen dyer of cloth, proves the capacity of Venetian art to shoot up from humble ground, as Ridolfi seems to emphasize.[32] Jacopo's family worked in color at the most basic level; we can see their house in Cannaregio still, sturdy but nonpalatial. Tintoretto shares Veronese's interest in crowds of internal spectators. Less concerned than either Titian or Veronese in pleasure, he is even more interested in representing and exploiting abrupt swooping movement.

One can see what he got from examples like Titian's leaping Bacchus. Titian appears in fact to have been somewhat hostile to Tintoretto (he is said to have kicked him out of his workshop); the two great painters differed in background and ethos. Unlike Veronese, who had adopted the spurious surname "Caliari" to get away from his familial stone-cutting origins, Tintoretto sustained the reference to his origins in his name—he is a *tintore*, or rather a *tintoretto*, a little dyer. His very name shrieks of color, and thus of Venice.

I see that my own 1961 postcard from Venice comments with odd admiration on the number of Tintorettos. I daresay this artist struck me particularly because he is so very Venetian, and one sees far fewer examples of his work elsewhere. Ruskin rightly says Venice is the only place in which to see him. Tintoretto remained in Venice essentially all his life; unlike Titian, he had few commissions from powerful courts and petty rulers on the mainland or in Europe. He was controversial, often appearing inelegant, particularly to some of the most classicizing theorists. His treatment of traditional scenes and themes was odd, sometimes even markedly comic: see the disciple getting his boots pulled off in the scene of Christ washing the feet of the disciples (Prado); the god Mars crouching under the bed of Venus, about to be given away by the yapping dog (Munich). Vasari was rather horrified at Tintoretto, a kind of monster, "extravagant, capricious, quick and resolute, with the most ferocious brain that Painting ever had."[33] Tintoretto with his strange concepts and lack of *disegno* seemed to be turning art into a jest, *una bai*, mocking the seriousness of the enterprise. If only he had studied properly in youth! Even Veronese feared (according to Ridolfi) that Tintoretto would bring the art of Venice into disrepute. His brushwork appeared too loose. One of the chief (and constant) charges against him was that he worked too fast. He seems to have broken with his former friend Pietro Aretino, perhaps over Tintoretto's disregard of the *littérateur*'s instructions to rein in his imagination, to be patient and paint *carefully*.[34]

At the same time, Tintoretto thought of himself as a champion of *disegno* since he was an enthusiast for Michelangelo. He is supposed to have put up the following ambitious motto over his studio door: "The design (*disegno*) of Michelangelo and the coloring (*colorito*) of Titian."[35] His contemporaries had to give way before his energies. Ridolfi says of him "bollivano continuamente nuovi pensieri nel fecondo ingegno suo" ("new ideas were always boiling in his fecund mind").[36]

Tintoretto is one of those big, dashing painters who require large subjects and canvases to be seen at their best. He is interested in crowds, as Carpaccio is, but he is not enamored of the appurtenances of wealth, like Veronese, and does not present us with fashionable company. We do not stop to inquire what kind of sweet silk this must be, or to marvel at the representation of delicate glass goblets. Tintoretto at last got his chance to show what he could do in the (controversial and disputatious) commission in 1564 to paint pictures for the walls of Scuola Grande di San Rocco. This exhibition of scenes from the Bible remains a necessary point of pilgrimage for all visitors, even though generations have complained about the difficulty of seeing such large and full paintings under the dim light. Once you do manage to descry them, they are so overpowering as to be hard to take in; as with Veronese—but how different in tone—we have crowds of figures at different levels. The ceiling panel of *The Brazen Serpent* has a divine or heavenly level, and below that a salvational level (Moses erecting the serpent on a pole, type of Christ on the Cross), and down again a human level of suffering and death, as the serpents are biting various bodies who have fallen and lie writhing on the ground. Allusion to the contemporary plague must have seemed uncomfortably immediate and real. The viewer cannot choose not to feel for the poor tormented bodies, even if their fate anticipates the Last Judgment. In *The Gathering of Manna*, a happier topic, manna rains down like snowflakes upon human need, out of a divine and golden sky, from something that looks like a boat made of stars. Everywhere is populous and full, movement is everywhere, in masses of shadow and masses of light. Strange colors, particularly fire colors, dominate these pieces, suitably enough in *The Pillar of Fire*, but they are equally present in *Moses Striking the Rock*.

In the scenes for San Rocco, Tintoretto apparently had a program in mind, to speak up for the needs of humanity and for humility—the Scuola had already been faulted for hypocrisy, vainglory, and wasteful expenditure. Rarely has a sermon been committed with so much passion. We feel exuberance as part of the motive power, and a constant sense of energy in the universe. That sense is not absent from Tintoretto's secular mythological paintings, but it is always urgently present in the works with a religious theme. In showing *The Creation of the Animals* (Accademia), Tintoretto revels in the multiplicity of animal life (Figure 17). His creation picture seems focused on the birds, though animals spring out of the earth and gambol beneath God's flying feet, and a Daliesque white horse is coming up behind Him. The sea is full of creatures shouldering each other, and above them the birds fly swiftly away, moving from right to left, as if shooting out of the picture. God appears deeply engaged in the delight of creativity, and seems

Figure 17. Jacopo Tintoretto, *The Creation of the Animals* (Scala/ Art Resource, NY)

to be jumping and saying, "Go! Go!" to the swift new birds, as to Olympic performers. Yet with all this excitement, some calm little rabbits unperturbed feed beneath God's skipping feet.

Tintoretto is attracted by flight. In *The Miracle of the Slave* (Accademia), one of a series presenting miracles of Saint Mark, the saint in crimson swoops in overhead to rescue a slave who is about to be tortured. The story is of a pagan lord of Provence, whose slave had dedicated himself to Saint Mark. Angry at the defection to the new faith, the lord ordered the slave's eyes to be put out, then that his mouth should be smashed in, but the executioners were powerless over the body of the dedicated man. Here we see the extended body of the slave supine on the pavement, his upturned face surrounded by the executioners. The scene is animated, and full of persons, including the lord and his attendants at our right (stage left as it were) and spectators at the viewer's left. Prominent among these spectators is a woman, well grown and even a little broad in the beam, dressed in orange and holding a child. This woman is one of the humble, for she is barefooted and even barelegged. It has been suggested that the recurrent woman and child in Tintoretto's works represent *Caritas*—Charity. However that may be, Tintoretto is notably open to including the lower orders in his scenes. Executioners are milling around, protesting as their instruments are breaking in their hands. One man in green on our right holds up the broken mallet, exclaiming indignantly to the glum authority dressed in dark red on the far right of the picture, ignorant of the swooping saint just above him. The slave's face seems to be illumined by the glory of the saint, but we cannot see Saint Mark's face—only the effect of his dive as he comes from an otherwhere into the here. It is a picture of an action. Moderns will inevitably be reminded of Superman and Batman, but such a painting reminds us that the origins of such personages are religious.

We have already glanced at one of the greatest paintings in the Accademia, *The Removal of the Body of Saint Mark* (see Plate 1). Tintoretto represents the foundational legendary episode in Alexandria when a terrific storm gave the Christians cover to take away and conceal the body of Saint Mark just after he had died. The square or piazza in which this action takes place looks amazingly like the Piazza San Marco, with a long arcade on the viewer's left extending toward a church, which seems to stand in the place of San Geminiano. Terrified Alexandrians are fleeing under the arches into the arcade to get away from the storm. These living people are pale and almost transparent, like ghosts, in contrast to the solid and unignorable flesh of the dead man. As in Giorgione's *La Tempesta*, lightning rends the air. In the background is a jumbled heap of wood, what remains of the funeral pyre on which the Alexandrians had proposed to eradicate the body of Mark. The group at the right is handling the body of Saint Mark, which is extended almost full length (save that the legs dangle). The body is white, powerful, and fully masculine. Behind this protective group of helpers there looms a camel. It evidently had some sort of business with the load of firewood intended for use in the burning of the saintly corpse. The camel is exotic (it tells us we are in Egypt, not in Italy). It seems agitated. Is the beast baleful or sympathetic? The driver of the camel is having much ado to restrain it, forced to lie almost recumbent on the ground, so fierce is the storm and so strong the pull of the beast. An androgynous figure in a purplish-red robe, this camel driver grasps the rope with left hand extended and right hand on the pavement, pulling with all his force. We cannot make out the profiled face very clearly, but this person has a shock of short red hair. It is an amazingly modern figure; if you abstract it from its context, it could have been painted by Toulouse-Lautrec. At the very front of the picture, next to us as it were, the cadent body of a human being, falling supine, clutches wildly at a swatch of pink fabric coming from nowhere. Odd energies are charging through the painting, energies left unresolved.

What might resolve these conflicting and unsatisfied forces is a new place—the building we cannot see, the church of San Marco, which will arise behind where the viewer stands in the real city of which this Alexandria is but an antitype and forerunner. The rescuers are really bringing the body of the saint toward the church of San Marco, in the future. So they are also lugging the body of Mark through time as well as space. A great and adorned Venice is the unseen prophetic location for which the body of Mark is destined. As David Rosand notes in *Myths of Venice*, this is "the kind of iconographic slippage and historical prolepsis that . . . we . . . expect in the world of Venetian imagery."[37]

It is a far cry from the action and drama of Tintoretto to the calm detail of the eighteenth century's Antonio Canal or Canaletto (1697–1768). For Canaletto, Venice is not a visionary future but a presence to be elaborately caught and interpreted again and again. Canaletto has come to seem a promoter of the tourist trade—which he undoubtedly was. His *vedute* were sold to travelers making the Grand Tour and also to admirers from other parts of Italy. His first "foreign" commission seems to have been from a merchant of Lucca who had collected views of Venice by an artist named Carlevaris, who had produced *Fabriche e Vedute di Venezia* in 1704. When the Luccan contacted his agent in Venice, Mareschini, the latter told him that there was a new painter who did the same sort of thing but better, as he could paint "the effects of sunlight."[38]

Born near the Rialto Bridge, Canaletto, like Tintoretto, is a true native of central Venice. Under his portrait, the frontispiece of his book of views of Venice, *Prospectus Magi Canalis Venetiarum* (1735), he placed the inscription *Antonius Canale. Origine Civis Venetus.* He was thus a descendant not of the patrician line but of the second class, the *cittadini*. His father was a painter of scenery for the theaters (which links him with the world of Goldoni and Casanova), and there is a theatrical quality to Canaletto's views. This connects the eighteenth-century artist with Veronese and Tintoretto, in a way, for the sixteenth-century painters' backgrounds often resemble theater sets, and Tintoretto made his own mock-ups of spaces, as stage designers do. Canaletto's views, like all *vedute*, have a theatrical element, and they are playful.

The young artist was lucky enough to be noticed by Owen McSwiney, who asked him to do some work for the Duke of Richmond. Then Canaletto had the even greater good luck to be noticed by Joseph Smith, a wealthy English merchant who had got himself made consul to Venice in 1744 and lived in great splendor in the Palazzo Balbi. The consul was a popular party-giver;

the hapless lovers Andrea Memmo and Giustiniana Wynne met at his house, and Casanova was one of his guests.[39] Smith was recognized by Venetians as a patron of the arts: Goldoni dedicated to him his play *Il Filosofo Inglese,* and, as we have seen, Smith encouraged the printer Pasquali to print the works of the *philosophes.* Something of a wheeler-dealer, Smith patronized artists and acted—not unrewardingly—as a middleman, commissioning works which he could sell on the foreign market. Smith now worked with Canaletto, getting him commissions from wealthy and even titled Britons, like the fourth Duke of Bedford.

Unlike their medieval and Renaissance predecessors, eighteenth-century Venetian painters could not rely on commissions from government offices with large new spaces to fill, or from churches, or from *scuole*; they needed private clients and commercial customers. Portrait painting, already a feature in Bellini's time, rose in importance, permitting a woman artist like Rosalba Carriera (1675–1757) to do more than make a living with her overtly modest but telling studies in pastels. Carriera, born in Chioggia, was to spend much of her life abroad, where she was admired, and hired, by some famous sitters. Her own self-portrait in middle age, now in the Accademia, gives evidence of a toughness of spirit and a kind of realism about personality and the body. Unlike Carriera, Canaletto would have lost his subject if he went abroad for very long (though he did eventually go to England, and painted English scenes). His genius really flourished in Venice, his inspiration and his subject, but he needed pipelines by which to export his various views of Venice. Canaletto's paintings are a kind of *poesie,* serving those in remote climes as creations of a place that appeals intensely to the imagination. *Vedute* permit a play of fantasy; this was an era in which painters like Guardi played with imaginary structures and fantastic towns. It is a mistake to expect all of Canaletto's scenes to be realistic representations, like photographs; they have something more in common with the portrait—or even with the mask— capturing an inner nature, or a different orientation, or a play of possibilities.

Canaletto was no mere recorder of the real canal before him; he could do that, but he could also vary or multiply perspectives, playing tricks with the sight lines and the proportion of the buildings. He could show you more than any real-life viewer could ever see from any one point of view. He used a camera obscura to capture the scene, and thus could see the 360-degree view that is impossible for the bystander in life. Canaletto's tricks with places and point of view infuriate Henry James, who considers his works as so many lies: "and here too . . . is San Simeone Profeta, I won't say immortalised, but

unblushingly represented, by the perfidious Canaletto. I shall not stay to un-
ravel the mystery of the prosaic painter's malpractices; he falsified without
fancy, and as he apparently transposed at will the objects he reproduced, one
is never sure of the particular view that may have constituted his subject. It
would look exactly like such and such a place if almost everything were not
different."[40]

Annoyed, James unjustly calls him "prosaic" but, like the other Venetians,
Canaletto is imaginative and in love with color. All of the Venetian artists
from the Bellini on are wrestling with the problem of representing movement
and light—especially in the terms of place. They prophetically perform in
their art the great suggestion of Isaac Newton in the celebrated thirtieth
"Question" at the end of his *Opticks:* "The changing of Bodies into Light and
Light into Bodies, is very conformable to the Course of Nature, which seems
delighted with Transmutations. . . . And among such various and strange
Transmutations, why may not Nature change Bodies into Light, and Light
into Bodies?"[41] Light may be turning into matter and matter may be becoming light—as they do in Venetian paintings, which may be one of the influences at work on Newton, too. "Place" then may be a temporary effect of
transmutation, the impermanent construction of light. It is the happy conjunction of energies that Canaletto rejoices to celebrate.

Canaletto may be considered as in the line of both Bellini and Carpaccio,
especially if we consider both those painters' cityscapes in the series on the
True Cross. The eighteenth-century artist of the cityscape can work on less
than glamorous scenes, and not all his works are effulgent depictions of the
Grand Canal. A painting presently in Ca' Rezzonico shows a scene by the
Canal dei Mendicanti (see Plate 7). Some fine folk walk on our left, on
the *fondamenta* between the canal and the giant handsome building which is
now the Ospedale Civile, but the right side (of the canal and of the painting)
is devoted to common persons. We are obviously looking at a modest *squero*
or boatyard. (The *squero* was still in the same area at the turn into the twentieth century, and the place is briefly described by Rolfe in *The Desire and Pursuit
of the Whole*.)[42] Canaletto's scene is abustle with lowly activity. Men and
women are pushing a beached boat out into the water. Above, a woman is
shaking her broom out the window, giving the folks below the benefit of its
gleanings. There are acres of laundry drying among the roofs and chimney-
pots. Here is Canaletto showing his Carpaccio side.

Another painting by Canaletto most interesting to me is the one that the
English National Gallery calls *The Stonemason's Yard* (Figure 18), though it

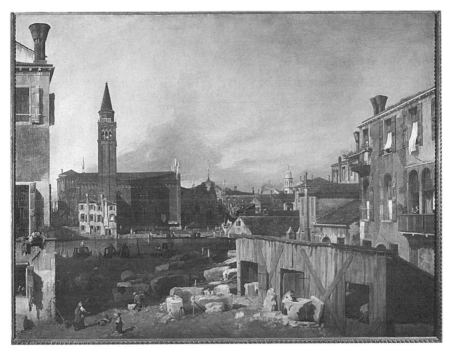

Figure 18. Giovanni Antonio Canaletto, *The Stonemason's Yard* (Erich Lessing/ Art Resource, NY)

should perhaps be called "Campo S. Vidal and Santa Maria della Carità." We are looking from a very raw Campo S. Vidal across the underemphasized canal toward the church of Santa Maria della Carità and the Scuola—that is, toward the set of buildings later turned into the Accademia. But the focus in this painting is not on finished buildings but on raw material, the stone heaps which the mason must make into shapes—pieces of the church of San Vidal in the process of construction, or it may be *palazzi* in the making. The buildings near us are by no means palatial. Nor are they in first-rate repair; the walls look blotchy. We realize that the dilapidated look—recorded, for example, in the narrator's view of peeling stucco in *The Aspern Papers* or in ominous film representations like *Don't Look Now*—must be a Venetian constant. There are always some walls with the stucco peeling off, or bricks crumbling. Laundry flutters from the windows. There is a jerry-built and flimsy shanty built up against the house on our right, where a woman is spinning on her balcony. In the foreground near us a woman has just issued from the door of the shanty to draw water from the well. On our left, a little child has fallen down and is mother rushes toward it, while a neighbor on the second floor cranes her neck to see what has happened.

This painting is a striking tribute to the mundane Venice of the workaday world. Canaletto's painting is a brilliant study in the play of horizontals at different angles. The campanile of Carità (soon to fall down) provides a unifying central vertical. The buildings may seem at first to take precedence over the people, and yet they do not; as we look we are more and more aware of seeing Venice's working people in the dawn light. We grasp their activities in detail, including the wash line on the opposite side of the canal. The painting's subject is the processes of making—of making Venice through the stones which will be the stones of Venice, of making new children, new fabric, a new day. Usually, the populace of Venice matter less to Canaletto than to Carpaccio; people are there but seldom individualized. In the glamour pieces made expressly for the tourist trade (or for rich foreigners who would like to fancy themselves in Venice), buildings take center stage—the buildings and their reflections in the water. Everything is translucent, liquid; the solidity of the buildings dissolves in the shifting reflections as light plays over them. Canaletto shows us that light itself both illuminates reality and creates fiction—and that seeing itself is always partly an act of fiction, that is of making. He is perfectly aware of what people are leaving out of their view—the common things and persons he sometimes puts back in, as in these two paintings.

With Canaletto's close contemporary Giambattista Tiepolo (Giovanni Battista, 1696–1770) we have an apotheosis of the fictional, an escape into the world of poesy itself. Here is an unusually patrician artist, a descendant of one of the first families of Venice (the Tiepolos gave the city a couple of Doges, and a famous rebel). Giambattista is confident and capable, able to handle large and lofty spaces with ease. Tiepolo senior is attracted to poised figures under or in the midst of extensive blue skies; he likes legendary scenes, pious or secular. He is very good on Tasso's Rinaldo enchanted by Armida (Chicago); His best characters are in repose, and—how unlike Giorgione's—not customarily engaged in conflict or ruffled by much anxiety. Tiepolo's colors incline toward complex pastels, and always there is a great radiant sky pouring down soft light. Tiepolo is "romantic" in the sense that his world resembles that of the French romances of the seventeenth century, possessing a great leisure, great space, and vibrant possibilities of adoration and peace. Tiepolo, all light and poesy, is at almost the furthest remove from

Carpaccio—save in his fondness for crowds. The crowds in Tiepolo are complex, one figure pressing over another so that we rarely see the whole form of a personage, but a face here, a shoulder and feet there. There is something of Bellini in him still, a kind of tenderness. But Tiepolo (in his great set pieces) cannot seem to bear any internal lack of tranquility. Compared to Tiepolo, Bellini is nervous.

Tiepolo has obviously studied the work of Veronese attentively. His architecture and color sometimes resemble Veronese's, but the colors are lighter, and his people are not expansive and assertive (like Veronese's), but quiet, even dreamy and introspective. There is usually something encouraging or consoling about a Tiepolo, but the artist does not rouse intense emotion. We don't have the sense of having been scrambled into something vast and urgent—if hard to comprehend—that we do with Tintoretto. Svetlana Alpers and Michael Baxandall point out that Tiepolo "favours . . . scenes of discovery that thematize beholding."[43] His crowds and heroic individuals prefer to have something to contemplate, rather than something to do.

Giambattista Tiepolo's son Giandomenico Tiepelo (1727–1804) will appeal to many of our contemporaries—as to myself—as the more interesting artist of the two, even if traditional classification has presented him as "minor." Giandomenico was under the shade of his father for a long while, but one can see him beginning to blossom out more and more into his own themes in midlife. Yet such a judgment is not exactly fair to Giambattista Tiepolo, who had other visions than sheer rococo allegory. In an embedded self-portrait as the artist in *Apelles and Campaspé* (Montreal) he gives himself a kind of caricature nose, a strong obstinate Venetian nose like Pulcinella (Punch) or Pantalone, an indication that he feels an affinity for such characters. Giambattista produced a series of puzzling etchings, starting with ten produced in 1743. Later, when father and son were both at Madrid, he got his son Giandomenico to do the actual etchings; this second set of twenty-four pieces was published by Giandomenico in 1775, after his father's death. In these playful and disturbing *Scherzi* the elder Tiepolo expresses material he wasn't usually able to get out—it strikes one at once that these disturbing capriccios must have been known to Goya. The *Scherzi* include some remarkable works, including *The Discovery of the Tomb of Pulcinella*, which adumbrates some favorite motifs of the artist's son. In that *Discovery*, it would seem that both primitive and civilized cultures seek something—something vital and humorous—that is needed and has been lost. It strikes you that Tiepolo, however languidly perfect he sometimes seems, is inwardly alert to the cost of civilization.

Giandomenico went further in the direction pointed to by the *Scherzi*; it is as if Giandomenico were determined to give more room to the disturbing reality that his father could let himself see in side glances, though both artists knew that "reality" can only be represented fantastically. Neither of the more famous Tiepolos (there was another painter-son as well) was greatly interested in painting legendary history or real-life scenes. Both of them went in for the fantastic and allegorical. Giandomenico painted frescoes for the family's inland villa, the Villa di Zianigo—a space not subject to commission or the ordinances of churches or princes. He was able there to paint what he wished to say—if only, so it must have seemed, for himself. These frescoes have now been collected and brought to Ca' Rezzonico. The most noted of these is *Il Novo Mondo*, but there are others, including the "Pulcinella" paintings and sketches of late works involving these Punch figures. Giandomenico makes up stories about satyrs and centaurs, male and female, and their families, humanized and sometimes rather desperate. Perhaps he picked up something of Titian's baby satyr in *Bacchus and Ariadne*, or Bellini's little centaur in the allegorical *Conversazione* or *Allegoria Sacra*. (Although in Bellini's picture the centaur is officially supposed to represent evil, there is something appealing about the little figure.) Giandomenico's commedia dell'arte figures are absurd, lonely (if ironic), and puzzled. For Giandomenico, Pulcinella or Punch seems to represent the average man or perhaps just the unidentifiable and unplaceable self, caught up in an act and acting absurdly, in a world that is itself absurd but manifests an underlying menace. This sense of things gives unusual power to his moving series of the *Via Crucis* in San Polo. (Tiepolo was one of the first pictorial inventors of the modern Stations of the Cross.) Christ's suffering (within the absurdity of social arrangements and flat cruelty) is, like that of Giandomenico's centaurs or commedia figures, unusually believable, and disturbing.

Giandomenico's *Il Novo Mondo* (see Plate 8), produced in 1791, ironically captures the eighteenth century's optimism about the future, about technology and control. In a flat white light, like the light of reason, we see a group of well-dressed people with their backs to us. None of these is poor; the ladies' shoes look like modern footgear by Ferragamo. It is quite a large group (I counted twenty-seven figures, but may have missed some); the crowding effect is achieved by adapting Giambattista's techniques of crunching figures together in suggestive parts. The effect of the painting resides partly in its horizontal stretch—an effect practically always severely under-mined by reproductions. These people are of various ages and sexes. Giando-menico has put himself and his father among the crowd at the right—spectators themselves par excellence, they too, like their companions, may be partly deluded by the act of looking at what they are seeing. On one narrative level, this little crowd is lined up to gaze through a mechanical contraption at a diorama, offered by a showman. They are not watching a sacred or civic event unfold, like people crowding a Carpaccio or Tintoretto canvas; they are just amusing themselves with speculation, an entertainment. But they seem quite serious, quite intent. On another narrative level, these people with their backs to us are gazing out to sea or at a distance. The woman in the center, broad in the beam with an orange jacket, may remind us of Tintoretto's poor woman, the spectator in the orange dress. Giandomenico seems to have stud-ied many of the crowd scenes in earlier Venetian works, and to have imitated or quoted them while swiveling everyone around to look away from the viewer. This is indeed a scene of "discovery and beholding."

On second thoughts, it occurs to us, these persons are in a sense behold-ing a sacred, new, and awe-inspiring event. Their sacred event in 1791 is the future, the "new world" that is coming. The French Revolution has already arrived. These happy people of the beginning of the revolutionary decade are looking to the future. Behind them, nearer us on our left, a Pulcinella figure, holding a sausage on a slightly diabolical fork, also looks out, but with a mixture of hope and knowing dubiety, sadly mocking their hopefulness and faith in the new. Little did they know—so we can reflect—those well-dressed Venetians looking so hopefully to the future, how very ugly and terrible the Venetian future was shortly to become.

8

———

Cybele-Venus-Venice
Women in Venetian Art

She looks a sea Cybele, fresh from ocean,
Rising with her tiara of proud towers
At airy distance, with majestic motion,
A ruler of the waters and their powers
—Byron, *Childe Harold's Pilgrimage*

Aut Venus à Venetis sibi fecit amabile nomen,
Aut Veneti Veneris nomen, & omen habent.
Either Venus from the Venetians made herself a lovable name,
Or the Venetians have their name and significance from Venus.

Color traditionally is feminine, design or drawing, like form itself, masculine. The Venetians visibly—even erroneously in the eyes of some non-Venetian theorists—tilted to the side of the feminine principle. Not only did they do so, they were very interested in depicting women, and the art of Venice, though not practiced by many women, has a strongly "feminine" slant in its subject matter. The feminine emerges as we gaze upon Venice as one of the tropes of this tropic. It is a trope not at all unselfconscious. It is manifest in the weathervane figure on top of the seventeenth-century customs house, the Dogana di Mare beyond Salute on the promontory of Dorsoduro; the figure is Fortuna, veering goldenly about at the head of the Grand Canal.

One serious rendition of the city's own nature is as personification of Justitia, the feminine figure of Justice, with her lion (or lions) by her side and her sword in her hand. Justitia appeals to the sense of value for Venetian law and constitution, but hers is a severe rather than an appealing image. It goes in almost the opposite direction from the most appealing image of all, which is that of the Virgin Mary. The most popular feminine image in Venetian art is undoubtedly the Virgin Mary. This hardly renders the Venetians singular in Europe. What is unusual, I think, is the fact that the Venetian representation of Mary is so thoroughly imbued from the beginning by the Greek ideas of the Mother of God. All Venetian images of Mary have their elder sister in the Church of Santa Maria e San Donato on Murano. Founded in the seventh century as the Church of Saint Mary, this church was rebuilt in its present form in the twelfth century; the apse mosaic, like the brilliant pavement mosaics, dates from that period. This Virgin of Murano in the apse has her hands raised in prayer. She is not tending her baby, or listening to an angel, but communicating steadily with the divine, erect and blue.

The first images of Mary on the islands are Byzantine in inspiration, Venetian in spirit. In the cathedral at Torcello, the central apse bears a large and long representation of Mary holding the Christ Child—so identified by the Greek letters above their heads. The figures, one holding and dwarfing the other, are in a golden field. The Virgin dominates the whole church, and towers above the apostles ranged in a meek line circling the apse on the level below. She stands on a cushion in a blue robe that falls in graceful folds about her knees. In her left hand, holding the Christ Child, there is a small oblong napkin or stole. Her robe has a kind of peplum with long gold fringes. She looks steadily out over the whole church, catching the viewer with that direct Byzantine gaze so disconcerting if we are used to the more modest or abstracted look of later saints. One imagines that the bishop in his chair would become nervously conscious of her eyes boring into his back. On the front of the arch that forms the apse, we have the Annunciation. On the left spandrel is the angel, and on the viewer's right the figure of Mary. She raises her right hand in greeting and in acquiescence—figuring the moment of conception. She is calm, erect, her dignified head not bowed. Her left hand holds a distaff, signifying her role as spinner of flesh—a symbol made more explicit in the Byzantine church of Kariye Camii in Istanbul, where the mosaics tell what had become the standard story of the early life of Mary, derived chiefly from the apocryphal Gospel of Saint James. According to that story, the girl Mary was given purple wool to spin to make the fabric of the veil of the Temple, prefiguring her sacred mission of spinning bodily life for the Messiah.[1]

The figure of Mary of the distaff (or spindle) appears elsewhere in Venice; the thirteenth-century church of San Giacomo dell'Orio has a delightful small Byzantine carving of the Virgin (stolen from Constantinople); she is holding the spindle of wool in her left hand. In honoring Mary as the life-spinner, artists and worshipers are declaring the value of physical and fleshly embodied life, of incarnation. Mary in such strong representation is not a meek and recompensing substitute for the erring Eve, but an important partner in creation with a life-giving skill of fabricating flesh, blood, and bone, giving human reality to idea. The Eastern Church (at least in its theory) never seems to have been quite as down on Woman as the Western Catholic church became, and it is less likely to be reminded of Eve and her sins when contemplating Mary. (*Ave fit ex Eva* doesn't work in Greek.) It was in the Council of Ephesus held in Greek Asia Minor that Mary was announced to have a peculiarly exalted state. Byzantine theology and art honor her as the godbearer—Theotokos.

The Byzantine cast of the early mosaic figures is noticeable. Yet many surviving Byzantine mosaics seem a little more restful than these Venetian images. If you look, for instance, at the tenth-century mosaic images originally in Hagia Sophia, you will see that the characters are as likely to be sitting as standing, and that they are more reposeful than the Venetian representations. Emperor Justinian and Emperor Constantine both stand beside the Holy Mother and Child, stooping under the weight of model buildings they are carrying, but looking quite patient. The Virgin sits with the child in her lap, blue gown in folds from knees to feet; she sits on a green cushion, and seems well settled. In comparison, the early works at Torcello and Murano seem electric and demanding. That restful quality of the truly Byzantine Madonna will be translated in the Quattrocento by Giovanni Bellini, Venice's most credible painter of benign Madonnas, but he also insists on the sternness, the dignity, the suffering and endurance.

One of Bellini's pictures of the Madonna and Child is in the apse of the Sacristy in the Frari—or to give the church its whole name, Chiesa di Santa Maria Gloriosa dei Frari. Bellini's painting here is a triptych with the Madonna and child (and attendant musical angels) in the center, between Saint Nicholas of Bari and Saints Peter, Mark, and Benedict. This picture (1488) is a modernized and Renaissance-minded version of the same idea that we find in tenth-century Constantinople. The Virgin, seated on a dais with a circular background of gold, holds her child, her blue-green mantle drifting down in interesting folds over her knees. But the baby is a toddler of full development, trying to walk away out of his mother's arms. He is naked; his belly is tubbed out and his genitals quite visible. Underneath the dais are two other chubby children, sassy little angels looking like little girls who have had a musical education, and have graduated into wings. Their hair is prettily arranged in crisping curls or ringlets. One plays the lute, the other blows a pipe. As they stand on the porphyry stairs, their Shirley Temple heads frame a plinth on which the artist has put his name in gold letters. (This, as much as the introduction of neoclassical pilasters and the naturalistic child, would tell us where we are in time. The Renaissance—to use a personification that annoys some—does not care for anonymity.) It is perhaps this picture that led to the sweet drink. But the Madonna is strong rather than pretty.

Bellini, as we have seen in the *Pietà* in the Palazzo Ducale, is not afraid of exhibiting the Virgin as changing under the pressure of circumstances. The Accademia possesses another Bellini *Pietà*, with no attendant saint. Here the Virgin is entirely alone with the corpse of her child. Sitting on the ground, an emblem of humility, she is a rather massive figure in robe and mantle. In her lap she holds the adult body of her dead son. The place where she sits is desert-like; only a few rough bits of herbage grow out of sandy soil. Beside her is the tall stump of a tree that has been cut off—as life has been cut off from the man. Across a tawny distance we see the walls of a city. We may take that to be Jerusalem, if we wish, but there are no geographical emphases. Neither is where we are, that sandy nowhere place, specified as Calvary (there are no crosses). The city with its walls and campanile seems like any Italian city of the mainland; it is going about its own business—who can doubt it?—indifferent to the two silent figures, one dead, the other grieving. The mourning Virgin wears a white scarf looped about her head and neck. Her hair is no longer completely covered, and we can see that it is thinning, the hair of a middle-aged woman. Her face has lines upon it, and bears the pinch of grief.

Besides this *Pietà* in the Accademia we can (imaginatively) set a Bellini painting in the National Gallery in London, of the *Madonna del Prato* or *Madonna of the Meadow* (see Plate 9). Here the Virgin, dominantly vertical, again sits on the ground, on a grassy patch of earth in the foreground like a strip of faded damask in comparison with the almost intrusively harsh, bare, gravelly earth behind her. The Virgin's baby is in her lap, but her hands are held touching in prayer, not fondling him; her white silk scarf has slipped and lets us see her auburn hair. Behind her, beyond the strip of sandy soil, there are laborers in the fields; one brown-skinned worker is sitting beside his ox, resting from the midday sun, perhaps watching a white stork trying to catch a snake. On a leafless tree, a dark vulture waits, scenting the death of the child.

On our right, moving toward the left, is a white figure in a headscarf, perhaps a female peasant, apparently releasing an ox and some goats from a penfold. Beyond these again there is a long fence, running the length of the picture on the horizontal, and behind that a small town or large fortified manor, with towers. Above this is a ribbon of curly cloud, another horizontal. Much of this painting is taken up by a delicate and fresh blue sky, creating the effect of a light wind blowing and an exhalation of earth in the air, like a morning in March. The freshness mingles with the sadness, as with an invalid at daybreak waiting to endure the painful day. To modern eyes, the clouds above the towers are reminiscent of industrial plumes, strangely adding to the effect a sense of threat and contamination, as well as to the contrast between busyness and quietness. The background and the foreground are in a certain tension, emphasized in the horizontals vying with the vertical.

Mother and child seem like outcasts. They are placed beyond the boundaries of normal human habitation and concerns, constricted in being shut outside fence and wall. Rejected by the smug walled city, disregarded by the working men and animals (in a kind of reversal of a Nativity scene), all they have is the inhospitable weeds besides an even hostile strip of sandy soil. "About suffering they were never wrong, / The Old Masters," as Auden says.[2] The world goes indifferently about its business while the momentous happens outside the pale. The Virgin sitting on the ground here goes beyond humility. The image shows what abjection may be.

Venetian reflections upon Mary as the centuries pass become more and more emphatic and usually more glorious, for the Mother of God becomes iconographically associated with the city itself. Venice had that heavenly birthday, 25 March, date of the Annunciation, and the words of God Almighty to Mark the Evangelist form a parallel particular Annunciation in which the City of Venice emanates in time and space from the Divine Mind—"fabricated by supernatural celestial plan," in the words of Veronica Franca. In any conflict with the papal power, Venice had reserves of strength to draw on in consciousness of itself as uniquely and divinely conceived, free of the contamination of old pagan Rome. Venice is the incarnation in matter and time of the fulfillment of divine will, a reflection in the mercy and grace of the feminine aspect of a not-merely-masculine God. Thus, Venice resembles Mary. Venetians took to their heart the idea of the Immaculate Conception in the fifteenth century. At the same time, as we have seen in an artist like Bellini, Venetians show Mary as human, in the flesh, under stress, growing old. She is divinely powerful, loving, and significant, yet at one with the human.

Every visitor to the city will note the hyperbolical number of churches dedicated to Saint Mary. Some of them are connected with special local miracles. The Madonna dell'Orto is so named because a statue of Mother and Child fell from the heavens into a garden or orchard here—*in orto*. Santa Maria Formosa is so named because its founder had a dream in which Mary appeared to him as a woman *formosa*—that is, not only beautiful but also "buxom," "well-endowed," "Saint Mary with the good figure." Venetian art inclines to pictures of strong women in representing its saints. For example, in the church of Santa Maria Formosa we find Saint Barbara as represented by Palma Vecchio (1480?–1528) (Figure 19). Barbara's tower is behind her, and at her feet are two disconcerting cannon; the artillerymen of Venice had their chapel in this church, and Saint Barbara had become the patron of those who work with artillery. This large Saint Barbara is a very strong, determined, and withal cheerful person able to stand up to storms and crises. She is not at all spindly—she too is "formosa."

The woman who is strong and "formosa" is not unlike that pagan image of the source of life and love, Venus herself. And Venus is the third powerful feminine image of Venice to itself. (Although there are other subordinate feminine images, like Ariadne, as we have seen.) It becomes progressively harder in the Renaissance to disentangle representations of the Virgin from representations of the divinely appointed and expressly conceived "mayden citie," the eternal glorious Virgin. (Did Elizabeth of England, the "Virgin Queen," take note of the effectiveness of some of the Venetian propaganda?) Venice and holy virginity become deliberately entangled. Thus, David Rosand argues, Thomas Coryat was both mistaken and correct when he (mis)identified the representation of Venice being crowned in the heavens as the Virgin Mary.[3] Artists such as Veronese begin to elide the images.

But Venice is not only assimilated to the Blessed Virgin. She is also a figure of Venus—or rather, Venus is a figure for her, a trope of Venetia. Part of the appeal lies in the chime of the goddess's name—Venice *sounds* like Venus. The city's name has had various explanations. Francesco Sansovino gives a conventional one: it comes from the Latin for "come again," "Veni etiam": "this word VENETIA would say *Veni etiam*, that is come again, and again, because however often you come, you will always see new things and new beauties" (a boast this, but quite true).[4] But more often than not, the city's name is "derived" from that of the goddess born of the sea spume,

Figure 19. Palma Vecchio, *Santa Barbara*, detail of polyptych in Santa Maria Formosa, Venice (Scala/ Art Resource, NY)

Venus, the Latin name of Aphrodite. Like Venus, Venice was spawned by the waves and arose from the deeps to startle and amaze all with her beauty.

Astrologers working with the year as well as the date of Venice's birthday found out that on 25 March 421 Venus was in the ascendant, which was also appropriate for the city's nature and future.[5] Venus has privileges because of her close connection with the city, of which she is a sort of special patron along with the Evangelist. The association with the lion is perhaps more properly hers even than Saint Mark's, because both Cybele and the lesser-known goddess of Asia Minor and the Middle East called "The Syrian Goddess" in antique times were associated with lions. Cybele was often depicted flanked by a lion, and this beast was taken over by the "sea Cybele." The lady-and-the-lion together compose an image of strength, control over physical nature, and harmony with Nature herself. The emblematology that Venice composed for itself associated the lady, mistress of the sea and of the land, with the lion of courage, invincible sun-spirit, and ruling power.

As Rosand explains in *Myths of Venice*, during the Renaissance the city very deliberately exploits this connection with Venus. And so it does to this day. One of the leading explanations for the great number of pigeons in Piazza San Marco is that they are descended from pigeons sent out from the Basilica weighted with paper on Palm Sunday, so that the poor might have something to feast upon for Easter. (If the poor were so needy, how come any of the gift birds survived?) A more appealing and even plausible explanation is that the birds are there because they are birds of Venus and thus suitable to Venice. They've been there for a good long time. Robert and Elizabeth Barrett Browning's child "Pen" was covered with them when he walked in the Piazza. We certainly can see them swooping and clustering there today, a multiple bobulation of amethyst necks. Some hate the birds—James Morris refers to them as "mindless grey parasites." When I first went to Venice, the city itself was still feeding them—a work of supererogation. The city is now quietly trying to quell their numbers, but no noticeable difference has been made, and the profits made from selling tourists corn to give them are too attractive to give up.[6] These lascivious and gregarious birds paddle and churr and shit about the Piazza, and about the Loggetta designed by Jacopo Sansovino (now partly a copy, since the falling Campanile destroyed the original in 1902). The original Loggetta, or porch to the Campanile, was created between 1537 and 1546. It displays Venice in three aspects: as Justitia (in Venice itself); as Jupiter (in Candia, i.e., Crete); and as Venus (in Cyprus). The lovely lounging Cyprian queen displayed on the Loggetta might be summon-

246 • CHAPTER 8

ing the pigeons to her as she summons a cherub or *putto*. But Venus in Venice is never just a pretty girl.

There are seldom any *merely* "pretty girls" in Venetian painting. A notable exception is the surprising *Woman Taken in Adultery* by Tintoretto, now in Prague Castle, in which the female referred to, surrounded by severe scholars and angry graybeards, is charmingly dressed in pink, with her Venetian-blond hair nicely done up. I presume this "Adultera" is the same as that described in the "Life of Tintoretto" by Ridolfi, who says that in her face can be seen a beauty that "without sin ravishes the soul."[7] I cannot agree; to me she looks like a Venetian courtesan got up as Barbie. Her little face with its rosebud mouth suggests she simply doesn't understand the situation of which she is the endangered center. Daringly, Tintoretto has placed Christ lower than all the other figures—the standing woman and the horde of angry or expository men. Jesus is sitting down, leaning back, almost amused at the moral indignation swirling about in a strange space at once open and enclosed, a columned semicircle, beyond which is a whorl of blue and white that might be air, land, or sea. Tintoretto seems deliberately to have passed up the opportunity to make the adulterous woman a figure of guilt, or of melancholy, of flamboyant defiance, or of alarm. She is one of the *very* few women in Venetian art to display looks but not strength.

Usually in a Venetian representation of a woman the strength is there in force. A good example is Titian's *Virgin and Child with Saints*, also known as *The Aldobrandini Madonna* (National Gallery, London); the freely moving Saint Catherine, beautiful in her subacid yellow dress with its charming pink sash (slightly Edwardian girlhood in style), plays with the responsive infant boy, who looks as pleased as babies usually do at the attention of a teenager. It is as if the favorite babysitter has just come. In a way, this is a lovers' meeting, for later (in a sense "later," in a sense "now") Saint Catherine will betroth herself to Christ. But in this painting both Christ Child and saint are relaxed and playful. Saint Catherine, unaccompanied by any wheel or other instruments of torture, seems free-spirited and all alive. Her youthful energy (which has an unselfconscious sexual component) dominates the scene. It is that unafraid energy of love which will make her the Bride of Christ.

Females with sexual energy are customarily favorably represented in Venetian art. The consistent identification of Venice as female, whether as Justitia or as a reflection of Mary, as an earthly avatar of Venus or as Aphrodite-Venus herself, ensures that the feminine is often represented, and positively.

(Or we could argue that the truth is vice versa, that the Venetians identified the city as female *because* they wished to represent the female in various aspects.) Venus is the pleasure and glory of the flesh. Giorgione's *Sleeping Venus* was finished by Titian, who, taking Giorgione's techniques aboard, made a number of paintings of lovely females with the "Titian-red" or golden blond hair (a color presumably achieved in something like the manner described by John Evelyn). But the Venetian Venus is not a mere passive object to the viewer's gaze. She is potency, the power of the state, the power of the future.

Even when a Venetian's Venus is "just Venus," as it were, her power is emphasized. In Titian's *Venus at the Mirror* (*Venere allo specchio*, 1555) in the Ca' d'Oro, the lady-goddess at her toilette is no simpering girl (Figure 20). Beside her is a box containing precious jewels from which she may choose to adorn herself. Her golden braids glitter like those of a Valkyrie, shining differently from the expensive drops in her ears. Her long and fleshy torso arises monumentally out of the robe, in which she is loosely dressed. She holds a contemplative large left hand near the top of her right bosom; the exposure of one breast reminds us pictures of lactating Madonnas, but this great female is not concerned with infants but with herself. Self-involved, absent, she gazes away, her very clearly outlined features made the more telling by a long furry—or almost furry—robe or throw, lapping against her like the hide of some friendly animal. The influence of Giorgione's suggestive *Laura* seems almost certain; in some ways this is a reading of the earlier painting. The furryish thing noticeably takes up the position some distance below the woman's belly-button, the area of her pubic hair, for which it is a metonym. Venus seems to enjoy the touch of her pubic hair. She arises out of the fuzzy mantle as if emerging from a beast form without any disturbance. Nor is there any apparent satiric intent. We are not looking down on Venus, mistress of animals, but admiring her ability to be at once human and animal and divine and a precious thing, as well as her power to command both natural and manmade objects composed out of organic and animal stuff. Like Madonna (the 1980s performer) this is "a material girl." Like Venice, Titian's Venus is proud of herself, and has only to decide what precious things she will take and enjoy.

In a late version of the Venice-Venus motif, Giambattista Tiepolo's *Neptune Offering Gifts to Venus*, in the Doge's Palace, Venice is a blond queen with a crown (Figure 21). She wears rich jewels about her throat, including the inevitable pearls. Her left hand, holding a scepter, rests on the head of her

Figure 20. Titian, *Venus at the Mirror* (Cameraphoto Arte, Venice/ Art Resource, NY)

Figure 21. Giambattista Tiepolo, *Neptune Offering Gifts to Venice* (Camera-photo Arte Venice, / Art Resource, NY)

lion, which looks rather like a dog—a Rottweiler rather than a lapdog—that has got on its mistress's bed. Her right hand is extended imperiously and dramatically toward Neptune, whose torso is bare in contrast to the brocades and flowing garments about the lady. Neptune looks anxious, and is hastily emptying a cornucopia. The gifts of the sea are not fishy, but substantially financial: round pieces of gold and silver, as well as pearls. Venice is the lady of desire, the queen who controls wealth, and takes rather than gives.

Taker and giver are balanced in Veronese's gigantic ceiling painting, *The Triumph of Venice* or *The Apotheosis of Venice* in the Sala del Maggior Consiglio in the Doge's Palace. In this apotheosis, Venice is rewarded and proclaimed, being crowned while sitting on a puff of cloud, while wealthy Venetians in contemporary dress on a loggia below gaze up admiringly at this vindicating spectacle. Venice has given power and security to Venice (herself) and thus is she rewarded. Here, as Rosand points out, she is like a Mary received into Heaven. She is also like a Venus in her blond beauty, though the rich brocades that swathe her ample figure may render her a little more a Juno than usual. The viewer, earthbound, has to crane his or her neck, standing admiringly with face tilted parallel to the horizontal plane, and thus fulfills a role by taking out a membership in a group lower than the lowest of the three represented. Admiring the scene, we become witnesses to the apotheosis, and submit in our own physical stance to the superiority of the Venetian state.

Reflecting on Venice itself is one of the favorite occupations of Venetian artists. Yet not all Venetian art is so self-reflexive. Certainly, representations of woman go beyond references to the city-state. There is one outstanding "apotheosis" of the Virgin which is free of political aggrandizement, and thoroughly exciting. This is Titian's splendid *Assumption of the Virgin Mary* (see Plate 10). After some peregrinations, this work has happily come back to the church for which it was originally designed, the Franciscan church of the Frari. As noted earlier, the Venetians embraced both the doctrine of the Immaculate Conception of Mary and of her bodily Assumption into Heaven long before these became official dogmas of the Roman Catholic church (in 1854 and 1950, respectively). This painting of 1518 is a relatively early work in terms of Titian's career, yet it is amazingly powerful and assured. This picture has the three levels imitated by Veronese: the earthbound, the mid-heaven cloud-floored area, and the upper heaven. On the earth the disciples stand, many reaching out agitated hands toward the ascending Virgin, who rises through the mid-heaven within a crescent of angels, toward God the Father enshrined in darkness at the very top. The Virgin is outlined against a glowing lemon-yellow sky. And she is wearing not blue but a strong red robe, with a black mantle floating about her. Her hands and eyes are raised, one can feel her motion upward. To come into the great church of the Frari and suddenly set eyes on this sight is electrifying. Not all the description in the world can catch its confidence of color, its terrific upward lift. It is like coming into the presence of a fired rocket, a space explorer soaring up from the earth.

Before I saw this painting, I had a rather condescending view of Titian as a pretty painter. Now, after having seen this work again and again, as well as a number of others, I give him a higher status—I would put him up there with Raphael—or even above—for power and invention, and for the suiting of creative means to significant ends. The two painters are obviously very different; for one thing, Titian is much more interested in movement than Raphael. At his best, Titian prefers power to prettiness, though Titian's power is always achieved through color. The Virgin in the *Assunta* is a big Madonna, fully developed, imposing—no child, nor slender teen. Her fiery satisfying red garb marks her final and unanswerable significance.

Before going on to discuss in detail one more big religious painting by Titian, *The Presentation of the Virgin at the Temple*, I wish to return to Bellini and his pupil Giorgione, and to try to do some justice to that alarming and fascinating picture *La Tempesta* (see Plate 11). Bellini's images of the Virgin are not altogether lacking in the power so startling in Titian; the younger artist patently learned much from Bellini. Titian too, like Bellini (and in another mode from that of the *Assunta*), is not afraid to show the Virgin as aging and suffering. There is an altarpiece at Ancona, a Crucifixion, which I have seen only once, at a Titian exhibition in London in 2003. That Ancona representation of the Virgin is a late work; Mary stands by the cross on the viewer's left, her face that of an elderly woman in such agony it reminds one of Munch's *The Scream*. This Mary also reminded me of my mother in her nineties, it has such terrible truth in it.

It is a relief after such a painting to go back to the scenes of Bellini, yet here also there is power and truth. In the Accademia's *Pala San Giobbe*, discussed earlier, the Virgin sits on her throne, foursquare, somewhat above the standing level of the accompanying saints. Among other things, this painting is a powerful and unsniggering statement of the power of female sexuality and reproduction. The viewer of this large picture finds his or her primary eye-line goes straight between the Virgin's powerful blue-draped knees. The viewer is swallowed up, knocked out, by this ocean of whelming blue. Beneath, a little angel plays a lute in the center, and the hole in the lute is suggestively directly in a line with the viewing point between the Virgin's knees. The viewer is really looking straight into the genital area of the Virgin.

Perhaps this work by Bellini arouses the reaction in me that it does because of the painting that now shares space with it in the Accademia. I interpret Bellini partly through a companion piece that he could never have known, a piece whose creator could never have seen it in such close juxtaposition with the Bellini *Pala*. Bellini's painting gains meaning by the proximity of *La Tempesta* by Bellini's pupil Giorgione, as *La Tempesta* also gains readability by proximity to Bellini's Madonnas, both the Mary of powerful generation in the *Pala San Giobbe*, and the bereft woman of the *Pietà*. At the very least, we can tell that *La Tempesta* was conceived and executed by someone who knew the work of Bellini extremely well.

One of his earlier works speaks clearly of the influence of Bellini upon Giorgione, and of the young artist's reinterpretation of his master. This is the altarpiece in his natal town of Castelfranco, *Madonna and Child Enthroned with Saint Francis and Saint Nicasius* (c. 1502). The chapel for which the painting was commissioned commemorates a young man lost in the wars, and the *pala* shares in mourning. The two male saints, Francis and that Nicasius who died to save others during the Vandal invasions, are somber dark columns standing beneath the throne. The Madonna and Child at first glance are simply extremely Bellini-like—but at second glance, they look exhausted and sad. In the background fresh-made ruins show the depredations of war, and on our left there is a sluggish and vaguely sinister gray canal. Giorgione likes turgid and somewhat stagnant pieces of water that may hide secrets. This *pala* represents a transposition of Bellini into a completely different key.

Giorgione doesn't seem to want to imagine a world with nothing to be afraid of. His women carry a certain valence of fear—they are scared for themselves, or they are scary. The woman in the painting known as *Laura* with her furry collar over her bare breasts seems to menace the viewer with a hint of the sexual savage. The old crone in *La Vecchia* (*The Old Woman*; Accademia) shrieks derisively of the passage of time and the loss of beauty. These things might be kept in mind as we look at *La Tempesta.*

Giorgione's most famous painting shows a naked woman with a baby at her breast, resting on a low hill, with a tall tree behind her. Beyond her and in the center-right of the painting we see the fortified walls of a city. To her left there is a small ravine with a little river or canal running through it. We know from infrared photography that there was once a woman or nymph in the river; as it is, one cannot be sure that there is not *something* stirring in the water, though the effect is partly that of the reflection of the white house or houses beyond. (The disturbing hint of unknown beings in the water connects this painting with *Il Tramonto,* with its horrible brown mere.) On the other side (our left), of this divide, there is a suntanned young man in a red jacket walking onward, away from the scene and almost toward us, but he gazes to his own left toward the woman. This man carries a staff like a pilgrim or perhaps a shepherd, and wears a shirt casually open, and a wallet, like a laborer, but his breeches seem to be of costly figured silk.

The landscape is depicted in detail; it is somewhat rough, uncultivated, certainly not a place of Arcadian beauty. Beyond, behind the pair in the middle distance, beyond a rickety bridge, there is a string of perhaps rather rickety houses (very like those in *Il Tramonto*); the human encampment is oddly related to the space, and alienated from the pair of figures we look at. The dominant colors in this piece—not excepting the red jacket and silk breeches—are both drab and aggressive. The sky above Giorgione's man and woman—one hesitates to call them a pair, and they are certainly not a couple—is dark and threatening. A jagged bolt of lightning bursts above the towers of the town and above the woman.

The earliest available description of this work (written in 1530) says it depicts "the storm, the gypsy and the soldier." The painting was at that time in the collection of Gabriele Vendramin, a man of a lofty patrician family (in itself an indication that Giorgione's work was already highly valued). In the 1560s the Vendramin heir had an inventory drawn up in which this picture is described as showing "a gypsy and a shepherd in a landscape with a bridge."[8] It is not wonderful that the woman in *La Tempesta* has been interpreted as being a "gypsy"—she is outside of human habitation and settlement, apparently removed from all human help. Giorgione's woman with a baby outside a fortified settlement is an echo of the motif of Bellini, in the *Madonna del Prato*. Unlike images of Mary, but very like images of Venus, the woman is naked. Venus, however, is never shown with a baby at her breast; this heavy-hipped female seems a violent, almost absurd, conflation of the two ideas.

This woman appears strong, but also helpless. The man seems interested but remote, and free. The most puzzling thing about Giorgione's picture is that the viewer cannot say anything certain about the affect of either character—something practically unheard of before, whether the artist is generating portraits, representations of pagan legends, biblical stories, or illustrations of a saint's life and deeds. This picture is *like* an illustration, but it doesn't clearly illustrate anything. The work is also immensely—even defiantly—unlike Carpaccio or Veronese in representing such lonely characters, persons who have no desire or capacity to form a group of any kind, let alone become part of a crowd. Eventually, and oddly enough, the piece becomes referred to as "the Family of Giorgione," and it is further suggested that it is a depiction of the artist himself and his mistress. Such an explanation, however, comes centuries after the artist's death. This sentimental family-stuff is nineteenth-century, though it took in Byron, who on seeing the painting in Manfrin's collection admires "Giorgione's wife."[9] Byron refers to the picture in *Beppo* (1817), declaring, "'Tis but a portrait of his son, and wife,/ And self; but *such* a woman! love in life!"[10]

The enigmatic painting seems to call urgently for explication, and a number of modern interpretations have been offered. I reject as preposterous the suggestion that the picture represents the finding of baby Moses, nor do I find the argument for classical Paris of Troy and his Oenone much more convincing. According to an ingenious suggestion by Jurgen Rapp, Giorgione's picture represents the fateful moment of Paris' departure from his little family.[11] But the painting does not suggest in any way any previous familiar tenderness between the man and woman. The early descriptions which say the man is "a soldier" or "a shepherd" (or—later—"a brigand") all indicate what the painting conveys—that the male in the picture has no important prior relationship to the female. The woman looks wary, lonely, for she is an alien, a stranger (hence, she is read as "a gypsy"). The man continues on his way on his own business; he has the staff of a pilgrim and sojourner, he too is a stranger (hence he is read as "a soldier"). Rather than the fondness or anger that would suit any kind of family relationship, the male seems to express an uneasy curiosity.

What I see in this painting is a deeply sexualized landscape. Like the jagged lightning bolt near its center, the painting carries a tremendous charge of energy. The chasm is a female genital crease and pit, referring to precisely what we cannot see in the naked body of the woman. The word for "storm" (*tempesta*) is female, and Giorgione may be playing upon a relation between the evident storm and the woman herself. Is it not she who is "La Tempesta"? Of course, *La Tempesta* is a name that we have given to the painting in later years, but the earliest written description mentions this element first; the storm itself is central to the picture, the bolt of lightning an innovation. It is worth noting that Francesco Sansovino's *Dictionary* of 1568 says that in Venetian use *tempesta* signifies "congealed water or hail as well as rain" and that *tempestare* is the equivalent of *grandinar* (to hail).[12] So a Venetian summer storm brings lightning winds, rain, and hail—we can flinch from the idea of hailstones pattering on those vulnerable naked bodies. Yet is the woman not at once both victim of the storm and the storm itself—is it not she who is "La Tempesta"?

As a woman can be referred to her surname with the article "La" before it, there is the curious possibility of a personal pun. The little neighboring town of Noale had been controlled by the Tempesta family until Venice secured it. The visual pun might refer to a member of the still-important Tempesta family. But how could that be, unless the woman had borne a child out of wedlock and was disgraced? In that case, such an insult as Giorgione's painting would not have gone unremembered, or unavenged. The woman at the center of the picture remains oddly powerful. She and her baby are marginalized like Bellini's Madonna and Child. Yet this woman represents such powers of fecundity, such vital energies, that the young man and the viewer alike are startled.

The young man, with the red jacket and red energy about his loins, has a prominent codpiece, or codpiece area—a sexually important fact that does not come out well when the painting is reproduced; the bulging genitalia hinted at reflect the frankly tumescent full breasts of the woman. Despite his undoubted sexuality, the young man apparently cannot connect with the naked woman, but glances toward her with a certain wariness in his turn, curiosity and speculation mixed with a kind of apprehension. He is not going to go in that direction.

This strong young man seems handsome and alert—yet is he not also one of Giorgione's troubled men? Which of these two sexually marked persons most fears the other? The storm of sexuality is evidently something to fear.

The two genders are split, dramatically, by the little ravine and the lightning bolt. Tintoretto uses Giorgione's lightning in his *Removal of the Body of Saint Mark* (see Plate 1), where it introduces divine astonishment, but he also uses it in a sexual context, repeating this electrifying bolt in his *Tarquin and Lucretia* (see Figure 12). Here, in a dark and dreadful space, a violent scene plays out by and upon a lavishly draped bed. Jagged bits of metallic lighting flash from the iridescent fabrics, angry statements of sexual stress and dissonance, as Tarquin grasps the struggling victim of his about-to-be-consummated rape, while the chaste pearls are falling, one by one, from her neck. In Giorgione's original and apparently unmythological (and hence incessantly puzzling) picture of an unknowable story, however, what is transpiring within violent sexual stress is not rape but a kind of opposite—avoidance. The woman is viewed coldly, if curiously. She herself also looks cool, estranged but apprehensive. She is undoubtedly a sexual creature, called "a gypsy" perhaps because viewers thought she has had a child out of wedlock, making her "a gypsy" in an older sense, "a tramp" in ours. But this woman knows the price of sex in giving birth. She does not want sexual union any more than a Virgin Mother does.

This painting feels like an allegory of a kind—an allegory unexplained. It seems to be neither a representation of an anterior narrative nor the illustration of a set of occult theories. If it represents anything, it is the great difficulty and stress of sexual passion, the enigma of passion and of sex itself. I would say the man who painted it was not happily heterosexual, and not able to take heterosexuality for granted, and is thus very different from Titian, who dwells in an often untroubled pleasure on fine Venuses and golden-haired courtesans. *La Tempesta* says that sexuality itself is stressful and alienating.

La Tempesta reminds us of the ironies and difficulties in the way of using Woman as a trope. Venice constantly calls upon the Trope of Woman, in consistently identifying itself as female. Or perhaps androgynous. The Doge may act the male part in espousing the sea, yet Venice rapidly turns once more into the marine feminine. Many feminists would find the symbolic use of the feminine in this manner objectionable, pointing out, rightly, that societies that draw on feminine imagery can still treat women very badly—some would argue for that very reason. The Venetian upper classes kept their women enclosed in the home (at least in theory). Venice did not produce numbers of women painters, though it did produce Rosalba Carriera, an artist in chalk and crayon whose popular portraits decorated no vast public spaces. My own broad if cautious agreement with this theoretical feminist position does not preclude a sense that the society which not only acknowledges woman in its midst but actively represents *itself* as feminine may indeed have a different "take" on things—a different sense of past, present, and future possibilities—than the society that does not. I do notice that Venetians seem rather less inclined than some other Europeans to find in Eve the root of all evil, and a relative shortage of puritanism makes Venice a refreshing change. That Venice was tolerant of its courtesans may from one view be seen as exploitative; from another, liberating. The questions the constant image of the feminine raises are, I think, all raised in *La Tempesta* itself, where we cannot tell if the naked woman is celebrated or repudiated.

La Tempesta is a very modern painting—so modern indeed that we may not yet have caught up with it.

I want to end with a Titian of an earlier period, one that is often dismissed as too simple for its time. This is the last painting the visitor to the Accademia sees upon leaving the gallery: Titian's *Presentation of the Virgin at the Temple* (see Plate 12). This was painted for the Scuola Santa Maria della Carità in the mid-1530s, and one sees it on the exact wall for which it was designed. An original commission to another artist some thirty years before had not been fulfilled because the artist had died. It has been suggested that the Scuola wanted to keep to the older plan and style, for Titian's painting has seemed to some art historians disappointingly old-fashioned for the High Renaissance, a reversion to the age of Carpaccio and linear processional scenes. I agree that Tintoretto's *Presentation* in the Madonna dell'Orto, a painting of 1552, is technically more exciting and more innovative, with its strange twist of perspective and odd use of the stairs. It is truly more "modern" than this work of Titian, though affected by it and in some ways a commentary on it. But the characters in Tintoretto's painting are not individualized, and for me Titian's painting says more. Titian's picture had a humble purpose; it covered the entrance wall of the *sala dell'albergo*, and would thus greet those coming to the hostelry of Charity.

Titian presents a picture with the effect of a procession, moving from the crowd at left to the right where the child Virgin ascends the thirteen steps up to the entry of the Temple of Solomon, toward the landing and entrance where the high priest and another cleric (possibly Zachariah) wait to receive her. Through the shiny marble columns of Solomon's porch we can see a wall in red-and-white stripes, reminiscent of the Palazzo Ducale, and the mountains behind the waiting crowd on the left intimate the Dolomites of Titian's own natal region of Cadore. As David Rosand points out, the work "resonates with obvious *venezianità*."[13] At the further left, however, we see an exotic pyramid; Rosand suggests this is an intimation of the wisdom of the East and that the whole fits in with the presentation of Mary as Divine Wisdom.

Yet Mary here is a child. Behind her in the crowd are her earthly parents Anna and Joachim, and also presumably Elizabeth, wife of Zachariah, as well as what are obviously some notable bigwigs. Yet these people cannot proceed with her. They have come to a halt at the foot of the stairs. Now, in Giotto's important treatment of the same scene at the turn into the fourteenth century (in his influential cycle of narrative paintings in the Scrovegni Chapel in nearby Padua), Saint Anna is pushing the child up the stairs, in an act of rather foolish maternal pride and loving officiousness. Titian makes clear that no one else can go where Mary is going. A child, in a plaid dress that looks rather 1850s, leans against the stairs, earnestly wishing to follow the other little girl, but she cannot, nor can the old or young men around her. Only one brave figure marches on, a child in a blue dress with a halo of light about her. An innocent procession of one, she stands alone, on the eighth step. Below her is an old woman with a basketful of eggs beside her.

Now, a number of commentators have seriously disliked this old woman and her egg basket. She seems to them quite hideous, a decided flaw in the sweetness and elegance of the composition. Erwin Panofsky, referring to her as "that repulsive old egg woman," sees in her a negative symbol of Judaism.[14] David Rosand elaborates on this interpretation, and determines that she represents the Synagogue, to be repudiated and cast out by the new Ecclesia; she is likewise the *mulier stulta et clamosa* of Proverbs, in contrast to Holy Wisdom.[15]

This reading gets rid of the basket of eggs. If this painting is seen as a retrogression to the era of Carpaccio, we might ask pertinently what Carpaccio does with such figures, and remember in the Ursula series the patient old lame nurse sitting on the steps outside the royal chamber. Carpaccio does not repudiate that old woman. I maintain that, although the traditional idea of the destruction and replacement not of the synagogue but of the Temple itself is indeed inevitably inherent in the subject of the painting, the concept is lightened by making the Temple resemble the Palazzo Ducale. Furthermore, I suggest the old woman does not represent the Old Law but new life coming at the end of an old one. The basket of eggs is placed directly beneath the figure of the Virgin, in a straight line down from her genital area. I have long doubted the truth of our contention that until very recent times nobody knew of the ovaries of the female—but let that pass. Remember the painting by Piero della Francesca (Brera, Milan) in which the Virgin holds an egg, representing the new life to which she will give birth, and the cosmic egg itself. The eggs in the basket are the future, and an allusion to the cosmic egg of Mary from which a new world comes.

The child Mary on the stairs still knows nothing of the life which is about to burst in and through her. But she marches bravely on, Titian's little Mary. A lone figure in a blue dress, the undaunted original for Tenniel's Alice, she is the child who will question everything by her existence and turn the world upside down. The painting is not as static as some interpreters make out. Those fine columns may begin to totter under the force of the fragile egg and the innocent child surrounded by her egg-shaped halo. She marches on to a world turned upside down, to a charity that has yet to reveal itself. The Trope of the Feminine can be used to investigate what change and transmutation may be and mean.

9

Labyrinth and Carnival

This is a city of mazes. . . . Although wherever you are going is always in front of you, there is no such thing as straight ahead. . . . The short cuts are where the cats go, though the impossible gaps.
—Jeanette Winterson, *The Passion*

It is the height of the Carnival—and I am in the estrum & agonies of a new intrigue—with I don't know exactly whom or what—except that she is insatiate of love—& won't take money . . . & that I met her at the Masque—& that when her mask is off I am as wise as ever.
—Byron to John Murray, Venice, 27 January 1818

The labyrinth, the Carnival (Carnevale)—these are undoubtedly two of the most well known and commanding of the tropes of Venice. One registers Venice as a place, a shape, a geographical phenomenon; the other registers behavior, indicating performance, with a subtext of gratified desire for lawlessness. They have something in common, however. Labyrinth and Carnevale alike inspire a degree of apprehension, and both engage a logic of excess, and of withholding.

It is almost inevitable that the visitor to Venice will refer to the city as "a labyrinth" or "a maze." Notoriously, no map small enough to be portable is capable of registering all the little side streets that rise and peter out before you are aware of them. The plan of the city is determined by the water, and what it will allow by way of islands and islets; the water has frequently to make its way in canal or *rio*, and then there are many small bridges, and twists and turns. John Evelyn, as noted earlier, observes that "this Miraculous Cittie which lies in the boosome of the sea in the shape of a Lute" is composed of "numberlesse Ilands tack'd together by no fewer than 150 bridges." Evelyn may have been wrong as to the exact number of islands and bridges, but it feels like that. One island is stitched to another, and then another, in a patchwork of areas that makes sense—but its own kind of sense, not the visitor's.

Veronica Franca said the city was built according to celestial divine plan, but the divine plan evidently favors the labyrinth. As Deborah Howard points out, Venice is in many ways like a city of the Middle East:

The general model, exemplified by such cities as Damascus, Aleppo and Cairo, all of which were frequented by Venetians over the whole medieval period, involves the separation of residential areas, public buildings (markets and religious institutions) and industrial functions. Shop-lined suqs fill the central circulation spaces, framed by khans and mosques. Suqs are usually open-ended thoroughfares, sometimes covered by wooden or stone vaults, sometimes open to the skies. The citadel, or centre of power, with its parade ground, lies on the perimeter of the main market area. Residential quarters, by contrast, are dense, secretive labyrinths, with narrow streets proceeding in short right-angled stretches, many of them dead ends. On the periphery lie the main manufacturing enterprises.[1]

Howard concedes that Venice is at once like and unlike these cities, for, until the Turks gained Constantinople, "the great cities of the Islamic world were not seaports," yet "the resemblance . . . remains very marked."[2] There are in Venice well-defined public areas, religious and governmental centers, contiguous with major markets; radiating from these are the intertwining streets and alleys where people live. We might also note that Aegean cities on or near the sea were often constructed on a rather secretive and inhospitable plan. Some settlements in areas afflicted by pirates actively determined to make their towns labyrinthine and difficult, which explains the odd layout of certain settlements in islands in the Aegean—the winding ways of Mykonos, for instance. Venetians took their facility with mazes to their empire, and improved by Aegean examples. On the island of Naxos the great Venetian fortification, the Castro, is a labyrinth unto itself. One would think Venice's labyrinthine quality could hardly be explained by a desire to foil enemy action, as for so many centuries Venice was safe from depredation by others. Yet at its foundation it was a refuge from invading armies, and some pinch of the old caution may have fostered the creation of a dense and yet obscure town threaded by twisting and enigmatic streets. At least, Venice found nothing inconvenient or antipathetic in such a layout, as long as its public spaces were emphatic, accessible, and capable of accommodating crowds.

Of course, Venice is singular among all mazy cities in being a labyrinth of watery ways as well as of footpaths. Small canals are folded in among the streets, and no street lasts for long without running into or over water. The effect is captured by the fantasizing Francesco Colonna when his hero is taken in a Borgesian fashion to look upon a garden which is also a wide maze: "We leapt nimbly up the spiral staircase to the flat top, where she showed me, and explained with divine eloquence, a wide circular garden made in the form of a complex and intricate labyrinth. Its circular paths were not walkable but navigable, for in place of streets there ran rivulets of water. This was a mysterious place with salubrious meadows . . . rejoicing in flowering greenery, and offering everywhere solace and recreation."[3] Mysterious, satisfying, labyrinthine, a maze of streets of water—this must be Venice. Here we have a reminiscence of the view as seen after ascending to the top of the Campanile. (The insistence on the presence of "flowering greenery" will strike us now as peculiar, but it matches Coryat's vision, and Colonna was writing more than a century earlier.) And in the novel this is also a dangerous place, for there is a dragon in the center, rather like the Minotaur in the original Cretan maze, and various routes through the waterways lead to various results, some most unfortunate. You have to be an Ariadne, and supply a clue.

Venice in resisting discovery can betray even—or especially—the heart that loves her. Nowadays the main routes are marked with loud signs: "Per Rialto—Per San Marco—Per Piazzale Roma." But even these can mislead. When you are near the Accademia in Dorsoduro, the Rialto and San Marco are in opposite directions, but you may suddenly see a sign saying "Per San Marco e Rialto"—which is utterly confusing, a kind of "Follow-the-Yellow-Brick-Road" injunction—unless you consider it may be the direction to a vaporetto stop. The main walking routes *ought* to be clear, especially to those who have been in Venice before—yet, even so, mistakes can occur at some crucial turn. But every lover of Venice gets lost by straying from the San Marco-Rialto thoroughfare in search of other things. A church may seem to elude a morning's search—or it may turn up incessantly when one is looking for something else. "Oh, not Santa Maria Formosa *again*," one exclaims pettishly as the street seems to have taken a shake and a jerk and tumbled you back to the same place. Of course, if you are searching earnestly for Santa Maria Formosa, you are likely not to find it, but something else instead, perhaps the Palazzo Querini Stampalia.

The courageous approach to Venice's maze is to plunge in, as Goethe boasts he did: "Towards evening I explored—again without a guide—the remoter quarters of the city. . . . I tried to find my way in and out of the labyrinth myself, asking nobody the way and taking my directions only from the points of the compass. It is possible to do this" (30 September 1786;

Journey, 79). Yet even the returning native may be foiled by the city's ways. In 1911 the Princess Marie von Thurn und Taxis-Hohenlohe (born in Venice of Austrian parents in 1855) was trying to show the poet Rainer Maria Rilke about Venice. As she describes it, they got lost:

One fine morning we were on our way to the Stampalia Gallery and Sta. Maria Formosa. I knew that Sta. Maria Formosa was not far from S. Zaccaria, and must be quite near the Riva del [*sic*] Schiavoni. So we started by taking the vaporetto (alas, the gondolas are becoming rarer and rarer!) and then walked on. A friendly little old man, who was roasting chestnuts, showed us the direction we must take. . . . Of course. . . . we promptly lost our way in a labyrinth of streets, passages, bridges and *sotto-portici*—a disgrace for a native of Venice like myself! Then suddenly we found ourselves in a very strange, completely unknown spot. A long street, which was not really what we call a *"calle"* in Venice, with a small fountain at either end, very high, large houses on both sides—sad, bare houses, devoid of the grotesque ornaments and open-work on the windows that abounds in the poorer quarters of Venice, and above all silence—a silence so deep that it seemed to be a legacy from time immemorial and which was further intensified by the shrill notes of a flute, on which someone was playing an interminable, Eastern melody. We both stood still and looked around us with the same sense of uncanny oppression, staring at the decaying pavement, from which grass was sprouting (grass in Venice!), the silent, poverty-stricken houses with their closed doors and barred windows, behind which no face appeared, the deserted street. Far and wide there was not a sound to be heard except the strange monotonous complaint of the flute. . . . In vain we looked for the name of the street. . . . I believe we shall never find that spot again, never again hear the little flute's long-drawn-out Eastern melody quavering through the empty streets.[4]

Modernity (embodied in the vaporetto) is troublesome, and apparent native friendliness (the chestnut vendor) will not help one through the maze. A sense of loss and disorientation is accompanied by a discovery, a seeing of something new. In this case, the new sight is disconcerting and inharmonious, the street of severe and silent houses—perhaps barred against her, an intruder, an Austrian? The intrusive "Eastern melody" serves as a reminder of something alien and "foreign" in Venice, its "Eastern" nature, which in nonverbal expression incessantly challenges the Western European princess and her German poet.

Descriptions of getting lost in Venice usually accompany some sense of discovery, which is likely to be represented not only as disconcerting but also as mysterious in some way, as in this passage of Proust:

After dinner, I went out alone, into the heart of the enchanted city where I found myself in the middle of strange purlieus like a character in the *Arabian Nights*. It was very seldom that, in the course of my wanderings, I did not come across some strange and spacious piazza of which no guidebook, no tourist had ever told me. I had plunged into a network of little alleys or *calli*, packed tightly together and dissecting in all directions with their furrows a chunk of Venice carved out between a canal and the lagoon, as if it had crystallised in accordance with these innumerable, tenuous and minute patterns. Suddenly, at the end of one of these alleys, it seemed as though a distension had occurred in the crystallised matter. A vast and splendid campo of which, in this network of little streets, I should never have guessed the scale, or even found room for it, spread out before me surrounded by charming palaces silvery in the moonlight. It was one of those architectural ensembles towards which, in any other town, the streets converge, lead you and point the way. Here it seemed to be deliberately concealed in a labyrinth of alleys, like those palaces in oriental tales whither mysterious agents convey by night a person who, brought back home before daybreak, can never find his way back to the magic dwelling which he ends by believing that he visited only in a dream.

The next day, I set out in quest of my beautiful nocturnal piazza, following *calle* after *calle* which were exactly like one another and refused to give me the smallest piece of information, except such as would lead me further astray. Sometimes a vague landmark which I seemed to recognise led me to suppose that I was about to see appear, in its seclusion, solitude and silence, the beautiful exiled piazza. At that moment, some evil genie which had assumed the form of a new *calle* made me unwittingly retrace my steps, and I found myself suddenly brought back to the Grand Canal. And as there is no great difference between the memory of a dream and the memory of a reality, I finally wondered whether it was not during my sleep that there had occurred, in a dark patch of Venetian crystallisation, that strange mirage which offered a vast piazza surrounded by romantic palaces to the meditative eye of the moon.[5]

The Oriental theme occurs irresistibly in the mind of Marcel—and of Proust: the vision of the moonlit piazza must be like the enchanted experience of a character in the *Arabian Nights*. The capacity to tease with illusory visions is felt to be "Oriental"—and thus estranging. Making beautiful trouble, reality, dream, and delusion mingle and become inseparable.

The discovery of Venice has a sexual analogy, as the visitor desires to see, to penetrate. But the visitor may also desire to be penetrated, to be taken. Morris, the Teiresias of travel writers, indicates that Venice inspires an emotion close to lust.[6] As Ian Littlewood notes, "The desire so often directed towards its inhabitants can be displaced with mysterious ease, so that lust for its creatures becomes lust for the hidden places and yielding textures of the city itself."[7] This lust or mixture of lusts, yearning for flesh and yearning for the city and its secrets, is expressed by Proust's Marcel as he goes on afternoon gondola journeys through winding back canals and *rii* in search of willing working-class women, like lacemakers. Fantasy indeed—for Proust it was not actually women who were the object of such searches. He is masking, hiding in his own labyrinth. Through the turning waterways the hero of *The Aspern Papers* greedily pursues his love-object also—the love letters of the dead poet.

The modern visitor to Venice is most likely to undertake exploration chiefly on foot, and thus to set himself or herself a-going within the maze. The sense of being lost or frustrated can be associated with a sensation of aching feet, or heat and thirst (or in the winter, damp and cold), as the poor wanderer struggles and winds haplessly about. This familiar experience was less likely to befall visitors of any standing in earlier eras; accounts of visits to Venice are full of references to gondolas, and most of the explorers are taking gondola rides. Each family of importance had a gondola and gondolier attached. "In Venice, it is always preferable to have one's own gondola, as it is preferable to have one's own car on land," Lawrence observes in *Lady Chatterley's Lover*; the two women are charged at the rate of "about thirty shillings a day, or ten pounds a week"—a sum not inconsiderable in the 1920s.[8] The gondola was certainly employed in past centuries primarily by native Venetians—as is now not the case, though wealthy Venetians or foreigners with homes here may keep their modern equivalent of the personal gondola, a motor launch.

The visitor who enters the maze of the city in a gondola is not going to be sore-footed or lost, or frustrated—at least, any frustration will be of a subtler kind. The gondolier who can thread the watery labyrinth is a wonder-worker, a secret-bearer, a quasi divine know-it-all, a Hermes or Psychopomp. The passenger is delightfully passive, able to lose the self in a vision of waters and reflections, of cornices and sudden lovely doorways. He or she can lose track of the craft's whereabouts, knowing only that with a strong swing the amazingly dexterous waterman can thread his way through the right sequence of canals and *rii*, coming with apparent ease to the objective. The power of the gondolier increases his already visible sexual attractiveness. He teases with his knowledge. The gondolier, already one of the tropes of Venice, carries several tropes in his image. He is the Secret Keeper, the Life Guide, the Bringer-to-Love, the Restorer of Youth, and the Conductor to the Shades. He is Hermes, Eros, Pan. He is a love-object in himself. It is no wonder that so many visitor to Venice have fallen in love or in lust with gondoliers—or with one of their number, like the high-born English lady we students had heard of in the 1960s. Or like the widow Aldini with her young boatman in Sand's novel. Or like John Addington Symonds, who had a long love affair with a gondolier. (Not to mention the notoriously promiscuous pursuer "Baron Corvo.")

Having a gondola at command may bestow a sense of power and privilege, a sort of freedom of the city and freedom of the seas expressed by that eccentric young traveler William Beckford, in his description of his first day in Venice, a hot day in August.

The pure exhilarating air of the morning drawing me abroad, I procured a gondola, laid in my provision of bread and grapes, and was rowed under the Rialto, down the grand canal, to the marble steps of S. Maria della Salute, erected by the senate in performance of a vow to the holy Virgin, who begged off a terrible pestilence in 1630. . . . The sun-beams began to strike against he windows of the cupola, just as I left the church, and was wafted across the waves to the spacious platform in front of St. Giorgio Maggiore, by far the most perfect and beautiful edifice my eyes ever beheld. When my first transport was a little subsided . . . I planted my umbrella on the margin of the sea, and reclining under its shade, my feet dangling over the waters, viewed the vast range of palaces, of porticos, of towers, opening on every side, and extending out of sight. . . . I contemplated the busy scene from my peaceful platform . . . and, whilst I remained thus calm and tranquil, heard the distant buzz and rumour of the town. Fortunately a length of waves rolled between me and its tumults; so that I eat my grapes, and read Metastasio, undisturbed by officiousness or curiosity. (*Dreams, Waking Thoughts, and Incidents*, 89–91)

There is something hippie-like in this young man's posture and activity. He is ostentatiously reading Metastasio—a Roman, not a Venetian, poet. He has pursued the Palladian beauty of San Giorgio Maggiore, yet he sits evidently with his back to it, and looks smugly across at the crowds around St. Mark's, his feet dangling over the water. But this is the hippiedom of privilege; Beckford can make his means of transport wait for him. After he has gone into the church for shade and examined the building and the Veronese in the monastic refectory, he returns to the patiently waiting craft:

I moved slowly out of the cloisters; and gaining my gondola, arrived, I know not how, at the flights of steps which lead to the Redentore, a structure so simple and elegant, that I thought myself entering an antique temple. . . . It was mid-day, and I begged to be rowed to some woody island, where I might dine in shade and tranquillity. My gondoliers shot off in an instant; but, though they went at a very rapid rate, I wished to fly faster, and getting into a bark with six oars, swept along the waters; soon left the Zecca [sic] and San Marco behind; and, launching into the plains of shining sea, saw turret after turret, and isle after isle, fleeting before me. (92–93)

Even the gondola did not suffice; Beckford can pay for a bark and six boatmen, just to gratify his whim to have a picnic lunch on a shady isle on an August day. On another occasion he goes to Torcello, providing himself with musicians and instruments so he can bring the concord of sweet sounds with him. His wealth lends a sense of enchantment, he does not mind not knowing where he is going, and the gondolier's path is a charming mystery—he arrived "I know not how" at Redentore.

Yet most travelers by water express a sense of anxiety about destination—if only about arriving at Venice itself. They have an object in view, they are drawn toward it through the watery maze, like the researcher in *The Aspern Papers*, seeking for Juliana Bordereau and her valuable secret archive. They may be driven by burning desire like Aschenbach, in his desperate pursuit of Tadzio, in a winding watery chase—it seems strange that Visconti did not use this scene in his film. Tadzio and his family are in one gondola, and Aschenbach follows in another:

So he floated and rocked, leaning on soft, black cushions, following the other black, high-powered boat, to the wake of which his passion chained him. At moments he lost sight of it; then he felt sorrow and unrest. But his guide, as if well versed in such assignments, was constantly able—thanks to sly manoeuvres, quick crisscross movements, and shortcuts—to make the object of his desire visible to him again. The air was still and odorous, the sun blazed strongly through the vapor that colored the sky a slate gray. Water lapped gurgling against wood and stone. The call of the gondolier, half warning and half greeting, was answered from afar out of the stillness of the labyrinth as if by some odd prearranged agreement.[9]

Aschenbach the pursuer is also a victim, a captive in his gondola, drawn ineluctably along, but he also hugs his secret knowledge of the sickness that is overtaking the ambiguous city, which is in some way a parallel to his own inner erotic sickness. (And the cholera that afflicts Venice in Mann's novel may be a euphemism, a metaphoric substitution for the venereal affliction that should be the fate of wicked sexual Venice.) A labyrinth, after all, has a secret—a deadly sexual secret—at its heart. In the original Cretan Labyrinth designed by Daedalus, there lay at the center the unspeakable, indescribable monster, product of an unnatural mixture between a beast and a queen. It was the monster, the Minotaur, which Ariadne helped the faithless Theseus to meet and kill. So Ariadne (who is, as we have seen, one of the figures of Venice), is Mistress of the Labyrinth. And she knows where and what the Monster is.

The labyrinth itself is at once point of departure and point of entry, an interval in time that makes time look like space. It is a topos of extension but no solidity. It is a temporary and resisted abode, which cannot be an abode at all—its own desire seems to be both to swallow up and cast out the alien intruder. The maze is a place in reality that manages to make itself imaginary. In showing that "place" is an elastic and variable idea, the labyrinth questions our notions of geographic space, and of all spatial order. The duty of the traveler who gets into a maze or labyrinth is to get out. But—there may be a mission to accomplish first. The first duty must be to get to a center—if only we knew where or what that is. There is thus a stress attached to being in the labyrinth itself, whether stumbling about on short hot streets or oozing along mysterious waterways with sudden turns.

Venice is really two labyrinths, one within another. There is the labyrinth of central or "proper" Venice—of Castello, San Marco, Dorsoduro, and so on—and then there is the meta-labyrinth formed by the pattern of islands that surround the city. At first these are indeed mysterious to the visitor. Even after taking a vaporetto or ferry trip to one or more islands, the first-time visitor may still be uncertain as to quite what island lies in which direction. Some isles are visible from Venice proper. Murano can be clearly seen from Castello. And small puzzling islands abound. One forlorn island off the Zuecca rejoices in the perfect name of San Giorgio in Alga—Saint George in the Seaweed. A more important island, visible from the Fondamenta Nuova, is San Michele, the island of the dead, which Dickens passed by in a gondola in the dark night of his arrival. Not so long ago, if you were in Venice for any length of time, you would see a waterborne funeral bound for that sober destination. A Venetian funeral is a procession by water.

San Michele was established as the Venetian cemetery by Napoleon. More exactly, he set aside the small island of San Cristofero for that purpose; when that rapidly became too small, it was joined to San Michele, whose fifteenth-century convent church became perpetually associated with funerals. I suppose San Michele is the only one of Napoleon's innovations that truly patriotic Venetians have made use of. The convent on the island was also used as a prison by the Austrians in the nineteenth century, so a visit to the cemetery was then made doubly lugubrious by the grim reminder of occupation and control. When you are in the San Zanipolo region, you may admire the tasteful practicality of the propinquity of hospital, undertaker's shop, and the burial island. San Michele is also to be passed as you come by motor launch from Murano or from Marco Polo airport. The little island punctuating the journey with its Renaissance church and dramatic dark cypresses warns you of your imminent arrival in Venice—and of your eventual arrival in the land of the dead. Modern interments, however, take place on the mainland.

A few rich or famous people like Stravinsky and Ezra Pound and now Joseph Brodsky are, we may suppose, buried there permanently (a silent tourist attraction), but little San Michele was traditionally mainly for temporary burial. After a corpse has been buried some years, it (or rather the remaining bones) must expect subsequent removal to an ossuary, a storage receptacle or area for bones, in accordance with the economical Mediterranean fashion. Venice never had land to throw away on permanent burial plots. Up until after World War II, the bones of common persons were taken from San Michele and piled up on the small island of Sant'Ariano, just off Torcello. In the late 1950s, Morris found skeletal bones and skulls piled up and crumbling together promiscuously in the bone yard of Sant'Ariano: "There was not a square foot of soil to be seen among the roots, only bones."[10]

A more cheerful—and much larger—island visible from the northwest side of Venice is the glassily famous Murano. This is several islands "tacked together" by bridges, like Venice itself, and parts of Murano are just as old. The churches are distinguished, particularly Santa Maria e San Donato, with its wavering lovely mosaics (and dry dragon bones). The revival of glassmaking means that Murano is once again dominated by the *vitreria*. Even though much of the work is done in Marconi, owners of the various firms are quite aware of the advertising value of Murano's Fondamenta dei Vetrai, and you can indeed see glass being made—and blown—in Murano factories. The warmth of their fires makes these a good place to visit in winter. These glassworks pose a true temptation to the shopper, especially as it is possible to order wine glasses, mirrors, and so forth made to order and shipped to you.

Mrs. Piozzi refused to be impressed, saying she had seen looking-glasses just as good or better in Paris, but even in her day Venice was still setting a tone for glassware, although new artists in France and in Bohemia had been vying with Venetian products. Murano is close enough to seem almost like part of the city of Venice. To go further afield—or further asea—is to venture into the archipelago of the laguna.

I once dared to hire a boat to take me about the islands. I was staying on the Lido at the time, at the very Hotel des Bains patronized by Aschenbach in Mann's novel—a hotel I can conscientiously recommend, with attractive sea views. After the relative stillness and quiet swell of the laguna, it is refreshing to see dashing white-capped waves under a blue sky. The long thin Lido is only one of several *lidi* (sandbanks) which keep the Adriatic at bay. If they went under, Venice would be inundated by the oceanic waters. Near the edge or point of the Lido, stretching southward toward Chioggia, is the even thinner winding strip of Pellestrina, another sandy line of defense. In the marshy islands about Chioggia there are still the occasional *cassoni*, little fishing huts like what the primitive tribes must have lived in. Once people went fowling here, like the boys in Carpaccio's picture; Pietro Longhi shows hunters shooting duck with guns, but one conservative gentleman still uses the traditional bow and arrow, even in the eighteenth century. The bird sanctuary puts an end to hunting around Chioggia. There are little islands scattered near Pellestrina and some good stories about these, not least the spooky folk tale "The Seven Dead Men" ("I Fondi dei sette morti").[11]

Pellestrina is inhabited if but lightly populated; its womenfolk, like those of Burano, were traditionally lacemakers. Its four quarters are named after families important in the fourteenth century. I daresay if you meet anyone with the last name "Vianello" even today, the chances are he or she will be from Pellestrina. Between 1751 and 1782, in order to protect Venice, Pellestrina was reinforced against the sea with strong walls or embankments build along its entire length (more than eleven kilometers). These embankments, called the *murazzi*, have been rebuilt after they were battered to pieces in the great flood (*la mareggiata*) of 1966.

On the southern coast of the Lido is the fishing village of Malamocco, where refugees from Metamocco, the first settlement on the lagoon, resettled after the old site was destroyed by a tidal wave in the early twelfth century. John Evelyn among others comments that Malamocco is the harbor where the English ships first make port in Venice. English ships didn't go further into Venice, and passengers must have gone to the city by sailboat or large passenger gondola-ferry. Otherwise, the Lido was pretty empty. It traditionally offered a convent with a church dedicated to San Nicolò, based on the rather lame story that the Venetians had after all stolen the bones of the famous Saint Nicholas (Santa Claus) from Bari (they really had not). There was also a fort (Fort San Nicolò) to guard the entrance into the lagoon, and a cemetery for Jews and another for Protestants. A large part of the Protestant cemetery was erased by the little airport added in 1930; any remains discovered were put into one large sarcophagus. A few Protestant tombstones were left; Morris found the neglected tomb of Consul Joseph Smith.[12]

One advantage of staying on the Lido is that you see more of the laguna. In traveling back and forth between the Lido and Venice (your hotel supplies a launch) you will pass close by some interesting places. For one thing, as you leave Venice and near the Lido on your right, you are perilously close to the infamous Orfano Canal, once discolored by the blood of Pepin's forces, and later the place of secret disposal so excitingly awful to visitors like Mme. de Staël, the canal into which bodies (living or dead) were dropped. (To fish in this canal was forbidden.) There are a number of small islands, including the Lazzaretto Vecchio, which has a history of vicissitude. Pilgrims once came here; in the fourteenth century the island turned into a quarantine hospital for invalids suspected of having the plague. The name of the church dedicated to St. Mary of Nazareth is supposed to have been distorted to *lazzaretto*, giving the world this word. A military depot during the occupation, it is now the site of a home for stray dogs, a voluntary charity. I have heard that the plague pit on the Lazzaretto Vecchio was recently discovered, and there is some thought of exhibiting the bones, but surely it seems best to let sleeping plague lie. San Clemente was a lunatic asylum in the nineteenth century, and later the site of a psychiatric hospital, not closed down until 1992. From 1725 until Napoleon's invasion noble persons who went insane were allowed to go to the hospital on San Servolo, and that institution eventually became the general asylum. The nearby Sacca Sèssola was until fairly recently the site of a hospital for the tubercular. It is a relief to come to the Lido, which has not been a madhouse or pest house (though it was once a cemetery).

One of the Lido's long sides faces Venice, and still feels Venetian. The other side faces the true sea, the Adriatic. It was off the two-faced Lido that the Doge, proceeding in the ducal barge the *Bucintoro* (all golden splendor and red velvet), from the twelfth century onward would annually wed the sea, throwing a gold wedding ring into the Adriatic, with the words *Desponsamus te mare, in signum veri perpetuique domini*: "We marry thee, O sea, in sign of true and perpetual dominion." This ceremony (in what the actors did not know was one of its last performances) was witnessed with pleasure by Hester Piozzi (*Observations and Reflections*, 130–133). The Adriatic thumps against lovely sandy beaches on the other side of the thin island from that which faces Venice. The Lido was for centuries practically a waste land, as William Beckford observed with disfavor:

A few minutes more brought me to a dreary, sun-burnt shore, stalked over by a few Sclavonian soldiers, who inhabit a castle hard by, go regularly to an ugly unfinished church, and from thence, it is to be hoped, to paradise; as the air of their barracks is abominable, and kills them like blasted sheep. Forlorn as this island appeared to me, I was told it was the scene of the Doge's pageantry at the feast of the Ascension; and the very spot to which he sails in the Bucentaur, previous to wedding the sea. . . . I shall only say, that I was obliged to pursue, partly, the same road as the nuptial procession, in order to reach the beach; and was broiled and dazzled accordingly. At last, after traversing some desart hillocks, all of a hop with toads and locusts (amongst which English heretics have the honour of being interred) I passed under an arch, and suddenly the boundless plains of ocean opened to my view. (*Dreams, Waking Thoughts, and Incidents*, 103–104)

At least Beckford, like Byron and other males after him, could enjoy what nobody gets now in the highly developed and determinedly bourgeois Lido, a swim in the nude.

It is amazing to think that his visit to Venice afforded Goethe at the age of thirty-seven his first contact with the sea, at the Lido: "Now, at last, I have seen the sea with my own eyes and walked upon the beautiful threshing floor of the sand which it leaves behind when it ebbs" (8 October 1786; *Journey*, 96). More appreciative, and more scientific, than the usual traveler, Goethe even enjoyed observing the flora in the sandy and salty Lido landscape. The insistent presence of the Adriatic at last brought about the establishment of a flourishing seaside resort in a full flush of upper-middle-class pleasure. The beach area with its hinterland has been developed since the late nineteenth century, erupting in seaside hotels, chief among them the Grand Hotel des Bains (which does not seem to have suffered in reputation from Aschenbach's notorious visit). The Lido also has cars, shops, the Cinema Festival Palace, and the Casinò (in the modern sense). The Lido's Casinò is only for summer. The grander casino in Palazzo Vendramin-Calergi in Cannaregio is used in the winter; you can remember or try to forget that it was in this palazzo that Wagner died. Inscribed on the exterior, as you can read from the Canal, are the words "Non Nobis." The uninstructed might idly surmise that these words form the beginning of a pious quotation, perhaps continued on the other side of the edifice: "Non nobis Domine sed Tibi gloria est" (Not unto ourselves O Lord but unto Thee be glory). But this is no spiritual reminder but a curt exhortation: "Not for us." Venetians are to remember that these gaming places are not for them. Venetians should not gamble; let the visitors lose their money. The Lido desired any amusements that would attract well-to-do tourists.

Development of this island sandbank postdates not only the era of Beckford's visit but also that of Alfred de Musset. The barren Lido seems to have inspired in the French Romantic poet a particular horror: "At Venice, at the horrible Lido [*l'affreux Lido*],/ Where on the grass of a tomb/ Comes the pale Adriatic to die."[13] Presumably when he saw the Lido it was exactly the same as in Beckford's time but even less lively, a wintry Lido with dry grass waving, not even "all of a hop with toads and locusts."

I daresay that temporarily residing on the Lido made me more island-conscious, and more desirous of taking a trip around as many islands as I could. In 1995 I gratified this wish. The owner of the handsome boat (larger and more comfortable than a *motoscafo*, with a bit of real deck) was devastatingly handsome himself. The Venetian boatman had brought his ten-year-old son with him, perhaps for protection, but more likely because his son always went with him on the water when he could. The son's name was David, and he had brought his own best friend, also named David, with him, so together we made up a party.

I had already visited one of the monastery islands, San Lazzaro degli Armeni, an Armenian monastery since 1717, when the Republic gave it to Armenian monks who had fled the Turks. At an earlier point the island had been a hospital for lepers. The monks built a fine church, monastery, and gardens, and established a printing press. They are still in possession, saving what they can of Armenian Christian culture. Their museum houses some interesting books, including one great illustrated manuscript of the *Alexander Romance*. Byron visited in 1816, admired the monks, and started to study Armenian (if not too seriously); the portrait of this quite unmonastic poet hangs on the wall. It is possible to get to San Lazzaro by vaporetto, though once there it is mandatory to take a guided tour.

We were going by motor power, but it is still possible to travel around the

lagoon solely by oar power, as people do in the Vogalunga, or "Long Row."
This new race, instituted in 1975, takes place on the first Sunday after Ascension Day, and in a sense replaces the Ascension Day celebration of earlier
centuries, but it is not a costume affair. People look like themselves, chewing
gum, wearing spectacles; they carry various kinds of insignia ("NoMose" has
recently figured). In origin, it is partly a protest against the damage done by
motorboats in creating destructive waves and exhaust. The "Long Row" entails a distance of some thirty-two kilometers, starting from St. Mark's Basin
at 9 A.M. (with a burst of music and the firing of a pistol shot), going around
Murano and Burano, past San Francesco del Deserto and Sant'Erasmo, and
returning via Cannaregio up the Grand Canal. The first arrivals return after
a bare two hours. The visitor may clearly pick out boats and rowing styles
featured in illustrations of centuries earlier, like the women's race in the *masc-
arete* (see Figure 7). The race is, however, a modern affair, open to a variety
of oared craft—the latest addition seems to be dragon boats (though there
is some protest against such innovation). There is a modern tendency toward
mixed-gender crews. The Vogalunga is also hospitable to foreign entries,
which in 2006 came from as far away as Estonia and Hungary. Most pleasing
to local people, however, is the sight of local teams, proclaiming themselves
as pertaining to "San Erasmo" or the Fire Brigade. The 2006 Vogalunga (the
thirty-second) attracted 5,190 rowers. There were three wrecks or sinkings,
but these, the *Gazzetino* says airily, were "of no consequence."[14] There are no
prizes except ribbons. Each participant who goes the whole distance receives
a certificate. This race is less a competition than a celebration of the lagoon.
For some precious hours no motor traffic is allowed on the relevant reaches
of the laguna, nor on the Canal Grande. The festivity and the number of
boats make you realize how truthful Canaletto can be, and if you want to get
the "Canaletto feel," don't miss the Vogalunga.

I was not going to require anything as luxurious as oared transport, but I
needed a special craft for my desired port. No *vaporetti* call at San Francesco
del Deserto (Saint Francis of the Desert, or of the Waste Land), an island
in a shallow part of the lagoon, just southeast of Burano. I stressed to my
boatman the fact that I wanted to go there specifically. There followed much
Venetian conversation with other boatmen encountered on the way about the
state of the tides today and the condition of the channels. It isn't always
possible, so I gathered, for even our light craft, ever so much smaller than a
vaporetto, to land at San Francesco del Deserto. Once we were out on the

lagoon, it became clear to me that the boatman had to keep the most extraordinary map in his head, a map of partially invisible pathways, of channels and deep spots and shallow places, of small currents and fresh silting-up, and tidal hours. He was teaching this lore to his son, and let young David take the wheel. In American circumstances I would have objected strongly to letting a ten-year-old do the driving of the boat, but there was no need for protest here; the boy was very serious and intent, by no means given to fooling or inattention, and his father was carefully (though not anxiously) supervising and informing. The lad was learning the lagoon in the traditional way of the boatmen of Venice, a process that has gone on for generations, back to the fifth century. The channels and mudbanks have changed enormously over time, but the need to learn the lore, to keep up-to-date with the current map, to know the invisible spaces and to sense tides and obstructions, does not change.

We passed Sant'Erasmo, now a truck garden much given to artichokes, a small isle formerly fortified against attack by sea. The artichoke island has its own Regata in June, a day of festivity and food and island hospitality, a homecoming event that has nothing to do with attracting foreign tourists. The paper reports that the women's race was won by "the cannaregiotta Gloria Rogliana and the pellestrinotta Debora Scarpa," the team who won the race in the 2005 Regata Storica, while in second place the rowers were from Murano and Sant'Erasmo.[15] The exact *sestier* or island to which someone belongs is obviously still of importance. Foreigners writing both for and against Venice overlook how much of local interest goes on—parish celebrations, island festivities—all taking place without us.

At length we stopped at San Francesco del Deserto, with its church and a monastery. A brother came to greet us and offer to show us around; he seemed a very senior personage. He promised a tour in English, but was obviously so much happier in Italian that I said Italian would do nicely. All four of us, *i due Davide* included, went about the little monastery, which is supposed to mark a place where Saint Francis stopped off in 1220. Some say it was here that he preached to the birds, or at least stopped a storm so that the birds sang. Our guide was very insistent that this is the oldest monastery dedicated to Saint Francis, and certainly predates that modern outfit in Assisi. Nowadays the brothers hire firms to do the rebuilding, and they let out the market garden. They host conferences and occasional retreats; the friar emphasized that people of various countries and religions and professions (he mentioned psychiatrists among them) came to those. The whole place has an extraordinary atmosphere of peace and good will about it. In the middle distance, we could spy Terraferma, and could actually see the planes taking off from Marco Polo, yet we seemed to be standing in a timeless space in the center of an everlasting sea. As we stood in the attractive little gardens, it became easy to believe Saint Francis had been here.

From San Francesco del Deserto we coasted within sight of Murano toward Burano, going through a cluster of islets, some nameless, and one bearing my favorite lagoon island name: San Giacomo in Palude (Saint James in the Marsh). The first major building on San Giacomo in Palude was a hospice for pilgrims, put up at the order of Doge Orso Bedoer in the twelfth century.[16] Burano is a bright island, with small houses painted bright primary colors, to an extraordinary cheerful effect, almost Mexican. Cheerful Burano is supposed to have retained Carnevale longer than other parts of Venice.[17] After Venice, there is something doll-housey about Burano. The streets are crammed with lace-sellers, including persons hawking large tablecloths, for Burano at one time was internationally famous for lacemaking. Most lace, including that of Chioggia and Pellestrina, is made with a bobbin, but the Venetians of Burano developed in the sixteenth century a method of making lace with a needle, a kind of embroidery. This method is called *punto in aria*, "point (or stitch) in the air." The aerial lace reminds one vaguely of delicate traceries on Venetian buildings, of crotchets that seem made *punto in aria*. It seems the ambition of much Venetian art and craft, loving effervescent delicate shapes, to pay tribute to foam. The lace industry was once the mainstay of Burano. During reconstruction the craft revived, but has languished again. Lacemaking is very demanding work, hard on the eyes; it takes a long time to make a ruffle, let alone a tablecloth. If you, O tourist, really manage to find a handmade lace tablecloth, you ought to pay thousands of dollars for it, considering the woman-hours (and eye-power) it would have devoured.

Although some women do practice lacemaking, much of what is made and sold by the time I got to Burano is not only machine-made but imported, from the Philippines or (more commonly nowadays) from China. If you like a tablecloth, buy it for itself, but don't imagine it was handmade in the laguna, even if (or especially if) you purchase it in the main square of Burano, where the statue of Baldassare Galuppi looks on, not at all judgmental. On my journey round the lagoon the boatman wished to stop at a particular bakery in Burano, where he bought for his children at home some *bussolai*, those round ring cookies that you occasionally see in eighteenth-century Venetian paintings. Other Venetians make unsweetened circles of bread, but Burano is famous for its sweet *bussolai*. And these at least are indubitably handmade on the island.

From Burano we threaded our way through little islets to Mazzorbo, once, as its name implies, a massive *urbs*, *maiurbium*, or "greater city." Formerly important in the northern lagoon, it is now merely the site of more market gardens, offering the pleasant view of green growing things. The lagoon islands are the source of a great many salads during the course of a Venetian day. Mazzorbo has the remains of a monastery and a pretty thirteenth-century church, but I didn't get off the boat to go and look at it. We coasted into Torcello, which I was glad to see again, and I had another look at the churches. No Cipriani's restaurant on this occasion; the boatman-father, the two Davids, and I had a humble something-to-eat at the humble modern snack bar by the landing place.

This excursion had—alas!—to come to an end with the return to the Lido. I was not gifted like Beckford with unlimited funds, and the cost had to be paid in cash, not by credit card. Indeed, I had to cash more traveler's checks at the hotel in order to stump up the required sum, and the limitations of my purse prevented my drifting on to Chioggia (Chiozza) as I should have liked to do.

I did at last get to Chioggia, but it was some years later, and in January, not June. Chioggia appears to be four or five islands, with three canals among them; the place is so close to the shore that it has inevitably been made a peninsula. Chioggia's blessing and curse has been its proximity and attachment to the land, which rendered it the only part of greater Venice vulnerable to invaders, just as, a couple of millennia ago, it was the abode of Romans who have left their grid-pattern layout. Despite its vulnerability, it is a most cheerful place, attractive even in winter. Everyone in Choggia seems just to have gone fishing, or to be just about to go fishing. Boats abound—unfortunately, the inhabitants have given over painting their boats with elaborate designs as they long used to do, as recently as the mid-twentieth century. The little port greets newcomers with a column bearing a small medieval lion atop, like a parody of the Piazzetta. The Venetians of central Venice jeer that this beast is more like a cat than a lion, and joke that the Chioggotti even sound like cats, speaking with their elongated vowels: "Maiou." It is true that the natives of the place do elongate their words (unlike the city Venetians who like to shorten things). Even the foreigner can notice the accent, hearing the dotted notes of the vowels, and the tendency to make "ch" and "gg" soft—so that "Chioggia" (in proper Italian "Key-*oh*-dgya") is pronounced more like "Chee-*owes*-jya" ("Chiozza").

Chioggia has a lot going for it. It has a sunny outlook, sweet little bridges, and a port like a front porch with a view of Pellestrina and of Venice in the distance. It has a cathedral, and the old church of San Andrea, with a campanile dating from the thirteenth century. It has its own Carpaccio in the charming small church of San Domenico. This painting, allegedly Carpaccio's last work, shows Saint Paul in a drapery of a remarkable color—yet another Carpaccio variant on red—an unusual orangey-vermilion.

As the fishing is diminishing, Chioggia is anxious to find other sources of income and nonpolluting industry. Naturally, tourism figures in its plans, but after looking at the horribly dull and soulless resort town of Sottomarina next door, I would urge local developers of Chioggia to go upmarket. They could do worse than build some elegant ultramodern luxury apartments, tastefully fitted in with the prevailing attractive but unostentatious style. Many people would love to live thus in Venice, with a view of central Venice itself, in a place yet approachable by road as well as by boat. They would acquire a famous home, the birthplace of Sebastian Cabot, Rosalba Carriera, and Eleanora Duse, home to Goldoni in youth and known to Casanova. Considering its associations, Chioggia might be a good place to set up a theater, even initiate a theatrical festival. The coast about Chioggia, the sort of marsh where young men like those in Carpaccio's picture must have done some of their bird-shooting, is now a wildlife reserve. This a perfect site for birdwatching. So what about some pleasant hostelries catering to birdwatchers? Of course the buyers (or leasers) of the luxury flats should live there the year round and spend their money there. If I seem a bit snobbish, at least I am disinterested, for the luxury flats, I fancy, would be well above my touch. But there—I fondly dream.

I regret that I did not first arrive in Chioggia by sea on that perfect June day. My quest, like so many quests, was partially frustrated, a love cut short. Samuel Johnson once remarked that if he had no thought of futurity (i.e., his eternal future), his idea of happiness would be to travel fast in a post chaise with a pretty woman. My idea of a similar state of perfection would be to travel by boat (preferably of course with a handsome boatman) all day about the Venetian lagoon. I did end that particular day with a better mental map, not only of the position of various islands—many without names and a number deserted—but also of the watery maze that is the lagoon itself.

This maze is Venice's long-term defense system. Its shallow lagoon, changeable winding channels, mudbanks, and sandbanks formed the security of Venice. King Pepin tried to invade and, so legend goes, asked an old woman in Malamocco for directions to Venice. She said "straight ahead," pointing him toward the treacherous mudflats; Pepin ran aground and his men were picked off by Venetians. Enemies just could not get at it. Genoa occupied Chioggia in 1379, but its forces couldn't make it across the lagoon. Any invading fleet would have had to disembark its warriors in small shallow boats, which would be easy to head off and destroy.

Even in 1797, the lagoon and the marshes posed some potential defense against Napoleon's army. Had the Venetians fought, they could have kept Napoleon's men busy for two or three months, though the ending seems still a foregone conclusion. And how many Venetians would have been killed, how much of Venice itself destroyed in that war! Perhaps Venice would have garnered more respect, but I have sympathy for Ludovico Manin, the old Doge who decided to yield without bloodshed. A few Venetians in the 1790s were rather fans of the French Revolution, and had some hopes of Napoleon—hopes to be altogether dashed. Had they known they were going to be sold to Austria, and for nearly a century, the Venetian nobles might have decided differently; the poorer *cittadini* and *popoli* seem to have been more in favor of fighting anyway. The marshes, small islands, and lagoon were still useful in World War II. Some young men avoided German conscription by hiding out there, and the few valiant partisans used the marshes as a base from which to harry the retreating German army as the British advanced.

This watery maze explains why Venice is not fortified, why the seat of its government and power, the Doge's Palace, is so unlike a castle. It may be that their positive feelings about the security provided by the mazelike configuration of their world induced the Venetians to adapt all the more readily to the labyrinth of their city. Strangers may find both the meta-labyrinth and the inner one surprising and disconcerting. As long as you are in Venice, you are in a labyrinth hidden within another labyrinth.

A labyrinth implies something about *space*—literal three-dimensional as well as psychic space. Carnival or "Carnevale" in its old acceptation refers to a human activity appropriate to a *time*. Both labyrinth and carnival tease the visitor, who, like the human who arrives in this world, cannot be a mere spectator but must be in some way a participant. Labyrinth and Carnival—both are existential. Carnival traditionally refers to the period before Lent in which the pleasures of the flesh are indulged, preparatory to a penitential giving-up of these, including the eating of meat. The word comes from the giving up: "Carne, Vale," "Farewell, Flesh." Carnival itself involves and evokes the headiest giving way to the activities of the flesh. Yet paradoxically it is not an occasion for mere solid gorging at a feast (Venetians never did go in much for that). Nor is it even a special time for getting gorgeously drunk and having sex, though such things may happen—even be supposed to happen—to individuals during Carnevale. The essence of the old Carnival lies in dressing up, particularly in masking. Venice had one of the liveliest carnivals in Europe, which eventually became *the* Carnival to go to. Maximilien Misson, the Protestant tutor from Lyon, gives a jaundiced account of it:

The Carnaval [*sic*] begins always the second Holiday after Christmas; that is, from that Time people are permitted to wear Masks, and to open the Play-Houses and the Gaming-Houses. Then they are not satisfied with the ordinary Libertinism, they improve and refine all their Pleasures, and plunge into them up to the Neck. The whole City is disguis'd. Vice and Vertue are never so well counterfeited, and both the Names and Use of them is absolutely chang'd. The Place of St. *Mark* is fill'd with a Thousand sorts of Jack-Puddings. Strangers and Courtesans come in Shoals from all parts of *Europe*: There is every where a general Motion and Confusion, as if the World were turn'd Fools all in an Instant.[18]

The convergence of masked persons can be seen in the celebratory picture of 1609, showing revelers capering outside San Stefano, with a caption assuring us that disguised persons of all kinds can be seen at almost any hour (Figure 22). Here we see the "general Motion and Confusion" that disgusted Misson. Less judgmental, young John Evelyn some forty years earlier left his studies in Padua to enjoy the delights of the season. "I stirrd not from *Padoa* till *Shrovetide*," he explains, "when all the world repaire to *Venice* to see the folly & madnesse of the *Carnevall*":

The Women, Men & persons of all Conditions disguising themselves in antique dresses, & extravagant Musique & a thousand gambols, & traversing the streets from house to house, all places being then accessible, & free to enter: There is abroad nothing but flinging of Eggs fill'd with sweete Waters, & sometimes not over sweete; they also have a barbarous costome of hunting bulls about the Streets & Piazzas which is very dangerous, the passages being generally so narrow in that Citty: Likewise do the youth of the severall Wards & parrishes contend in other Masteries or pastimes, so as it is altogether impossible to recount the universal madnesse of this

In questa guisa si ueggono le maschere in Vinegia nel Carnouale, d'ogni qualita di persone
le quali sogliono quasi tutte alle hore 23. ridursi su la piazza di san stefano, è quiui passeggi-
ando tratenersi fino a quasi due hore di notte
Giacomo Franco Forma con Priuilegio

Figure 22. "Le Maschere in Vinegia" ("Masks [or Masqueraders] in Venice"), from *Habiti d'Huomeni et Donne Venetiane*, 1609 (Permission of British
Library: C 48.h.11, f. 15)

place during this time of licence: Now are the great banks set up for those who will play at Basset, the Comedians have also liberty & the Opera to Exercise: Witty pasquils are likewise thrown about, & the Mountebanks have their stages in every Corner. (February 1646; *Diary*, 240)

There had been attempts to make laws against the egg-flinging, the "game (or joke, *gioco*) of the egg," as early as 1268. This was the first law regarding Carnevale, but not the last. From the thirteenth century on there is a cascade of such rules. For example, in 1443 a law is passed against men going in travesty as women. In 1444 there is another law forbidding women to go about in travesty as men. These attempts at regulation tell us that Venetians in the fifteenth century, like Goldoni and some of his characters in the eighteenth century, were fond of gender-bending. There had been earlier laws against going masked at night. None of these seems to have had much effect. By 1502 the Council is legislating only against going masked while armed.[19]

Thus, most attempts at regulating the exuberance of Carnevale, even in relatively well-governed Venice, were visibly fruitless. Carnevale is the production of the creativity of the Venetian people—of all classes, certainly not just of those at the top. The core of this celebration seems to be not ingestion (feasting and drinking) but almost its opposite—activity, the release of power in activity. Sex itself may seem but a metaphor for the importunate general desire to release energy. We note connecting the activities referred to by Evelyn and others—music and dancing; fighting or running with bulls, encountering Fortune or Chance—a display of vital force, an invocation and expenditure of energies customarily kept in reserve. At the heart of the occasion and the concept is the fact that people of all classes and sexes go in disguise, entertainingly in "antic" (or "antique") dress. The standard differences between one person and another are set aside, there are no barriers: "All places being then accessible"—even the houses are not shut and barred. There is visibly some aggression in the playfulness, hurling the perfumed filled eggshells at somebody else. And yet it is an egg, a promising egg, a new beginning, such as Titian introduces in his picture of the child Mary.

Central to Carnevale is the fact of disguise and masking. Some suggest that Italian masks have some affinity with, and perhaps some linear descent from, masks from sub-Saharan Africa. The Roman great families had masks of their illustrious dead, to be worn in funeral processions. Both Greek and Roman drama used masks, a tradition continued in commedia dell'arte. Probably the Venetian mask is a mixture of Greek, Roman, and African elements.

A commonly told historical story of origins is that the mask came to Venice from Constantinople as the Byzantine ladies wore masks as protection against the sun. After the Venetian conquest of Constantinople in 1204 the returning conquerors brought these *larvae* back with them. But such cosmetic protectors don't sound very exciting. Several cults of late antiquity held festivals in which celebrants wore masks, including the mask of the lion, and a hint of this comes through the modern Carnevale. Revelers who wear lion masks (like the doorknocker lion face so commonly found on Venetian front doors) are perhaps reflecting ancient homage to the Sun, as well as paying tribute to Venice's lions. And nowadays you can observe at Carnevale a variety of masks of the Sun itself.

Venetians had one standard traditional mask, called the *bauta*. It was actually a complete head outfit, a hood largely of lace, going over the head and shoulders, and held in place by a tricorn hat at the top of the head; the remaining part of the face would be covered by a plain white mask, or *volto*, giving the wearer a sharp white peaked visage. This was convenient in that the lace part permitted breathing and even eating without the need to remove the false face. A certain gender change was involved. "Every man or woman in costume," Mario Belloni informs us, "was greeted, indifferently, with the title 'signora maschera' ['lady mask']."[20] We can watch this happening in Goldoni's *I Rusteghi*, when Filipetto in a *bauta* is greeted as "Siora maschera."[21] Here is a trick with language playing on the fact that the word for "mask" is always feminine. Another mask, the "Gnaga" was especially for men who were disguising themselves as women; the word comes from the Venetian for cat, "gnau"—which may explain why cat masks are so popular now.[22] A woman of the eighteenth century going out in public might wear the "Moretta," a small dark mask also called "la Muta," as the wearer had to remain silent, holding the mask in place with teeth clamped around a button. It looks rather as if the woman had received a black pie in the center of the face. An example can be seen in Longhi's picture of the spectators of the rhinoceros; the Muta-wearer is in tempting décolletage (see Figure 2).[23] But there were other masks as well, some emanating from the playhouse characters of the commedia: Arlecchino (Harlequin); the Plague Doctor; Pantalone, Pulcinella; Columbina. Not only is drama allowed, the play in which nobody is who he pretends to be, but the theater and the street, citizen and play-actor, are amalgamated. Everyone is putting on his act, all is theater.

A number of preachers took a dim view of the Carnival celebrations, and there were sermons and appeals against it, which must have come to seem

part of the ritual. It was not moralists' complaints that silenced and ultimately shut down the Venetian Carnival, however, but the grim insult of occupation. Many ordinary Venetians preferred not to sing and dance as clowns
to entertain their new masters. True, there were some efforts at Carnival during the earlier Austrian rule; Byron enjoyed Carnival in 1817: "up all night
at the masked ball of the Fenice—. . . it was a fine sight—the theatre illuminated—and all the world buffooning."[24] He enjoyed the Carnival perhaps
even more in 1818, when he caught the clap. But the Austrian rulers and
military officers were themselves rather suspicious of some of the Carnival
activities, which offered too good a chance for subversive activity. The Austrians too issued laws against going masked except within private indoor celebrations. This time, such a law, now enforced by a hostile military, would be
obeyed. The prohibition makes one realize how self-confident the old Republic really was in allowing the Carnival with its masking, its rowdiness—
and its hordes of foreigners—to take place year after year.

After the brave and disastrous revolt under the leadership of Daniele
Manin in 1848, Austrian rule became much harsher and Venetian resentment
more intense. The Venetian Carnival shut down almost completely as a *Venetian* affair from 1848 to 1867. (The Austrians could celebrate it—Effie Ruskin refers to it—but celebration was enclosed in spaces like theaters, and no
longer spread out over the city.) Upon their liberation, the Venetians at once
thought of reinstating Carnevale. The first free Carnival since 1797 was held
in 1867. Aleksandr Herzen, Russian liberal and political exile, approvingly
observed the phenomenon:

The crowd keeps growing, *le peuple s'amuse*, plays the fool heartily with all its might,
with great comic talent. . . . The absence of everything indecent surprises one. . . .
This is the recreation, the diversion, the playfulness of a whole people, and not the
dress-parade of the brothels. . . . Here . . . their sister, wife and daughter are diverting
themselves, and woe to him who insults a mask. . . . Nothing is too nonsensical to
happen when Saint Vitus' Dance takes hold of a whole population in fancy dress.
Hundreds, perhaps more, of mauve dominoes were sitting in the big hall of a restaurant; they had sailed across the Square in a gilt ship drawn by bulls.[25]

One can feel the delight, the relief, as the whole people of Venice united in
creating their own Carnival once more. The Carnival's flickering flame was
blown upon by the Great War, and it was to run up against severe prohibition
again between the wars. Mussolini absolutely forbade the Carnival. One can

see that siphoning popular attention from Il Duce and Fascist demonstrations was not to be encouraged. And besides, the license allowed in the Carnival and the confluence of people would allow opportunity for subversive doings or at the very least satiric and subversive thought. Nobody likes comedy less than a dictator.

In the late 1950s James Morris observed that the Carnival was practically defunct:

Just before Lent each year the city enjoys a brief season of Carnival, last remnants of the city's legendary festivities. Nowadays only the children of the place, in a pitiful last fling, buy their funny faces and moustaches from the chain stores and emerge to saunter through the city in their fancy dress: here a devil, here a harlequin, a three-foot-three Red Indian, an infant Spanish dancer. . . . The costumes are often elaborate, but the general impression is forlorn. Each exotic little figure walks along with its family . . . and they parade the Riva degli Schiavoni in prim and anxious demurity.[26]

Morris very obviously believes the Venetian Carnevale was at its last gasp in this stiff and pathetic children's show. On the contrary. One must not sing swan songs too soon. The Venetian Carnival has been revived in recent years. Wisely considering the popularity of Carnival in the modern world, in places like New Orleans and Rio de Janeiro, in the light of the deep history of Venice, some creative spirits got together in the late 1970s and planned its return. The city fathers were solidly behind it (as they had been indeed in the seventeenth and eighteenth centuries, when, as Misson notes, the Carnival was a money-spinner). Venice returned to the festive business with a bang, and the new Carnevale sprouted and then bloomed in the 1980s.

My first Venice (in 1961) was maskless—no masks, no mask shops. I have no nostalgia for that aspect of the past, preferring the proliferation of faces. The art of mask-making had to be resurrected. As one of the founders of the famous mask firm of Ca' Macana explains: "At the time, we were architecture students in the city and partly out of necessity and partly for fun we tried creating the first models and selling them in the squares and along the alleys. These were only attempts at mask making, since nobody really knew what materials to use or what techniques to adopt."[27] The old Venetian mask was made chiefly of waxed linen (linen being an easy product to obtain for artistic purposes in a city full of sails); as Venice prospered a special class of workers arose to make and decorate the objects, making this one of the industries of the Renaissance city.[28] From the late twentieth century, the good masks are customarily made of papier-mâché, in a special process. Materials, techniques, and styles both change and remain constant.

The revived Carnevale is a genuine Venetian party, arising from Venetian desire. It is, however, no longer a spontaneous popular creation, but takes place under civic eyes, with a good deal of organization. But then, a certain amount of organization was always required (coordination of transport and hotels, marshalling of foot traffic in crowded streets). And, as always, the success of Carnevale depends not just on venality but also on a good-humored inclination on the part of the populace to see that the foreigners have a good time, and a wish on the part of the foreigners to entertain as well as to be entertained.

As the modern Carnevale is a revival, some purists are disgusted at it. Not I. "Revival" is one of the ways we humans arrange our affairs. If we did not revive the past we would have no "classics." I was, on the contrary, curious to see it, and in February 2002 I persuaded my younger sister to go with me. Freda made herself a costume at home, based on fashions of the 1780s; I contented myself with a black velvet cape and a wig. Both of us bought masks in Venice. It is chic in some circles to despise "those dreadful mask shops" in Venice, but I shall never do so. True, some of the shops have the uninteresting plastic imported things, but there are plenty of shops where genuine handmade and individually designed masks are sold. You can even stand around and watch them being made. As Venetians insist, mask creation is a local folk art.

I think what makes the scorners scoff is not the fact that the masks are imported, or ugly, but the intrusive and somehow distressing fact of masks themselves. Masks are aggressive, faces without responsibility. To choose a mask is to defy nature in choosing an appearance, a manifestation, different from what Nature gives. It is a trick, and a conscious choice. Venetians love conscious tricks, as we see in the stories they tell about themselves: the old woman who directed Pepin's fleet to the mudflats, the thieves with Saint Mark's body disguising it under a load of pork, Bellini in a toga pretending to be the gentleman requiring a portrait. Masking at one important level is conscious trickery—for it is impossible unwittingly to be masked. The choice both deceives and reveals, for the appearance you choose says something "truer" about who you are than you would ordinarily be willing to admit—or even know. But even that would be only another possible truth among many. The mask is not only the solid substance—disembodied yet embodied—of willed deceit. The Italian (Latin) word for mask is *larva*, which is also a word for "ghost."

In choosing a mask you become a specter. There is something ghostly and haunting about masks. You can hardly go half a mile in Venice without seeing a great number on display, so many faces laid out for your delectation, weird or fantastic, grotesque or beautiful, the face of the Sun, the face of Panta-lone, the face of a cat. . . . In Stanley Kubrick's last film, *Eyes Wide Shut* (1999), based on a story by Arthur Schnitzler, the sex orgy scene, though apparently taking place in New York State, utilizes genuine Venetian masks, produced by top maskmakers like Ca' Macana and Mondonovo. The effect of the masks atop of naked bodies in crowds is perverse and chilling. There is no way of knowing a person, even when the body is thrown open, as long as the face is masked. With spangles, velvet, embroidery, and plumes of feath-ers, the masks in the mask shops rise in their ranks and stare at you with hollow eyes, each asking the mocking question, "And who are you?" Each mask invites, "Be me—whoever I am." The array of mask shops offers the first of Carnevale's many tweaks and twitches to the concept of identity.

The chief pleasure and occupation of Carnevale in Venice nowadays is to wander about, dressed in your costume and masked, looking in your turn at all the other folk who go masked and in costume. They are polyglot and multicolored (Figure 23). It is a new experience to meet stiff gold faces in the street, to pass various *larve*, a *larva* oneself, as if all are engaged in some metamorphosis of which this is a phase leading to the unknown. Each new passerby may add to the delight and strangeness of the scene. Strikingly at-tired entities choose squares and church walls as beautiful backdrops for their effects, and the most beautifully costumed bow graciously and silently while others exclaim and crowd round them. Without language we performed and admired (Figure 24). Everyone was gracious about allowing everyone else to take photographs, and you knew you were always figuring in the back-ground in somebody else's version of the event. Celebrities whose real face and name were unknown were born every hour, costumed beings eagerly an-ticipated and followed.

The modern Carnevale is supposed to last only ten days. By the weekend preceding the last weekend before Shrove Tuesday, hordes of visitors have arrived and are parading *en costume*. In 2002 the crowds were freshly enriched by visitors from Russia and Eastern Europe, as well as from Western Europe, the Americas, Australia, and Asia. There were also visitors from all over Italy. Some people in Europe must spend their entire winter designing a startling costume for these few extraordinary days, and in most cases it appeared to be the job of couples to carry out their theme. Gender transformation seemed old hat by this time. Some costumes seemed both beautiful and oddly mournful, as if lingering over a loss unidentified. The costumes reflected, perhaps, the fears and hopes of Europeans, including East Europeans and especially Russians, and their aspirations for a new structure in the post–Cold War world. Some apparel was no longer human costume as such, but more like the dress of a building or an idea, suggesting an ice palace or some fantasy structure such as might be found beyond the moon.

Momentary scenes: rich, elegant, disconcerting. A vision of the Danieli at night, a crack of light over the landing stage and a party of people in eighteenth-century dress getting into a gondola. The young lawyer in gown and bands walking in front of the Carità—Venice seemed relaxed with him, as if it had seen him many times over the centuries. A person in a *bauta* crossing a bridge at night seems to have stepped out of the Cinquecento. It was startling to go into the Caffè Florian and see those eighteenth-century rooms full of people in eighteenth-century dress, taking material real chocolate and coffee in their phantasmal ruffles and white wigs. Reality and theater had merged. Bits of the twenty-first century slid into the dream-vision—a young man in a pink suit, eighteenth-century style, and gorgeous pink hat, with a *telefonino* at his be-plumed ear. It both was and was not what we are accustomed to call "reality"; it seemed on the far side of something indefinable.

On the weekend before Shrove Tuesday Venice became positively uncomfortable. What Europeans term "Pullmans" (giant bus coaches) from all over the Continent pulled into Piazzale Roma and disgorged hordes of passengers. There cannot have been fewer than thirty thousand people suddenly added to the mixture. Local papers called it an invasion, and the streets were so congested it took an age to pass down any section of the Merceria. Most of these newcomers, alas, did not make any effort to costume themselves; they changed the mixture for the worse by being present only to gawk and not to make the show—a kind of cowardice rather than the effect of poverty. It seems only right that anybody coming to the Carnival at Venice might make a tiny, cheap effort to keep in the spirit of the thing.

There was music in the Piazza and a long contest for the best costumes. The costume-judging was both pleasing and discordant. Pleasing, because the event offered a chance to view a parade of effective costumes. Disconcerting, because the contest supplied a teleology to an event that absolutely resists the functional, the purpose-driven. It is the essence of Carnival masking that

Figure 23. Maskers celebrating Carnevale in Venice, February 2002. Photo by the author.

Figure 24. Maskers celebrating Carnevale in Venice, February 2002. Photo by the author.

it has no serious object in view external to itself. The playfulness of dramatic comedy may bestow on the purposelessness a function (as in *I Rusteghi*'s story of the young man who comes masked to the house in order to see the proposed fiancée). It is comic because there is a discord between rational external purpose and masking for the sake of masking. True Carnevale is non-teleological, and that is in a way frightening in itself—the contest tames it.

At the end of that last congested weekend most of the crowd disappeared as suddenly as they had come, and Venice was again a passing and repassing of elegant or bizarre costumed persons. On the Monday and Shrove Tuesday the Venetians themselves come out to play, folk from Mazzorbo and Burano and the further islands. They come with their children and homemade costumes to greet one another, and I think this is one of the pleasantest times of the whole event.

It is indeed strange to be going about in a costume and masked. To wear a mask all the time is to be aware of masking as a fact, and to recognize the masks not made of linen or papier-mâché that we wear all the time. The Venetians in the past had become used to going about masked, including the gamblers at the Ridotto. Indeed, you could be admitted as a gambler only if you wore a mask—except, oddly enough, patrician ladies, who enjoyed the privilege of showing themselves unmasked. (The patricians who acted as bankers, in guarantee of the honesty of the house, were barefaced and wore the toga, that costume of respectability.)[29] Ladies of the higher classes, as we have seen, tended to go out in public, when they went out at all, in masks. Masking is freedom—with an edge. In masking, it is impossible to delude oneself that one *knows* people. Can one really estimate the character and worth of the person in mask and costume sitting next to you?

A world of certainties is put on hold. I think this must have been always part of the charm of the Venetian Carnevale. Strange energies are released in a peculiar way. These energies are not the same as those unloosed in, for example, seeking earnestly after sex (which is a purposeful and often a solitary pursuit, though men do it in packs). Nor is it like cheering on a football team (communal and procedural). Rather, one seems to meet forces within that nebulous entity that we like to think of as "the self," energies customarily involved in constructing what we call the "personality" but which now (briefly) do not have to manufacture a personality in the same way. These energies are free-floating, not teleological; they drive to no objective through no procedure.

I have neared the end of my consideration of Venice by summoning two disconcerting entities. Labyrinth and Carnival both make unusual demands on the individual's sense of self, even asking you to let it go for now. You release your sense of your own importance. If your masked personage is a success, it is precisely because you have convincingly escaped your "you." Since Mikhail Bakhtin's theoretical works appeared on our academic scene, we have been talking a mite too cheerfully about Carnival—which itself is masked in Bakhtin, who evades Soviet controls by making Carnival do a deal of work as a political code. The participation in Carnival is *not* necessarily a purely happy experience, though it may be an important and rewarding one. Neither is it an experience that exists on one level alone. If it can be a difficult experience to lose oneself in a maze, it can also be painful to lose oneself in a mask. The mask is a piece of "Venetian appliqué," an encrustation applied to what is, one begins to realize, another surface. Once you have grown used to your "false" surface you are less certain about the front you more ordinarily wear. The boundaries between subjective and objective are blurred or broken, for you become an object of your own gaze, and the mirror returns you a mask.

Both self and space are fantasticated. The masked wanderer in the labyrinth uneasily knows that what is required for the perception and creation of what we desire to call reality—desire to *be* reality—may be withdrawn. That "reality" may deny itself altogether, and prove to be another mocking or delusive dead end. Or a mirror reflecting nothing—or something surprising. Yet there is always that insistent flesh, the real which we must always hail in saying farewell.

Conclusion

Venice and London—London's Death the Bony
Compared with Life—that's Venice! What a sky,
A sea this morning! One last look! Good-bye . . .
              —Robert Browning, "Sighed Rawdon Brown"

*I*t is hard to say good-bye to Venice—hard even to end a book about it. I would rather linger a while longer on the various pleasures, and the various ways in which people take them. It amuses me that Charles Burney enjoyed Venetian paintings chiefly for their informative display of musical instruments.[1] There is room for various enjoyers and enjoyments. Spotting a great crested grebe on the way back from Torcello, for instance. Waiting glumly for a vaporetto on a sleety morning and hearing a Venetian boat crew on the water, youthful and laughing, out practicing for the Vogalunga. Or popping into San Zaccaria late on a January day to see the great *Virgin and Child with Saints* (painted by Bellini in his seventies) only to find a service about to begin. I sit quietly, hearing a sermon and trying to sing new hymns, with the Bellini beside me, a presence and a friend. It seems both stirring and restful to have that intimacy with the painting, and not to glare at it in a culture warehouse.

The fact that we are able to look at Venice at all is the result of decisions and accidents. Unlike Carthage, which ended its days in massacre and fire, Venice in 1797 fell quietly. The unhappy Doge doubtless felt he was sparing the people and their beautiful city. That we can see Venice as we know it is partly the result of his sad decision. Could Ludovico Manin have seen the ferocity of Austrian attack in 1848–1849, perhaps he and the Council would have decided differently. Some critics and historians like to speak as if Venice departed from history in 1797, but this is a view of history as consisting only of world dominion and great successful deeds. The Venetians were heroic again, in 1848–1849, but they were not successful. Even an Italian guidebook omits that period from the "Cronologia storica."[2]

Venice has not departed from history. We might pause in our repetitive chatter about the imminent disappearance of Venice to consider what it has to offer the world now and in the future.

For one thing, Venice offers us a model of what may be done by two hundred thousand people—or actually fewer than that. We have been so bound up for the last five hundred years in the grandeur of the mega-nation-state, whose population is counted in the tens or hundreds of millions, that we may have forgotten something to which we need to return: that human creativity and human satisfaction can be achieved by much smaller groups working with a certain degree of harmony. Perhaps our notion of the state may be due to change yet again—perhaps it is changing now. Venice among others could point out a way. That might be one benefit, but only one among many. I would maintain that what Venice itself offers has only become more important as our modern world continues. It is of major importance as a creation and an idea.

If we count our Venetian tropes, we come to something like the following list: slime and viscous substance, polyglot crowds, the Orient, encrustation, reflective surfaces, broken lights and tesseration, water, mixed substances, the feminine, impurity, labyrinth, carnival mask, color. The confusing list is a list of the confusing. Substances are not to be solid and graspable; the underpinning of the world seems in question.

What we see in Venice, I think, is a tribute to matter—a tribute reflected also in its painting. But the Venetian version of matter is inclusive and unorthodox, as it includes without reprehension the seaweed and mud which can still be sanctified (Saint George in the Seaweed, Saint James in the Marsh). Matter does matter. So also do fleeting phenomena. Fluctuation, momentary appearance, is also sacred. Venetian architecture and art play with light, but it is light coming into contact with various surfaces and disturbances and being broken up and refashioned by them, in an unstable play of changeability. This hylic performance comes from a culture which had to begin by sitting lightly to place, like seabirds on islands. Its relation to the material substances of this world is not conditioned by solid experience of the paternal acres, but of engagement in adventure, commitment to making, re-making, imagining, and remembering. Its tenuous and hard-won relation to its own substratum, its knowledge of both abundance and scarcity—scarcity of land, above all—teaches it to hold each thing in the world free of contempt.

This means that the aesthetic of Venice admits of what is usually excluded—the element of the disgusting. We find that coming through strongly, for example in Casanova's proclamation, cited earlier, that he had

Figure 25. Drunken Noah vomits into Venice. Photo by the author.

always loved savory dishes, "game on the very edge . . . cheeses . . . when the little creatures which inhabit them become visible," and the accompanying observation that he always loved women who smelled strongly. He is challenging us in an ultra-Venetian manner when he says such things. Venetian aesthetics make room for the strong, the nauseating. The story of the rescue of Saint Mark's body by hiding it in a load of pork is, when you think of it, truly revolting. The mosaic showing the ship with its cargo of pork and the Muslim inspectors holding their noses, makes revulsion evident. It is worrying, this image, because it shows how closely a saint's body or any human body resembles—or just *is*—meat.

The fine carvings, dating from the fourteenth century, at the corner of the seaward loggia of the Doge's Palace show Adam and Eve and the Archangel Michael, a representation of the Fall of Man. And on the corner nearest the Ponte della Paglia, we see a very fine and graphic statue of the same period representing the Drunkenness of Noah. Truly, we find exhibited a Noah who is very drunk indeed, so that this patriarch appears to be vomiting—or about to vomit—into the Riva (Figure 25). The conventionally disgusting is incorporated, like the "slime" and "seaweed" that gave poets like Otway and Byron a handle with which to berate Venice. The "disgusting" is also found in the representations of an aging Madonna, by Bellini, or the distraught old Madonna of Titian's Ancona altarpiece, reminding us of the human aspect of the Virgin, and honoring the inevitable movement of life toward decay. So too we have the obstinate lame old nurse sitting on the stairs outside the king's room in Carpaccio's Ursula sequence. And the old crone selling eggs in Titian's *Presentation of the Virgin.*

The disgusting reflects and reflects upon what is saliently physical and corporeal, the intimately peculiar, like Veronese's dwarf and the man with the bloody nose in the *Feast at the House of Levi*, the monkey and the aging mother in the San Sebastiano picture. This sense of the intimately peculiar and vulnerable is reflected in Giandomenico Tiepolo's male and female satyrs and centaurs—in their vulnerable mixture of the human and the animal. We see this quality also in his Pulcinellas, and in all the characters of commedia dell'arte.

The disgusting mingles in Venetian art with the tender, with the concern that the humble and bodily not be quietly abandoned or haughtily thrown away. The physical is treated as holy, and as changeable—it is not an immoveable solid, even drunkenness and pork have their *punta in aria* aspects. The foamlike nature of nature, forming and reforming, demands tenderness. It is important that nothing be left out. That concern and something of the tenderness can be seen in Goldoni's interest in the value of the coffee house owner and his work, or the humble and homely labor (cooking, ironing) of the landlady in *La Locandiera*—where this worker is not a secondary or tertiary character but the heroine. There is no abjection.

We have been pursuing the question "Why do some love Venice so much?" As we have seen, not everybody loves Venice. Even those who have done so may express twinges of fear or anxiety, like the traveler who finds a strange irrecoverable *campo* in moonlight, or who gets lost in the maze. A good deal of literature about Venice is touched, at least a little, by fear or something like fear—odd, so one might think, in a place so transparently light, so rippling with color.

I cannot mock it, this fear, for I too have been, at least once and most decidedly, touched by *Horror Venetiae.* I had been walking at night with a companion through the Dorsoduro, from the Accademia Bridge to the Salute. We were proceeding toward the Dogana beside the black water when I was suddenly seized by a shivering and a sense of darkness, stopping me in my tracks. I felt as if I were walking through a malign atmosphere—as of a place where some bad scene, a murder perhaps, had transpired in the past. But that is probably a rationalization in itself. Certainly this was not one of the famous historical murder sites in Venice (there are several). We had recently passed near the site where Constance Fenimore Woolson plunged to meet her doom, but were not aware of this. And how could I be truly frightened of the black water itself, when, even if pushed in, I could certainly have swum? The chilling moment was all the more surprising as I have always enjoyed the snail-curls of cheerful Salute. At that moment I could not go on, nor did I want to turn back. Dorsoduro seemed suddenly a trifle sinister, and I did not want to walk back through the winding dimly lit ways. But it was late, and the vaporetti had ceased to ply, likewise the *traghetto* gondola. My companion was surprised, as he had no reason to think me given to such fantasies and mollygrubs. Being the sort of person who could whistle up a cab in New York in a thunderstorm, he amazingly managed to whistle up a boat, just to take us to the hotel immediately opposite. I was heartily grateful, but could never explain the fear or horror that momentarily overcame me. Fortunately, my friend did not (as I expected) tease me unmercifully about the incident; he later said he had felt something of the same sensation himself.

A certain subconscious sense of lacking perfect safety fosters a touch of fear, or at least stress, in visitors to Venice. Perhaps not only the tourists in *The Comfort of Strangers* but even Dante felt it, as he gazed into the viscous pitch. That fear may be projected upon treacherous strangers, con men like Volpone, but the con artist we truly fear is found in the mirror. Giorgione knows about mixed emotions, about fear and desire, and of apprehension as to what may lurk in the waters of a canal or mere. We apprehend ourselves in Venice, our own emotions, and confusedly know them to be mixed, and tinged with various hues. We may wonder if we know ourselves, as we recognize that we are constantly in the process of changing. To cross water is an emblem of making a life change. The crossing of living water is a significant—and scary—moment. To cross a river (Styx or Jordan) is to die. Many descriptions of arrival in Venice contain open or veiled references to crossing the Styx. Any crossing of water may be a figurative death. A space by a shore—of river or sea—is traditionally, in fiction and in art, a threshold of new possibility, a site of crisis, the scene of salvation or love or desolation. We see all of these in Titian's *Bacchus and Ariadne*, in a scene by a shore. We note how the tourists in Venice gather in cafés around Saint Mark's Square, where they are all able to look out at something dry and not watery. But the illusion of being on Terraferma is indeed an illusion. In Venice you are perpetually crossing water, as if you were instant by instant making a life change,

metamorphosing, with some new spiritual or physical revelation (and the two
are blended) around every corner, across every rio. The area is a multiplicity
of shores, one great viscous marshland of sex, death, and change. It is not a
slough to be shunned and ignored, however, but a sparkling and gleaming
ebullition of creativity, unignorable even when not dear. Every *fondamenta*
speaks of a new baptism, a rebirth. We encounter two fears: the fear of changing and the fear of not changing.

The cityscape itself inclines toward changeability. The constant play of
light, sky, mist, and sun on the broken fragments of water all make for disturbance, a shifting scene. The disturbance is connected with possibilities of
high excitement, noted in the work of painters as various as Carpaccio, Canaletto, and Turner. The excitement is also registered by fictional characters
who approach their dreamed-of Venetian objective. The first time he was to
go to Venice, Proust's young Marcel became so excited by the prospect that
he became ill, and the trip had to be postponed.

Even in contemplation, Venice can be dangerous. Some demand is being
put on the self, to explore, to let go. There is always a scent of the promise
or menace of estrangement. A certain elation or heightened sensitivity connected with Venice is associated with the loss of the self. This loss, or the
sense of oncoming loss, can be blamed on the wickedness or decadence of
Venice, as in the case of the speaker of "A Toccata of Galuppi's." It is always
tempting to *blame* Venice. Aschenbach in the gondola in his labyrinth seems
to himself to see deeply into the iniquity of Venice:

The call of the gondolier, half warning and half greeting, was answered from afar
out of the stillness of the labyrinth as if by some odd prearranged agreement. From
small gardens, situated at a height, clusters of flowers, white and purple, smelling of
almonds, hung down over crumbling walls. Arabic window enframements could be
seen in the murk. The marble steps of a church descended into the water; a beggar,
squatting there, attesting to his destitute state, held out his hat and showed the
whites of his eyes, as if he were blind; a dealer in antiques, standing in front of his
wretched shop, invited the passerby with cringing gestures to stop and look around,
in hopes of cheating him. That was Venice, the obsessive and untrustworthy
beauty—this city, half fairy tale, half tourist trap, in whose reeking atmosphere art
had once extravagantly luxuriated and which had inspired composers with music that
gently rocks you and meretriciously lulls you to rest. The adventurer felt as if his
eyes were drinking in this luxuriance, as if his ears were being wooed by those melo-

dies; he also recollected that the city was sick and was disguising the fact so it could go on making money.[3]

Venice is a deceiving woman, a "treacherous beauty." Venetian frailty seems to be illustrated in the orientalizing existence of the "Arabic" windows, the eastern, alien quality. This aspect of Venice also repels—something felt obscurely by many travelers, and very consciously by others. In the film version of *Comfort of Strangers,* in an important scene involving the two women, both the thematic music accompanying the scene and Caroline's parlor by the balcony are markedly "oriental"—thus dangerous. Caroline, victim and predator, pained and voluptuous, seems to sit amidst and upon the luxurious fabrics of a harem, with a background of similarly "Moorish" Venetian windows.

In Mann's novel the Oriental jars as a sign of the sinful and the repulsive, and the disgusting and out-of-place is emphasized as well in the physical presence of the beggar and in the fact that the wretched antiques dealer has memorials of the past for sale. Even the greatest Venetian art is felt to be voluptuous and erring; it participates in weakness, and shares the inner disease to which Aschenbach himself, a martyr to love—a figure ridiculous but not without pathos—is haplessly succumbing, leaving his old respectable, rational self in his pursuit of Tadzio. Venice itself is presented as inwardly corrupt, stagnant and diseased. It is a metamorphosing place where bad things happen. This seems to be not just Aschenbach's vision but Mann's, who needed Venice as an objective correlative (to borrow T. S. Eliot's term) of the transformation of Aschenbach and his spiral toward erotic enlightenment and death—about which Mann himself has a dual consciousness. (The novel is great but it is not in good faith.) The power of Eros, Mann's novel indicates, can be comprehended only in a negative setting. For Aschenbach the Platonist, the fall into the flesh is ultimately fearful and humiliating.

If the most notable case of self-alienation, loss of the known self, in fiction about Venice, is the figure of Aschenbach, there are plenty of others. Venice, with its expertise in masking and Carnival, plays with that exciting and most disturbing possibility of slippage of the self, loss of the sole and solid and well-known identity. Estrangement is the name of the game. The experience of the crowd, so diverse and various, is a premonitory taste of the Dionysian Carnevale. We have seen how important, in different ways, the crowd is to artists like Gentile Bellini, Carpaccio, Veronese, and Tintoretto. Experience is not just a private matter. Nor are experiences identical in a homogeneous world. Still more startling—an entity (thing or person) need not be solid and uniform, the same all through, but may luxuriate irides- cently in a glow of appliqué. Thin marble sheets, cladding to light brick, shine brilliantly in the sun, and their reflections dance on the water. Every- thing changes, moment by moment. Marble shines and surprises, and so does the person in the mask, cladding to a face. The presence of the polyglot and variously arrayed crowd, both in the daily life of the Piazza San Marco and in Venetian art, is a constant reminder that the way one is oneself (in the way one is *today*) is not the only way of conducting the business of being. Hence, Venice appears to some as Babylon. When we call it "Babel or "Baby- lon" we mean that it ought to fall—that it is unbearable. Not supporting solid unity, normal order, it—or she—has already "fallen." She must then be meretricious, a courtesan. We feel the constant menace of loss of normal- ity—and may be charmed by this too, as we go through abnormal streets of water. The heightened sense of consciousness to which we are brought by Venice is flickeringly illuminated by the threat that we may approach the brink of what we know, that an accustomed order of things might vanish, that consciousness itself may slip and change. This obscure threat—-or promise?—-breeds a kind of underlying dread. The greatness of Venetian art incorporates and releases some of this fear, in grandeur and bursts of change- ful color.

Travelers to Venice feel disorientation. Some hate it, and avoid it as much as may be, while others go to Venice perhaps in order to feel a sort of divine confusion. The Maori novelist Witi Ihimaera in *The Matriarch* has his Maori narrator reflect on his visit: "I had left the real world and crossed some threshold between reality and fantasy . . . in which the senses were heightened by the conjunction of both. Venice . . . was the product of two worlds in collision, the supernatural with the real, the fantastic with the natural, the bestial with the sublime."[4] Or rather, we might argue, Venice gives a new sense of reality, the possibilities of what reality might mean, by refusing to subscribe to our normative view of it. Venice will not endorse our common taxonomy of division between the real and the fantastic. The palazzi are real, artificial, and fantastic, built of imagination and memories of the East. We are dis-oriented partly because the Orient has come here, affronting our Western sense of what is and should be. The line between the East and West, like the line between solid earth and sea, has become blurred and indetermi- nate. In contemplating the mixed styles of Venice, the traveler is being asked if such lines of demarcation are as important as we customarily suppose. Do they really matter? Or matter in the "normal" way?

We, travelers to Venice, are being put out of our frame. What we usually take for granted (solid earth for a start) isn't here. When we try to catch the bus, a vaporetto, we stand on a platform that is really a kind of raft, and bob up and down in the wash of boats; we may wobble, we may feel our equilibrium threatened, there on the landing stage and on the vaporetto itself. We constantly leave solid ground. In the architecture all about us, the trope of incrustation teaches us that no edifice needs to be solid, and that the artificial, complex, and multiple may work as well as the straightforward and simple. It is fitting that one of the great literary moments on Venice concerns disequilibrium. Proust's Marcel suddenly recollects Venice through a moment of shifting stones beneath his feet, which offers him a key event in constructing his theory of memory and time:

I put my foot on a stone which was slightly lower than its neighbour, all my discouragement vanished and in its place was that same happiness. . . . A profound azure intoxicated my eyes, impressions of coolness, of dazzling light, swirled round me. . . . And almost at once I recognized the vision: it was Venice, of which my efforts to describe it and the snapshots taken by my memory had never told me anything, but which the sensation which I had once experienced as I stood upon two uneven stones in the baptistery of St Mark's had, recurring a moment ago, restored to me complete with all the other sensations linked on that day to that particular sensation, all of which had been waiting in their place.[5]

Being thrown off balance is a disconcerting form of rescue. Marcel in Venice was thrown slightly off balance on the uneven ancient floor of the Baptistery. The stones of Venice are shifting stones.

What Venice stands for—what Venice is—must go beyond a set of aesthetic principles, for a city or city-state is a community of persons and thus cannot help being constituted of what we call moral principles as well as of political beliefs and usages. But these are not abstractions in the city itself. All cities intrude with their physical presence. And all cities represent themselves, speak of what they are in multiple narrations. A city cannot help telling its stories about itself in its patterns and habits, in its punctuating ornaments and narrative points. Cities have been very self-conscious about that, erecting monuments we are supposed to look at—but these conscious signs must go with what has to be there. Venice tells many stories about itself (there is no one "myth of Venice") but what has to be there is the water, and it will not be subsumed in mathematical squares or other abstract forms.

What we have been pursuing in the question "Why do some love Venice so much?" is the related question "What does Venice give to the world?" And the answers are—in the broadest and deepest terms—aesthetic. Venice is Western aesthetics' loyal-disloyal Opposition. It is the most signal and complete opposition to the aesthetic principles that have long been dominant in the West. In that dominant aesthetic, reaching back to Plato and perpetually accompanying us in various kinds of formalism, Idea is superior to Matter, and Form triumphs over Color, just as Male is superior to Female, and West superior to East. The permanent is noble; the changeful is base. The spontaneous, iridescent, and unstable are unfit to rule. The principles of Andrea Palladio (his invented surname waving like a banner to proclaim his classical sympathies) took Venice in the formal Western direction, at once classic and modern, which is why I sympathize more than just a little with Ruskin's dislike of Palladian buildings in Venice. The Venetians were happier with the baroque and the rococo than with the neoclassical. They got along better with something less abstract, to which they could give their own playful twist. Burnet thought the Venetians valued Christ less than His Mother, and that is why Redentore was so uninteresting and Salute so attractive. He was comically out in his reasoning, but right in his impression—Salute is more suited to Venice than the cold triumph of Redentore. The imposed "return" to Western principles is a distortion of Venice's own dominant statements.[6]

These are not merely aesthetic but moral considerations—or impulses—moral in their aesthetics, not aside from them. The principles possess enormous significance for the ways in which we order our lives. Venice the strange Republic is a hold-out for another order of being, imperfectly understood, and even, very often, detested. It is natural that we should find a grain or two of antipathy, even suppressed shock, lurking in our response to Venice. Venice is not what a city should be: "Streets Full of Water Please Advise."

There are some sobering practical implications to this observation, that Venice is constructed and lives on different aesthetic and moral principles. It is truly *strange*—different from much else that is Western and familiar. It differs from what was dominant in the great Roman empire, and from what is dominant now. A corollary to this observation is that Venice requires truly Venetian approaches to its continued existence and well-being. One of the greatest dangers to Venice is the application of un-Venetian principles to "solving" her "problems." Those who adhere to the West's dominant aesthetic think of the water as an enemy, an exterior element to be held or controlled or contained by some new manmade objects and assertive force. We will come in from outside with our good ideas and intentions and want to push the water away—hold it off somehow. We Westerners like dry land and railway bridges. The Mose Project is a truly and hideously "Roman" idea. It is Palladianism rushing into the sea. The truly Venetian engineering is a way of living *with* the water, which flows through this cloven city.

Tried by strict orthodoxy, Venice is always going to be abnormal, unnatural, "queer." It is Babylon as opposed to Jerusalem, or Rome. It is not safe. It speaks of the new, the potential, of shifting and estrangement and disequilibrium. "Io non so', non so' Roma." Venice is not Rome—which is a way of saying that Venice lives and produces somewhat outside of the dominant notions that have been so central, and sometimes so comforting, to the West. My *figura* of the Venetians as Phoenicians, Carthaginians, is an elaboration, an ornament (perhaps playful, perhaps serious) of my main point. The Venetians seem to come to us from outside the box in which we usually sit—from a culture outside the Western European. They do not intend to answer to some basic cultural assumptions. They know, the Venetians, that what we call Form is as changeable as Color, that Color in proper conditions (see Giorgione and Titian) can be Form. They understand that intermediate states are the real thing and not just some junction through which we are supposed to proceed with eyes wide shut. They see that life is not a matter of Platonic Ideas and stately eternal truths, and steadfast rest of all things firmly stayed, but a flow and a flux. The transient glimmer lost in a moment is a reality, and not something to be discarded and ignored in the face of a higher Truth. Surfaces are real, and every real thing is a play of surfaces. Light becomes matter, and matter, light. Subject and object cannot be neatly split.

If Venice were to leave our map of the world, too much would go with her for our loss to be easily borne. For not only would we lose many beautiful things—the city itself as a beautiful Thing—but we would lose ideas, concepts, approaches to the work of living that are more needed now than ever before. Venice's work is not done. It may be that the glorious and checkered past was just a prologue to an instruction of the world, giving intimations of how to bear with what is new and foreign and fleshly and uncertain.

Venice's sense of the holy is a sense of the moving and flowing. I think that sense of the holy was present to Pope John XXIII, once Patriarch of Venice. Pope John XXIII, born in Bergamo (once within Venice's expansive reach), expresses a sense of the holy at work in the world, and chides the "prophets of doom" who cannot see good in the world, when he believes that Divine Providence is leading us to "a new order of human relations" including an acceptance of difference.[7] His sense of the holy encompasses the need to avoid exclusion and overlordship, making him in some ways as Venetian as Tintoretto and Veronese, if a puzzle to some of his co-religionists. In acknowledging movement and including slime, yielding to that flux, that glow and flow, we may feel we are losing ourselves and what we call "our principles," not in uncertainty or doubt but in something like the positive and alarming force of a wave or current of the sea. So some of Venice's lovers have not been able to remain and live with her, so stressful is the task of living in sparkle and change, with the animal and the organic viscousness of things as companions.

My own thinking latterly has been much taken up with the attractions and dangers of the Gnostic. I was tardy myself in fully recognizing this new interest, which grew at first unconsciously, but was slowly brought to awareness by my thinking about the novel in my book *True Story of the Novel*. Gnosticism tends to "spiritualize" what seems central, and to discard other things or elements completely, or almost completely. The Gnostic moves thorough a horror of the flesh toward dry transcendence which a few chosen special souls can reach. The world tempts with extras, like roses, but one must disregard these dangerous things, for matter is touched by the Devil. Other persons, the low and the unenlightened, may not be real people, but vessels of clay, androids not destined for eternity. Few beliefs are more dangerous, or at bottom more warlike, than Gnosticism. It is suited to the justification not only of war but extermination of others, as well as to complete disregard of the reality of the many, and of the despised earth.

I see in Venice a highly spiritual city—of its own kind. I don't think Veronica Franca was wrong when she said it was built to a celestial plan. In its central principles—though goodness knows not always in its behavior—it is opposed to this destructive dismissal of the material and the human. Venice is at the opposite end, as it were, of some sort of scale starting with Gnosticism. So far away is Venice from the "spiritual" that Venice is also not going to appear quite orthodox or even good to those who tie orthodoxy and goodness to uniformity, regularity, and stability, and to the superiority of Form to Matter, Design to Color, Male to Female. Venice's deep opposition to the Gnostic is for myself a kind of ultimate answer to my question as to my own attraction to it, an explanation for my affection for its colored art, for its animals and slime and mud. Venice's stance is so far from Gnosticism that to some the city has not seemed spiritual at all. To my Platonic philosophy teacher, it was always to be Babylon. If we face Venice theologically—that is, if we face it in terms of the holy—it must be with a theology of immanence. We will then begin to comprehend its revelation of the divine energy within matter, and within our relation to the stuff of the world.

Notes

Chapter 1. Discovering Venice

Note to epigraphs: "Le immagini della memoria, una volta fissate con le parole, si cancellano,—disse Polo.—Forse Venezia ho paura di perderlar tutta in una volta, se ne parlo. O forse, parlando d'altre città, l'ho già perduta a poco a poco." Italo Calvino, *Le città invisibili* (Turin: Giulio Einaudi Editore, 1972), 94. Translations are my own unless another translator is indicated.

1. Two thousand lire is the right fare for the period, though it seems incredibly little, just a few dollars. But as Venetians old enough to know have informed me, at that time salaries for many jobs in Italy were ten or twelve thousand lire per month, so such a train fare could easily be 15 or 20 percent of the monthly wage. (In 1961 I was living on £50 sterling a month.)

2. The Czech composer Christoph Willibald Gluck (1714–1787) wrote the opera *Orfeo ed Euridice* (1762); Ranieri de' Calzabigi was the librettist. The aria sung by the bereft Orfeo just after his wife Euridice's death contains the repeated lines "Che farò senza Euridice?/ Dove andrò senza il mio ben?" (What shall I do without Euridice?/ Where shall I go without my treasure?) (Act III, sc. i). As "ben" means anything that is good, including "goods," it might have been applied to my luggage and traveler's checks.

3. The Basilica comes off badly in the picture. One surprise in looking over these old materials is the dullness and even blurriness of the postcard images. Postwar postcards were perhaps inferior to those of earlier decades.

4. James Morris, *The World of Venice* (New York: Pantheon Books, 1960), 73–76. "Venice is one of the world's supreme cat-cities" (73). Although James Morris has become Jan Morris, I use the earlier name for the book first published under that name.

5. Thomas Otway, *Venice Preserv'd, or A Plot Discover'd* in *The Works of Thomas Otway*, ed. J. C. Ghosh, 2 vols. (Oxford: Clarendon Press, 1932), Act V, line 369; II, 281.

Chapter 2. Ever-Vanishing City

Note to epigraphs: Alexander Pope, *Dunciad* (1743 version), Book IV, lines 307–310, in *The Poems of Alexander Pope*, ed. John Butt (London: Methuen, 1970), 282. Ann Radcliffe, *The Mysteries of Udolpho: A Romance, Interspersed with Some Pieces of Poetry*, 4 vols. (London: G. G. and J. Robinson, 1794), II, 36.

1. Radcliffe, *The Mysteries of Udolpho*, II, 36–38.

2. Johann Wolfgang von Goethe, headnote to Venetian section in *Italian Journey* (*Die Italienische Reise*, 1816), trans. W. H. Auden and Elizabeth Mayer (London: Penguin Books, 1970), 74. As this work will be frequently quoted, future citations will be given with the text according to date of diary entry (where applicable) and page number.

3. John Ruskin, *The Stones of Venice*, illustrated edition, 3 vols.: vol. I. *The Foundations;* vol. II. *Sea Stories;* vol. III. *The Fall* (London: George Allen & Unwin, 1925), I, 352. Subsequent citations will be given within the text, according to volume and page number.

4. Byron, *Childe Harold's Pilgrimage*, Canto IV (first published 1818), lines 1–2, in *Byron: The Complete Poetical Works*, ed. Jerome McGann, 4 vols. (Oxford: Clarendon Press, 1980–1986), II (1980), 124. Subsequent quotations from this poem will be accompanied by reference within the text.

5. William Beckford, *Dreams, Waking Thoughts, and Incidents; In a Series of Letters from Various Parts of Europe* (London: J. Johnson and P. Elmsly, 1783), 105–106. (Beckford tried to suppress this book just before publication, his future in-laws apparently not approving.) Subsequent references will be accompanied in the text by date and page number.

6. "I repaired to the statue of Neptune, and invoked it to second my enterprize" (*Dreams, Waking Thoughts, and Incidents*, 106). Beckford must mean the large statue of Neptune by Jacopo Sansovino, which, along with his statue of Mars, adorns the Scala dei Giganti (Giants' Staircase) and gave it that name. Beckford is evidently quite aware that Neptune is customarily invoked in Venice as a supporter—not a destroyer—of the city-empire.

7. Germaine de Staël, *Corinne ou l'Italie,* ed. Simone Balayé (Paris: Gallimard, 1985), Book xv, ch. viii, 426.

8. Ibid. This is the Orfano canal, which evokes such satisfying horror in a number of subsequent visitors, including (as we shall see) Gautier. Perhaps the French particularly enjoyed lamenting wicked Venice's horrid use of this canal since that erased memories of the canal's first historical appearance as the site of the defeat of King Pepin of France.

9. For the relation of the poem to the song, see John Julius Norwich, *Paradise of Cities: Venice in the Nineteenth Century* (New York: Doubleday, 2003), appendix, 315–317.

10. Robert Browning, "A Toccata of Galuppi's," in *Robert Browning: The Poems*, ed. John Pettigrew, 2 vols. (New Haven: Yale University Press, 1981), I, 550–552.

11. Byron, "Venice. An Ode," in *Works*, ed. McGann, vol. IV, 201–6. We may note that Byron thinks Venice's empire beneficent, or at least harmless: "She was the voyager's worship;—even her crimes/ Were of the softer order–born of Love,/ She drank no blood, nor fatten'd on the dead,/ But gladden'd where her harmless conquests spread" (stanza 3, lines 110–113; ibid., 204). Byron must here choose to forget the Fourth Crusade.

12. Alvise Zorzi, *La Repubblica del Leone: Storia di Venezia* (Milan: Tascabili Bompiani, 2005), 566. Much of the information in the next two paragraphs is derived from Zorzi's chapter 13, "La rovina" ("Ruin"), 533–581.

13. Anthony Trollope, "The Last Austrian Who Left Venice" (first published in *Good Words*, 1867), in *Later Short Stories*, ed. John Sutherland (Oxford: Oxford World's Classics, 1995), 56–74.

14. Alexander Pope, *Essay on Man*, lines 291–292, in *The Poems of Alexander Pope*, 544.

15. Percy Bysshe Shelley, "Lines Written Among the Euganean Hills" (written 1818,

published 1819), in *Shelley: Poetical Works*, ed. Thomas Hutchinson (Oxford: Oxford University Press, 1968), 555–556.

16. Thomas Moore, "Extract II: Venice," first published in *Rhymes of the Road*, 1819; here as published in Moore's *Fables for the Holy Alliance, Rhymes of the Road, etc.* by "Thomas Brown the Younger" (pseudonym) (London: Longman, Hurst Rees, Orme and Brown, 1823), 85–86.

17. Benjamin Disraeli, *Contarini Fleming: A Romance* (Leipzig: Tauchnitz, 1846), 189.

18. Jonathan Keates, *The Siege of Venice* (London: Chatto & Windus, 2005), 112.

19. See Mary Lutyens, *Effie in Venice* (London: John Murray, 1965), 132–134.

20. Alvise Zorzi, *Venezia Austriaca: 1798–1866* (first published 1985; Gorizia: Libreria Editrice Goriziana, 2000), 106.

21. William Dean Howells, *Venetian Life*, new and enlarged edition (Boston, 1895; reprinted New York: AMS, 1971), 414. Subsequent references will be given in the text by short title and page number.

22. Letter of Ralph Curtis to Isabella Stewart Gardner, 2 September 1915, printed in Henry James, *Letters from the Palazzo Barbaro*, ed. Rosella Mamoli Zorzi (London: Pushkin Press, 1998), 202.

23. Zorzi, *La Repubblica del Leone*, 608–609.

24. See John Berendt's account of his first interview with Giovanni Volpi in *The City of Falling Angels* (New York: Penguin Press, 2005), 81–89.

25. Complaints about the damage to the lagoon by the huge channel, as well as about the smog resulting from the plant itself, have become fairly common, but, considering the large vested interests involved, there seems sadly little chance of any basic change being made at present. For the plan to cut down on cars, including the three-day stoppage, and reactions to it, see almost any issue of *Il Gazzetino di Venezia* from late 2005 or early 2006.

26. De Staël, *Corinne*, Book xv, ch. vii, 420–421.

27. Byron, *Beppo, A Venetian Story*, stanza xix, line 151, in *Works*, ed. McGann, IV (1986), 135.

28. Mark Twain (Samuel Clemens), *The Innocents Abroad*, ed. Tom Quirke and Guy Cardwell (London: Penguin Books, 2002), 154–155.

29. Thomas Mann, *Der Tod in Venedig (Death in Venice)*, trans. Stanley Appelbaum, Dual Language Book: *Death in Venice and A Man and His Dog* (Mineola, N.Y.: Dover, 2001), 34–35.

30. Alfred de Musset, *Poésies complètes*, ed. Maurice Allem (Paris: Gallimard [Bibliothèque de la Pléiade], 1957), 448. Translations are my own.

31. George Sand (Mme. de Dudevant), "Fragment d'un roman qui n'a pas été fait," in *Sand et Musset: Le roman de Venise*, ed. José-Luis Diaz (Arles: Babel, 1999), 114–115. Diaz has collected and assembled primary material (including lovers' letters) relating to this Venetian visit in this book, presumably entitled *Le roman de Venise* in honor of the "roman" that Sand did not complete.

32. Ibid., 116.

33. Charles Dickens, *Pictures from Italy*, in *American Notes and Pictures from Italy*, Oxford Illustrated Dickens (Oxford: Oxford University Press, 1997), 330–331.

34. Théophile Gautier, *Voyage en Italie,* in *Italia: Voyage en Italie,* ed. Marie-Hélène Girard (Paris: La Boîte à Documents, 1997), 79. Translations are my own.

35. Ibid., 80–81.

36. H. E. Tidmarsh, "The Boats of Venice," *The Graphic* (16 January 1892), 75–78.

37. Gabriele D'Annunzio, *The Flame,* trans. Susan Bassnett (London: Quartet Books, 1991), 6. Cf. "Conoscete voi . . . qualche altro luogo del mondo che abbia, come Venezia, la virtù di stimolare la potenza della vita umana in certe ore eccitando tutti i desiderii sino alla febbre?" *Il Fuoco,* ed. Niva Lorenzini (Milan: Arnoldo Mondadori, 1996), 6. (The power and potential of human life are stimulated almost to fever pitch at certain times, certain special hours, it is implied, not at every Venetian moment.)

38. D'Annunzio, *The Flame,* 301.

39. Luchino Visconti's film (*Il Morto in Venezia*) with Dirk Bogarde as Aschenbach appeared in Italian in 1971, and was reissued in English in 1990. Visconti is evidently attracted by the opportunity to use Mahler, as he effectively does, but he sinks Aschenbach in the process.

40. Euphemia Ruskin, letter to Mr. and Mrs. Gray, 20 October 1851; Lutyens, *Effie in Venice,* 204.

41. Henry James, *The Aspern Papers* (London: Penguin Books, 1986), 49–50.

42. Ibid., 51.

43. Kai Meyer, *Die Fließende Köningen* (2001), translated as *The Water Mirror: Dark Reflections, Book One,* by Elizabeth D. Crawford (New York: Margaret K. McElderry Books, 2005).

Chapter 3. A Dream of Pleasure, a Nightmare of Spies

Note to epigraph: Robert Browning, "A Toccata of Galuppi's," line 34, in *Robert Browning: The Poems,* ed. John Pettigrew, 2 vols. (New Haven: Yale University Press, 1981), I, 552.

1. "Sur les lagunes," section ii of "Variations sur le Carnaval de Venise," lines 10–19; in *Émaux et Camées* (first published 1852) ed. Claudine Gothot-Mersch (Paris: Gallimard, 1981), 37–38 (translation mine).

2. Austen's version, under the title "Arietta Veneziano," can be heard on the CD *Jane Austen's Songbook* (Albany Records, 2004). The "I" of the song may be taken as the gondolier rowing the blonde. In Sand's novel, "La Biondina" is sung by the rowing hero in an effort to seem manly and careless; see *La dernière Aldini* (Brussels: Meline, Cans et Compagnie, 1858), 80.

3. Gautier, *Voyage en Italie,* 131 (translation mine).

4. Gautier, "Sur les lagunes," lines 12–31 (translation mine). A note by the editor explains the connection with Paganini: see Gothot-Mersch in *Émaux et Camées,* 232–233.

5. Venice had pulled itself together after losing its spice empire, and by the latter eighteenth century had increased its shipping so that "the total tonnage moving through the port of Venice was larger in 1783 . . . than ever before in the thousand years of the city's history" (F. C. Lane, *Venice: A Maritime Republic*; quoted in John Julius Norwich, *A History of Venice* [New York: Vintage Books, 1989] [originally published in United Kingdom as *Venice,* 1982], 591).

6. Bishop Gilbert Burnet, *Bishop Burnet's Travels Through France, Italy, Germany, and Switzerland: Describing their Religion, Learning, Government, Customs, Natural History, Trade, &c. And illustrated with curious Observations on the Buildings, Paintings, Antiquities, and other Curiosities in Art and Nature. With a detection of the Frauds and Folly of Popery and Superstition in some flagrant Instances* (London: T. Payne, 1750), 144.

7. For *barnabotti*, the concentration of wealth in endogamic matches, and the devolution of patrician power into mere bureaucratic control, see Zorzi, *La Repubblica del Leone*, 443–447. See also Norwich, *A History of Venice*, 596–597.

8. Hester Lynch Piozzi, *Observations and Reflections Made in the Course of a Journey Through France, Italy and Germany* (Dublin: Chamberlaine, White, 1789), 141. Subsequent reference will be made within the text giving short title and page number.

9. Giacomo Casanova, *Histoire de Ma Fuite des Prisons de la République de Venise, qu'on Appelle les Plombs* (written 1787; published Leipzig, 1788), 22 (translation mine). Subsequent references will be made within the text giving short title (*Ma Fuite*) and page number.

10. Letter to Lady Pomfret, 6 November 1739, in Lady Mary Wortley Montagu, *Complete Letters of Lady Mary Wortley Montagu*, ed. Robert Halsband, 3 vols. (Oxford: Clarendon Press, 1966), II, 159.

11. P. G. Molmenti, *Storia di Venezia nella vita privata* (1926–1929), quoted by Danilo Reato, *Le Maschere Veneziane* (Venice: Arsenale Editrice, 1988), 15 (translation mine).

12. Samuel Richardson, *The History of Sir Charles Grandison*, ed. Jocelyn Harris, 3 vols. (Oxford: Oxford University Press, 1972), II, 458.

13. Ibid., 459.

14. "Venice's superb communications and the almost legendary stability of her government had made her Europe's principal centre of espionage, an international clearing-house for secrets of state" (Norwich, *A History of Venice*, 521). In the early seventeenth century, Spain was making a very determined effort to overthrow Venice, and there were numerous genuine plotters: "For years the Spanish Embassy had been the busiest centre of intrigue in the whole of Venice" (ibid., 523). It is on the most important of these attempts that Otway's *Venice Preserv'd* is based. That Spanish plot was foiled, but there were other plots—not to speak of industrial espionage: Joan DeJean gives an amusing and detailed account of the efforts of Louis XIV to lure Murano glassmakers to France in *The Essence of Style* (New York: Free Press, 2005), 177–200.

15. [Maximilien Misson], *A New Voyage to Italy. With Curious Observations on Several Other Countries*, 4th ed., 4 vols. (London: R. Bonwicke, J. Tonson, 1714), I, 268. The author's name is not given on the title page, nor is that of the translator. The work is presented as a series of letters (the Venetian letters are dated early in 1688), with marginal additions written later by the author. Misson's book was still being read as a kind of guide in the mid-eighteenth century.

16. Misson, *A New Voyage to Italy*, 269.

17. Montagu, letter to Wortley Montagu, 11 December 1739; *Letters*, II, 163.

18. Judith Summers, *The Empress of Pleasure: The Life and Adventures of Teresa Cornelys—Queen of Masquerades and Casanova's Lover* (London: Viking Penguin, 2003). Teresa Imer called herself "Mrs. Cornelys," after the last name of a Dutch lover, but there is no record of their marriage.

19. Giacomo Casanova, *Histoire de Ma Vie*, translated and annotated by Willard Trask as *History of My Life*, 12 vols. (Baltimore: Johns Hopkins University Press, 1966), III, 141–142. Subsequent references will be made in the text, giving short title followed by volume and page number. Trask's translation is based on the edition of *Histoire de Ma Vie* published by F. A. Brockhaus (Paris, 1960). Casanova's scandalous self-narrated life story, left incomplete in manuscript at his death, took a long while to get into print.

20. Monteverdi's first opera was *Orfeo* (1607) followed by *Arianna* (*Ariadne*) (1608), both produced in Mantua. In 1640 *Arianna* was revived for a Venetian audience; of this work only the "Lament of Ariadne" survives. Monteverdi went quickly to work producing more operas: *Il Ritorno de'Ulisse in Patria* in 1640, *Le Nozze d'Enea con Lavinia* (lost), and *L'Incoronazione di Poppea* (1642).

21. There is perhaps a political flavor to *I Quattri Stagioni* (*The Four Seasons*). This four-season conceit could be seen as making a claim to the mainland of the Veneto and its rural fields, orchards, and groves. Venice has seasons (including sharp winters), but the green growing things, farm animals, and birds conjured up in the concept of "seasons" were scarce in central Venice.

22. These include composers such as Domenico Albert (c. 1710–c. 1740); Giuseppe Jozzi (c. 1710–1770), and the Naples-born Pietro Guglielmi (1728–1804). Their work is most readily to be found in Venetian recordings, such as *Il Clavicembalo a Venezia: Sonate del Settecento dai manoscritti delle biblioteche veneziane* (Venice: Nalesso Records, 2001).

23. Charles Burney, *The Present State of Music in France and Italy: Or, The Journal of a Tour through those Countries, Undertaken to collect Materials for A General History of Music* (London: T. Becket and Co., 1771), 170.

24. Ibid., 187.

25. Ibid., 138.

26. Ibid., 150–152.

27. There is a good discussion of it with illustrations in Nelli-Ellena Vanzan Marchini, *Venezia: Luoghi di Paure e Volutà* (Venice: Edizioni della Laguna, 1984), 82–83.

28. Goethe, 7 October 1786: "For this evening I had made arrangements to hear the famous singing of the boatmen, who chant verses by Tasso and Ariosto to their own melodies. This performance has to be ordered in advance, for it is now rarely done." Goethe refers to Rousseau's notation in his *Recueil d'Airs, Romances et Duos,* 1750; this work was reprinted after Rousseau's death in *Les Consolations de Misères de ma Vie,* where "Tasso alla Veneziana" can be found on page 199. A work of that name, an arrangement by based on this notation, can be heard sung by Ursula Mayer-Reinach on the CD *Music Around the Mediterranean* (Lausanne: Gallo, 1992).

Having already written that now *gondolieri* don't sing anything better than "O Sole Mio," I was electrified to hear a remarkable performance from three gondoliers one late afternoon in March 2006; I think they were enjoying themselves, chiefly, and they knew opera, but it strikes me that perhaps some few families in Venice may retain memory of the old vocal music.

29. Horatio Brown, *In and Around Venice* (New York: Charles Scribner's Sons, 1905), 42–43. Subsequent reference will be made in the text, with short title and page number.

30. Brown observes: "The long monotonous chorus, each verse punctuated by the

thud of the drive, must be familiar to all who love the lagoon of Venice" (131). In the days when dredging and pile-driving were all carried out by manual labor, this must be one of the many work-songs that visitors heard all the time without knowing precisely what the words meant.

31. *The Rule of Four* by Ian Caldwell and Dustin Thomason (New York: Dial Press, 2004), a surprising bestseller with a basis in *Hypnerotomachia*, meets a response from Joscelyn Godwin, recent translator of Colonna's book into English. Godwin favors the Venetian monk as author, pointing out that there are references to the Veneto and traces of the Venetian dialect, though she does not enumerate these. See *The Real Rule of Four* (New York: Disinformation Co., 2004).

32. William Shakespeare, *As You Like It*, in *The Oxford Shakespeare: The Complete Works*, ed. Stanley Wells and Gary Taylor (Oxford: Clarendon Press, 1998), 638. This edition of Shakespeare's plays will be used for all Shakespeare quotations, and referred to subsequently as *Works*.

33. "Facanapa is a modern addition to the old stock of dramatis personae, and he is now without doubt the popular favourite in Venice. He is always, like Pantalon a Venetian, but whereas the latter is always a merchant, Facanapa is any thing that the exigency of the play demands. He is a dwarf . . . a coward, a boaster, and a liar; a glutton and avaricious, but withal of an agreeable bonhomie that wins the heart. To tell the truth I care little for the plays in which he has no part, and I have learned to think a certain trick of his—lifting his leg rigidly to a horizontal line, by way of emphasis, and saying 'Capisse la?' or 'Sa la?' (You understand? You know?)—one of the finest things in the world" (*Venetian Life*, 78–79). Howells adds, "the standard associates of Facanapa" are "Arlecchino, il Dottore, Pantalon dei Bisognosi, and Brighella"—the traditional commedia characters. Plainly, Goldoni did not eradicate them. In this instance, Howells expresses (as so rarely) a positive view of the talents of contemporary Venetians.

34. Smith, whose wealth brought him the position of British consul, rented a great palace and was a well-known host and patron of the arts and letters, entertaining alike the high-born, the creative, and the charmingly louche. Casanova was one of his guests, and in his house the unfortunate lovers Andrea Memmo and Giuistiniana Wynne first met. See Andrea di Robilant, *A Venetian Affair: A True Tale of Forbidden Love in the Eighteenth Century* (New York: Random House, 2003), 17–19. See also Norwich, *History of Venice*, 586–587.

35. Carlo Goldoni, *Delle Commedie di Goldoni*, 16 vols. (Venice: G. B. Pasquali, 1761–1768), "L'Autore A Chi Legge," IX, 8 (translation mine). The picture of the interrogation serves as the frontispiece to volume IX. Each volume is prefaced by Goldoni's own account of a certain phase of his life and works; thus, the collected *Commedie* represents an autobiography before the *Mémoires*. Goldoni's prefaces are collected (without the illustrations to which they so often refer) as "Prefazioni di Carlo Goldoni" in *Il Teatro Comico e Memorie Italiane*, ed. Guido Davico Bonino (Milan: Arnoldo Mondadori, 1983).

36. Goldoni, *Commedie*, IX, 8–9 (translation mine).

37. Goldoni, *Mémoires de M. Goldoni, pour servir à l'Histoire de sa Vie et à celle de son Théâtre*, 3 vols. (Paris, 1787), I, 147.

38. Goldoni, *Commedie*, Pasquali edition, frontispiece of volume III, "Una figura di Giovanetto in abito femminile" ("Image of a youth in feminine dress"). In the preface, "The Author to the Reader" ("L'Autore A Chi Legge"), Goldoni speaks of his being "al prediletto esercizio" (III, i). Cf. *Prefazioni*, 104.

39. *I Rusteghi*, translated by I. M. Rawson as *The Boors* in *Three Comedies* (Oxford: Oxford University Press, 1961), I.i.105–106; cf. Pasquali edition, vol. III, p. 2.

40. *The Boors*, trans. Rawson, I.vi.120. In original: "Mai una volta alla Zuecca, mai a Castello, mi no credo de esser passà in vita mia tre, o quattro volte per piazza." *I Rusteghi*, in *Commedie*, Pasquali edition, vol. III, p. 14.

41. *Il Bugiardo* (*The Liar*) appears in volume IV of *Commedie* in the Pasquali edition; the illustration (facing page 93) provides a view of what is described: "Notte con luna. Strada con vedute del Canale." The author provides a footnote to the entry "Barcajuoli di Peota" in the dramatis personae (*Personaggi*): "La peota in Venezie e una barca assai comoda [*sic*], capace per multe persone, coperta di un panno rosso, con buoni sedeli ed una Tavola in mezzo. Serve per . . . piccioli viaggi, e per divertimento in Città" (*Il Bugiardo*, IV, 93).

42. Casanova presumably paid for the production of this little book printed in Leipzig and took some care with the production. There is a frontispiece, as well as the illustration of the escape on the roof (see Figure 4); the pictures were presumably drawn according to the author's direction and design. Subsequent references will be given in the text with short title and page number.

43. The written report or deposition of Giovanni Battista Manuzzi (jeweler and spy) submitted to *Messer grande* appears translated as an appendix to volume IV of Trask's edition of *History of My Life* (355–358). Manuzzi appears most willing to act as an informant, and is—or makes himself out to be—shocked at Casanova's carryings-on. The jeweler claims that Casanova (never without funds from some mysterious sources) is not only a cardshark who induces others to gamble, but also an unbeliever in Christ and a dabbler in the occult: "The said Casanova boasts that he is a cheater at cards, a freethinker, and believes in nothing in matters of Religion, that he has all the suppleness necessary to ingratiate himself with people and deceive them" (356). Apparently, relatives and heirs of Bragadin were pushing the state to do something in order to prevent their elderly and sickly relative from being fleeced. The mother of Andrea Memmo and his brothers also laid a complaint against Casanova, fearing his bad influence on her boys.

44. According to Willard Trask, on 12 September 1755, Giacomo Casanova was formally sentenced by the tribunal of three Inquisitors to five years' imprisonment for atheism (note 33 to chapter xii of volume IV of *History of My Life*, 345). Casanova appears to his enemies as no quiet theoretical atheist or philosophic materialist but a missionary of the occult who uses the occult to rob others. Manuzzi says in his report: "with these damnable impostures of the Rosicrucians and Angels of Light he bewitches people, as he did . . . Ser Zuanne Bragadin and other Noble Patricians to get money out of them" (ibid., 355).

Secrecy would appear to have dominated trials either for high treason or for injury to a patrician family whose name would be dragged through the mud by trying a criminal case against the accused in a court of law. This is undeniably repulsive to human rights, and Casanova got his own back in his book. The most that can be said for the legal authorities is that Casanova knew what he was doing and must have known the risk he was running in trying to exploit Bragadin.

45. Of recent years there has been a strange disposition to argue that the "macaroni" Casanova refers to was not our macaroni but gnocchi. I see no justification for this belief. Giuseppe Baretti, in his *Dictionary*, defines *"maccherone"* [*sic*] as "a kind of paste meat, made of round pieces of pasta boiled in water, or meat broth, and so put into dishes with fresh butter and grated cheese" (*A Dictionary of the English and Italian Languages*, 2 vols. [London: W. Strahan, J. Rivington et al., 1771], I [n.p.]). This is entirely correct, but someone may have been misled by Baretti's use of "meat," a word employed in the old standard English sense of "substantial human food," which need not refer only to animal flesh. Gnocchi would have been almost impossibly hard to prepare in the given prison conditions; moreover, Casanova is quite detailed in his description of the cookery.

46. Sándor Márai, *Conversations in Bolzano*, trans. George Szirtes (London: Penguin Group, 2005), 72–73. The novel was first published in Hungarian in Budapest in 1940.

47. Friedrich von Schiller, *Der Geisterseher*, translated by Andrew Brown as *The Ghost-seer* (London: Hesperus Press, 2003), 8. The first installment of this unfinished fiction (Schiller's only novel) appeared in a magazine, *Thalia*, in January 1787, and the last in May 1789. It was first translated into English in 1795, as *The Ghost-seer, or Apparitionist, an Interesting Fragment.*

48. Schiller, *The Ghost-Seer*, trans. Brown, 9–10.

49. The first edition of Casanova's work was published in Leipzig in 1788; the dates seem too tight, as Schiller published the first installment of his story in January 1787, but a friend in Leipzig may have given him advance word (or even an advance glimpse) of the Venetian's book. And Casanova had told the story many times (while he still had teeth) so word of it would have got about. But *Der Geisterseher* sounds to me like the work of someone who has actually read *Ma Fuite.*

50. Schiller, *The Ghost-Seer*, 26.

51. One critical interpretation of Schiller's Gothic tale is that the mysterious Armenian, like the Sicilian trickster unmasked fairly early in the story, is simply an impostor, playing fantastic tricks in order to pervert the Prince from Protestantism to Catholicism. Some real German princes at the time were balancing between the two forms of religion, but such an unriddling of the plot seems inappropriate to the setting, for Venetian piety, if ardent, was never proselytizing.

52. James Fenimore Cooper, Preface to *The Bravo* (London: Richard Bentley, 1834), v–vi. The preface is dated October 1833.

53. Gautier, *Voyage en Italie*, 81.

54. Radcliffe, *Mysteries of Udolpho*, II, 57–58.

55. Zorzi, *La Repubblica del Leone*, 611.

56. Norwich, *History of Venice*, 625.

57. There is a potboiler of a romance by Max Pemberton, *Beatrice of Venice: A Romance of the Last Days of the Venetian Republic and of Napoleon's Campaign in Italy* (London: Hodder and Stoughton, 1904). The winsome heroine persuades Napoleon not to raze the city.

58. For a good description of Napoleon's dreadful visit to Venice, 30 November–8 December 1807, see the second chapter of Norwich's *Paradise of Cities*, 25–49.

59. Pacifico Valussi, in *Dalla memoria d'un vecchio giornalista dell'epoca del Risorgimento italiano*, as quoted and translated by Keates, *The Siege of Venice*, 315.

Chapter 4. Happy and Unhappy Travelers

Note to epigraph: Henry James, letter to William James, 26 September 1869, *Letters from the Palazzo Barbaro*, 66–67.

1. Francesco Petrarca, letter to Francesco Bruni, 9 April 1363, in *Seniles (Rerum senilium libri)*, trans. Aldo S. Bernardo, Saul Levin, and Reta A. Bernardo, 2 vols. (Baltimore: Johns Hopkins University Press, 1992), Book II, letter 3; I, 62. The *Seniles* or *Rerum senilium (Epistles of an Old Man)* seems to be the title Petrarch gave to his own letters written in later years.

2. Ibid., letter to Pietro Bolognese, Book IV, letter 3; I, 132.

3. Pietro Aretino, letter to Domenico Bolani, 27 October 1537, in *Lettere*, ed. Gian Mario Anselmi (Rome: Carocci Editore, 2000), 110–112.

4. Quoted by Patricia Fortini Brown, *Private Lives in Renaissance Venice* (New Haven: Yale University Press, 2004), 153.

5. The original full title of this play is *The Comical History of The Merchant of Venice, or Otherwise Called the Jew of Venice*. Gobbo's statement is a comic mix-up; most people would have said: "You may tell every rib I have with your finger."

6. Ben Jonson, *Volpone*, IV.i, lines 27–28, in *The Complete Plays*, ed. G. A. Wilkes, 4 vols. (Oxford: Oxford University Press, 1982), III, 71. Future references to this play will be to this edition; act, scene, volume, and page will be given parenthetically in the text.

7. Brown, *Private Lives*, 153.

8. For recipes (including one for *sarde'le in saòr*) and for description of Venetian food over the centuries, see Pino Agostini and Alvise Zorzi, *Venice: Tradition and Food* (Venice: Arsenale Editore, 2004); note especially the historical introduction by Alvise Zorzi, "Venetian Life, Then and Now," 8–31. By the eighteenth century, French cuisine, itself partly a product of the Italian, has combined with native traditions, as Zorzi points out in comments on the dishes referred to in Goldoni's plays. The book by Agostini and Zorzi is informative, but many photographs show beautiful dining rooms and elegant tables rather than eatables, thus bearing out Brown's observation that, in Venetian banquets, display takes precedence over food.

9. Desidirius Erasmus, *Colloquiorum Desidirii Erasmi Roterdamai Familiarum Opus Aureum*, ed. Samuel Patrick (London: J. Walthoe et al., 1733), 462, 459.

10. Burnet, *Travels*, 146–147.

11. Euphemia Ruskin, letter to her father (from the Danieli), 10 December 1849, quoted in *Effie in Venice*, 84.

12. Sir Henry Wotton in letter of 2 January 1607, cited in Gerald Curzon, *Wotton and His Worlds: Spying, Science and Venetian Intrigues* (n.p.: XLibris, 2003), 107.

13. Charles Dickens, *Little Dorrit,* 1856–1857, Book II, ch. 5 (London: Penguin Books, 1975), 524.

14. Burnet, *Travels,* 147.

15. Misson, *A New Voyage to Italy,* I, 264–265.

16. Mark Twain, *A Tramp Abroad,* ed. Robert Gray Bruce and Hamlin Hill (London: Penguin Books, 1997), 364–365. Twain is being slightly self-mocking here—this is what Americans expect to be like, and to like. He adds, too, that a family dinner in Venice is much better than hotel fare, target of his chief objections.

17. Morris, *The World of Venice,* 203.

18. John Evelyn, *The Diary of John Evelyn,* ed. E. S. De Beer (London: Oxford University Press, 1959), June 1645, 227. Further references to this work, noting date and page, will be given parenthetically in the text. John Evelyn, born in 1620, was the son of an English country gentleman. He was studying medicine at the University at Padua during much of his time in the Veneto, and was thus able to avoid some of the evils of the English Civil War.

19. Thomas Coryat, *Coryats Crudities. Hastily gobled up in five Moneths travells in France, Savoy, Italy, Rhetia commonly called the Grisons country, Helvetia alias Switzerland, some parts of high Germany and the Netherlands; Newly digested in the hungry aire of ODCOMBE, & now dispersed to the nourishment of the travelling members of this Kingdome* (London: Printed by W.S., 1611), 262. Further reference to this work (by page number) will be made parenthetically in the text.

These stilt-shoes must often have been quite striking (the one or two now in the Correr Museum are rather plain). Despite disparagement, the fashion had some sway in Europe, if we can judge by the remark by Hamlet to the Player who plays the female roles: "By'r Lady, your ladyship is nearer heaven than when I saw you last by the altitude of a chopine" (*The Tragedy of Hamlet, Prince of Denmark,* II.ii; *Works,* 667).

20. Edward Gibbon to Dorothea Gibbon (his stepmother), 22 April 1765, *The Letters of Edward Gibbon,* ed. J. E. Norton, 3 vols. (London: Cassell and Co., 1956), I, 193.

21. See *The Letters of Rupert Brooke,* chosen and edited by Geoffrey Keynes (London: Faber & Faber, 1968), letter to St. John Lucas, April 1906; *Letters,* 50–51; letter to Katharine Cox, January 1912, 345.

22. Guido Fuga and Lele Vianello, *Navigar in Laguna: Fra Isole Fiabe e Ricordi* (Venice: MarediCarta, 2001).

23. Patricia Fortini Brown picks up Ridolfi's observation that young Giorgione painted cupboards, headboards for beds, and chests, and cites Marco Boschini's amplification explaining "that when the artist did not have other commissions he painted chests for a certain Rocco della Carità, who had his *bottega* beneath the Procuratie Vecchie on Piazza San Marco." See Brown, *Private Lives,* 107. As shops were very small, much of the work of furniture painting would have been done outdoors—in Rocco's case, in the Piazza. *Ciarlatini* or charlatans were positively encouraged to perform in the Piazza in the Renaissance. Mrs. Piozzi comments on "the street orators and mountebanks in Piazza San Marco" as well as poultry auctions (*Observations,* 142). Howells notes the selling of puppies, etc., in *Venetian Life,* 344–345. Goethe meditates on "uncleanliness" and begins mentally to devise "sanitary regulations" on 1 October 1786 (*Italian Journey,* 80).

24. D. H. Lawrence, *Lady Chatterley's Lover* (London: Penguin, 2000), 258–259.

25. Francesco Sansovino, *Venetia Città Nobilissima et Singolare, Descritta in xiii Libri* (Venice: Iacomo Sansovino, 1581), 3V.

26. Gasparo Contarini, *De Magistratibus et Republica Venetorum* (Paris: Michael Vascosani, 1543), p. I.

27. Francesco Sansovino, *Dialogo di Un Venetiano e di Un Forestiero* (Venice, 1564), A4R.

28. Patricia Fortini Brown, *Venetian Narrative Painting in the Age of Carpaccio* (New Haven: Yale University Press, 1988), 136–139. Jacopo dei Barbari's woodcut "View of Venice" was made in 1500. Marin Sanudo completed the first version of *De origine, situ et magistratibus urbis venetae* (also known as the "Cronachetta") in 1493, very shortly after Marcantonio Sabellico's *De Venetia urbis situ* appeared in 1490.

29. Gasparo Contarini, *De Magistratibus et Republica Venetorum* (Venice, 1589), translated as *The Commonwealth and Government of Venice* by Lewis Lewkenor (London, 1599), 5. The English translator includes some of Sansovino's material in *Venetia Città Nobilissima,* especially on marriage, as an appendix to Contarini's book.

30. Sansovino, "Matrimonii," in *Venetia Città Nobilissima,* Book X, 153R.

31. Giacomo Franco, *Habiti d'Huomeni et Donne Venetiane* (Venice, 1609). The author or designer in collecting these interesting pictures is obviously creating visual propaganda for Venice, and his book goes well beyond explaining what clothing the Venetians wear.

32. Sir Philip Sidney to Robert Sidney, n.d., *Correspondence* in *Prose Works of Philip Sidney,* ed. Albert Feuillerat, 4 vols. (Cambridge: Cambridge University Press, 1962), III, 124–127.

33. "Farewell, Monsieur Traveller. Look you lisp and wear strange suits, disable all the benefits of your own country . . . and almost chide God for making you that countenance you are, or I will scarce think you have swam in a gondola." Rosalind's words to Jacques indicate that travel—especially to Venice—was thought to endanger young males, effeminating them with foreign fashions, making them discontented with their English identity and English appearance. But does not the man in the Chandos portrait (allegedly Shakespeare) look rather Italian, or possibly Jewish? Was this painted after foreign travel?

34. Miguel de Cervantes, "Novela del Licendiado Vidriera," as "The Glass Graduate," trans. Lesley Lipson, *Exemplary Stories* (Oxford: Oxford University Press, 1998), 111.

35. William Lithgow, *The Totall Discourse, Of the rare Adventures, and painefull Peregrinations of long nineteene yeares Travailes from Scotland* (London: I. Okes, 1640), 37–38. I cannot get up much sympathy for this traveler when he was threatened later with burning alive and underwent torture at the hands of the Inquisition at Malaga, even though he includes illustrations of his chains and the rack (462, 471).

36. Morris, *World of Venice,* 210.

37. Sand, *La dernière Aldini,* 51.

38. Euphemia Ruskin, letter to Mrs. Gray, 13 November 1849; *Effie in Venice,* 65.

39. George Grant, letter to Maud Grant, n.d. [summer 1938], in *George Grant: Selected Letters,* ed. William Christian (Toronto: University of Toronto Press, 1996), 31.

40. See *The Autobiography of a Seventeenth-Century Venetian Rabbi: Leon Modena's "Life of*

Judah," ed. and trans. Mark R. Cohen (Princeton, N.J.: Princeton University Press, 1989), introduction, 29.

41. Gautier, *Voyage en Italie,* 78.

42. Marcel Proust, *A la recherche du temps perdu,* trans. Scott Moncrieff and Terence Kilmartin, as *Remembrance of Things Past,* 3 vols. (New York: Random House/Vintage Books, 1982), I, 425.

43. Ibid., 423.

Chapter 5. Venice-Venus

Note to epigraph: Alexander Pope, *Essay on Man,* lines 291–292, *Poems,* 544.

1. Otway, *Venice Preserv'd,* II.iii, lines 292–295, in *Works,* II, 225.

2. Byron, *Childe Harold's Pilgrimage,* canto IV, ii, line 10; 229.

3. In *City of Falling Angels* Berendt takes as one of his themes the complex wrangles and acerbic split within the American organization Save Venice. In 1998, Count Marcello gave the group in New York what Berendt calls "a dressing-down": "A few members of the board do not consider Save Venice an association of friends who do good work for Venice but rather as a means to gain personal prestige and power. We Venetians regard our city with the same ancient civic sense with which we have built, governed and loved it for centuries, and it is very painful to see it being used in this manner. . . . [W]e Venetians are loath to accept help from those who have so little respect for us" (315).

4. Cassiodorus for Theodoric, in *Variarum,* book XII, letter 24, as translated in Norwich, *A History of Venice,* 6–7.

5. Zorzi, *La Repubblica del Leone,* 9.

6. Ibid., 29–30.

7. In the edition of *The Merchant of Venice* edited by W. Moelwyn Merchant (London: Penguin Books, 2005), a note discusses the "traject" as a ferry (237); Peter Holland in his introduction to that edition comments that while Bassanio has to borrow a lot of money for his extravagant journey to Belmont, Portia suggests "a rather different way of navigating these ventures: one simply checks the timetable and catches the next ferry" (xlix). Such a touch confirms my impression that Shakespeare himself actually had been to Venice.

8. Sansovino, *Venetia Città Nobilissima,* f. 3R.

9. Henry James, "The Grand Canal" (first published 1892), in *Italian Hours* (Boston: Houghton Mifflin, 1909), 65.

10. John Ruskin, "The Burden of Tyre," chapter 1 of *St. Mark's Rest, The History of Venice, Written for the Help of the Few Travellers Who Still Care for Her Monuments,* first book edition (Orpington, Kent: George Allen, 1884), 5. This work first emerged as pamphlets in the 1870s.

11. The founding of the Correr Museum is a late example of aristocratic obligation. Patrician Teodoro Correr in the time of the occupation contributed his private collection to keep the memory of Venice alive. "His example created proselytes, many Venetians turned into collectors of mementos rescued from the wreck in order then to donate them to the city" (Alvise Zorzi, *Venezia austriaca,* 68). Numerous items dating from the great

period of wealth can be found in the Correr Museum, including early Renaissance maps, as well as rich imports and sumptuous fashion accessories.

12. Burnet, *Travels*, 126.

13. See, for examples, articles in *Il Gazzetino di Venezia*, 14 January 2006, citing recent documents urging a reconsideration of Mose.

14. See Peter Popham, "Venice Rescue Plan Sunk by Berlusconi," *Independent on Sunday*, 19 March 2003, 24. Popham describes the cost of the project and its long delay, suggesting the war in Iraq has set back payment for the expensive caper. He discusses the possible merits of Arca, a more modest system "nicknamed 'Mose's little brother.'" The engineer Alfo Massaro declares Arca "would be gradual, experimental and reversible." Popham is impatient at the introduction of another plan at this late date—but something less ruinously final is surely worth considering.

15. The *Legenda Aurea* or *Golden Legend* ("Golden Reading Matter") is a hagiographic and encyclopedic collection of tales about the miraculous lives and works of saints compiled in the thirteenth century.

16. Norwich, *History of Venice*, 106–107; Zorzi, *La Repubblica del Leone*, 84.

17. Norwich, *History of Venice*, 183.

18. Aristotle, *Politics*, book II, cap. viii, Loeb Library edition of Aristotle, vol. 21, trans. H. Rackham (Cambridge, Mass.: Harvard University Press), 156–163. Aristotle criticizes the Carthaginians for thinking that only wealthy rulers should be chosen: "For this law makes wealth more honoured than worth" (161).

19. Garry Wills, *Venice: Lion City: The Religion of Empire* (New York: Simon and Schuster, 2001), 112. The Venetians certainly preferred that their Doges and councilors should be wealthy men—indeed, the Doge was supposed to show off his wealth by largesse the day of his installation. But the personal wealth was a resource, to be used for Venice in case of necessity. It is interesting that, according to Aristotle, Carthage had the original democratic elements that Venice had—in that the males in a general assembly were allowed to speak and make decisions—a right given up after the *Serrata*.

20. For *Compagnie della Calza*, see Norwich, *History of Venice*, 334, and Brown, *Private Lives*, 20–21; Brown translates and comments on Sanudo's description of a show put on by one of these companies, 123.

21. Wills, *Venice: Lion City*, 112–113.

22. Geoffrey de Villehardouin, twelfth-century historian and contemporary of Dandolo, in his history published as *La Conquête de Constantinople*, as cited by Norwich, *History of Venice*, 134.

23. Thomas F. Madden, *Enrico Dandolo and the Rise of Venice* (Baltimore: Johns Hopkins University Press, 2003), 161.

24. For the stripping of the *Bucintoro*, see Norwich, *Paradise of Cities*, 17–18.

25. Norwich, *History of Venice*, 561.

26. Margaret Oliphant, *Makers of Venice: Doges, Conquerors, Painters and Men of Letters*, "Extra Illustrated Edition" (first published 1887; London: Macmillan, 1892), 125–126.

27. Petrarch, letter to Boccaccio, late 1360s; see *Seniles*, trans. Bernardo et al., Book V, letter 2; I, 164–165.

28. Oliphant, *Makers of Venice*, 358–359.

29. For the life and fate of Marino Faliero, see Zorzi, *La Repubblica del Leone*, 181–189, and Norwich, *History of Venice*, 223–229. The doggerel insult the young man (traditionally if improbably identified with the future Doge Michel Steno) left on the Doge's chair is given by Zorzi as follows: "Marin Falier de la bella moier./ Altri la galde, e lui la mantien" (Marin Falier of the beautiful wife,/ Others enjoy her while he maintains her) (182). Falier was seventy-nine when he became Doge and his second wife was over forty. The distich would seem to belong to the category of general insult.

30. For an account of the affair of the two Foscari, see Norwich, *History of Venice*, 334–340. See also Zorzi, *La Repubblica del Leone*, 232–240. Zorzi and Norwich agree that the government was embarrassed when old Foscari died so soon after they had humiliated him, stripping him of office (and electing another Doge); they illogically tried to make recompense by giving Francesco a state funeral as Doge. For a dramatic representation, there is Byron's *The Two Foscari: An Historical Tragedy* (1821).

Giuseppe Gullino, discussing the mysteries of the case in *La saga dei Foscari: Storia di un enigma* (Verona: Cierre Edizioni, 2005), thinks Jacopo, subjected to repeated charges, "was but the pretext for an initiative which was mounted against his father and the entire family of Foscari, of which the old doge was chief." He proposes (elaborating on Zorzi) two political groupings fighting for control: one in favor of moving into Italy, the other in favor of keeping to the Mediterranean base. Like Byron, Gullino thinks young Jacopo was murdered, but adds a twist, suggesting that members of his own party, who feared he knew too much, assassinated him.

31. Norwich, *History of Venice*, 282.

32. Giovanni Boccaccio, *Decameron*, "Tenth Story of the Sixth Day" and "Second Story of the Eighth Day" in volume 4 of *Tutte Le Opere di Giovanni Boccaccio*, ed. Vittore Branca, 12 vols. (Milan: Arnoldo Mondadori Editore, 1976); Berto della Massa, accomplished liar, "come disperato a Vinegia, d'ogni bruttura ricevitrice," IV, 367.

33. *The Merchant of Venice* is a dramatic story of almost unrelieved cheating. Shylock pretends his bond is a joke, whereas it really is—or he decides to make it—a trap. Jessica and Lorenzo steal Shylock's jewels and live high on the proceeds. Bassanio wants to woo Portia only on account of her money; having spent all his inheritance, this *barnabotto* is willing to borrow unmercifully from his best friend in order to pretend to be a wealthy suitor. Portia herself wins her law case by disguise and trickery.

34. Petrarch, letter to Pietro Bolognese, 10 August 1364, describing celebrations at victory over rebellious Crete: *Seniles*, trans. Bernardo et al., Book IV, letter 3; I, 135.

Chapter 6. The Engineering of Color

Notes to epigraphs: William Wordsworth, "On the Extinction of the Venetian Republic," first published 1807, in *Wordsworth's Poetical Works* (Oxford: Oxford University Press, 1969), 242; Herbert Asquith, *The Volunteer and Other Poems* (London: Sidgwick & Jackson, 1915), 22. Ruskin, *Stones of Venice*, II, 43, discussing the Basilica on Murano.

1. Dante, *Inferno*, Canto XXI: "restammo per veder l'altra fessura/ di Malebolge e li altri pianti vani;/ e vidila mirabilmente oscura./ Quale nell'arzanà de' Viniziani/ bolle

l'inverno la tenace pece/ a rimpalmar li legni lor non sani,/ chè navicar non ponno; e 'n quella vece/ chi fa suo legno novo e chi ristoppa/ le coste a quel che piú viaggi fece;/ chi ribatte da proda e chi da poppa;/ altri fa remi e altri volge sarte;/ che terzeruolo e artimon rintoppa;/ tal, non per foco, ma per divin' arte/ bollìa là giuso una pegola spessa,/ che 'nviscava la ripa d'ogni parte." *Inferno*, Canto xxi, lines 4–18, in *La Divina Commedia*, ed. Giovanni Fallani (Messina-Firenze: Casa Editrice G. D'Anna, 1970), I, 235–236.

2. Appian, a second-century Greek of Alexandria, wrote a history of Rome. He drew on the narrative of the fall of Carthage set down by the Greek historian Polybius (a narrative no longer extant). Polybius, who accompanied Scipio to Carthage, was an eye-witness to the fall and destruction of Carthage described in Appian's eighteenth book.

See *Appian*, ed. and trans. Horace White Loeb Library, 2 vols. (Cambridge, Mass.: Harvard University Press, 2002), book VIII, chapter xviii, caps. 121–122; I, 614–619). The ruins of Carthage visible at present show the island just off shore where the Carthaginians customarily assembled their ships, apparently according to division of labor. The little island is now a museum.

3. "Qualis apes aestate nova per florea rura/exercet sub sole labor": Virgil, *Aeneid* I, lines 430–431.

4. See Wills, *Venice: Lion City*, especially chapter 2, "Declarations of Independence," 37–45.

5. Ruskin expresses his theological views on architecture very directly (with diagrams) in the twenty-seventh chapter of the first book of *The Stones of Venice*: "These cornices are the Venetian Ecclesiastical Gothic; the Christian element struggling with the Formalism of the Papacy. . . . Now, observe. The cornice *f* represents Heathenism and Papistry, animated by the mingling of Christianity and nature. The good in it, the life of it, the veracity and liberty of it, such as it has, are Protestantism in its heart; the rigidity and saplessness are the Romanism of it" (I, 314).

6. Ruskin, *St. Mark's Rest*, chapter v, "The Shadow on the Dial," 67.

7. Curzon, *Wotton and His Worlds*, 118–119.

8. See Wills's *Venice: Lion City* for Venice's opposition to the Index, and the role of Sarpi and others (including Wotton) in its resistance to the Interdict, 343–355.

9. Norwich, *History of Venice*, 282–283.

10. "One of the chief Ornaments of *Venice* was the famous young woman that spake five tongues well, of which the *Latin* and *Greek* were two. She passed Doctor of Physick at *Padua*. . . . Her extraordinary Merit made all People unwilling to remember the Blemish of her Descent on the one side; for tho' the *Cornaros* reckon themselves a Size of Nobility beyond all the other Families of *Venice*, yet her Father having entertained a *Gondolier's* Daughter so long, that he had some Children by her, at last . . . married the Mother, and paid a considerable Fine to save the Forfeiture of Nobility" (Burnet, *Travels*, 132–133).

11. See Jan Morris, *The Venetian Empire: A Sea Voyage* (London: Penguin Books, 1990); Larry Wolf, *Venice and the Slavs: The Discovery of Dalmatia in the Age of Enlightenment* (Stanford, Calif.: Stanford University Press, 2001).

12. Mariano Fortuny (1871–1949), born in Granada, settled with his family in Venice in 1889, partly for the sake of his health, and he remained. With the help of his wife,

Henriette Negin, he invented the method of printing upon fabric, in imitation of the effects of medieval and Renaissance textiles. His fifteenth-century palazzo (once the Palazzo Pesaro degli Orfei) is now the Fortuny Museum; fabrics in his style can be bought elsewhere in Venice.

13. For the search for transparent glass see Paul Hills, *Venetian Colour: Marble, Mosaic, Painting and Glass, 1250–1550* (New Haven: Yale University Press, 2000).

14. Joan DeJean in *The Essence of Style* has described the efforts made by France under Louis XIV to outstrip the Venetians in mirror-making; the French succeeded in making larger mirrors, though the famous Hall of Mirrors was actually constructed by fitting plates of Venetian mirrors together. Big pier glasses and cheval glasses were made in France, but not before Louis XIV had spent a fortune on acquiring Venetian mirrors for himself, and then on wooing Murano glassmakers to France.

15. See Brown, *Private Lives*, 147; the same page has a color photograph of the ship-pitcher in the Museo Vetrario. It seems odd that Harmonia was a glass designer, since she was the daughter of a painter, not a glass-blower, nor did she marry into a glass-making family.

16. Francesco Colonna, *Hypnerotomomachia Poliphili*, trans. Joscelyn Godwin (1999) (New York: Thames & Hudson, 2005), book I, 123–124.

17. See Ian Caldwell and Dustin Thomason, *The Rule of Four* (2004), a modern campus story with a basis in *Hypnerotomachia Poliphili*. Joscelyn Godwin argues for a Venetian author of the 1499 fiction, not only because of references to Venice and the Veneto but also Venetian qualities in the language; unfortunately these qualities are not specified in detail: *The Real Rule of Four* (New York: Disinformation Company, 2005).

18. *Everyman Guide to Venice* (2004) has two pages of effective illustration, including a photograph of Alberto Valese, 62–63.

19. See entry in the *Diarii* of Marin Sanudo for 26 March 1516, for an account of the original motion, in which Dolfin said that "the Jews brought evil on the country, as the preachers preached that the perverse accidents that befell the State come from this, and that the synagogues go against the form of our laws," and urged that therefore they should be enclosed. Sanudo also gives an account of what Anselmo, the leader of the Hebrews, argued in his address to the Council, but reports that after Anselmo left "Dolfin was hotter than ever."

On 6 April 1515 Sanudo had recorded his own anxiety about "a wicked custom of continued commerce with the Jews," so that they could be found in this land in great numbers, in various parishes "and nobody says nay to them, because during the war, we have need of them, and they do what they will." He also reports that "The preacher at the Frari, Fra Zuan Maria di Arezo [*sic*], preaches vociferously against them and against the Hebrew doctors and especially [*maxime*] Maestro Lazaro, who has made Christian women abort." Marin Sanudo, *I Diarii (1496–1533): Pagine Scelte* (Vicenza: Neri Pozzi Editore, 1997), 276, 256.

20. According to Patricia Fortini Brown, Wotton's expensive rental included "figured tapestry wall hangings for the audience chamber, leather wall furnishings for the main reception area, tapestries for the dining room, thirteen beds with bedding, velvet covered seats, a bed canopy for his bedroom, a billiard table, and a gondola" (*Private Lives*, 89).

21. For the petition, see Keates, *The Siege of Venice*, 86. Keates describes the circumstances of Daniele Manin's grandparents' change of name (64).

22. Musset, *Poésies complètes*, ed. Allem, 375.

23. Gautier, *Voyage en Italie*, 234.

24. Cristiana Moldi-Ravenna and Tudy Sammartini, *Secret Gardens in Venice*, trans. Joseph A. Precker and Tudy Sammartini, photographs by Gianni Berengo Gardin (Venice: Arsenale Editrice, 2001), 43.

25. Ibid., 88.

26. Zorzi, *La Repubblica del Leone*, 568.

27. Ravenna and Sammartini, *Secret Gardens*, 88.

28. Francesco Sansovino, *Dialogo di Un Venetiano e di Un Forestiero*, f. A2R.

29. Michelangelo Mariani, *Le Meraviglie della Città di Venetia* (Venice: Giacomo Zattoni, 1666), ff. A3V–A4R.

30. "Senza discorrer poeticamente,/ Senza usar l'hiperbolica figura,/ Ch'è pur troppo bugiarda apertamente,/ Si poteva impiegar la vostra cura /In lodando Vinegia singolare,/ Meraviglia, e stupor de la natura:/ Questa dominatrice alta del mare/ Regal Vergine pura inviolata,/ Nel mondo senza essempio, & senza pare." Veronica Franca (or Franco), "Risposta della S. Veronica Franca," in *Terze Rime di Veronica Franca* (Venice, 1575), f. 23V. For a biography see Margaret F. Rosenthal, *The Honest Courtesan: Veronica Franco, Citizen and Writer in Sixteenth-Century Venice* (Chicago: University of Chicago Press, 1992).

31. Franca, *Terze Rime*, f. 24R.

32. Ruskin, "St. James of the Deep Stream," *St. Mark's Rest*, 31.

33. Ibid., 36–37.

34. Petrarch, letter to Pietro Bolognese, 10 August 1364, *Seniles* IV.3; I, 132.

35. Horatio Brown is here quoting and summarizing the report in *Archivio Veneto*, vol. XXIX. Giacomo Boni (1859–1925), a Venice-born archaeologist, was already famous for excavation of the Roman Forum.

36. De Staël, *Corinne*, Book V, ch. viii, 424.

37. Twain, *A Tramp Abroad*, 363.

38. Cooper, first chapter of *The Bravo*, 2.

39. Gabriele D'Annunzio, *The Flame*, trans. Bassnett, 169.

40. Deborah Howard, *Venice and the East: The Impact of the Islamic World on Venetian Architecture, 1100–1500* (New Haven: Yale University Press, 2000), 142–143. The magnificently illustrated book conveys visually as well as verbally the resemblances, echoes, modifications, understatements, and exaggerations playing through the varying relations of Venetian architecture to the architecture and other arts of the Near East.

41. Ibid., 133.

42. Hills, *Venetian Colour*, 81.

43. Ibid., 87.

Chapter 7. Venetian Painting

Note to epigraphs: Joseph Brodsky, *Fondamenta degli Incurabili*, first published 1989 (Milan: Adelphi, 1991), 20, English translation mine; Ruskin, *Stones of Venice*, III, 184.

1. Patricia Fortini Brown, *Venetian Narrative Painting*, 15.

2. Ibid., 20.

3. Brown is led by an interest in what she sees as a development of a new way of painting, "a whole stylistic movement—called here an 'eyewitness style'" (ibid., preface [i]).

4. [Carlo Ridolfi], *Le Meraviglie dell'Arte ovvero Le Vite degli Illustri Veneti e dello Stato*, reproduction of Padua edition of 1835; 2 vols. ([Milan]: Arnoldo Forni Editore, 1999), I, 87.

5. Giovanna Nepi Scirè, "La Scuola di Sant' Orsola," *Carpaccio, Pittore di Storie*, ed. Giovanna Nepi Scirè (Venice: Marsilio Editori, 2004), 36.

6. Gabriele D'Annunzio, *The Flame*, trans. Bassnett, 49; see *Il Fuoco*, 52. The word *larvato* can also mean "masked," and the young shooter's face is concealed from us.

7. Claudia Cremonini, "La Scuola Di San Giovanni Evangelista," in *Carpaccio, Pittore di Storie*, 67.

8. Brown, *Venetian Narrative Painting*, 3.

9. Cremonini, "La Scuola Di San Giovanni Evangelista," 68.

10. "The guidebooks to the city, written by Sabellico and Sanudo, came out within a few years of the beginning of the True Cross campaign and the Barbari map. They, too, may be seen as products of a common desire to display the city in all of its *sestieri*. In his *De origine*, Sanudo moved away from the encomiastic perspective of earlier panegyrists like Sabellico, toward a concrete approach which portrayed the city as an organic and realistic totality." Brown, *Venetian Narrative Painting*, 137.

11. The episode is taken from *Hieronymus: Vita et Transitus* (Venice, 1485). See Linda Borean, "San Agostino nello studio," in *Carpaccio, Pittore di Storie*, 86.

12. Ruskin, *St. Mark's Rest*, supplement I, 2nd ed., 1887, "The Shrine of the Slaves," 38–39.

13. Brown, *Private Lives*, 91.

14. Terisio Pignatti says, regarding *Two Women*, "at least once, however, he [Carpaccio] consented to compete with Giorgione on the latter's own ground." *Carpaccio*, trans. James Emmons (Lausanne: Editions d'Art Albert Skira, 1958), 95–96. A surprising judgment; the color in the picture of the women, though warm, has none of the soft haze and quasi-twilight of Giorgione (haze being saved for the accompanying lagoon scene), and Carpaccio here insists on repetitive hard edges and outlines (part of the comedy of the thing) not typical of the soft shadings of Giorgione.

15. Ridolfi, *Le Meraviglie dell'Arte*, I, 199. See also *The Life of Titian*, a translation of Ridolfi's biography with an introduction, by Julia Conway Bondanella and Peter Bondanella (University Park: Pennsylvania State University Press, 1996).

16. For an example of our contemporary assurance, see Carol Vogel, "A Titian Travels to Washington," "Inside Art" column, *New York Times* (20 January 2006), B32. Titian's stock has apparently risen while Giorgione's has slowly fallen, though to the Victorians Giorgione was the greater genius. Titian probably completed the painting after Giorgione's sudden death. The difficulty of distinction was already well known to Ridolfi, who comments that Titian imitated Giorgione's manner: "Titian transformed himself in ap-

pearance in the manner of Giorgione, so that no one could detect any difference. Thus it is that many paintings are confusedly held to be without distinction by one or the other." Ridolfi, "Vita di Tiziano," *Le Meraviglie dell'Arte*, I, 199–200.

17. Marco Boschini in 1664, cited by Annelisa Perissa Torrini, "Documents and Sources," in *Giorgione: Myth and Enigma,* ed. Sylvia Ferino-Pagden and Giovanna Nepi Scirè (Milan: Skira Editorio, 2004), 23. This book commemorates an exhibition held jointly by the Kunsthistorisches Museum, Vienna, and the Soprintendza Speciale per il Polo Museale Veneziano.

18. For Giorgione's possible Jewishness, see Augusto Gentili, "Traces of Giorgione: Jewish Culture and Astrological Science," in *Giorgione: Myth and Enigma,* 57–69; and Mino Gabriele, "'The Three Philosophers,' the Magi and the Nocturnal," ibid., 79–83.

19. David Rosand, *Painting in Sixteenth-Century Venice* (Cambridge: Cambridge University Press, 1997), 25. Rosand is recording the frustration not only of Renaissance critics puzzled by a lack of closure and "iconographical illegibility," but also of our own contemporaries struggling to make sense of paintings that don't clearly follow known stories and the emblematic lexicon.

20. David Rosand, citing Ridolfi's "Vita di Tintoretto," in explicating the Venetian identification of Ariadne with Venice, in *Myths of Venice: The Figuration of a State* (Chapel Hill: University of North Carolina Press, 2001), 143–144.

21. Ridolfi explains that the goat-foot child is Pampino the little satyr (*satiretto*), Bacchus' favorite; the calf's head is a sacrifice of the feast of Bacchus in memory of Pentheus, rent asunder by Maenads as a penalty for his hostility to Dionysius/Bacchus. See "Vita di Tiziano," *Le Meraviglie dell'Arte*, I, 205. There are thus disturbing hints of pedophilia and blood sacrifice contained within the picture.

22. Ibid.

23. See Giorgio Vasari, *Le Vite de più eccelenti pittori, scultori ed architettori nelle Redazioni de 1550 e 1568,* 9 vols. (Florence, 1568).

24. Hills, *Venetian Colour,* 91–92.

25. Ruskin, *St. Mark's Rest,* "The Shrine of the Slaves," 29–30.

26. Rosand, *Painting in Sixteenth-Century Venice,* note 49 to chapter 4, 224. This note gives the original record of the interrogation of the artist.

27. John Ruskin, *Praeterita and Dilecta,* with an introduction by Tim Hilton (New York: Everyman's Library, 2005), vol. 3, chapter I, 441.

28. Ibid., chapter II, 442. If you pursue the Queen of Sheba on the Internet, you will find Ruskin's copy of a section of the picture.

29. Ibid.

30. Peter Schjeldahl, "The Colorful Paolo Veronese" (review of a Veronese exhibition at the Frick), *New Yorker* (14 April 2006), 172–173.

31. David Rosand tells us about the steps in a note to his discussion of Veronese's way with perspective: "The nineteenth-century restorer of the San Sebastiano canvas . . . apparently found the dissociative quality of Veronese's perspective—technically correct in this case—rather disturbing, for he 'corrected' it by substituting a flight of steps

for the original pavement, thereby offering a rationale for the seeming break in spatial continuity." *Painting in Sixteenth-Century Venice,* note 40 (to pp. 116–117), 123.

32. "Jacopo was born in Venice, theater of all marvels, in the year 1512, and his father was Battista Robusti, Venetian *cittadino* and dyer of cloth from whom the son took the cognomen [or nickname] of Tintoretto." Ridolfi, *Le Meraviglie dell'Arte,* II, 173. In reminding us that Venice is the "theater of marvels," Ridolfi, writing a whole book about Venetian marvels, defies Vasari and his successors. He likes a David-and-Goliath scenario. The child Jacopo manifested precocious ability: "While still a child he gave himself to drawing with charcoal and his father's colors upon the walls, delineating puerile figures which nonetheless possessed a certain grace. Upon seeing this his parents were stimulated to cultivate his natural inclination" (ibid.). So—low things serve high things, and a humble father's dyes can produce a child who will out-do Titian, and all the Florentines.

33. Rosand says that Vasari thought Tintoretto "an affront to art." See Rosand, *Painting in Sixteenth-Century Venice,* 15–16. Rosand cites in full Vasari's negative description of Tintoretto (Vasari, *Vite,* vol. 6) in note 85 to chapter 1, 187–188. According to Vasari, Tintoretto is "nelle cose della pittura, stravagante, capriccioso, presto e risoluto, e il più terribile cervello che abbia avuto mai la pittura."

34. Rosand, *Painting in Sixteenth-Century Venice,* 134. Pietro Aretino wrote to Tintoretto in April 1548, after the young painter's *Miracle of Saint Mark* had been completed and shown. Aretino joins in the general acclaim, regarding himself as one of Tintoretto's early discoverers. He says that the *spectaclo* in the painting seems more true than feigned, "più tosto vero che finto." But Aretino urges Tintoretto not to cease to climb toward a higher step on the ladder of perfection, "maggior grado di perfezione." Youth is too precipitous, it is necessary for the young painter to rein in, to exchange quickness of execution for patience. (Aretino's letter is given by Rosand in note 3 to chapter 5, 233–234.) Vasari, Aretino, and others agree that Tintoretto was not patient and humble; he failed to follow the appropriate career trajectory.

35. Ridolfi, *Le Meraviglie dell'Arte,* II, 174.

36. Ibid., 182.

37. Rosand, *Myths of Venice,* 88.

38. See David Bomford and Gabriele Finaldi, *Venice Through Canaletto's Eyes* (London: National Gallery Publications, 1998), 14. This little book was published for an exhibition in London and Swansea in 1998.

39. See di Robilant, *A Venetian Affair,* 18–20.

40. James, "The Grand Canal" (first published 1892), in *Italian Hours* [1899], 68–69.

41. Isaac Newton, *Opticks, Or, A Treatise of the Reflections, Refractions, Inflections and Colours of Light,* 3rd ed. (London: William and John Innys, 1721), 349–350. Newton's *Opticks* was first published in 1704, and again, enlarged in Latin in 1706. He considered the edition of 1717 the second edition, and in this he entered his new "Questions."

Newton's theory of color was of great interest to painters. Francesco Algarotti, a curious champion of Newton (and inheritor of his famous prisms) suggested that, rather than using the earth-color ground, an artist should create a white ground and then paint over it, thus obtaining an increase in *lucidezza*. See Svetlana Alpers and Michael Baxandall, *Tiepolo and the Pictorial Intelligence* (New Haven: Yale University Press, 1994), n. 7 to the second chapter, 179.

The artists got there first. Experiments with light in their own métier conducted in former centuries by painters, including the great Venetians, must have contributed to shaping Newton's own imagination. The artist who creates an oil painting palpably turns matter into light.

42. Frederick Rolfe ("Baron Corvo"), *The Desire and Pursuit of the Whole: A Romance of Modern Venice* (New York: New Directions, 1953), 52–53.

43. Alpers and Baxandall, *Tiepolo and the Pictorial Intelligence*, 33.

Chapter 8. Cybele-Venus-Venice

Note to epigraphs: Byron, *Childe Harold's Pilgrimage*, Book IV, stanza ii, lines 10–13; anonymous verse in *Venetia trionfante et sempre libera* (Venice, 1613).

1. The Life of Mary used by painters has extensively drawn on an iconography given in the apocryphal *Gospel of Saint James* (*Protevangelion*), with its *Gennesis Marias tes Hagias Theotokou* ("Nativity of Mary, the Holy God-Bearer"). According to this story, which fills in Mary's birth and childhood, when the priests of the Temple in Jerusalem called together the virgins of Israel to weave a curtain for the Temple, Mary was one of the maidens; offered a choice of stuffs to work with, the Virgin Mary chose "the true porphyry and the scarlet (cochineal)": chapter 10 in *Le Protévangile de Jacques*, ed. Emile Amann (Paris: Letouzey et Ané, 1910), 220. It has been suggested that this apocryphal work exhibits the influence of Egypt, and even that its real author was a devotee of Isis. It affected numerous representations of the holy story.

2. W. H. Auden, "Musée de Beaux Arts," lines 1–2, in *Selected Poems*, ed. Edward Mendelson (New York: Vintage Books, 1979), 79.

3. Rosand, citing *Coryats Crudities* in *Myths of Venice*, 44.

4. Sansovino, *Venetia, Città Nobilissima* (1581), f. 4R.

5. Rosand, *Myths of Venice*, 117.

6. Morris cites the Palm Sunday explanation, and describes the "municipal feeding" by "the maize man" at nine o'clock on winter mornings (Morris, *World of Venice*, 80–83). John Berendt describes the tactfully quiet efforts the city is now making to catch and kill pigeons, and the paradoxical value of the pigeon feeding to the touristic economy (*City of Falling Angels*, 70–74).

7. Ridolfi, *Le Meraviglie dell'Arte*, II, 234.

8. Giovanna Nepi Scirè summarizes the history of the painting's whereabouts and the accounts given of it in a succinct and well-illustrated article in *Giorgione: Myth and Engima*, 188–196. I quote her translations of the early descriptions.

9. Byron, in a letter to John Murray in 1817, describes his view of the paintings in Girolamo Manfrin's collection, and approves among them some "very fine Giorgiones": the pictures of "The queen of Cyprus & Giorgione's wife–particularly the latter . . . are Venetian as it were of yesterday—the same eyes and expression—& to my mind there is none finer" (*Letters and Journals*, ed. Marchand, V, 213).

10. He also celebrates this woman's beauty as "not . . . ideal beauty . . . but something better still, so very real": *Beppo: A Venetian Story*, stanzas 12–13, *Complete Poetical Works*, ed. McGann, IV, 133. For a discussion of the versions of the painting's subject known to Byron's contemporaries and to Byron, see Nepi Scirè, *Giorgione: Myth and Enigma*, 188.

11. Paris, son of King Priam of Troy, according to one legend, lived in his youth an idyllic existence in the wilds with the nymph Oenone, by whom he had a son, Korythos. But he forsook them both when he went off to be judge in the famous beauty contest among the three goddesses, and disaster followed. See Jurgen Rapp, "The 'Favola' in Giorgione's *Tempesta*," in *Giorgione: Myth and Enigma*, 119–123.

12. Sansovino, *Ortografia delle Voci della Lingua Nostra ovvero Dittionario Volgare et Latino* (Venice, 1568), N8R, DdV.

13. Rosand, *Myths of Venice*, 111.

14. Rosand, *Painting in Sixteenth-Century Venice*, 85; he cites Erwin Panofsky's *Problems in Titian, Mostly Iconographic* (1969).

15. See Rosand, *Painting in Sixteenth-Century Venice*, 85–87; Rosand, *Myths of Venice*, 115.

Chapter 9. Labyrinth and Carnival

Notes to epigraphs: Jeanette Winterson, *The Passion* (London: Penguin, 1988), 49; Byron to John Murray, Venice, 27 January 1818; Byron's *Letters and Journals*, ed. Leslie Marchand, VI, 9.

1. Howard, *Venice and the East*, 5.

2. Ibid., 6.

3. Francesco Colonna, *Hypnerotomachia Poliphili*, trans. Joscelyn Godwin, 124.

4. Princess Marie von Thurn und Taxis, *Memoirs of a Princess*, ed. and trans. Nora Wydenbruck (London: Hogarth Press, 1959), 142–143.

5. Proust, *Remembrance of Things Past*, trans. Moncrieff and Kilmartin, III, 665–666.

6. "The allure of Venice . . . is distinct from art and architecture. There is something curiously sensual to it, if not actually sexual." Morris, *World of Venice*, 323.

7. Ian Littlewood, *A Literary Companion to Venice* (New York: St. Martin's, 1991), 152.

8. Lawrence, *Lady Chatterley's Lover*, 256–257.

9. Mann, *Death in Venice*, trans. Appelbaum, 98–101.

10. Morris points out that a 1904 guidebook says the bones are used in the refining of sugar. Presumably, later sensibilities ended this industrial application, but when Morris came in the 1950s the island had only just fallen into disuse: "It is only a year or two since the monthly bone-barge plowed its way to Sant' Ariano" (*World of Venice*, 306–307).

11. Francesco Seni, *Leggende di Venezia* (Venice: Edizioni Helvetia, 2001); Guido Fuga and Lele Vianello, *Navigar in Laguna: Fra Isole Fiabe e Ricordi* (Venice: MarediCarta, 2001), 22–23)

12. Morris, *World of Venice*, 310–311.

13. Alfred de Musset, "La Nuit de Décembre," *Poèmes complètes*, 312.

14. See *Il Gazzetino*, section "Nord Est," 5 June 2006, I–II.

15. *Il Gazzetino*, 3 June 2006, V.

16. Fuga and Vianello, *Navigar in Laguna*, 116.

17. Ibid., 124.

18. Misson, *A New Voyage to Italy* (1714), I, 265.

19. The old laws regarding Carnevale in Venice are summarized by Danilo Reato, *Le Maschere Veneziane*, 11–13.

20. Mario Belloni, *Maschere a Venezia* (Venice: Una Tantum Editore, 2003), 16.

21. Goldoni, *I Rusteghi*, II, sc. xi, in *I Rusteghi e Sior Todero Brontolon*, ed. Pietro Gibellini (Milan: Arnoldo Mondadori, 1993), 53. This comedy was first performed in the Venetian Teatro San Luca toward the end of Carnevale, 1760.

22. Belloni, *Maschere a Venezia*, 24–26.

23. Ibid., 20–22.

24. Byron to Augusta Leigh, February 1817; *Letters*, ed. Marchand, V, 171.

25. Aleksandr Ivanovich Herzen, *My Life and Thoughts*, trans. Constance Garnett, as cited by John Julius Norwich in *A Traveller's Companion to Venice*, first published 1990 (New York: Interlink Books, 2002), 365–367. Herzen, an exile from Russia because of his liberal views, and a friend of Garibaldi, was fully prepared to rejoice in the liberation from Austrian rule.

26. Morris, *World of Venice*, 121–122.

27. Belloni, *Maschere a Venezia*, 66.

28. Reato, *Maschere Veneziane*, 38; Reato cites C. Musatti, *Le Maschere Veneziane* (Venice, 1931).

29. P. G. Molmenti, *Storia di Venezia nella vita privata*, III, 277–278, quoted in Reato, *Maschere Veneziane*, 14–15.

Conclusion

Note to epigraph: "Sighed Rawdon Brown," *Poems of Robert Browning*, ed. Pettigrew, II, 964.

1. "I frequently, in the old masters, met with representations of musical instruments, either of their own times, or at least such as they imagined to be in use at the time when the action of the piece happened; thus I observed in a famous picture of the Marriage of Cana by P. Veronese . . . a concert, with a variety of instruments, of all which I have made a memorandum," Charles Burney, *The Present State of Music in France and Italy*, 164.

2. "Cronologia storica" in *Venezia e provincia* (Milan: Touring Club Italiano, 2004), 16–17. The chronology takes note of the advent of the railway bridge in 1846, and the next item is the annexation of Venice and the Veneto to the Kingdom of Italy.

3. Mann, *Death in Venice*, trans. Appelbaum, 99–101.

4. Witi Ihimaera, *The Matriarch* (Auckland: Pan Books, 1990), 431.

5. Proust, *Time Regained*, trans. Kilmartin, III, 899–900.

6. "The latter [Salute] is much the finer; it is to the Virgin and the other is only to our Saviour: so naturally doth the Devotion of that Church carry it higher for the Mother than the Son. It is true, the *Salute* is later than the other; so no wonder if the Architecture and the Riches exceed that which is more ancient" (Burnet, *Travels*, 129). Burnet seems a natural believer in progress, if he can assume that the later building

would likely be better. However, many visitors in the seventeenth and eighteenth centuries went on excursions especially to see Palladio's work, as Beckford did in his first days in the city.

7. Pope John's Opening Speech to the Council, 11 October 1962, translated; see www.christusrex.org.

Index

Acknowledgments

I am happy to express a profound sense of connection with all the writers over the centuries who have written about Venice, especially transient, opinionated, and idiosyncratic visitors like myself. Here's to the small, the great, and the odd who have added their reflections to the reflexive sparkles of the Grand Canal.

It is only right to express my gratitude to the Institute for Scholarship in the Liberal Arts, College of Arts and Letters, University of Notre Dame, without whose help the illustrations would not be what they are. It is also my pleasure to express my deep personal sense of gratitude to the following persons who in various ways and at various times have helped and encouraged my project: Francesco Berenato, Marcangelo Berenato, Stephanie Cabot, Ted Cachey, Robert Coleman, C. Kinian Cosner, Christopher Fox, William Franke, Anthony Grafton, Eamon Jones, David Lyle, Robert Mack, Collin Meissner, Douglas Murray, Robin Rhodes, Francesco Santini, Roger Short, John Sitter, Giuliano Vidilio, Marigold and Michael Wace, and Marina Warner. I am grateful to the "Eighteenth-Century Group" of graduate students and faculty at Notre Dame, and especially to Eileen Hunt Botting of the Political Science Department for discussions of Contarini. I owe something to Greg Kucich and Larry Wolf for severally pointing out that the Dalmatians didn't necessarily appreciate being the first block of Venice's empire. Warm thanks to the distinguished historian John Julius Norwich for his interest in my book in progress. Particular appreciation is extended to the unflappable Jessica Monokroussos, who has tidied unruly pages and rescued me from various computer snarls.

Tante grazie to Enrica Villeri, who is happy enough to live in Venezia, for meals, including Acqua Pazza dinner, and for good conversations over the years. Thanks also to Flavio Gregori, also for Acqua Pazza, and for account of growing up in Grado. Many thanks to Ugo Camerino and Marinella Columni Camerino for the Venetian dinner party.

Special thanks are due to my sister Freda Bradley who joined me for a delightful Carnevale in February 2002. Over the years I have enjoyed talking about Venice with my cousin John Williams, to whom this book is dedicated.

I am obliged to Noreen O'Connor-Abel for conscientious copyediting. Finally, I owe Jerry Singerman my thanks for being such an encouraging general editor.

3M